Glorious War

Glorious War

The Civil War Adventures of George Armstrong Custer

Thom Hatch

ST. MARTIN'S PRESS
New York

Photo credits: West Point Cadet Custer (p. 1), Elizabeth Bacon "Libbie" Custer (p. 3), General Sheridan with his staff (p. 5), and James Ewell Brown "Jeb" Stuart (p. 6) are courtesy of the author's collection. Commander Pennington (p. 1), Artilleryman Pelham (p. 2), *Harper's Weekly* (p. 3), Confederate Colonel Mosby (p. 6), and Commander General Robert E. Lee (p. 6) are courtesy of the Library of Congress. Lieutenant Washington and Custer (p. 1), General Rosser (p. 2), Newlyweds George and Elizabeth Bacon Custer (p. 2), General McClellan (p. 3), Custer and Major General Pleasonton (p. 4), General Sheridan (p. 4), General Grant (p. 5), General William Henry Fitzhugh Lee (p. 7), General Hampton (p. 7), General Kilpatrick (p. 7), Thomas W. Custer (p. 8), and Major General George Armstrong Custer (p. 8) are courtesy of a private collection.

www.stmartins.com

Maps by Paul J. Pugliese

LIBRARY OF CONGRESS CATALOGING-IN-PUBLICATION DATA

Hatch, Thom, 1946–
    Glorious war : the Civil War adventures of George Armstrong Custer / Thom Hatch.—First edition
        p. cm.
    ISBN 978-1-250-02850-1 (hardcover)
    ISBN 978-1-250-02851-8 (e-book)
    1. Custer, George A. (George Armstrong), 1839–1876.   2. Generals—United States—Biography.   3. United States—History—Civil War, 1861–1865—Cavalry operations.   4. United States—History—Civil War, 1861–1865—Campaigns.
5. United States. Army—Biography.   I. Title.
    E467.1.C99H39 2013
    973.8'2092—dc23
    [B]

                                                      2013024013

St. Martin's Press books may be purchased for educational, business, or promotional use. For information on bulk purchases, please contact Macmillan Corporate and Premium Sales Department at 1-800-221-7945, extension 5442, or write specialmarkets@macmillan.com.

First Edition: December 2013

10 9 8 7 6 5 4 3 2 1

To Lynn and Cimarron,

two very special people

Contents

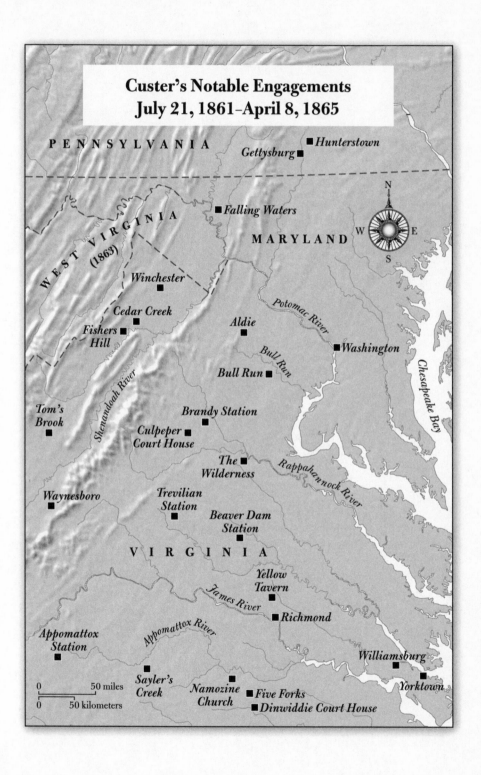

**Custer's Notable Engagements
July 21, 1861–April 8, 1865**

PENNSYLVANIA

Gettysburg ■ ■ Hunterstown

- - - - - - - - - - - -

■ Falling Waters

WEST VIRGINIA (1863)

MARYLAND

N W E S

Winchester ■

Cedar Creek ■

Fishers Hill ■

Aldie ■

Potomac River

■ Washington

Bull Run

Bull Run ■

Chesapeake Bay

Tom's Brook ■

Shenandoah River

Brandy Station ■

Culpeper Court House ■

The Wilderness ■

Rappahannock River

Waynesboro ■

Trevilian Station ■

Beaver Dam Station ■

VIRGINIA

Yellow Tavern ■

James River

■ Richmond

Appomattox Station ■

Appomattox River

Williamsburg ■

■ Yorktown

| 0 | 50 miles |
| 0 | 50 kilometers |

Sayler's Creek ■

Namozine Church ■

■ Five Forks

■ Dinwiddie Court House

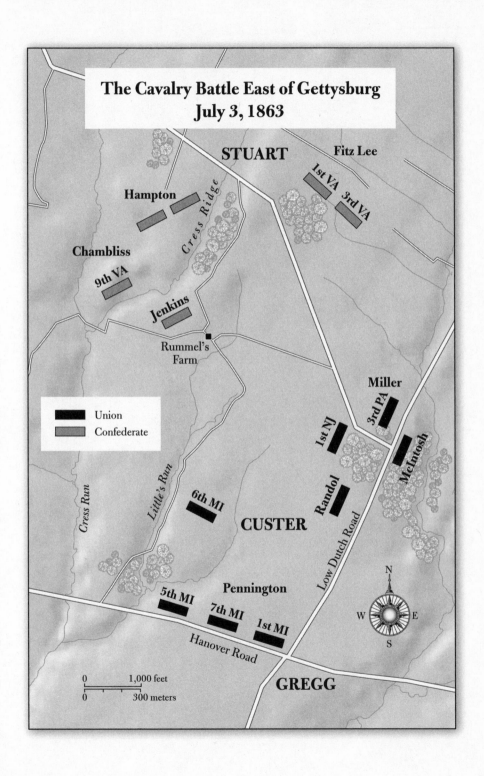

The Cavalry Battle East of Gettysburg
July 3, 1863

STUART

Fitz Lee

1st VA

3rd VA

Hampton

Cress Ridge

Chambliss

9th VA

Jenkins

Rummel's
Farm

Miller

3rd PA

1st NJ

McIntosh

Union
Confederate

Cress Run

Little's Run

6th MI

CUSTER

Randol

Low Dutch Road

N

Pennington

5th MI

7th MI

1st MI

W   E

Hanover Road

S

0   1,000 feet

GREGG

0   300 meters

Glorious War

Prologue

————◆————

On the afternoon of July 3, 1863, Confederate Major General George E. Pickett led over thirteen thousand gray-clad soldiers on a brazen—some say suicidal—charge across an open meadow toward the center of the Union line at Cemetery Ridge. It was apparent to both sides that the outcome of the three-day battle for Gettysburg, and possibly the Civil War, would be decided by the success or failure of this audacious maneuver.

The tactic had been brilliantly designed by General Robert E. Lee as a coordinated effort with a detachment of Confederate cavalry that would simultaneously strike the Union rear from another direction and cause havoc along the lines. If this collaborative plan was successful, Pickett and his mile-wide line of men would smash through that blue-clad front to rout the Yankees and place the future of the Army of the Potomac and the Union itself in dire jeopardy.

Three miles east of Gettysburg down the Hanover Road, legendary Confederate cavalry commander Major General James Ewell Brown "Jeb" Stuart and his six thousand horsemen—known as the "Invincibles"—were poised to support Pickett by attacking the Union rear. When the cannon barrage was fired from Gettysburg, Stuart would lead his mounted troops down Cress Ridge on a purposeful ride toward the Yankee lines.

Stuart had been a thorn in the side of the North throughout the first two years of the war. As commander of the Army of Northern Virginia's elite cavalry, he had redefined the role of horsemen as an independent arm capable of wreaking havoc upon his enemy and had not come close to being challenged by the outclassed Union cavalry. His bold raids into enemy territory had disrupted communication and supply lines, gathered vital intelligence, and destroyed millions of dollars' worth of property—in addition to bloodying his enemy at will. His spectacular 1862 ride around McClellan's army had embarrassed the North and instilled confidence in the South's belief that it could prevail. Stuart had been elevated to a lofty position in the hearts of his Southern admirers that rivaled that of a knight of King Arthur's court and had gained at least grudging respect from his Northern opponents. Now he had been called upon to play a significant role in the pivotal Gettysburg battle.

Blocking Stuart's access to the battlefield in support of Pickett was only one brigade of Union cavalry—about twenty-three hundred men. This brigade of "Wolverines" from Michigan was commanded on the field by twenty-three-year-old Brigadier General George Armstrong Custer, who had been promoted from brevet captain to his present rank only three days earlier. Custer had never before commanded a large unit in combat, having served mainly as an aide-de-camp on the staffs of several generals.

Although Custer had personally distinguished himself under fire, he was now placed in the precarious predicament of facing the finest cavalrymen and cavalry commander the Confederacy had to offer with only a small detachment of battle-weary, outnumbered troops at his disposal.

History has recorded and analyzed in scrupulous detail virtually every footfall taken by Pickett's men across that open field and the resoluteness of the Union soldiers entrenched along the line on that day. The same cannot be said for this engagement three miles east of Gettysburg.

What, if anything, could Custer, the young, inexperienced cavalry officer, devise to stop Stuart's determined troopers from reaching the field and supporting Pickett's charge?

With perhaps the destiny of the Union at stake, it was evident to observers that the old cavalry master Stuart was about to teach the upstart Custer a bloody lesson on his way to attacking the Union rear and securing victory for the South.

Or, by some miracle or quirk of fate, could this skirmish become the stuff from which legends are born?

George Armstrong Custer, known for only one day in his life—the day he died, which has invariably tarnished his entire career—was on the threshold of becoming a legend.

One

※※◈※※

West Point Cadet

In January 1857, a letter addressed to George A. Custer, Esq. arrived in the mail at the Emanuel Custer residence in New Rumley, Ohio. This official-looking correspondence, which had been postmarked from the nation's capital, was known to contain potentially life-changing news that the entire family had been anticipating with some anxiety.

Seventeen-year-old George—known to his family as "Armstrong" or "Autie"—tore open the envelope to remove a form letter written on crisp, white stationery and signed by Secretary of War Jefferson Davis. The boy quickly scanned the words, his fair-skinned face flushing and his mischievous blue eyes lighting on fire.[1]

Armstrong handed the letter to his father, who, after absorbing each word, in turn gave it to his wife, Maria, who read the message with a sense of sadness. This was the news that Maria had been dreading—not so Armstrong.

The letter informed him that he had been awarded an appointment to the United States Military Academy at West Point, New York. There was a good chance that by this time the boy could no longer contain himself and let out a series of joyous whoops. He was a spirited boy who was prone to such displays of enthusiasm.

This coveted appointment, which would take effect in June, had not come without a great measure of surprisingly good fortune—against seemingly insurmountable odds—that has baffled historians to this day.

Young Armstrong had arrived at the conclusion that he would require some sort of assistance in order to further his education at an institution of higher learning. Otherwise, due to the family's meager finances, he might be relegated to make his way in the world on merely a high school education and whatever skills he could muster on his own. There was a good chance that out of necessity he would be compelled to learn a trade, which was not to the liking of a young man with great dreams and high ambitions.

Armstrong had always been an avid reader of adventure novels and envisioned the glory that might be attained by a military career. On a more practical note, he believed that being a graduate of a prestigious school like West Point would open endless doors of opportunity. So he had made up his mind to shoot for the top. To that end, he wrote to his district's Republican representative, John A. Bingham, and requested an appointment to the United States Military Academy at West Point.[2]

This audacious act by the son of an outspoken, lifelong Democrat demonstrates the undaunting determination that would be Custer's lifelong hallmark. The odds that a son of Emanuel Custer, whose politics were the polar opposite to those of Bingham, could gain political patronage from a Republican were astronomical. And Armstrong himself did not help his cause in the least when he participated in a rally for Democratic presidential hopeful James Buchanan and later protested an appearance by Republican John C. Fremont.[3]

Differing stories have been written about why Armstrong Custer was even considered for this prestigious appointment from a man whose politics were contrary to those of the staunchly Democratic Custer family. Bingham later related—after Custer had become famous—that the "originality and honesty" of the young man's letter "captivated" him. Others have speculated that the father of a girl—Mary Jane "Mollie" Holland, with whom Custer was romantically involved—pulled strings with the congressman in order to remove Custer from his daughter's life.[4]

Regardless, this letter signed by Secretary of War Davis meant that Armstrong could now further his education at an institution where his tuition would be paid. But, alas, his acceptance to the military academy at this point was contingent upon the approval of his close-knit family.

The decision for Armstrong to enter the Academy became a matter of family discussion. Mother Maria, who had hoped that her son might become a minister—an idea likely long forgotten—was strongly opposed to her boy becoming a soldier, especially with rumors that war could be on the horizon. Maria was outvoted by the other family members, and finally acquiesced. Emanuel went to the bank and borrowed against his farm, receiving two hundred dollars to pay for his son's expenses and admission fee.[5]

There was one more obstacle between Custer and West Point, however—entrance examinations. And those exams, to which each aspiring cadet was subjected before acceptance, were not merely a formality but a rigorous experience with no mercy shown for those who were not up to standards. The candidates would be tested individually, and it was known that nearly half of them would be rejected for one reason or another.

The entrance examinations for admittance to this class at the Academy were scheduled for June 20, 1857. George Armstrong Custer boarded a train in Scio, Ohio, and arrived at Albany, New York, where he boarded a boat for a trip down the Hudson River to West Point.

The journey downriver by Armstrong was perhaps best described by his future bride, Libbie, when she wrote:

I cannot imagine anything more delightful to a susceptible imaginative temperament than to sail on the Hudson, a beautiful river, and to follow the outlines of the mountains on either side whose reflection was mirrored in the river, thus giving double delight. Such an approach to a spot where four years of one's life were to be spent filled out a picture to a boy full of romance that lasted until life ended.

The Academy site was so well chosen; all the buildings, the parade and drill ground, the cemetery, the fortifications lie on a level plateau, but at the background rise the soft, lovely hills covered with trees and

verdure, forest trees that have been cared for since West Point started
with its corps of professors and one pupil. To look daily upon such
mountains, to see, from barrack windows, camp, parade, drill ground,
the broad blue river in all its moods, the majestic mountains rising
before them, was inspiration to those country lads who came from
some obscure inland town.[6]

The history of West Point dates back to the Revolutionary War, when
General George Washington regarded the plateau on the west bank of the
Hudson River to be the most important strategic location in the country.
Washington established his headquarters at West Point in 1779, and directed
his Continental soldiers in the building of the fortification and the placement
of a 150-ton iron chain that spanned the Hudson above the narrow S curve
to control river traffic and prevent British ships from sailing upriver and dividing the colonies. Although West Point commander Benedict Arnold committed his act of treason by trying to sell the post to the British, the fortress
was never captured and has been the oldest continuously occupied military
station in American history.

In 1802, at the urging of Washington, Alexander Hamilton, and John
Adams, President Thomas Jefferson signed legislation that established and
funded an institution devoted to the art of warfare and military leadership.
It was called the United States Military Academy and would be located at
West Point. The level of academics provided to the cadets was equal or superior to the country's leading colleges and universities—and by teaching subjects about warfare and establishing military discipline and traditions,
exceptional officers were trained for the United States Army.[7]

In the early decades of the young country, it was West Point graduates
who designed the majority of America's bridges, roads, railway lines, canals,
river levees, and harbors. In addition to engineering feats, graduates of the
Academy participated in the War of 1812—the first conflict that tested the
training at West Point—and distinguished themselves in such battles as
Crysler's Farm, Fort Erie, Craney Island, and the defense of Norfolk.[8]

During June 1857, 108 candidates, including George Armstrong Custer, would be examined for entrance into the United States Military Academy. These young men would be interviewed at Academic Hall by an examining board comprised of about two dozen professors and other interested parties, who stood out in their classy dress-blue army officer uniforms with fringed golden epaulets.

The examination may have seemed more like an inquisition to those whose fate depended on a good showing. One right after another, the young men entered the examining room and later exited wondering if they had passed muster.

Eventually, it was Custer's turn to step inside the inner sanctum, which he found to be a semicircle of desks with imposing figures seated and standing behind them. Among those present were Superintendent Richard Delafield; Albert Church, the head of mathematics, who was said to have roomed at The Point with Jefferson Davis; and Chaplain John French, professor of geography, history, and ethics.

There can be no question that Custer was to an extent intimidated and had some measure of self-doubt when all eyes focused on him seeking any reason to find fault and dash his dream. But he had not made it through the difficult application process just to be turned away before he had a chance to prove that he could indeed become an army officer. In the end, after the professors had put their heads together and discussed the applicants, George Armstrong Custer was judged to be worthy of his appointment—although he ranked in the bottom ten of those selected.[9]

On July 1, 1857, Custer and sixty-seven other plebes—also known as "animals," the lowest form of humanity—out of the original 108 who had been examined, reported for duty as the class of 1862. The blue-eyed boy stood almost six feet tall, weighed about 170 pounds, and was soon good-naturedly nicknamed "Fanny" by his classmates due to his wavy, yellow hair and fair complexion.

The inherent urge of Custer to be the fun-loving prankster was immediately at odds with the strict Academy code of conduct, which was calculated by a system of demerits. Demerits or black marks—called "skins" by the cadets—were awarded for various offenses, such as being late for parade, not keeping eyes to the front, throwing stones on post, not properly carrying a musket during drill, talking after taps, an unshaven face or untrimmed hair, inattention, unkempt quarters, untidy uniform, dirty equipment, failure to salute an officer, altercations or fights with fellow cadets, and many other instances of unacceptable military behavior. One hundred skins in a six-month period would be grounds for dismissal from the Academy.

Custer's offenses ranged from "boyish conduct" to an unbuttoned coat to improper handing of his musket to inappropriate attire.[10] He accumulated seventeen demerits by the time his class broke summer camp at Camp Gaines and moved into the permanent barracks, and he would test the limits of this code before his tour at West Point had been completed.[11]

Students were organized into sections according to their academic abilities, and Armstrong found himself for the most part among Southerners and Westerners, whose knowledge was regarded as being generally inferior to the New Englanders. He was assigned a tower room in the Eighth Division at Cadet Barracks, a four-story stone building with gothic turrets that overlooked a forty-acre plot of grass located at the center of the Academy grounds that was known as the "Plain." Each room had a window facing the Plain; was furnished with a fireplace, two beds with thin mattresses, a table with two chairs, clothes press, gun rack, washstand and slop bucket; and was illuminated by an oil lamp.[12]

Custer's first roommate was James "Jim" Parker, a rather homely, rough-hewn, plodding sort from Missouri. Other close friends who resided in neighboring rooms were Kentuckians William Dunlop and George Watts, Pierce M. B. Young of Georgia, John "Gimlet" Lea of Mississippi, and Southern sympathizer Lafayette "Lafe" Lane, whose father was an Oregon territorial delegate to Congress.

Custer also befriended a number of upperclassmen, such as Alabaman John Pelham and Texan Thomas Lafayette Rosser from the Class of 1861, and North Carolinian Stephen D. Ramseur, who was a third classman. Other upper classmen with whom Custer's future would be linked were Judson Kilpatrick, Wesley Merritt, and Alexander Pennington. The tall, bull-strong, swarthy-complexioned Tom Rosser, who roomed next door, could be considered Armstrong Custer's best friend.[13]

At the present, these cadets were comrades in arms, sharing the unique adventure that was West Point. In the future, however, each of them would be taking sides with the advent of war, and friendships would be strained if not dissolved. Their geographic differences may not have seemed important now, but those differences in culture and beliefs would eventually come to the forefront as the politics of the outside world escalated beyond reason and called these young men to choose sides.

The rigorous curriculum, which had been expanded to five years, emphasized military courses, such as infantry, artillery, cavalry tactics, military science, gunnery, ordnance, administration, veterinary science, horsemanship, and use of the saber, but did not lack for challenging traditional college-level subjects. Among the courses Custer would be required to master were algebra, geometry, trigonometry, spherical astronomy, English, French, Spanish, chemistry, drawing, electrics, civil engineering, philosophy, geology, mineralogy, history, and ethics. The cadets would also serve as valets for the upperclassmen and were afforded the dubious privilege of blacking boots, hauling water, maintaining uniforms, and other physical tasks—all the while never speaking unless spoken to.[14]

At the end of his first year, Custer ranked fifty-second in mathematics and fifty-seventh in English in a class of sixty-two—six members had departed either by choice or dismissal. His placement was partially due to the fact that he had accumulated 151 demerits, the highest number in his class. His offenses now included tardiness, inattention, throwing snowballs, visiting after hours, unauthorized card playing, and failure to keep the section at attention during a formation.[15]

Despite this dismal showing, Custer was not discouraged and wrote to his sister Lydia Ann Reed of Monroe, Michigan, on June 30 saying, "I would not leave this place for any amount of money because I would rather have a good education and no money, than to have a fortune and be ignorant." With that said, he did have some misgivings about being away from home—his parents' welfare, "If there is one reason why I wish I were through here it is that I might be of some aid to them." He did have a personal grievance, however, "I am surprised at Pop not signing my permit to use tobacco. I said distinctly I did not want tobacco for myself, but for my room-mate who smokes, and would give me things I want. Nothing could induce me to use tobacco, either in smoking or chewing. I consider it a filthy, if not an unhealthy practice."[16]

Armstrong Custer's less than glowing academic record was not the result of a lack of intelligence on his part—he likely could have been an honor student. In fact, he regularly checked out literary books from the library that he read for pleasure. He made his way through James Fenimore Cooper's Leatherstocking Tales, and, perhaps in an effort to understand his closest friends, he borrowed *Swallow Barn*. This novel by John Pendleton Kennedy described Virginia plantation life from the standpoint of a dashing hero named Ned Hazard, who was always followed by a pack of hounds. Incidentally, the slavery described by Kennedy depicted a kindly institution, with blacks as almost comical figures. In addition to being a devoted reader, Custer became a skillful writer, as evidenced especially by his later works.

His downfall in formal education can be attributed to his propensity for pranks and an immaturity and rebelliousness that gave him a devil-may-care attitude. He studied not to excel but only enough to keep from flunking out of school. In addition to receiving a load of demerits, Custer spent time in the guardhouse. Found in his portfolio of sketches saved from West Point was a drawing of the guardhouse with bars at the window and a cadet standing behind them that was labeled G. A. CUSTER'S SUMMER HOME ON THE HUDSON.[17]

"It was all right with him," a classmate recalled, "whether he knew his lesson or not: he did not allow it to trouble him." Fellow cadet Peter Michie wrote, "Custer was always in trouble with the authorities. He had more fun, gave his friends more anxiety, walked more tours of extra guard, and came nearer to being dismissed more often than any other cadet I have ever known." Tully McCrea reflected that "the great difficulty is that he is too clever for his own good. He is always connected with all the mischief that is going on and never studies any more than he can possibly help." Cadet Morris Schaff, who was a year behind Custer, remembered, "West Point had had many a character to deal with; but it may be a question whether it ever had a cadet so exuberant, one who cared so little for its serious attempts to elevate and burnish.

And yet how we all loved him." Another cadet wrote, "He was beyond a doubt the most popular man in his class."[18]

Custer was prudent and disciplined enough when his total of demerits would reach levels of dismissal, however, to behave for long periods of time or choose to work off minor infractions by walking extra guard duty. "If my memory serves me," he wrote, "I devoted sixty-six Saturdays to this method of vindicating outraged military law during my cadetship of four years."[19]

Although his "boyish, but harmless frolics kept him in constant hot water," Custer excelled in popularity and leadership. Many a fellow cadet followed Custer into the "skin book" of demerits. One of his favorite haunts was Benny Havens' Tavern at Buttermilk Falls, an off-limits establishment a mile below the post, where the adventurous Custer would lead late-night forays following taps and lights-out. After a hot day on the drill field, Custer and his revelers would savor a cool beverage and sing along with the music, and then try to flee before authorities could catch them in the act or possibly find them missing in a bed check. These pleasure-loving cadets had learned how to stuff and arrange their bedclothes to make it appear as if they were sound asleep in their beds.[20]

There was no end to the imaginative pranks that Custer dreamed up, many of which not only amused and entertained the cadets of his time but became part of West Point lore. He was known to wear a tan-colored wig to hide his shaggy hair, but still received demerits for the long hair. As a result, he once shaved his head, and then endured the razing of his classmates, who would shout during an inspection, "Hair out of uniform!" In another instance, he covered his ankle with iodine and limped around in order to escape drill—just to see if he could get away with it.

His pranks were numerous and varied. One time he tied tin pans to the tail of a dog owned by a professor, which had the predicable effect. He and a coconspirator were known to sneak into a sleeping cadet's room and roughly pull the unwitting victim from his bed onto the floor and flee before anyone knew what was going on. One day in Spanish class, Custer asked the instructor to translate the phrase "class dismissed." When the phrase was spoken in Spanish, Custer led a mass exodus from the room.[21]

Armstrong Custer's second year was little improvement over the first. He had accumulated 192 demerits—only eight short of the two hundred that would have resulted in his dismissal—for such offenses as having cooking utensils in the chimney and gazing about in ranks. His class standing was fifty-sixth out of sixty. He did, however, prove his skill as a horseman by, according to tradition, executing the highest jump of a hurdle ever at the Academy while slashing at a dummy with his saber.[22]

The end of this school year meant that Custer's class would receive their first furlough since entering the Academy. He spent his two months alternating between his family home in New Rumley, Ohio, and his sister's home in Monroe, Michigan, where he would for the first time see his new nephew, Harry—also nicknamed Autie by the family—who would perish with Custer at the Little Bighorn. Whether or not his romance with Mary Holland was resumed during this time would be a matter of speculation. The two had corresponded, but it appears that the flame was at least flickering and would soon be extinguished.[23]

Custer's third year at West Point recorded another poor performance. He studied optics, natural philosophy, astronomy, drawing, French, and Spanish, among other subjects—and earned 191 demerits, one less than the preceding year, and ranked at the bottom of his class. His offenses this year ranged from making a boisterous noise in his sink and talking and laughing in drawing class to throwing snowballs outside and throwing bread in the mess hall.

He had, however, proven that he could discipline himself, if necessary, by remaining demerit-free for a three-month period when threatened with dismissal. Also to his credit, Armstrong was never assessed a skin for fighting or an altercation with another cadet throughout his West Point career. That does not mean, however, that he did not believe in violence toward his fellow man when necessary. Once, when a cadet taunted him through a window, Custer punched the boy through the glass and somehow escaped detection by authorities.[24]

As Custer's fourth year approached, the atmosphere at West Point would undergo a dramatic change, however. Politics and sectionalism were about to enter into the daily regimen, and no one—from the most studious cadet to the class clown—would be able to escape its portentous presence.

Two

Rumors of War

In October 1860, the entire cadet corps passed in review for Albert Edward, Prince of Wales, in front of an estimated six thousand spectators. The cadets had waited in ranks with muskets in hand for three hours until the prince finally presented himself, which predictably soured their opinion of the distinguished royal visitor from across the Atlantic Ocean.

Cadet Tully McCrea summed up the sentiments of the cadets when he wrote that the prince "is a grand humbug in the shape of a well dressed Dutch boy with monstrous feet." This rather unflattering description should serve as fair warning not to make military men stand in ranks for excessive periods of time—a practice known to all soldiers as "hurry up and wait."[1]

It was at about this point in time that the affairs of the country could not be ignored, and the cadets began paying more attention to their geographic roots. Political disagreements on a national scale had provoked a widening abyss of social standards between elected officials separated by the Mason-Dixon Line, and sectionalism became an issue at West Point. Southern cadets had always been resentful toward their Northern contemporaries, who they believed had an advantage at the Academy due to receiving a superior early education. But it was not the issue of education that was invading the ranks at this time; rather, all eyes and ears were focused on the escalating debate about the immediate future of the United States of America that was occurring in the nation's capital. Most cadets, especially those from Southern states, were taking a greater interest in the volatile political scene as it played out on the national stage.

The most radical of rumors circulating warned that the South would secede from the Union if Abraham Lincoln was elected president. Northern cadets stood behind Lincoln, and dissention gradually spread throughout the ranks. Although it seemed unthinkable that the representatives from both sides would not solve their problems and avert this drastic measure, the debate became more and more invective until secession became a real possibility.

For this reason, the school administration decided to eliminate sectional issues, such as slavery, from classroom debate. To the credit of the staff officers, none of the cadets formed groups and isolated themselves, and outspoken abolitionists still remained friends with advocates of slavery.

But then an event occurred that strained relationships almost to the breaking point between the two factions of cadets.

John Brown's raid on Harpers Ferry in October 1859 caused a wave of turmoil at West Point, and an attitude of polarization pervaded through the ranks. Brown believed that he was God's appointed instrument to rid the country of the sin of slavery. To that end, he had attempted to start an armed slave revolt by seizing the U.S. Arsenal at Harpers Ferry. Brown had been thwarted by U.S. Marines led by Colonel Robert E. Lee and assisted by Lieutenant Jeb Stuart. The fighting ended with ten of Brown's men killed and seven others captured, including Brown. John Brown was subjected to a sensational trial and was found guilty of treason against Virginia. On December 2, 1859, amid much fanfare, he was hanged at Charles Town, western Virginia.

Southerners were furious at this attempted slave insurrection at Harpers Ferry, and blamed Northern Republicans for allowing it to happen. Spokesmen for Southern states then took an unprecedented step and put the country on notice that if a Republican president was elected in 1860 they would secede from the Union.

At West Point, discussion and heated arguments about Brown's motives and the issue of slavery caused a collision of ideals—and the occasional shoving match or fistfight—with Northerners and Southerners forced to take sides and defend their positions. This attitude was decidedly contrary to the military discipline that was necessary for an army or an army-in-training to operate properly.

In time, a truce of sorts was declared, esprit de corps prevailed, and the atmosphere of confrontation gave way to more of a sense of friendship and comradeship. With the guidance of staff officers and upperclassmen, the young men made a concerted effort to refrain from engaging in political discussions. The corps gradually returned to a routine calmness but with the knowledge that the separation of loyalties—the bad blood of sectionalism—could flare up and longtime friendships could at a moment's notice be strained and even irrevocably broken.[2]

With all of these factors playing out, the school year was anything but business as usual. Armstrong Custer and his classmates received good news when Congress voted to reduce the school term from five to four years—meaning they would graduate in 1861 instead of 1862. The negative aspect of that decision was that the reason for this change was the growing threat of war between the North and the South and new officers might be required to fight to preserve the Union.

Custer was torn between loyalties. After all, his father was a dyed-in-the-wool Democrat, which caused him to be outspoken against the Republicans. Custer condemned John Brown's raid, but claimed his rancor was due to the fact that the abolitionist had captured the father of an Academy friend from the class of 1859, James Washington, and would have killed the man. James Washington, the great-grandnephew of George Washington, would later describe Custer as being "the rarest man I knew at West Point."[3]

The presidential election was nearing, and one night the Southern cadets hanged a dummy of Republican presidential candidate Abraham Lincoln in effigy. This insulting display was cut down by Northern boys before daylight, but word spread and the flag of truce between the two sides was severely tattered and torn. Emotions once again ran high, perhaps beyond the point of no return, and even the best efforts of corps leaders and staff officers could not quell the antagonism.[4]

Examinations were at hand, but Custer and his friends chose to argue politics rather than study until long after taps. He wrote a letter on May 5, 1860, in which he said, "I will change the subject by saying a few words on politics." His few words filled two and a half pages, and claimed that the Republicans "will either deprive a portion of our fellow citizens of their just rights or produce a dissolution of the Union." He went on to say that Southerners had been insulted until "they determine no longer to submit to such aggression."[5]

It would appear that Cadet Custer was caught in a sticky web of geographic and political loyalties that could have him fighting alongside his Southern comrades if war broke out. Could it be that only a Democratic victory in the presidential election would solve his problem of allegiance to his northern roots as opposed to his newfound friendships and political leanings? Perhaps his happy-go-lucky personality saved him from having to publicly choose sides, and he was able to appease most of his classmates with his sense of humor and comical antics.

On November 6, the fears of the South were realized when Lincoln won the election with 39.8 percent of the popular vote over a splintered trio of Democratic candidates—Dickinson, Lane, and Hunter, all supporters of slavery. As was expected, this victory caused serious rumblings of discontent to spread throughout Southern states.[6]

"The election has passed," Custer wrote to his sister, Ann Reed, "and I fear there will be much trouble." Southern cadets, to a man, vowed to resign from West Point if and when their states seceded. Although it was rarely spoken aloud, most cadets believed that this event was only a matter of time. "You cannot imagine how sorry I will be to see this happen," he continued, "as the majority of my friends and all my roommates except one have been from the South."[7]

The inevitable soon became reality. Southern secession was initiated by South Carolina on December 20, 1860, and before long was followed by Georgia, Alabama, Mississippi, Louisiana, and Texas. Custer's friend, John "Gimlet" Lea of Mississippi, was one of the first of his class to leave, and others who had resolved to join the Confederate forces were torn between loyalty to their states and the desire to remain at West Point long enough to earn their diplomas. They had worked hard for almost four years and were deserving of official recognition for their efforts. But letters from home and national headlines nagged them. Tough decisions by young men, most of whom had not yet approached full maturity, would have to be made.

West Point's librarian, Oliver Otis Howard, recalled: "Probably no other place existed where men grappled more sensitively with the troublesome problems of secession."[8]

One day when Custer was walking one of his extra guard duty tours, two of his classmates from the South chose to leave their diplomas behind and depart the Academy. John Kelly and Charles Ball were carried on the shoulders of friends toward the gate that led to the steamboat landing. Custer explained, "Too far off to exchange verbal adiex, they caught sight of me and raised their hats in token of farewell, to which, first casting my eyes about to see that no watchful superior was in view, I responded by bringing my musket to a 'present.' "[9]

Meanwhile, classes continued, and the cadets made an effort to maintain their normal routine. In January 1861, Armstrong Custer was involved in an incident that furthered his reputation as the unofficial Academy prankster. Apparently there was this particular rooster that crowed too much and too loudly for the likes of Custer and his companions. The rooster belonged to Lieutenant Henry Douglas, whose quarters—and chicken coop—lay across the Plain from Custer's tower room in the Eighth Division.

Cadet Morris Schaff wrote, "Custer slipped down one night, took him from his perch, and later he was in a kettle boiling over the gas-burner, his feathers on an outspread newspaper. When the feast was over, the one delegated to dispose of the feathers was not careful as he carried them off, and the result was that the next morning there was a string of yellow feathers from the Eighth Division clear across the area. This delinquency, not recorded in the Military Academy's Records, helped break the routine, offering a pleasant relief and contrast at a time when clouds hung dark and passions were stirring deep."[10]

Had this delinquency been recorded and Custer's role found out by the authorities, the resultant demerits would have pushed him over the number allowed and he would have been dismissed from the Academy. It seemed that nothing, not even the threat of war or the possibility of dismissal, could keep the class prankster from his appointed duties.

In February, the Confederate States of America was formed in Montgomery, Alabama, with Jefferson Davis, the man who had signed Custer's appointment to West Point, as president. The Provisional Confederate Congress authorized raising an army and established a financial basis to support the new nation.

Predictably, this act had a profound effect on the cadets, as well as the administration. West Point Superintendent Pierre G. T. Beauregard, a Louisianan, was relieved of duty after only five days in that position. The separation of allegiances became even more evident than before at the Academy with impromptu and intense contests of regional pride.

In one instance, on February 22, to honor George Washington's birthday, the corps assembled at the chapel to listen to the farewell address by outgoing president James Buchanan. Following the speech, the cadets were marched back to their barracks and dismissed for the day.

At about 9:30 that night, while they were in their quarters, the band down in the Plain below performed "The Star-Spangled Banner." This stirring tune evoked wild cheering from those Yankee cadets who stood in their windows facing the band, which was a clear violation of regulations. Cadet Schaff wrote, "It was begun at our window by Custer, for it took a man of his courage and heedlessness openly to violate the regulations."

The playing of "Dixie" followed, and the Rebels—led by Custer's boisterous friend, Tom Rosser—tried to outshine their comrades in volume. Every window was filled with cadets yelling at the top of their lungs in a passionate competition.

There can be no doubt that the young men on either side who participated were aware that the camaraderie the corps had enjoyed in the beginning was rapidly coming apart at the seams due to the whirlwind of national events. These primal screams were as much a protest of that dilemma as a show of support for their cause.[11]

Sadly enough, as winter turned into spring, these rivalries more often than not escalated into arguments that resulted in blows being exchanged. There were no secrets about loyalties between classmates, and tensions mounted with each day. One can only imagine the emotions that passed from room to room as these young men struggled to come to terms with the notion that today's friend and comrade in arms would likely be tomorrow's enemy on the field of battle.

Armstrong Custer wrote, "The cadets from the South were in constant receipt of letters from their friends at home, keeping them fully advised of the real situation and promising them suitable positions in the military force yet to be organized to defend the ordinance of secession. All this was a topic of daily if not hourly conversation."[12]

At the dinner table one evening, Cadet Pierce M. B. Young addressed Cadet Custer, "Custer, my boy, we're going to have war. It's no use talking: I see it coming. Now let me prophesy what will happen to you and me. You will go home, and your abolition Governor will probably make you colonel of a cavalry regiment. I will go down to Georgia, and ask Governor Brown to give me a cavalry regiment. And who knows but we may move against each other during the war." Young may not have actually thought that his boyish prediction would be fulfilled. He and Armstrong Custer would indeed be meeting under adversarial circumstances.[13]

In a letter to his sister on April 10, Custer predicted that he expected the outbreak of war within a week—and for the first time proclaimed where his loyalties would take him. "In case of war," he pledged, "I shall serve my country according to the oath I took here." In spite of his friendship with his Southern classmates, he would honor the oath of allegiance to which he had sworn upon entering West Point and offer his services to the governor of Ohio.[14]

George Armstrong Custer would fight on the field of battle to preserve the Union, if necessary, even if it meant facing off against his closest friends. This decision must have been agonizing to someone known as being fiercely loyal to his friends. And it can only be speculated as to what extent his Southern comrades had gone when trying to persuade him to follow them to the South and serve in the Confederacy. Custer may have been known as being happy-go-lucky but this decision would have been made in dead seriousness, likely over sleepless nights filled with tormenting thoughts.

On April 12, the spark of rebellion ignited into full-fledged conflagration when Southern artillery under the command of former West Point Superintendent Beauregard opened up on Fort Sumter in Charleston harbor. The fort fell two days later, which compelled President Lincoln to call for seventy-five thousand volunteers to preserve the Union.

The months and days of waiting had come to an end. Southerners at West Point had no choice but to head for home. Thirty-seven cadets, including Custer's best friend, Texan Tom Rosser, departed the academy to offer their services to the Confederacy.[15]

The class of 1861 was graduated early, on May 6, with Judson Kilpatrick delivering the valedictory address. Four days later, Kilpatrick would participate in the opening skirmish of the war at Big Bethel in Virginia and suffer a severe wound, making him the first Regular Army officer wounded in action. He would be sidelined until September.

Custer's class of 1862 was subjected to an abbreviated curriculum that would supplant the final year of studies and was scheduled to graduate on June 24, 1861.[16]

Cadet Custer had racked up an additional 192 demerits during his academic year. Throughout his years at West Point he had been in constant danger of dismissal, and had tallied an impressive four-year total of 726 demerits. Nevertheless, the class mischief-maker, who excelled in horsemanship, athletic prowess, and leadership skills but lagged behind in academics, had overcome his own outrageous pranks and antics to qualify for graduation from West Point. George Armstrong Custer had satisfactorily completed his studies and was commissioned a second lieutenant. Incidentally, his best subject in that final year was artillery tactics—his worst, cavalry tactics.[17]

Custer's record at West Point can best be summed up in his own words, "My career as a cadet had but little to commend it to the study of those who

came after me, unless as an example to be carefully avoided. The require-
ments of the academic regulations, a copy of which was placed in my hand
the morning of my arrival at West Point, were not observed by me in such a
manner at all times as to commend me to the approval and good opinions
of my instructors and superior officers. My offences against law and order were
not great in enormity, but what they lacked in magnitude they made up in
number. The forbidden locality of Benny Havens possessed stronger attrac-
tions than the study and demonstrations of a problem in Euclid, or the prosy
discussion of some abstract proposition of moral science. My class numbered
upon entering the Academy about one hundred and twenty-five. Of this number only thirty-four graduated, and of these thirty-three graduated above me.
The resignation and departure of the Southern cadets took away from the
Academy a few individuals who, had they remained, would probably have
contested with me the debatable honor of bringing up the rear of the class."[18]

It was no wonder that when Superintendent Richard Delafield handed
Custer his diploma his fellow cadets exploded in riotous applause and cheering.

Perhaps predictably, however, Custer found himself in trouble before
even receiving orders assigning him to his first duty station. On June 29,
he was Officer of the Guard when an argument over whose turn it was at
the water faucet broke out between two cadets—one of whom was William
Ludlow, who would be chief engineer on Custer's Black Hills Expedition of
1874. The incident escalated into a fistfight. Inexplicably, Custer disregarded
his duty to break up the fight and send the combatants to the guardhouse.
Instead, he told the surrounding crowd of cadets, "Stand back, boys; let's
have a fair fight."[19]

The Officer of the Day, First Lieutenant William B. Hazen, a West Point
instructor and future Custer critic, was one of two officers who happened
along to witness the event, and Custer was placed under arrest. Within a few
hours, his classmates departed the Academy and proceeded to Washington
for further orders—but without Custer. He was detained, and the uncertain
status of Second Lieutenant George Armstrong Custer's future career wasn't
settled until July 5, when his court-martial was convened at West Point.[20]

Nine officers listened to evidence regarding the charges of neglect of duty and "conduct to the prejudice of good order and military discipline" for Custer's failure to "suppress a quarrel between two cadets." First Lieutenant Stephen Vincent Benet—namesake grandfather of the Pulitzer Prize–winning author—served as judge advocate.[21]

The cadets involved in the altercation—Ludlow and Peter Ryerson—testified that their disagreement was but a minor "scuffle" and not a serious breach of military discipline. Custer prepared a four-page statement, and argued that the discord between the two cadets was but a "trifling" matter of little consequence. He also noted, "I plodded my way for four long years," and now he only desired to be permitted to serve his country and march off to war. Custer was aided by First Lieutenant William B. Hazen, the officer who had reported the incident, who acted as a character witness.[22]

The court was not impressed by Custer's defense. On July 15, he was found guilty on both counts. His sentence, however, was the ruling that he only be "reprimanded in orders." This leniency was "owing to the particular situation of Cadet Custer represented in his defense, and in consideration of his general good conduct as testified to by Lieutenant Hazen, his immediate commander."[23]

Under normal circumstances, Custer likely would have been dismissed from the service, but the Union needed trained officers to fight a war. The fact that he escaped severe punishment was the beginning of "Custer's Luck," the term Custer and others would employ to characterize the favorable events that occurred to him until the day he died. In this case, his luck had been supported by influential friends in Washington. Congressman John A. Bingham had learned of the court-martial and interceded to help save his appointee's fledgling military career.[24]

Three days after the verdict, on July 18, a telegraphic order was received that directed the superintendent of the Academy to release Second Lieutenant Custer at once and have him report without delay to the adjutant-general of the army for duty. Custer departed West Point by steamer destined for Washington by way of New York City—the final member of his class to leave that post.[25]

At almost the last possible moment, the military career of George Armstrong Custer nearly ended before the ink on his diploma had even dried, but now he was free to apply the lessons that he had learned at the military academy on the battlefield. He was about to experience combat for the first time, and it would not be the glorious event that he may have envisioned as a West Point cadet dreaming of bombs bursting in air. And it was likely that no one—Northerner or Southerner—could foresee that this first major battle would only be the beginning of an escalation of hostilities that would last for years and cause immeasurable suffering and hardship.

Three

———◆———

Bull Run

George Armstrong Custer spent several hours in New York City to visit the well-known military equipment firm of Horstmann's and purchased a lieutenant's uniform, saber, sash, Colt side-hammer pocket pistol, spurs, and other accouterments—and had his photo taken for his sister. He then boarded a train to complete his journey to the nation's capital, where he would receive orders directing him to his first duty assignment.[1]

Custer arrived in Washington on Saturday morning, July 20. His first stop was at the Ebbitt House, a hotel where he briefly visited with Jim Parker, his former roommate. Parker had accepted a commission in the Confederate army. Custer made an effort to persuade his friend to reconsider his decision on the grounds that he had sworn an oath of allegiance at West Point. The argument fell on deaf ears. Perhaps part of Parker's decision to shun the Union was because he had received 102 demerits during his final semester and had been denied graduation from the Academy. Regardless of reasons, good friends Parker and Custer were now on opposite sides of the war.[2]

That afternoon, Custer reported to the adjutant general's office at the War Department. He was informed that he had been assigned to Company G of the Second United States Cavalry, commanded by Major Innes Palmer. His unit was presently part of General Irvin McDowell's Union forces at Centreville, where the battle for possession of nearby Manassas Junction, Virginia, was presumed imminent. The adjutant general was about to direct a subordinate to write out Custer's orders when he paused to ask, "Perhaps you would like to be presented to General Scott, Mr. Custer?"[3]

Lieutenant General Winfield Scott, the seventy-five-year-old hero of the Mexican War from Virginia, had turned down a Confederate commission and was serving as President Lincoln's chief military advisor. "Old Fuss and Feathers," as he was known for his meticulous dress and attention to military protocol, was a virtual legend, having served in every U.S. conflict since the War of 1812, where he had been severely wounded in the shoulder.[4]

Custer was certainly impressed. "Scott was looked up to as a leader whose military abilities were scarcely second to those of Napoleon," he wrote, "and whose patriotism rivaled that of Washington." This green second lieutenant was doubtlessly taken aback to imagine that he would be deemed worthy of being introduced to the country's most celebrated soldier, but "joyfully assented" to the adjutant general's invitation.[5]

Custer was ushered into Scott's office, which was occupied by a number of other officers as well as several congressmen, all of whom were studying maps of the vicinity of Manassas Junction. Scott was an imposing figure, standing six feet, four inches in height, although one shoulder drooped from the war wound. "General," the adjutant general introduced, "this is Lieutenant Custer of the 2nd Cavalry. He has just reported from West Point, and I did not know but that you might have some special orders to give him."

A cordial General Scott shook hands with Custer and asked if he would prefer drilling volunteers, which had been one of the duties assigned to recent West Point graduates, or did he desire something more active? The drill assignment would keep him out of harm's way and utilize the training he had received at the Academy. But Custer had also been trained for war, and could not imagine being left behind in the rear when the bugles sounded and the battle had begun.

"Although overwhelmed by such condescension upon the part of one so far superior in rank to any officer with whom I had been brought in immediate contact," Custer wrote, "I ventured to stammer out that I earnestly desired to be ordered to at once join my company as I was anxious to see active service." Scott was pleased with that answer, saying, "A very commendable resolution, young man." He ordered Custer to secure a horse and return that evening to carry dispatches from Scott to General McDowell in the field on his way to duty with the Second Cavalry.[6]

Custer spent several hours searching for an available mount without success until finally happening upon an enlisted man whom he recognized from the Academy. The soldier was a member of Captain Charles Griffin's artillery battery and had been retrieving an extra horse that had been left behind when the battery had moved out. Custer was offered the mount, which, ironically, had been a favorite of his from West Point named Wellington.

With the important dispatches from Scott to McDowell secured in his tunic, Custer and the soldier crossed the Potomac on the Long Bridge as darkness descended, rode through the night, and arrived in Centreville at about 3:00 A.M.[7]

Custer delivered the dispatches to McDowell's headquarters, and learned over a breakfast of steak, coffee, and Virginia corn bread that the general intended to attack the Confederates in the morning. It would not have dawned on him that there was the distinct possibility that he had been carrying the orders that would initiate the first major battle of the war.

Custer remounted and made his way alone through the darkness in search of his unit, eventually coming upon a line of mounted cavalry. He located Major Palmer, and after introductions with his fellow officers—who were quite hospitable—was directed to his platoon to await orders for the march.

George Armstrong Custer, three days removed from West Point and forty-eight hours without sleep, was about to participate in the first grand struggle of the Civil War.[8]

The Southern forces, some twenty-two thousand strong, commanded by General P. G. T. Beauregard, were deployed along the right bank of Bull Run, the stream that would give its name to the battle. These Rebel troops were protecting the strategically vital railroad intersection at Manassas Junction, Virginia, located twenty-nine miles southwest of Washington D.C., and held every bridge across Bull Run for some twelve miles.

There were gaps between this line of men and artillery, however, and Brigadier General Irvin McDowell and his thirty-five-thousand-man army hoped to exploit that fact. McDowell planned to strike with one division to draw the enemy's attention, while sending two other divisions farther up Bull Run to cross at a predetermined place, circle around, and attack the flank.

On Sunday, July 21, 1861, a clear, hot day, the two armies engaged in a long-awaited showdown. Armstrong Custer and the Second Cavalry had been relegated to supporting artillery batteries throughout the early action. He heard the thunder as the eleven guns were fired, watched the cottony clouds of smoke fill the sky, and felt the rumble of the cannons as they shook the ground. Those Union guns were answered by the roar of enemy artillery. His first thought was that the sound was much different than a West Point drill. The experience made a lasting impression on the young cavalry officer.

"I remember well the strange hissing and exceedingly vicious sound of the first cannon shot I heard," Custer wrote about protecting Captain Griffin's battery, which was under fire from enemy artillery. "Of course I had often heard the sound made by cannon balls while passing through the air during my artillery practice at West Point, but a man listens with changed interest when the direction of the balls is toward instead of away from him. They seem to utter a different language when fired in angry battle from that put forth in the tamer practice of drill."[9]

That artillery barrage to which Custer paid such attention may have been launched by the battery commanded by Tom Rosser, his West Point friend. Rosser had departed the Academy on April 22, 1861, and traveled to Montgomery, Alabama, where he enlisted in the Confederate army. He had been commissioned a first lieutenant, and was assigned to New Orleans to become an instructor for the famous "Washington Artillery," which had been organized in 1838 and was manned by the best of Creole society.

Incidentally, Thomas Lafayette Rosser was known as a Texan but had actually been born in Campbell County, Virginia, on a farm known as "Catalpa Hill." In 1849, the family moved to a 640-acre farm in Panola, Texas, about forty miles west of Shreveport, Louisiana. At the time, Rosser's father had business dealings that detained him in Virginia, and thirteen-year-old Tom was in charge of the wagon train that carried his mother and younger siblings to their new home. Rosser was appointed to West Point by Congressman Lemuel D. Evans and became a proponent of Texas secession, leaving a scant three weeks before graduation. Rosser and Custer had shared many experiences together—such as escapades to Benny Havens'—during their years at the Academy, and their parting must have been quite emotional.

Now, three months later, Tom Rosser was in command of a company of the Washington Artillery at Bull Run and lobbing deadly artillery shells at his former roommate and best friend, George Armstrong Custer.[10]

At one point during this vicious battle, Custer's regiment formed in a column of companies and prepared to move to the crest of a hill, where it was presumed the order would be given to charge to protect the guns from an enemy assault. There can be no doubt that Custer's heart was pounding against his newly purchased uniform tunic. This was the real thing, not a West Point exercise designed by instructors. Blood could be spilled on this ground before the day, not to mention the hour, was over.

Custer wrote, "When it is remembered that but three days before I had quitted West Point as a schoolboy, and as yet had never ridden at anything more dangerous or terrible than a three-foot hurdle, or tried my saber upon anything more animated or combative than a leatherhead stuffed with tan bark, it may be imagined that my mind was more or less given to anxious thoughts as we ascended the slope of the hill in front of us."[11]

Second Lieutenant Leicester Walker, who had been appointed from civilian life and outranked Custer by a few days, waited at the head of the next platoon. Custer and Walker had chatted earlier and now engaged in small talk as both made an effort to mask their apprehension about engaging in actual combat. Walker called out from his position, "Custer, what weapon are you going to use in the charge?"

Custer, the West Pointer, who was expected to know such things, promptly answered, "The saber," and drew his blade. Walker instantly imitated Custer and drew his own saber.

As the formation moved at a walk up the hill, Custer began debating in his mind about the comparative merits of the saber as opposed to the six-shot revolver, and came to the conclusion that the firearm would be best at close quarters. Without a word, he replaced his saber in its scabbard and drew his revolver. Walker noticed, and copied Custer's actions.

Custer's mind resumed its debate—a revolver quickly emptied in the midst of the enemy would be less effective than a saber, he judged. With that realization, he holstered the revolver and drew his saber. Walker had observed the exchange, and again followed Custer's example.

In truth, Custer had no idea which weapon to use and became amused by his own indecision and his comrade's imitating actions. It was as if the former class clown had planned this saber charade for fun, which assuredly was not the case. The episode, however, had served as a distraction to bolster his nerve for the impending charge.

The company arrived at the crest of the hill and prepared to charge. But, lo and behold, there was no enemy within sight. Consequently, the charge was canceled. The need for either saber or revolver had been, for the time being, postponed. The cavalrymen returned to a sheltered place to await further orders. In time, the company was dispatched to guard the artillery when it moved, and endured hour after hour of inactivity.[12]

Both armies fought gamely throughout the day. The Union had initially gained the upper hand when the undermanned Confederates wavered under a series of determined assaults. The Confederate soldiers, however, had been inspired by the courage of Thomas Jackson, who had held his position on Henry House Hill "like a stone wall," thus earning him the nickname "Stonewall."

Custer wrote, "With the exception of a little tardiness in execution, something to be expected perhaps in raw troops, the battle plan marked out by General McDowell was carried out with remarkable precision up 'til about half-past three p.m. The Confederate left wing had been gradually forced back from Bull Run. But at this crucial moment, with their enemies in front giving way in disorder and flight, a new and to the Federals an unexpected force appeared suddenly on the scene. The next moment the entire line leveled their muskets and poured a volley into the backs of our advancing regiments. The Union lines, but a moment before so successful and triumphant, threw down their arms, were seized by panic, and began a most disordered flight."[13]

The battle was being contested by untrained, undisciplined, green recruits, which resembled two armed mobs rather than professional soldiers. Although both sides fought with zeal and patriotism for their cause, the complexity of McDowell's plan became too much for the Yankee troops to follow. And when Confederate reinforcements arrived on the field—perhaps as many as ten thousand men—the day became bleak for the Union, which had envisioned a quick, romantic victory.

The exhausted Federal troops could not withstand the assailment and the day ended in a rout. Although some Union outfits were able to maintain some semblance of military discipline, most virtually dissolved like dust tossed into the wind and scattered about. These terrified men discarded their weapons and equipment so they would not impede their flight, and headed northward.[14]

The Confederate cavalry chased the retreating enemy for miles, and soon had captured so many prisoners who required escorts to the rear that the force was reduced to one squad and was compelled to abandon its efforts. Throughout the evening and into the night the panicked Yankee troops filled the roads to Washington. In fact, it was reported that some Union soldiers did not stop running until they reached the streets of New York City, where they could lose their military identity and blend in with the civilian populace.[15]

Custer's company acted as rear guard during this disorganized retreat, and was one of the last to leave the field. His unit arrived at the Cub Run Bridge, the main route of retreat to Centreville, to find that artillery shells had struck a number of wagons and carriages to block passage with debris. To add to the confusion, a panicked mob of troops had jammed the bridge in their haste to cross. If the enemy appeared, or if the Confederate artillery opened up again, these bunched-up soldiers would be easy targets and a great amount of casualties would be sustained.

Custer immediately took charge and soon cleared the way for an orderly withdrawal. He then led the cavalry company up Cub Run until he found a place where the waterway could be forded. The troopers finally halted at Centreville, and waited for hours in pitch-black darkness until orders arrived. Too many men had fled from their outfits, they were told, and there would be no way the Union could re-form and make a stand. They were ordered to re-treat the twenty-five miles back to the Potomac.

Custer rode at the rear of his company in the driving rain throughout the night, acting as a personal guardian as they retreated down the pike. Company G bugler Joseph Fought noted, "The roads were jammed with people clamoring for news of the fight. But, though famished, exhausted, spent, Custer never gave up, never slackened control."[16]

To the shock and dismay of authorities in Washington, the day was irrevocably lost for the Union. The Bluecoats had lost 460 killed, 1,124 wounded, and 1,312 missing, compared to Confederate losses of 387 killed, 1,584 wounded, and 13 missing—numbers that fail to provide a clear view of the engagement. The Federals had not just been defeated, they had been severely demoralized.[17]

The battle of Bull Run, or First Manassas—as the North and South respectively called the engagement—had concluded with a tactical and moral victory for the Confederacy. The people of the South could not have been more jubilant at the outcome of this conflict. They had always believed that Southerners could outfight Northerners, and this was testament to that fact. In their minds, this victory signified the birth of a nation. Any indecision about whether to continue this fight until the Union cried uncle had been thoroughly dismissed, and any doubters had been won over to the cause of war.[18]

The coolness under fire and ability to maintain orderliness among the troops by Second Lieutenant George Armstrong Custer—who experienced no actual combat—during this every-man-for-himself retreat was also viewed with great regard by his superiors and earned him a citation for bravery.

His actions even came to the attention of Congressman John A. Bingham, the man who had nominated Custer to West Point. "I heard of him after the First Battle of Bull Run," Bingham wrote. "In the report of that miserable fiasco he was mentioned for bravery. A leader was needed to re-form the troops, and take them over a bridge. Like Napoleon at Lodi young Custer sprang to the front—and was a hero." This statement was quite an exaggeration, of course, but typical of praise from a politician with a vested interest who wanted to pat himself on the back for the actions of others.[19]

The outcome of the battle, however, was a bitter disappointment to Custer. "I little imagined," he wrote, "when making my night ride from Washington on July 20th, that the night following would find me returning with a defeated and demoralized army."[20]

By midmorning on July 22, Custer's G Company had returned to its camp at Arlington Heights. The green second lieutenant who had experienced his first taste of war dropped from his horse, curled up under a tree in the pouring rain, and for the first time in thirty hours slept.

Although thoroughly disappointed, Custer had to be proud that he had made it through his first day of battle without making any mistakes and had accomplished what he could for the cause. The war had only just begun. And, if that day's battle was any indication, it was not going to be the quick or romantic victory that Northern politicians had predicted. Consequently, there would be many more opportunities for an ambitious young officer to distinguish himself in battle and gain glory and promotion. He had likely fallen asleep dreaming about someday wearing those general's stars that were the goal of every West Pointer, but would awake in the morning to the reality that to attain this lofty goal he must endure the hardships and apprehension that were unique to combat.

Four

The Cavalry Charge

The disaster at Bull Run spelled doom for the command of General Irvin McDowell. The Lincoln administration had lost confidence in McDowell's abilities to lead the army, and he was replaced by Major General George Brinton McClellan on July 27, 1861.

McClellan, the thirty-four-year-old Pennsylvanian and West Point graduate —second in his class of 1846—was well known in the upper echelons of the military, having served on General Scott's staff during the Mexican War. He had subsequently been assigned as a West Point instructor, an engineering officer, and as an observer of tactics during the Crimean War in Europe. The general was the inventor of the famous "McClellan saddle," a comfortable and practical alternative to the traditional saddle, which was presently standard equipment for mounted units.

In 1857, McClellan had resigned his commission and accepted a position in the railroad industry, eventually serving as president of the Ohio & Mississippi Railroad. He rejoined the army when Fort Sumter fell, and had been assigned command of the Ohio volunteers in Kentucky and western Virginia. During June and July, he had led his troops to victory in several skirmishes in western Virginia while guarding the strategically located Baltimore & Ohio

Railroad, which brought him national attention. At that time, the general also had been instrumental in persuading the local citizens to follow their own principles and establish the state of West Virginia.

Major General McClellan—known as "Little Mac"—had been chosen by President Abraham Lincoln to reorganize every element of the army in order to restore sagging morale and produce a cohesive fighting force. He would be expected to transform an undisciplined mob of raw recruits into an army capable of withstanding whatever the Confederates could throw at him— which would be no small task.[1]

In creating his vision of the Army of the Potomac, however, McClellan's innovative approach to cavalry saddles apparently did not translate into tactical ingenuity with mounted troops. Brigadier General George Stoneman was named chief of cavalry, but would serve in a purely administrative role. While Confederate colonel James Ewell Brown "Jeb" Stuart would redefine the purpose of cavalry as an independent arm, the mounted Union regiments were assigned to infantry generals who could find no better use for the horsemen than, in the words of one Pennsylvania cavalryman, "as escorts, strikers, dog-robbers and orderlies for all the generals and their numerous staff officers from the highest rank down to the second lieutenants."[2]

George Armstrong Custer's Second Cavalry was renumbered the Fifth Cavalry, and attached to Brigadier General Philip Kearny's New Jersey brigade. Kearny had rejoined the army after Bull Run, and was a battle-tested officer, having lost an arm in the Mexican War while on duty as an aide-de-camp to General Scott. In 1859, he had served in Napoleon III's Imperial Guard in the Italian War, and had been awarded the French Legion of Honor for bravery at Solferino.[3]

Presently, Kearny's brigade was primarily detailed as part of the capital defense force, and the general was in need of staff officers. Second Lieutenant Custer, as the junior lieutenant in the Fifth Cavalry, was assigned to Kearny's staff as an aide-de-camp. Custer wrote of his new duties, "I found the change from subaltern in a company to a responsible position on the staff of a most active and enterprising officer both agreeable and beneficial."[4]

Kearny was also the strictest disciplinary Custer would ever encounter, quick-tempered with those who neglected their duty in the slightest—but he was lenient with the troops, blaming their faults on their superiors. Kearny paid close attention to training his men, a trait that Custer noticed. In fact, Kearny went as far as to send three hundred of his men against an enemy picket in an unauthorized raid to allow them to experience live fire for the first time. Custer accompanied this nighttime detail as an observer, and watched as the result of the ill-advised mission was Bull Run all over again—the Union troops turned tail and ran when the entrenched Rebels fired at them.[5]

Custer, however, closely followed Kearny's manner of commanding troops and learned valuable lessons. The second lieutenant described this general, the first with whom he had daily contact, as "a man of violent passions, haughty demeanor, largely the result of his military training and life, brave as the bravest men can be, possessed of great activity, both mental and physical, patriotic as well as ambitious, impatient under all delay. He constantly chafed under the restraint and inactivity of camp life, and was never so contented and happy as when moving to the attack. He was always to be found where the danger was the greatest." Ironically, much of that description would fit the future General Custer as well.[6]

In a short time, the capable and enterprising Custer had risen from aide-de-camp to assistant adjutant general. He remained on Kearny's staff until an order was issued that fall that forbade regular army officers from serving on the staffs of volunteer officers. The War Department reasoned that volunteer officers, who often organized their own units and had little or no formal military training, were not as professional as regular officers. It became desirable for junior officers to be tutored by the best men available in order to assure that the future staff officer corps would be as competent and experienced as possible.[7]

In early October, Custer was stricken with a mysterious illness—the nature and extent of which are unknown—and was granted a leave of absence. He first visited the Reed household in Monroe, Michigan, to see his sister and her husband, and then traveled to his parents' newly purchased eighty-acre farm in northeastern Ohio.

At that time, Custer learned that his brother, Tom, sixteen, had run away

from home a month earlier and lied about his age to join the army. This impulsive act by the boy had greatly distressed his parents. Emanuel Custer
had thwarted Tom's initial attempt to enlist in Monroe by informing the recruiter that the boy was underage, but the determined youngster had slipped
across the border to the state of his birth to accomplish the task. Tom was six
years younger than Armstrong and worshiped his older brother. He imitated
just about everything Armstrong did—in this case joining the army and
marching off to war. For the next three years, young Tom Custer, as a member of Company H of the Twenty-first Ohio Infantry, would participate as a
common foot soldier in such bloody battles as Shiloh, Stones River, Chickamauga, Missionary Ridge, Chattanooga, and the Atlanta Campaign.

The brothers had gone their own ways as they sought to establish their
careers. One day there would be a joyous reunion for Armstrong's wedding,
and then the opportunity to serve together, with actions that would have
Armstrong bursting with pride over Tom's performance under fire.[8]

Armstrong Custer returned to Monroe, where he was welcomed as a local
war hero, and enthusiastically immersed himself in the social scene. The
dashing young officer was invited to parties, patriotic rallies, and community
dances. He could be found on most nights romancing an adoring young lady
or carousing with friends and other soldiers on furlough at any one of the es-
tablishments that served up alcoholic beverages and the merriment of music.[9]

This reckless behavior, however, led to an episode that would greatly
affect the future of George Armstrong Custer—negatively in the short term
but positively for the remainder of his life.

On one particular evening, Custer had frequented a local tavern and im-
bibed to excess. He and a male companion staggered through the streets of
Monroe on their merry drunken way toward Armstrong's sister Ann's house.
The two soldiers created quite a ruckus as they loudly laughed and sang without any regard whatsoever for the delicate ears of those within listening distance of the boisterous serenade.

The two revelers happened to pass the Bacon residence, where they
were observed by Judge Daniel Bacon and his nineteen-year-old daughter,
Elizabeth.

Circuit Court Judge Bacon was one of Monroe's most respected citizens. The judge had recently shaken Custer's hand publicly at a rally and hailed him a hero for his service. That evening, this proper gentleman was appalled by the uncouth behavior displayed by the young army officer.[10]

Custer was unaware of it at the time, but Elizabeth "Libbie" Bacon—who would always remember "that terrible day"—would in time become the object of his affections. Partially due to the improper public display of the young man on that winter's night, Judge Bacon would forbid any contact between his daughter and this raucous cavalry officer.

In addition to his disgusting drinking habit, however, Custer would face another seemingly insurmountable obstacle to winning the affections of Libbie Bacon and the approval of her widowed father. Judge Bacon may have been cordial with Custer publicly, but he would never entertain the thought of inviting the young army officer into his home. Custer, through no fault of his own, had been born on the wrong side of the tracks. Under no circumstances could he be an acceptable suitor for such Monroe "royalty" as Elizabeth Bacon. Although he had attended West Point, his recent behavior had demonstrated that he may have received an education but due to his breeding and upbringing had retained his working-class habits—and no commoner would ever win the hand of Libbie Bacon, the prettiest girl in Monroe, Michigan.[11]

George Armstrong Custer had been born on December 5, 1839, in the back room on the first floor of his parents' house in New Rumley, Ohio. He was the first child born to Emanuel Henry and Maria Ward Kirkpatrick Custer, who each had lost a spouse and brought two children to their marriage.

Emanuel Custer had been born in Cresaptown, Maryland, on December 10, 1806, the oldest of seven children. His namesake grandfather, who was of German descent, had served in the Revolutionary War, and his great-grandmother was a cousin of the mother of George Washington. Emanuel moved to New Rumley in 1824 to follow in the family tradition and learn the blacksmith trade from his uncle. When his uncle left blacksmithing to work a farm, Emanuel took over as the village smithy. He was respected throughout the community and had served as a justice of the peace. He did not drink or gamble and smoked tobacco only in a pipe. If Emanuel had a vice, it would be politics. He regarded his loyalty to the Democratic Party, which could be called nothing less than militant, to be as sacred as his church ties—he had helped found the New Rumley Methodist Church and was deeply committed to that faith. Emanuel was also a member of the New Rumley Invincibles, the local militia. He lost his first wife in 1835, leaving him with two young sons, Brice and John.[12]

Custer's mother, Maria Ward Kirkpatrick Custer, was born in 1807 to Scotch-Irish parents in Burgettstown, Pennsylvania. The family relocated to New Rumley, Ohio, in 1816, where Maria's father, James Ward, opened an unlicensed tavern. After being arrested and fined, James obtained the proper paperwork for his establishment, which was attached to the family home and located adjacent to the town square.

The tavern was not a friendly neighborhood bar by any means, however. James, who was highly volatile and had a habit of settling matters with his fists, along with his two sons, was often involved in frequent brawls with patrons, and the place soon became quite notorious. It was in this rowdy and vice-ridden environment that Maria was reared. At the age of fifteen, she escaped the tavern by marrying a twenty-seven-year-old customer named Israel Kirkpatrick. She soon gave birth to a son, David, in 1823, and a daughter, Lydia Ann, two years later. In 1825, her husband died, and she was left a widow with two young children.[13]

Emanuel and Maria had probably known each other for years and eventually began dating. On February 23, 1836, the couple married, and the combined family moved in together in Maria's ancestral log home that had been the tavern until her parents died.[14]

The first two children born to Emanuel and Maria Custer died in infancy before five healthy children were born—George Armstrong (1839), Nevin (1842), Thomas (1845), Boston (1848), and a daughter, Margaret (1852).

The Custer family was not by any measurement well-to-do, but Emanuel and Maria compensated for the lack of material possessions by creating a home full of love and family unity. The children from the three families bonded together with true affection, and to which family a child belonged was never an issue. Each child was loved and disciplined equally.

The Custer household was said to be always in a happy uproar. Emanuel acted like a big kid around his children—romping, wrestling, and playing as aggressively as any of them. He also made them the target of practical jokes and dodged their mischief in return, which became a lifelong practice between them. The class prankster at West Point had been well schooled.

In later years, Emanuel lamented about his inability to provide more for Armstrong and the other children, to which Custer replied, "I never wanted for anything necessary. You and Mother instilled into me principles of industry, self-reliance, honesty. You taught me the value of temperate habits, the difference between right and wrong. I look back on the days spent under the home-roof as a period of pure happiness, and I feel thankful for such noble parents."[15]

Maria, who was thin and frail, was often referred to as being in ill health or an invalid. Custer adored his mother throughout his life and was certainly her favorite child. He had been named after a missionary, and constant prayers were offered for him by Maria to let the boy grow up to serve God in the ministry. Perhaps due to this doting, Armstrong never quite severed that invisible umbilical cord between him and his mother, and some of his most painful experiences as an adult would be parting with Maria.[16]

From an early age, Custer would work around his father's blacksmith shop, riding the newly shod animals and tending to them, which enabled him to develop an early skill in horsemanship. Young Autie also attended the "cornstalk" militia musters and parades, and Emanuel would proudly show off his little son executing the military manual of arms. Young Armstrong viewed these days with his father as holidays, and the colorful uniforms, the sound of the fife and drums, and talk of war apparently made a lasting impression on him. Emanuel was so proud of his son's interest in the militia that he had the town tailor make a miniature reproduction of his own uniform for Autie to wear.[17]

The Custer children attended school in New Rumley, and Armstrong gained a reputation as a competent student who took his studies seriously enough to satisfy his teachers. He had a penchant for sneaking adventure novels, such as *Jack Hinton*, or *Tom Burke of "Ours,"* or *Charles O'Malley, the Irish Dragoon*—which was also a childhood favorite of future Little Bighorn comrade, Irishman Myles W. Keogh—into class and reading them instead of his textbooks. Emanuel would purchase a book for Armstrong to read whenever he could squeeze out a little money from the family budget.

The boy was not a bookworm, however, but a spirited and fun-loving youngster who was a natural-born leader and quite a favorite with the young ladies. One classmate remembered, "Custer was what he appeared. There was nothing hidden in his nature. He was kind and generous to his friends; bitter and implacable toward his enemies."[18]

In 1849, Emanuel sold his blacksmith shop in town, and the family moved to an eighty-acre farm on the outskirts of New Rumley. Armstrong and his siblings worked the farm—plowing, sowing, harvesting, and tending to the livestock. One by one, however, the older Custer children left home to find jobs or get married.

Whether it was his disinterest in education at the time or the cost of sending the children to a subscription school, Armstrong was soon apprenticed to a furniture maker in Cadiz, the county seat. This arrangement was not to his liking, however, and he was sent to live at the age of ten with his half-sister Lydia Ann Reed and her husband, David, in Monroe, Michigan. Ann, as she was called, became a surrogate mother and trusted confidante to Custer, a relationship that would continue throughout his life.

Armstrong lived with the Reeds for five or six years, and attended Stebbins' Academy. He was not a model student by any stretch of the imagination, disliking homework and cramming at the last minute before tests. He had started his pranks and mischief at an early age and became a popular leader. One classmate, a teacher's son, said, "He was a rather bad boy in school, but one thing would be said of him, he *always* had his lessons, yet he was not considered an unusually bright lad."[19]

In 1856, at age sixteen, the recent graduate accepted a job teaching in a one-room schoolhouse at Locust Grove, earning twenty-eight dollars a month.

Known as a "big-hearted, whole-souled fellow" with a fun-loving disposition, he then moved on to teach at Beech Point, near Athens, Ohio, and earned two extra dollars a month by chopping wood for the school fireplace. It was at Beech Point that Armstrong boarded with a prosperous farmer and became enamored with his daughter—Mary Holland. The relationship would become a casualty of his appointment to West Point.[20]

Although Custer could call two towns his childhood home, much of his formative years were spent in Monroe with the Reeds. Monroe, one of the oldest settlements in Michigan, was located on the western shore of Lake Erie, twenty-five miles south of Detroit. This former trading post, established by French-Canadian trappers in 1785, was named Frenchtown but had undergone a name change in 1817 after a visit by President James Monroe. The city was connected to the outside world by lake steamer and the railroad, and the residents regarded themselves as being quite cosmopolitan, which created a society of the upper crust—and beneath that elite class existed those whose lives were of little or no consequence except to cater to those who mattered.

David Reed operated a successful draying business, but the family belonged to the Methodist Church while the "socially acceptable" people were Presbyterians. These aristocratic families—many of which were headed by military veterans—were quite snobbish and unwelcoming to newcomers, especially those of the plebeian class. One member of Monroe royalty stated, "We did not associate with the [Reeds and] Custers. They were quite ordinary people, no intellectual interests, very little schooling."[21]

Monroe had sent comparatively few young men off to fight in this war. Most of those of fighting age had gone off to big cities like Detroit or Toledo, where school or business opportunities were greater. The women and girls, however, pitched in to the war effort, forming Societies for Knitting and sending innumerable socks and undergarments to the front lines. The faithful workers also made linen havelocks—a cover for a military cap with a long rear flap as a protection from the sun—and were quite indignant to learn that the troops were using them to clean their rifles. Although Monroe suffered with the sorrowful sight of funeral cortéges on the streets for those who had served and died, a young officer like George Armstrong Custer on furlough was treated like a hero—until proving otherwise.[22]

Now, perhaps predictably, this West Point graduate with lower class roots had shamed himself and his family by carousing through the streets of Monroe like a common drunk—and it was his trusted confidante who would come to his rescue. On that same night that he had been observed by the judge and his daughter, the overindulgence in strong drink by her brother came to the attention of Ann, who was deeply religious. She was shocked and dismayed by the condition of Armstrong when he reached her doorstep.

A determined Ann Reed—with Bible in hand—took Armstrong into her bedroom, shut the door, and evidently delivered a temperance lecture for the ages. Apparently, she made her brother promise before God that he would never touch another drop of intoxicating beverage as long as he lived. Perhaps amazingly, her efforts were successful. From that day forth, Custer never again touched alcohol, not even wine at formal dinner parties.[23]

In February 1862, after four months away, a sober Second Lieutenant George Armstrong Custer returned to Washington with renewed ambition. He had heard that several former West Point friends in the Confederate army— Tom Rosser, who had distinguished himself at Bull Run, John Pelham, and Stephen Ramseur—had already been promoted to captain, and it was rumored that Jim Parker had become a lieutenant colonel, only two ranks below general. It appeared that Custer once again lagged at the rear of his class.

Custer reported back to his company to find that they had been quartered in canvas-roofed huts with mud and stick chimneys and stone slab stoves. The winter had been consumed with monotonous drilling and constructing fortifications that stood a scant twenty miles from those of their enemy. The officers and men were anxious to resume the war and get it over with once and for all now that the weather would be improving.

During this slow period, army commander General George McClellan, who was exceedingly popular with the men, had been working out the details of creating a viable army that could not only compete with the Confederates but defeat them. He had organized regiments, brigades, and batteries that would complement the intense training of his men, which he had placed first on his agenda. He did not want to experience another debacle like Bull Run.

This was a complicated role, but one that McClellan had been born to play. In the midst of this, however, he was being pressured by President Lincoln to advance on the enemy without delay. Thus far, the general had resisted. McClellan may have been rightfully called overly cautious—even obsessed with caution—but, conversely, Lincoln was motivated to order action by the hammering of bad press his administration was suffering through and hoped that an operation against the Rebels would stifle critics. McClellan remained adamant that he needed more time for training and preparation before undertaking an extensive mission, which left the president fuming and had strained relations between the two men.

It was not just the president who had lost patience with McClellan, however. Even the public, which had provided his most ardent support, as well as the press and his allies in Congress and members of the president's cabinet, urged him to take action against the enemy. McClellan understood that his position was now at risk in such a political climate—he would likely be replaced as commander if he did not acquiesce to the consensus of Northern opinion.[24]

On March 9, Confederate general Joseph E. Johnston decided to abandon his lines around Centreville, near Manassas, and withdraw his army south of the Rappahannock River toward central Virginia. Johnston feared that an offensive by Union forces up that river could cut him off, leaving his men in an indefensible position. This movement made its way to the ears of General George McClellan.[25]

McClellan, who had already prepared a plan to advance on Richmond, was finally compelled to act. He would send 155,000 troops by ship to Union-held Fortress Monroe at the tip of the Virginia Peninsula, situated between the James and York rivers. Upon arrival, these troops would march fifty miles up the Peninsula and attack Richmond from the southeast.

Lincoln had argued for an overland route, but Little Mac firmly believed that on such a march as that his communications would be placed at risk.

Further, the navy could easily deliver supplies to his men on the water route. The president grudgingly agreed to the plan—at least his army commander was taking to the field.

McClellan set his plan in motion after hearing about General Johnston abandoning his position. He ordered the cavalry to trail the retreating Rebels in an effort to gather intelligence.[26]

Custer had endured the routine of daily duty throughout February, but now the opportunity for possible glory presented itself. On March 9, the Fifth Cavalry rode out, leading a Union column southwest toward Centreville. Custer was baffled—and likely disappointed—by the fact that his unit was marching overland rather than traveling by water with the main body of troops. What he did not know was that this ride was an essential part of McClellan's master plan. The general not only wanted the cavalry column commanded by General George Stoneman to provide reconnaissance, if possible, but to act as a feinting movement to attract the enemy's attention while the transports were being loaded for the trip down the river.

Custer's disappointment at not being part of the larger movement was appeased when he learned that he was the only commissioned officer in his company—the other field officers were off on assignment—and he would therefore for the first time in his career command a troop of cavalry. Company commander Custer would be in charge of about one hundred horsemen who had been assigned to four platoons of twenty-five men each.[27]

On the second day out, the blue column approached Bull Run, and the advance guard reported that there were fortifications with artillery ahead but no soldiers in sight. Custer and several others cautiously rode up to investigate, and discovered that the "artillery" was nothing more than blackened logs—known as "Quaker guns"—set up to deceive Union forces. It was noted that the enemy had only recently abandoned this position and had burned their supplies—the air was filled with the odor of burned bacon—to keep them out of Yankee hands. Not only that, but scouts had detected Confederate pickets entrenched on the hill beyond the railroad line at nearby Catlett's Station.

Word of those discoveries was sent back to General George Stoneman, who was still seething about the embarrassing disaster at Bull Run and wanted nothing more than to retaliate against the enemy. Stoneman ordered regimental commander Major Charles J. Whiting to dispatch a company to attack those pickets and strike a blow for the Union.

George Armstrong Custer had been waiting at Major Whiting's location when Stoneman's courier arrived with the order to "Drive in the pickets." Custer immediately volunteered his company for the assignment and was accorded permission.[28]

Second Lieutenant Custer formed his company in a column of twos, and rode down the road toward a showdown with the enemy. The Union horsemen pushed fencing out of their way and advanced across the pasture to the base of the hill where the pickets were known to be posted. Bullets were being fired from the enemy position, which convinced Custer that he must order a charge up this slope without delay—there would be no time to bring in artillery to blast them out of there. He ordered his men to "Draw sabers!"

George Armstrong Custer, his own saber pointed toward the enemy, dug his spurs into his horse's flanks and yelled, "Charge!"

Every horse sprang forward as the company eagerly followed their young commander up the sloping terrain. Hooves tore up the ground and threw clods of dirt in every direction while the adrenaline-fueled cries of men with hearts thundering filled the air. The blue-clad riders were met with a ferocious fusillade of bullets from the Confederate picket line. Custer stated that "the bullets rattled like hail," but the cavalrymen pressed forward toward their objective.

By the time they topped the crest of the hill, they found that the Rebels were now fleeing for their lives in fear that their position would be overrun by the audacious charge. Custer urged his horsemen onward and maintained his pursuit until encountering a skirmisher line of about three hundred of his enemy, who opened up with a blistering volley of small arms fire.

At that time, with at least one man slightly wounded and one horse down, Custer prudently ordered his men to retire. The troop and its jubilant commander returned to camp, where Custer reported directly to a pleased General Stoneman that the mission had been accomplished—they had driven in the pickets.

For the first time in his military career, George Armstrong Custer had led a troop of men on a successful cavalry charge—it would not be the last.[29]

Five

———◦◉◦———

Balloons and Battle Flags

T he Union cavalry had pushed the Confederates away from Washington, and now the entire army—120,000 men, 14,500 horses and mules,
44 artillery batteries, and over 1,000 wagons and other vehicles—were being
loaded aboard about 400 vessels for the purpose of moving on Richmond.[1]

On March 17, Armstrong Custer wrote a letter to his parents to tell them
about his first cavalry charge, and how he had confiscated a black foxhound
from the abandoned Confederate camp, and that he now weighed 176
pounds—and had not had his clothing off in a week. He added that the present operation by the Union would assuredly result in victory due to the leadership of George McClellan. "I have more confidence in him than any man
living," Custer wrote. "I am willing to forsake everything and follow him to
the ends of the earth and would lay down my life for him if necessary."[2]

On March 26, Custer boarded the *Adele Felicia* on what he described as
"the greatest expedition ever fitted out." He may have been confident in the
hands of George McClellan, whom he called "the greatest and best of men,"
but he also demonstrated a twinge of apprehension about the pending mission. He finished a letter to his sister Ann just before embarking by writing a
dramatic, "Good-bye my darling sister. Good-bye all of you."[3]

The flotilla of steamboats, schooners, and barges, each one packed tight with troops and equipment, sailed past Mount Vernon and then beyond Robert E. Lee's birthplace in Stratford and out into Chesapeake Bay. This massive floating caravan finally began docking and unloading a few days later at Fortress Monroe, located at the tip of the Peninsula between the York and James rivers. Although troops and equipment continued to arrive, this area was almost at once built up into a good-sized city, with thousands of men, animals, wagons, and supplies spread across its expanse.[4]

An operation this extensive could not be kept secret from the enemy, which had learned about it soon after it commenced. General Joseph Johnston's main body of troops was presently stationed behind the Rappahannock River, about fifty miles north of Richmond. Major General John B. Magruder was holding Yorktown, about twenty miles up the York River from Fortress Monroe, with only around twelve thousand men. This unit was all that stood between McClellan and the Confederate capital. Magruder, however, devised a strategy that called for moving his troops from one position to another in the heavily wooded terrain with deep ravines to create the impression of greater troop strength.

Upon learning about the operation, Johnston's army—with Jeb Stuart's cavalry attached—was sent racing through sleet and snow to reinforce Magruder before McClellan could figure out the ruse and overpower that small force. Some officers, including Stuart, believed that Yorktown would escalate into a major battle—comparable to the Siege of Sebastopol in the Crimean War— and could very well decide the outcome of the war. After all, this was the historic place where Lord Cornwallis had surrendered to George Washington in the American Revolution.[5]

As it was, there was no need for Johnston to hurry. Magruder's strategy of deception was serving its purpose to the fullest. The ever-cautious George McClellan fell for the ploy. He overestimated the Confederate strength, and refused to order an assault of Yorktown. Instead, the Union commander chose to initiate a siege intended to blast the enemy into submission with artillery before sending in troops.[6]

On the Union side of the lines, Custer's cavalry unit was deployed on reconnaissance missions during this siege, and came under fire on two occasions. In the first, Custer and another officer located an enemy artillery battery by crawling up a hill and returned safely to report their findings. The second encounter, in which casualties were sustained, was more intense and made a lasting impression on the young second lieutenant.

In a skirmish that lasted an hour, Custer and his men withstood a pitted battle against enemy sharpshooters. "Everyone got behind a tree and blazed away as hard as he could," he described in a letter to Ann Reed. "But the rebels made their bullets so thick it was all we could do to look out for ourselves." In time, reinforcements arrived and forced the Rebels to withdraw.[7]

Custer was deeply affected by the burial the next day of those troopers who had been killed in the firefight. For the first time, this happy-go-lucky young man had become intimately involved with the tragic consequences of war. "We buried our dead slain in the skirmish, in the clothes they wore when killed, each wrapped in his blanket," he wrote to his sister. "No coffin. Some were quite young and boyish, and, looking at their faces I could not but think of my own younger brother." The sight of one particular trooper evoked Custer to emotionally write, "As he lay there I thought of the poem: 'Let me kiss him for his mother . . .' and wished his mother were there to smooth his hair."[8]

His graphic description of this dangerous mission and its aftermath was received with predictable concern by his family. Emanuel Custer wrote that Maria, Custer's mother, "troubles hir self so much about you and Thomas and she doant like to here of you being so venturesom." Ann Reed responded with, "My dear brother I want you to be very careful of yourself. Don't expose yourself you know how much your parents depend on you and how much we all love you."[9]

The war not only raged in the North, but Union forces under Generals Ulysses S. Grant and Don Carlos Buell were campaigning in Tennessee, and had captured Forts Henry and Donelson, which opened up the middle of the state. Combined Confederate forces under Generals Albert Sidney Johnston and P. G. T. Beauregard were dispatched to halt the movements of these Yankees, but were outnumbered sixty thousand to forty thousand by their enemy. On April 6, however, the Rebels attacked inexperienced troops under General William T. Sherman, which were camped at Pittsburg Landing in a wooded area surrounding Shiloh Meeting House. The fierce battle escalated as reinforcements arrived on both sides, and after two days of desperate fighting the Union troops beat back the Confederates, forcing them into retreat toward Corinth, Mississippi.

In this first great bloody battle of the war, the North lost a total of 13,047 with 1,754 killed and the rest either wounded or captured, as opposed to the South's losses of 10,694, 1,723 of that number dead. The Confederates mourned the loss of General Johnston, who failed to promptly treat a leg wound and subsequently bled to death. His death would be almost as devastating as that of Stonewall Jackson, leaving a vital loss of leadership in the West.

Back in the North, the troopers manning the Union fortifications at Yorktown settled in for a long siege. General McClellan hungered for intelligence, and one manner in which to spy on his enemy was by hot-air balloon. The Balloon Corps, under the command of Brigadier General William F. "Baldy" Smith, was stationed about a mile from Confederate lines. The technical aspects of the operation were under the direction of "Professor" Thaddeus S. C. Lowe, who had developed a portable hydrogen generator for the gas that was necessary to send the balloons aloft. Professional balloonists were sent up daily, weather permitting, to observe anything of note about the enemy that was visible.

Confederate gunners occasionally fired cannon rounds at the balloons, but only one had been hit and downed. Custer's friend Tom Rosser, the Confederate artillery officer, was credited with shooting down one of McClellan's balloons and was rewarded with a promotion to captain for the feat.

General Smith eventually became dissatisfied with the quality of the information provided by these men. It was in the interest of job security for these "acronauts" to embellish their observations, and they often reported sights and scenes from their imagination without fear of contradiction. Smith decided that he needed to put a trusted military man into the basket, and

Brigadier General Fitz-John Porter, commander of the Fifth Corps, was chosen for the task.

On April 11, Porter was sent aloft—and an unexpected easterly wind captured the balloon and blew the general over the enemy line. The Rebels scrambled to aim their artillery at this target floating through the air, but the wind changed direction and Porter was saved, although he crashed roughly into a tree. This near tragedy convinced General Smith that the life of a general should not be taken so lightly. He needed a more expendable man for balloon reconnaissance.[10]

Orders were cut to assign Second Lieutenant George Armstrong Custer to the staff of General "Baldy" Smith as an assistant to the chief engineer, Lieutenant Nicholas Bowen. In this capacity, Custer would serve as a military observer from a hot-air balloon.

Custer approached this unusual duty with some anxiousness. "I was told to take with me in my balloon ascent a field glass, compass, pencil, and note-book. With these I was supposed to be able, after attaining the proper elevation, to discover, locate, and record the works and encampments of the enemy. The balloon was kept but a short distance from General Smith's headquarters, fastened to the earth by numerous ropes, like a wild and untamable animal. Thither I proceeded, my mind not entirely free from anxious doubts as to how the expedition would terminate."[11]

Custer had mentally prepared himself as well as possible for ground warfare in the event that a bullet would cut him down or an artillery shell might explode beside him in battle, but he had not planned for this manner of death. He not only feared that shots from below could hit and penetrate the willow basket, or car as it was called, in which he rode but that the fragile bladder of gas vapor could suffer damage or malfunction and send him plummeting to earth. He tried to act nonchalant on his initial voyage, but admitted that he was suffering from a bad case of the jitters. When the anchor ropes were cast off, Custer soared off above the trees into lower space, and could observe the tiny specs that were upturned faces below him. "I had the finest view I ever had in my life & could see both armies at once," he later wrote of that first experience.[12]

After a number of ascents, Custer soon overcame his fear and became comfortable with the procedure. He was quite adept at noting enemy gun emplacements, counting campfires, and plotting the number of white tents and sketching their position in his notebook.

Custer also had the presence of mind to appreciate the view from a perspective that few of his generation were privileged to witness. "Gradually I became more familiar with the car, and was able to turn to the contemplation of the magnificent scenery which lay spread out beneath and around us as far as the eye could extend. To the right could be seen the York River, followed which the eye could rest on Chesapeake Bay. On the left, at about the same distance, flowed the James River. Between those two rivers extended a most beautiful landscape, and no less interesting than beautiful; it was being made the theatre of operations of armies larger and more formidable than had ever confronted each other on the continent before."[13]

At about 2:00 A.M. in the wee hours of May 4, Custer had made his second ascension of the night when he observed indications that the enemy had abandoned Yorktown. His suspicions were basically confirmed by dawn when he could not see any breakfast fires. He signaled to bring his balloon back down to earth and hurried to report his findings to Baldy Smith.

General McClellan was notified by telegraph, and ordered Smith to dispatch troops to investigate. Custer and another officer volunteered to cross the river over the dam by themselves and approach the enemy camp. It did not take them long to discover that the Confederates had indeed vacated the earthworks and the entire town. McClellan, who understood that he would be vilified by his superiors, the press, and the public for allowing the enemy to escape without inflicting any damage, ordered an immediate pursuit.[14]

The day was cold and dreary, and heavy rain had turned the countryside into a quagmire, but McClellan believed that he could escape the considerable criticism for his hesitancy to attack Yorktown by striking and defeating his enemy wherever they chose to make a stand. General Stoneman's cavalry—without Custer, who remained with General Baldy Smith—was ordered to immediately pursue the retreating enemy. General Joseph Hooker's division was sent to support Stoneman by moving down the Yorktown and Williamsburg Road. Baldy Smith's division would move forward by the Lee's Mill and Williamsburg roads.[15]

Confederate General Joseph Johnston had chosen to withdraw from Yorktown in order to seek a more favorable location with which to engage McClellan's huge army. The cavalry under Jeb Stuart once again acted superbly as rear guard and screened the departure of the Confederates, who slogged through muddy roads up the Peninsula. On the afternoon of May 4, Stuart's scouts informed him that the Yankees were in hot pursuit on the road behind them. Stuart left the road and traveled along the sandy shore of the James River.

In 1861, the Confederates had erected a system of crude earthworks, consisting of thirteen redoubts, with the heavily fortified so-called Fort Magruder—named after Major General John B. Magruder, who oversaw its construction—at the center, about two miles from Williamsburg, the old colonial capital of Virginia. Jeb Stuart and his cavalry reached Fort Magruder, and he attached his command to Major General James Longstreet, whose division was presently entrenched at that location.[16]

That same afternoon, Custer could hear distinct sounds of battle originating from the south side of the Peninsula. Evidently, one of the Union detachments had encountered the enemy and was engaged in a vicious fight. General Smith did not respond with concern to the distant action and continued riding through the rain until dark, when he called a halt and the men went into a soggy bivouac.

Before long, a messenger rode into Smith's headquarters with the word that the cavalry, including Custer's Fifth Regiment, had taken a beating that afternoon and sustained heavy losses. No doubt Custer was moved by this terrible news, and may have even contemplated requesting permission from the general to rejoin his old outfit.

On the chilly morning of May 5, however, Custer remained with Smith's column as it marched through the miserable conditions. Eventually, Custer was assigned the duty of riding ahead on roads that had become hazardous with thick mud to seek out more passable detours that would lead the troops to Williamsburg in the fastest possible manner. The sounds of battle were already emanating from the direction of that town, and Smith was anxious to enter the fray.

When Custer approached the Skiff Creek bridge, which he discovered had just been set on fire, a sniper targeted him from the surrounding brush. Custer leaped from the saddle and fired off a number of rounds with his pistol at this invisible arsonist. Then, leading his horse and all the while shooting, he reached the bridge. The sniper-arsonist was by that time discouraged from making a stand, and vanished into the woodlands. Custer stamped out the flames, burning his hands in the process, but saved the structure for the column to cross. This heroic action was recognized by General Baldy Smith, who officially cited Second Lieutenant George Armstrong Custer for gallantry.[17]

The Battle of Williamsburg had begun that morning at about 7:00 A.M., when Union troops under Brigadier General Joe Hooker attacked Longstreet's position at Fort Magruder and were met with fierce opposition. On both sides of the line, artillery shells whistled overhead and tore into the rain-drenched woodland, while bullets zipped through the trees, ripping leaves and branches apart and sending debris flying in every direction.

Another of Custer's West Point friends, Confederate captain John Pelham, would be singled out for his actions in commanding the artillery battery. Pelham had only three guns at his disposal, but fired off 360 rounds in succession that pinned down the Union troops and made it impossible for them to maneuver close.[18]

The men entrenched in the rifle pits along the Rebel stronghold, which stretched for almost four miles in length, were determined to hold their position against Hooker's pressure. Bold charges by Hooker's troops into the midst of the gray line were repelled one right after another. Jeb Stuart's cavalry was called upon to check the enemy at various locations along the line, and responded admirably. Ultimately, counterattacks by General Longstreet's men had started taking a toll on the Yankees.[19]

Baldy Smith's division was positioned on Hooker's right covering the

Yorktown Road. Smith received word about a route through the woods that crossed a dam on Cub Creek beyond the enemy's flank that was said to have been left unguarded. Second Lieutenant Custer was dispatched to investigate, and returned to confirm the information. Smith sought permission to cross the dam with his entire division, but that request was denied because his outfit was holding the center of the Union line. He did, however, obtain approval to advance a brigade across the dam. Smith selected Brigadier General Winfield Scott Hancock's brigade—thirty-four hundred men and eight artillery pieces—for the movement. Armstrong Custer volunteered to accompany Hancock, and was granted permission.[20]

Custer, who had made the initial reconnaissance, was at the front riding with the leading regiment—the Fifth Wisconsin—as it crossed the dam and then deployed within about a mile of Longstreet's left flank in two abandoned redoubts to prepare for contact with the Rebels. General Hancock, with Custer at his side, readied his artillery on the crest of a hill above a wheat field and placed skirmishers on the right and left of the road, reinforcing the Wisconsin regiment with the Sixth Maine. It was not long before their presence was contested. Confederate riflemen from Fort Magruder turned their weapons on Hancock's men and laid down a ferocious base of fire to pin them down.

Several hours later, Hancock's entrenched men were faced with a daunting sight—Confederate soldiers, their rebel yells sending chills down the spines of the surprised Federals, burst from the trees and raced toward Hancock's position. "The Confederates," Custer wrote, "with courage which has never been surpassed by the troops upon either side, boldly advanced, delivering their fire as rapidly as possible, and never ceasing to utter their inspiring battle cry."[21]

Before long, the ranks of the advancing Rebels were being decimated by small arms fire, and the charge began to waver. Hancock rode along the line exhorting his men to counterattack with a bayonet charge into the faltering enemy. The Union soldiers were still intimidated by that mass of howling gray-clad men, however. Hancock's troops slowly began to form ranks for a charge, but orders from their officers to move forward were largely ignored.

The soldiers feared that they were outnumbered and would be slaughtered if they moved closer to that Rebel force.

The anxious Union troops refused to obey orders and were losing an opportunity to deal a severe blow to their enemy—until Second Lieutenant George Armstrong Custer decided to take the initiative to encourage the men.

Custer boldly rode out where everyone along the line could see him. He waved his hat and shouted to urge the troops forward—an act that likely none of them, officer or enlisted, had ever witnessed before then. But Custer was not finished. He spurred his mount and, hunched down in the saddle, his pistol raised and ready to fire, his yellow hair flowing behind him, burst from their midst and rode on a collision course with the enemy.

This brazen act by the lone rider inspired and rallied the men, and renewed their fighting spirit. The roar from the Union lines drowned out those terrifying rebel yells. The soldiers poured from their positions and, following Custer, charged after their enemy. General Hancock wrote in his official report that with "Lieutenant Custer, Fifth Regular Cavalry, volunteering and leading the way on horseback," the Confederates broke into a retreat.[22]

Hancock's ability to flank the Confederates had for all intents and purposes ended the battle for Williamsburg. The fighting ceased soon after dark when Johnston withdrew and resumed his escape up the Peninsula, allowing the Union army to secure that picturesque town, which boasted beautiful colonial buildings belonging to the College of William & Mary. The day's losses totaled about twenty-two hundred for the Union army and at least seventeen hundred for the Confederates, but the Federals held the field, a requisite for victory.

Back on the battlefield, Second Lieutenant Custer emerged from the destruction—dead horses, overturned ambulances, abandoned artillery pieces, and dead and wounded men from both sides—in high spirits. He had not only led the gallant charge of Hancock's troops, but had played a major role in beating back the enemy.[23]

Custer wrote, "I was in the thick of the fight from morning till dark. The Battle of Williamsburg was hard fought, far more so than Bull Run. I captured a Captain and five men without any assistance, and a large rebel flag. It was afterwards sent up by McClellan to the President at Washington."[24]

If this "large rebel flag" was indeed a battle flag—although none was reported missing by the Confederate regiments—it would have been the first enemy colors taken by the Army of the Potomac. That feat would have been quite an honor for George Armstrong Custer. Nineteenth-century combatants regarded the capture of enemy battle colors to be the highest measure of glory that could be bestowed upon an individual. This resulted from the belief that the loss of a flag was a unit's greatest shame. Consequently, had Custer indeed successfully captured this flag, it would not have been surprising that none of the Confederate regiments would admit to the loss.

Perhaps Second Lieutenant Custer also learned a valuable lesson about charges that day that he would carry with him in the future. While most officers would order a charge and send their troops forward, themselves lagging behind, as was the custom, Custer had emboldened the men into action by his visible presence at the front. In other words, he learned that a leader should lead and not expect his troopers to charge the cannon's mouth while he watched from a safe distance. Of course, few officers shared the propensity for action and calculated risk that flowed through the veins of Armstrong Custer.

One of the Confederate prisoners taken at Williamsburg was Custer's former classmate and friend, Captain John "Gimlet" Lea from Mississippi, who had been badly wounded in the leg. Upon seeing Custer, Lea cried and hugged him. Custer went out of his way to make sure his friend was as comfortable as possible. The two young men then talked at length about old times and exchanged information about classmates on both sides of the conflict. Custer received permission to remain with Lea for two days, and carried his meals to him and generally watched over him.

Upon leaving, Armstrong gave Gimlet Lea much-needed stockings and some money. Lea reciprocated by writing in Custer's notebook that, if captured, Armstrong should be given good treatment by the Southerners. Custer remarked, "The bystanders looked with surprise when we were talking, and

afterwards asked if the prisoner were my brother." Despite those political
and sectional differences that had led them to serve on opposite sides of this
war, the youthful West Point friendship of the two young men had endured
onto the battlefield.[25]

On May 20, Second Lieutenant Custer rejoined his outfit for the march
up the Peninsula, which reached the swollen Chickahominy River—a waterway that flowed into the James River. The river was normally forty feet across,
but due to recent rains had overrun its banks and flooded nearby woodlands.
McClellan's troops needed to cross this river, but the Rebels had burned all
the bridges and placed sharpshooters to guard potential crossing locations.
Union engineering officers were detailed the task of scouting out potential
crossing sites.

Custer was assigned to accompany Brigadier General John G. Barnard,
the army's chief engineer, on this potentially dangerous mission. On a number of occasions, Custer would not simply guess at the depth of the water but
would wade right into the river to find out for certain—in spite of being exposed to enemy sharpshooters. With his revolver held over his head and
without removing his clothing, he would move across that river to the opposite bank in water up to his chest. This was typical of the way Custer went
about his daily responsibilities, wherever he was assigned—with a guarded
fearlessness and dedication to duty.[26]

At one point, Custer and Lieutenant Nicholas Bowen happened upon
an ideal place at a bend in the river that could support the crossing of a raiding party into enemy-occupied territory. Custer crept closer and spied pickets walking their posts, as well as the main guard post, which he believed
could be captured by a small force. That information was passed back to
headquarters.

On May 24, an infantry and cavalry operation was mounted at that position seven miles below Mechanicsville at New Bridge. Custer and Bowen led
two companies of the Fourth Michigan to this newly found ford on the Chickahominy River. One company crossed, while the other headed downstream
to New Bridge, where the remainder of the regiment was engaged in a firefight
with Confederate pickets from Louisiana and Georgia.

Custer attached himself to the company that crossed the stream and struck the enemy on the flank. The attack forced the surprised Confederates back, and resulted in fifty of the enemy being captured. Custer advanced with a line of skirmishers, and battled the Rebels for three hours before Lieutenant Bowen ordered a withdrawal. Bowen wrote in his official report that Armstrong Custer "was the first to cross the stream, the first to open fire, and one of the last to leave the field." [27]

General George McClellan was informed of every aspect of the raid—including the process of testing water depths and the foray across the stream—and requested the presence of that heroic second lieutenant named Custer.

The commanding general remembered seeing Armstrong Custer for the first time: "He was then a slim, long-haired boy, carelessly dressed [his uniform was likely still covered with mud from the stream]. I thanked him for his gallantry, and asked him what I could do for him. He replied very modestly that he had nothing to ask, and evidently did not suppose that he had done anything to deserve extraordinary reward."

McClellan then asked if Custer would be interested in serving as an aide-de-camp on his personal staff. "Upon this," McClellan wrote, "he brightened up, assured me that he would regard such service as the most gratifying he could perform; and I at once gave the necessary orders."[28]

So, George Armstrong Custer, at the bottom of his West Point class, had been chosen to be an assistant to the top general in the army. His bravery under fire and desire to be at the front in every battle had finally paid off for him. An assignment like this was not handed out to just anyone. Custer must have been bursting with pride as he reported to the commanding general, ready to prove once again that he could assume any role thrust upon him and excel. And he would more than live up to expectations.

Six

———◆———

Aide-de-Camp

The position of aide-de-camp at army headquarters, which carried with it the brevet, or temporary, rank of captain, entailed great responsibility. George Armstrong Custer would report directly to General McClellan and take orders only from him. As the top commander's representative, he was required to be knowledgeable about troop positions, movements, routes, and locations of the officers and to possess the ability to modify orders on the battlefield if McClellan was unavailable. He would spend long hours in the saddle without food or sleep and, if necessary, ride into the thickest of the fighting to gather information or deliver the commander's orders.

The adventurous Custer was perfectly suited for this position, which would also serve as a valuable learning experience for him from the man whom he had previously sworn that he would "follow to the ends of the earth."

The admiration and devotion that Custer held for McClellan would soon become mutual. The general wrote, "In those days, Custer was simply a reckless, gallant boy, undeterred by fatigue, inconscious of fear. His head was always clear in danger and he always brought me clear and intelligible reports of what he saw under the heaviest fire. I became much attached to him."[1]

In some respects, this relationship between McClellan and Custer was quite odd. The most glaring contradiction was how the two men differed in their approach to combat. McClellan was overly cautious and hesitant when it came to attacking, whereas Custer was a man of action who bordered on recklessness and was prone to charge rather than wait. Nevertheless, the two men quickly established a close bond, with Custer clearly engaging in hero worship of his older mentor.

By the end of May, McClellan's 105,000-man army had approached to within six miles of Richmond—close enough to observe church spires rising above the city. McClellan placed two corps south and three north of the swollen Chickahominy near the crossroads of Seven Pines and Fair Oaks Station on the Richmond & York River Railroad. The Federal commander was confident that he could now administer "one desperate blow" to destroy the Confederacy.[2]

It was Confederate general Joseph Johnston, however, who seized the initiative and on May 31 attacked one of McClellan's isolated corps with his sixty thousand fighting men. Johnston had been pressured by President Jefferson Davis to mount an offensive against the Union forces, which had not been the best idea. The general's hastily devised battle plan was perhaps too complicated to be effectively executed. The two-day battle of Seven Pines and Fair Oaks resulted in enormous casualties on both sides. The Federal troops suffered 5,031 casualties and the Confederates 6,134—including the wounding of Johnston, who was struck in the chest with a shell fragment. In the end, the Yankees held the ground when the Rebels withdrew.[3]

General George McClellan, however, could not savor the victory. This was the first battle under Little Mac's command that his troops had suffered serious losses. He wrote to his wife after the fight was over, "I am tired of the sickening sight of the battlefield, with its mangled corpses & poor suffering wounded! Victory has no charms for me when purchased at such cost."[4]

During the battle, Confederate Lieutenant James B. Washington, an aide-de-camp to General Johnston, was carrying messages when he happened upon Union troops and was captured. Washington was escorted to McClellan's headquarters, where Armstrong Custer cared for his West Point class of '59 acquaintance. The two men were photographed together—in one photo Washington called out to a small black boy standing nearby, and placed the child between the two men, saying the picture ought to be called "Both sides, the cause." This photo later appeared in *Harper's Weekly*. When Washington was sent to the rear, Custer gave him some money, a gesture the prisoner and his family never forgot.[5]

On June 1, Confederate president Jefferson Davis replaced General Johnston with fifty-five-year-old Robert E. Lee—West Point class of 1829—who had been called by Union general Winfield Scott "the best soldier I ever saw in the field."

Robert was the fourth child of "Light Horse Harry" Lee, who had been a Revolutionary War cavalry hero. Harry, however, subsequently had been imprisoned for debt and died from wounds he received in trying to suppress a riot in Baltimore. Young Robert was reared by his widowed mother in Alexandria, Virginia, where he attended private schools until being appointed to West Point in 1825. He graduated second in his class, without a demerit to his name, and was commissioned a second lieutenant. Two years after his graduation, he married heiress Mary Custis, the great-granddaughter of Martha Washington. The couple would have seven children.

Lee would toil at various civil and military engineering projects until the Mexican War, when he was assigned to the staff of General Winfield Scott. He distinguished himself in several battles, including the assault of Chapultepec, where he was wounded. He was promoted to brevet colonel for his heroism, and in 1852 assumed a three-year term as superintendent at West Point. He was on leave from his assignment in Texas in 1859 when he was placed in command of a detachment of United States Marines and recaptured the Harpers Ferry arsenal from John Brown and his followers.

After the fall of Fort Sumter, President Abraham Lincoln offered Lee the field command of the Union army. Lee, a loyal Virginian, declined and instead accepted command of his state defenses. On August 31, 1961, he was promoted to full general with the assignment as special advisor to President Jefferson Davis. Now, he was commander of the forces he named "The Army of Northern Virginia."

Robert E. Lee's first order was to withdraw his army to the outskirts of

Richmond in order to defend that city while he planned an offensive intended to crush McClellan's army.[6]

Meanwhile, Confederate cavalry commander Jeb Stuart was disappointed with his role thus far in the campaign, and sought an opportunity to help his country and distinguish himself in the process.

Virginia plantation born, twenty-nine-year-old James Ewell Brown Stuart—known to his friends as "Jeb"—was educated at home by his mother, his aunt, and various tutors until the age of fifteen, when he entered Emory & Henry College. After two years of college and a failed attempt at enlisting in the army, Jeb received an appointment to West Point, where he graduated in 1854, ranked thirteenth in his class of forty-six.

The newly commissioned lieutenant served on scouting duty in Texas, but was soon transferred to the First Cavalry Regiment at Fort Leavenworth, Kansas Territory. At that post in 1855, he met Flora Cooke, the daughter of the commander of the Second Dragoon Regiment. The couple was married in November of that year. He engaged in fighting Native Americans on the Plains, as well as participating in the violence of Bleeding Kansas.

In one notable 1857 skirmish with the Cheyenne on Solomon's Fork, or the Smoky Hill River, in northwest Kansas, Stuart was chasing a fleeing group of warriors when he came upon several troopers battling with a dismounted warrior who had leveled his revolver and was about to shoot one of the men. Stuart instinctively drew his saber and charged to protect his comrade. Stuart swung his blade, feeling the steel strike its target, but simultaneously, the warrior discharged his weapon from a distance of about one foot. The bullet struck Stuart squarely in the chest. He was carried three miles to the doctor, who announced that the bullet had bounced off a bone and lodged in fatty tissue without causing serious damage to any vital organ. Stuart was back to duty in several weeks.

In 1859, Stuart invented and patented a new piece of cavalry equipment, a saber hook, which improved the manner in which sabers were attached to belts. While in Washington to discuss a government contract for his invention, Stuart served as an aide-de-camp to Colonel Robert E. Lee at Harpers Ferry and read the ultimatum to John Brown before the assault.

Jeb Stuart was promoted to captain in April 1861, but resigned from the

U.S. Army in May with the advent of war. He was made a lieutenant colonel in the Virginia infantry, promoted to lieutenant colonel of cavalry soon after, and now served as a brigadier general commanding a brigade of gray-clad horsemen.[7]

Stuart was a jovial man who loved to laugh and sing. He viewed himself as the ultimate cavalier, and played the role to the hilt. He was described by author Mark Nesbitt, "In stature he was six feet, and weighed about one-hundred and ninety pounds. A complexion somewhat ruddy from exposure, with light brown hair, worn rather long, and full flowing beards. His regulation gray uniform was profusely decorated with gold braid, and was topped with a broad-brimmed felt hat, pinned up at the side with a star from which drooped an extravagantly large ostrich feather. On his left breast was a shield, about two inches in width, which held a chain attached to the handle of a small stiletto, the blade being passed through the button holes of his coat." He was also known to wear a red-lined gray cape, a yellow sash, and a hat cocked roguishly to the side, and he placed a red flower in his lapel.[8]

Now, this dashing cavalier craved adventure and achievement. To that end, he decided to initiate a reconnaissance of the area to determine whether the enemy had any glaring weaknesses.

John Singleton Mosby had been assigned to Jeb Stuart's cavalry as a scout. Mosby, who had attended the University of Virginia until being imprisoned for shooting a fellow student—the details of which are elusive to this day— had left his law practice in Bristol, Virginia, to fight at Bull Run, and was as anxious for action as the cavalry commander.

Mosby was dispatched by Stuart on a mission to find out if McClellan had protected his army's supply line on the right flank. Mosby returned from his scout to report that the Union had only a few cavalry outposts in that area, which rendered the supply line quite vulnerable. An elated Jeb Stuart immediately rode off to General Lee's headquarters at Dabb's Farm.

The commanding general was impressed with the information, but required confirmation. Stuart would lead his cavalry—1,200 men—on a raiding expedition into the Union rear for the purpose of gaining intelligence, disrupting supply and communication lines, and destroying wagon trains.[9]

At 2:00 A.M. on June 12, a cheerful Jeb Stuart awakened his staff and announced, "Gentlemen, in ten minutes every man must be in the saddle!" He told no one of their destination, and when asked how long they would be gone, replied, "It may be for years and it may be forever."

The morning was sweltering and muggy as Stuart and his cavalry rode steadily northward up the Brook Turnpike. Stuart could never have dared imagine the extent of accolades that would be showered upon him for this mission—but he was about to ride into the annals of Southern legend.[10]

On Sunday morning, June 15, after three days in the saddle and a distance of 150 miles, General Stuart, with Mosby scouting the way, returned home after riding all the way around McClellan's army. He had obtained vital intelligence, confiscated or destroyed millions of dollars' worth of Union property, bloodied the enemy at will, and captured 165 prisoners and 260 horses and mules—all the while thoroughly embarrassing the Northern army. And he had lost only one man—Captain William Latane, who would become a martyr for the Confederate cause for losing his life in a cavalry charge at Old Church. Stuart's amazing feat gained him overnight celebrity status in the South.[11]

Beneath headlines such as "A Magnificent Achievement," Southern newspapers were filled with embellished accounts of this dangerous expedition. Stuart was hailed a hero by an adoring Confederate public to the extent that when he was recognized while viewing a military drill, he obliged requests to make a speech from the steps of the Governor's Mansion, which was received "amidst the ring of deafening cheers." But perhaps the most significant praise came from General Lee, who called Stuart a "gallant officer" and expressed "his admiration of the courage and skill so conspicuously exhibited throughout" the raid that he proclaimed "a brilliant exploit." From that point forward, Lee would regard Stuart's cavalry as the trusted eyes and ears of the Confederate army.[12]

General Lee planned to act immediately on the intelligence that Stuart had provided by confirming that his enemy indeed had a weak spot that could be exploited. This action would entail bringing General Stonewall

Jackson down from the Shenandoah Valley to join three other divisions that together would strike the vulnerable Federal right flank.[13]

General George McClellan had abandoned his headquarters at White House and was in the process of moving twenty miles away to the James River by the time the Confederates attacked at Mechanicsville on June 26—without Jackson, who inexplicably continued to slowly march southward and failed to arrive according to his commander's wishes.

Captain George Armstrong Custer was sent by McClellan to determine the extent of the situation on the battlefield. He reported back that certain units were under immense pressure, and then was told by McClellan to pass the word to the beleaguered Pennsylvania Reserves to "maintain the honor of Pennsylvania." Custer rode along the entire line under fire repeating McClellan's words of encouragement to each regiment he passed, and was showered with cheers from the troops.

On the following day, Custer was conferring with McClellan when Stonewall Jackson finally arrived from the Valley to strike a corps five miles downstream from headquarters at Gaines' Mill. Custer was asked by McClellan if he knew of any crossing sites suitable to send in reinforcements. When Custer replied that he did, McClellan sent him out to guide two brigades across the river; the crossing was not completed until late that afternoon amidst a scene of confusion that reminded Custer of the mad scramble across Cub Run Bridge at Bull Run.

McClellan kept his aide-de-camp busy moving brigades into position and assisting in the removal of the wounded. Armstrong Custer would later write to his sister, "I was in the saddle four consecutive nights and as many days. I generally had but one meal—coffee and hard bread—breakfast."

The stamina of George Armstrong Custer was remarkable. He may have been on the slender side, but he was physically strong and could stay awake and alert for long periods of time. One officer remarked that Custer could "eat and sleep as much as anyone when he has the chance. But he can do without either when necessary."[14]

During this vicious battle, the Confederate artillery was commanded by

Tom Rosser, Custer's best friend at West Point, who had been promoted to lieutenant colonel on June 10. Rosser had distinguished himself throughout the conflict, and was singled out for official praise by General Beverly Robertson, "Rosser received a severe flesh wound in the arm, which, though did not prevent his commanding the pieces while the engagement continued. [He] displayed much judgment in placing his pieces, which, under his personal supervision, were served in the most handsome style."[15]

Captain John Pelham also received a complimentary report from Jeb Stuart, "[He] displayed such signal ability as an artillerist; such heroic example and devotion in danger and indomitable energy under difficulties in the movement of his battery. I feel bound to ask for his promotion, with the remark that in either cavalry or artillery no field grade is too high for his merit and capacity." Pelham, stripped down to his shirtsleeves, had helped load, aim, and fire his guns.[16]

It was no wonder that these two Custer friends from West Point would distinguish themselves. Former roommates Rosser and Pelham were flamboyant extroverts, known as aggressive commanders who demonstrated raw courage under fire and would risk their own lives to inspire their troops. No doubt Custer had heard of their exploits, and was eager to prove that he belonged alongside them as a battlefield commander. But for now, Custer understood that his role as McClellan's aide was a vital part of Union military operations.

Rosser, however, was not destined to remain in artillery. At the Academy, Rosser, Pelham, and Custer were known as the best riders on the post. On June 24, Rosser was promoted to full colonel and assigned command of the Fifth Virginia Cavalry Regiment in Jeb Stuart's division. Rosser would be in the saddle for the remainder of the war, and would prove himself to be an invaluable cavalry officer.[17]

With Lee's army on two sides of him, McClellan abandoned his advance on Richmond and began to withdraw down the James River. On July 1, Union forces successfully repulsed Confederate assaults at Malvern Hill, which brought to an end the so-called Seven Days' Campaign. McClellan marched his army through the rain that night to Harrison's Landing, where gunboats on the James River could protect the troops.

While McClellan's men rested and recuperated, the general dispatched messages to Washington imploring President Lincoln to supply more men, that the lack of troop strength was the reason the operation had not been successful. Regardless of the Southerners' victories, McClellan's frustration, and the president's lack of patience, morale amongst the Federal troops was high and their commanding general personally remained popular.[18]

During this time of relaxation, Custer loafed around the encampment, spending most of his time with his new best friend, Lieutenant Nicholas Bowen. Both men had taken on paid "servants" from the scores of former slaves who had poured into the camps to seek Union protection. Custer's horse was well taken care of, his uniform was neat and tidy, and his boots were shined daily. He had also acquired a dog named Rose, which would start the custom of him keeping animals, including packs of dogs, at his duty stations throughout the rest of his life.[19]

On August 2, First Lieutenant George Armstrong Custer—his new regular army rank dated to July 17—was detailed by McClellan to accompany a reconnaissance mission toward Southern lines comprised of three hundred cavalrymen under the command of Colonel William W. Averell.

By late morning, the patrol had traveled forty miles. Custer was scouting ahead when he came upon a regiment of Confederate cavalry near White Oak Swamp. He reported his discovery, and Colonel Averell ordered a charge. The surprised Rebels scattered in the face of the assault, many of them surrendering when realizing that their escape route was cut off.

At one point, Custer chased a Confederate officer who was riding a bay horse with a black saddle and a morocco breast-strap, and called for the man to surrender. Their harrowing ride took them hurdling over fences and racing through treacherous pastures and shrub-clogged woodlands. Custer urged his mount to greater speeds, and gained on his enemy. He called out once more for the man to halt and surrender. When there was no reply, Custer pulled out his pistol and shot the officer from the saddle—probably the first man he had killed in the war in a one-on-one situation. He later wrote, "I had either shot him in the neck or body. In either case the wound must have been mortal. It was his own fault; I told him twice to surrender, but he compelled me to shoot him."

Custer also captured a soldier and confiscated a double-barreled shotgun and a bright bay horse, which he planned to send home to his brother, Boston. He also captured or was given a sword—a coveted Toledo blade—from the saddle of a riderless mount. This heavy sword was inscribed with the Spanish sentiment: NO NI TIRES SIN RAZON, NO MI ENVAINES SIN HONRA. "Draw me not without provocation. Sheathe me not without honor." In the tradition of King Arthur's Excalibur, Custer was said to have been awarded the special sword by virtue of the fact that he was the only one strong enough to easily heft the blade above his head.

The raiding party returned without losing a man, and Custer was cited for "gallant and spirited conduct."[20]

But all was not well at headquarters when Custer reported back to General George McClellan. The general had promised President Lincoln that he would resume his advance on Richmond—only after he was reinforced with fifty thousand additional troops. This excuse of not enough manpower irked Lincoln, and he decided to take action.

The president and his advisors had devised a plan to reorganize the army. McClellan's corps was recalled to the capital, and would be combined with the armies of Major General Nathaniel Banks, General John C. Fremont, and General Irvin McDowell to create the Army of Virginia, under the overall command of Major General John Pope. McClellan, predictably, was opposed to the plan, and lingered until mid-August before marching his troops toward Fort Monroe for transport to Washington.[21]

The Southern cavalry had also undergone reorganization. Jeb Stuart received a commission to major general, and in accord with his rank would command a division of cavalry comprised of two brigades. One brigade would be led by Stuart's close friend, twenty-seven-year-old newly commissioned brigadier general Fitzhugh Lee, Robert's nephew, a veteran of the Indian wars, and one of Cadet Custer's instructors at West Point. The other brigade went to new brigadier general Wade Hampton, a forty-four-year-old South Carolinian whose management of his family's plantations had made him one of the largest slave owners and wealthiest men in the South. Incidentally, the Fifth Virginia Cavalry regiment now would be commanded by newly promoted Colonel Tom Rosser.[22]

When Custer arrived in Williamsburg with McClellan's staff, he learned that his Confederate friend Gimlet Lea was on parole from Fortress Monroe and recuperating in that town. Lea had been given his conditional release after another West Point acquaintance, Alexander Pennington, happened upon him lying in a barn.

Custer was granted permission to visit Gimlet Lea, and found his old friend at the home of his fiancée, whose mother had nursed Lea back to health in the hospital. This "secesh" family warmly received Custer with typical Southern hospitality and invited him to return that evening for supper.

While they dined, Lea related that the couple had planned to marry the next week, but now that Custer had unexpectedly arrived Lea wanted his West Point friend to stand up for him as his best man. Custer agreed, and the nuptials were hastily set for the following evening.

Custer wrote in a letter to his sister, "I was at the residence of the bride long before the appointed hour. Both [the bride and her bridesmaid and cousin, Maggie] were dressed in white with a simple wreath of flowers upon their heads. I never saw two prettier girls. Lea was dressed in a bright new rebel uniform trimmed with gold lace; I wore my full uniform of blue."

After the traditional Episcopalian wedding ceremony, Custer went on, "Every one seemed happy except the young lady who had been my partner on the floor. She kissed the bride and sat down crying. Lea, observing this, said, 'Why, Cousin Maggie, what are you crying for? There is nothing to cry about.—Oh, I know. You are crying because you are not married; well, here is the minister and here is Captain Custer, who I know would be glad to carry off such a pretty bride from the Confederacy.' She managed to reply, 'Captain Lea, you are just as mean as you can be.'"

Later, Armstrong and Maggie evidently had been flirting, while enjoying each other's company. He escorted her out to dinner and asked how it was that so strong a secessionist as she could take the arm of a Union officer. She coyly answered, "You *ought* to be in *our* army." After dinner, Maggie played the piano and enthusiastically sang "For Southern Rights, Hurrah," as well as "Dixie," while a laughing Custer turned the pages of the sheet music for her.[23]

Gimlet Lea would soon be exchanged, and according to Custer would be "fighting for what he *supposes* to be right!"[24]

Another Confederate West Point comrade had also found love. Artillery officer extraordinaire John Pelham had begun seriously courting Sallie Dandridge while training his men at Jeb Stuart's headquarters on the plantation owned by her father, Colonel Adam Dandridge, situated along the Opequon Creek near Martinsburg. The Dandridges were a wealthy and influential family—Martha Washington had been born a Dandridge and had spent time during her youth at that plantation.

Pelham romanced Sallie relentlessly—riding through the countryside with her, dancing exclusively with her, strolling through the fields hand in hand with her. The romance became so intense that Stuart asked his trusted subordinate if Sallie was going to spoil John's love of fighting. Pelham truthfully replied that he still loved to fight, but would be glad when the fighting was over and he could settle down with Sallie and raise a family. Pelham gave Sallie his most prized possession—the Bible his mother had given him to take to West Point. It appeared that another wedding would be taking place in the near future—but the couple would have to plan it around the operations and battles of a very active cavalry.[25]

In late August, General Pope's sixty thousand troops faced off across the Rappahannock River with Lee's fifty thousand, and engaged in the familiar battleground of Bull Run, or Manassas, the scene of the first major battle of the war. With Stonewall Jackson and Jeb Stuart leading the way, the Rebel army crossed the river, and by August 30 had caved in Pope's flank, which resulted in a Union defeat. Pope's army suffered 16,000 casualties, while inflicting 9,200 on its enemy. Lee resumed his march toward the Potomac, preparing to raid into Maryland.[26]

Two days after this Second Battle of Bull Run, in a move hailed by the rank-and-file troopers, President Lincoln restored George McClellan to command of the Union forces. With Lee invading Maryland, Little Mac quickly marched with his energized army to meet the challenge, arriving in Rockville on September 7, but slowed his pace the closer he came to his enemy.[27]

McClellan cautiously pursued Lee's army. By a quirk of fate, he acquired a copy—one of nine given to the various commanders—of Lee's Special Order No. 191, which outlined Confederate plans for the Maryland campaign. A Union private had discovered the orders wrapped around three cigars in a meadow where Confederate soldiers had previously camped. The wary McClellan thought it might be a trap, and waited two days before confronting Lee's army. That hesitation on McClellan's part afforded Lee time to position his men on the crest of a four-mile ridge east of Sharpsburg, beside a creek called Antietam.[28]

Perhaps remarkably, Custer would maintain that McClellan had used good judgment by not throwing his reserves against Lee's weak spots, which would have left his own line vulnerable. This opinion must have been made from blind loyalty—Custer the commander would later prove that he believed just the opposite and would send his last man toward the cannon's mouth against hopeless odds if there was even the slimmest chance that he might score a victory.[29]

The battle for Antietam on September 17 was the bloodiest single day of the war. Seventy thousand Union troops faced 39,000 Confederates, and when the acrid smoke had cleared, the field was littered with more than 26,000 casualties—13,700 Confederates and 12,350 Union soldiers were dead, wounded, or missing.

McClellan received reinforcements on September 18, but hesitated again, which gave Lee time to escape across the Potomac into Virginia during the night—with Stuart's cavalry screening the retreat. McClellan followed without much enthusiasm, never close enough to engage his enemy.[30]

While the Union army recuperated in the vicinity of Sharpsburg, President Lincoln used his war powers to issue his preliminary Emancipation Proclamation. This executive order did not outlaw slavery and did not make former slaves—now called freedmen—citizens. The act, however, called for another goal to attain in this conflict of states' rights, in addition to preserving the Union—that of human freedom. This insult outraged white Southerners and some Northern Democrats, invigorated abolitionists, and warned Europe not to intervene in the conflict on the side of the Confederacy.[31]

At Antietam, George Armstrong Custer had been kept busy at McClellan's headquarters but still managed to get into the fray. In one instance, he and another aide, Lieutenant James P. Martin, were detailed to General Alfred Pleasonton and attached to the Eighth Illinois at South Mountain. Near Boonsboro, Custer and a detachment were returning to headquarters when they encountered and captured several hundred Confederate stragglers and two abandoned cannon. Pleasonton cited Custer and Martin for heroism, and McClellan later reported the incident to President Lincoln.[32]

On September 26, Custer escorted a group of paroled Confederate soldiers across the Potomac under a flag of truce, and happened upon several of the enemy who had been classmates or friends. The gregarious Custer and his Rebel acquaintances "had an hour's social chat, discussing the war in a friendly way." Custer learned that in recent action he had been fighting Fitzhugh Lee and Tom Rosser, as well as Georgian Pierce Manning Butler Young, a West Point comrade who had prophesized that they would meet in battle, and who had been wounded in the engagement.[33]

In his role as a general's aide, Custer was traveling on the fringes of danger, but he no doubt would have preferred to have been in the thick of the fighting. He wrote a letter of a curious nature to his cousin on October 3 while President Lincoln was visiting the camp, which read in part, "You ask me if I will not be glad when the last battle is fought. So far as my country is concerned I, of course, must wish for peace, and I will be glad when the war is ended, but if I answer for myself *alone,* I must say that I shall regret to see the war end. I would be willing, yes glad, to see a battle every day during my life."[34]

Skeptics might comment that these words were merely the false bravado of a young man who, due to his position with McClellan, had not endured the daily hardships of war when compared to the average cavalry officer. That opinion, however, fails to take into consideration the fact that Custer possessed the character of a natural born cavalier—bold, daring, and ambitious almost to a fault. His revealing statement truly demonstrated how he yearned to prove his ability on the field of battle and feared that hostilities would end before he had the chance to attain the glory that he envisioned for himself.

There certainly had been no lack of battle experience or glory for Jeb Stuart, but he did not intend to remain idle when the opportunity for further distinction was only an expedition away. General Lee approved a plan by Stuart to lead a raiding party to Chambersburg, Pennsylvania. The purpose of the mission, in addition to gathering "all information of the position, force, and probable intention of the enemy," was to collect horses, snatch hostages for exchange, if possible, and destroy military stores.[35]

At dawn on October 10, Stuart's 1,800-man cavalry, reinforced with four artillery pieces under John Pelham, crossed the Potomac at McCoy's Ford heading north. The Southern cavalry returned home to Leesburg on October 12 after traveling 126 miles, and capturing about 1,200 horses and leaving in their wake at least $250,000 in damage. In the process, the Confederate horsemen had for the second time ridden around the Union army.[36]

Jeb Stuart had embarrassed McClellan once again with this bold raid, and that fact was widely reported to his admiring public. Stuart himself officially commemorated the event with a grand ball, where he received a gift of a pair of golden spurs from a woman in Baltimore. Stuart would adopt the sobriquet "The Knight of the Golden Spurs," and even sign some correspondence with the abbreviation "K.G.S."[37]

While Stuart and his cavalry celebrated this great success, all was not well on the Union side of the lines. On November 5, President Lincoln relieved General George B. McClellan as commander of the Army of the Potomac due to their continued disagreements over strategy. Major General Ambrose E. Burnside, a man with a bluff manner and elaborate side whiskers, would now be in charge of the Federal troops.[38]

The loyal George Armstrong Custer was predictably shocked and saddened by this unexpected turn of events. Rather than recognize the military faults of his beloved commander, he blamed the politics of the Republican administration for deposing the Democrat McClellan, which might have been a factor. Regardless of the true reason, there was little for Custer to do but return home to Monroe, Michigan, and await orders.

Custer's disappointment with McClellan's fate, however, would quickly become secondary in importance when another special person would reenter his life. The next best thing to fighting for a young man was to fall in love with a young lady, and Custer was about to fall as hard as anybody ever had.

Seven

Libbie

On Thanksgiving Day, George Armstrong Custer attended a party at the Young Ladies' Seminary and Collegiate Institute in Monroe, and was introduced to Elizabeth Clift "Libbie" Bacon—and his life would never be the same again.

Twenty-year-old Libbie Bacon had that effect on countless adoring boys who dreamed of being chosen as her romantic suitor. To call her merely attractive would be doing an injustice to this refined and spirited young lady. She stood a willowy five feet four inches tall with a dangerously thin waist and a well-rounded bustline. Her ivory face was framed by thick chestnut-brown hair and highlighted by luminous light blue-gray eyes that flashed with humor and mischief. But Libbie was more than just a rare beauty in terms of physical appeal. She was highly intelligent, strong-willed, properly educated—especially in literature and the arts—and was comfortable engaged in either serious conversation or whimsical flirtation. It was no wonder that she was considered the prettiest and most eligible young lady in that Lake Erie town.

From the above description, it would appear that Libbie Bacon had enjoyed a special upbringing of happiness and contentment, but, in truth, her early life had been far from idyllic.[1]

Libbie was the only child of Daniel S. Bacon, one of the most influential and respected citizens of Monroe, Michigan. Daniel, a descendant of the Plymouth Colony, had been reared on the family farm in Onondaga County in upstate New York, but departed at the age of twenty-four to seek greater opportunities. He carried with him a teaching certificate and dreams of finding a community where he could invest in cheap land and then fulfill his political ambitions. By the spring of 1823, his journey exploring small towns by stagecoach and steamship brought him to Michigan Territory, where he taught school by day and read law at night in a small settlement called Monroe.[2]

Daniel Bacon soon invested his money in a ten-acre parcel of land along the river Raisin, and planted apple, peach, and plum trees. In time, he passed the bar examination and opened a law office in town. With a partner, Levi S. Humphrey—whom Bacon had taught to read and write—he continued to buy government land, subdividing it into city lots and selling it for profit.

In 1831, Daniel entered politics and won election as county supervisor. A year later, that victory was followed by his election as inspector of schools, and in 1835 and 1836 as the Whig representative to the Fifth and Sixth Territorial Legislatures. Now that he had achieved an element of financial success and had earned the esteem of the community, Daniel decided at age thirty-nine that he could support a wife and family.[3]

The object of his affection was Eleanor Sophia Page, the twenty-three-year-old daughter of a nursery owner from Grand Rapids who had recently arrived from Putney, Vermont. Abel Page and his wife had the distinction of successfully marketing the "love apple," a decorative fruit that had long been rejected as being poisonous. Page had transplanted this fruit to his vegetable garden, bravely bit into a sample as an experiment, and thought it delicious. The love apple soon became known as the "tomato," and became a specialty of Page nurseries.[4]

Following a proper courtship, in June 1837 Daniel asked the Pages to sanction his engagement to their daughter, promising "protection and affection due from husband to wife." The couple was married in September, and honeymooned with a visit to Daniel's family in Onondaga County.[5]

Shortly after the nuptials, Daniel suffered his first political defeat when he ran for lieutenant governor. On the positive side, he took advantage of the recently passed free banking law to establish himself as president of the new Merchant and Mechanics Bank, and also assumed the position as assistant judge of the Monroe County Circuit Court.[6]

The Bacons' first child, Edward Augustus, was born on June 9, 1839. Soon after, the bank became a victim of the national economic depression and closed, but due to circumstances that did not tarnish the reputation of its president. Daniel was then elected to the Michigan Senate, and by November 1840 had risen to associate judge of the circuit court. Real estate may have been risky at the time, but the Bacons built a fashionable Greek Revival–style home on South Monroe Street in the center of town.

It was in this house that three daughters were born—Libbie, on April 8, 1842, and Sophia and Harriet, both of whom died in infancy. In 1848, the Bacons suffered another tragedy when their son, Edward, died from disease, likely cholera or diphtheria. With the death of Edward, six-year-old Libbie became an only child.[7]

No doubt the Bacons doted on their only surviving child, although Libbie was taught values and virtues and punished when necessary. Her mother, Sophia, as she was called, was a quiet woman who was involved with the Presbyterian Church as a Sunday school teacher, perhaps finding solace for her losses in her belief in God's will. Libbie may have been strong-willed, but she went out of her way to please her parents and was an obedient child.

Libbie was also immersed in the church, often attending services twice on Sundays, and freely offering her opinion regarding sermons. By her tenth birthday, she also attended other churches—Catholic and Methodist, in particular—as she searched for truth among the various faiths. Libbie attended Boyd's Seminary primary school during the week, and played with her friends after school, mainly in her own backyard, where Daniel had set up a swing.[8]

Her father had given Libbie a diary on her ninth birthday with the inscription: "to be kept and preserved by her as a wish of her Father Daniel S. Bacon." He had also admonished her to be sure to write legibly. After a year, she felt confident enough in her handwriting and thought process to begin making entries.

Her observations displayed a youthful eye for reporting details of local news. "It has been more like Spring today than any we have had this month," she wrote. "A dissipated german by the name of Mr. Aulwringden living near the depot committed suicide by hanging himself this after-noon near tea time." She would write about P. T. Barnum coming to town with little person Tom Thumb, and noted that the stands collapsed under the weight of so many people in attendance. She chronicled one person's failed trip to the California gold fields, remarking about the hardships of travel across the Plains and observing that California was not the Promised Land after all.

This diary would also become her confidant for personal thoughts and dreams as she struggled with the ideals and morals suitable to a good Christian girl. She would copy down favorite lines of poetry and possibly song lyrics.[9]

Twelve-year-old Libbie's journal was the recipient of a sorrowful entry on August 27, 1854, "When I last wrote you my Mother sat comfortably in her dear rocking chair by the fire. My dear mother is sleeping her last great sleep from which she never will awake no never! Not even to correct my numerous mistakes. Two weeks ago my mother was laid in the cold ground, & as I stood by that open grave and felt—oh! God only knows what anguish filled my heart. O! Why did they put my mother in that great black coffin & screw the lid down so tight? I hope the Lord will spare me to my father for I am his only comfort left." Before the casket had been closed, Libbie slipped the wedding ring off her mother's finger and clipped a lock of her hair.[10]

Sophia had died from "bloody dysentery, the second case in town." Daniel wrote to his family, "My poor wife is no more. Her physicians were unacquainted with the nature of her disease. She bore sufferings with great composure and Christian fortitude." Before Sophia had lapsed into a coma, she had been gazing lovingly upon a portrait of her daughter.[11]

Soon after her mother's death, Libbie was sent to live with Sophia's sister, Loraine Richmond, in Grand Rapids, while Daniel moved into a room at the Exchange Hotel. Libbie would be in the company of two cousins, Rebecca and Mary, who could help comfort her. After several months, however, this arrangement did not suit Libbie, and Daniel brought her back to Monroe.

In November, Libbie was enrolled in the Young Ladies' Seminary and Collegiate Institute, a boarding school established by and for prominent Monroe citizens. The principal, Reverend Erasmus Boyd—who also ran Boyd's Seminary primary school—demonstrated great sympathy for Libbie. He gave her special privileges, such as a room on the third floor with spectacular views of Lake Erie and the surrounding city, which she shared with a teacher, Miss Thompson. Boyd also offered the girl a small garden where she could tend flowers as a diversion to her gloomy thoughts.

Libbie soon learned that she could take advantage of others as "poor motherless Libbie Bacon." She wrote years later, "How shamelessly I traded on this. What an excuse I made of it for not doing anything I didn't want to do! And what excuses were made for me on that score." Part of her exploitation of sympathy was the fact that Daniel had left for New York and Vermont, leaving her "quite lonely all alone."[12]

In spite of the misery brought on by circumstances, Libbie was an excellent student. She performed quite well in literature and mythology, but had problems with math and French. Although talents such as needlepoint and music were emphasized, the girls were not taught domestic skills. They were from the upper class and would be hiring cooks and servants. The curriculum was centered on the belief that the educated young lady would make her home comfortable for her husband.[13]

Libbie became a voracious reader, but not classics like Shakespeare or Milton; rather, her tastes were more common with modern authors—Fanny Fern and Grace Greenwood. Fern (real name Sara Payson Willis) wrote scandalous books, such as *Ruth Hall* and *Rose Clark,* that shocked readers by introducing an independent female protagonist and sermonizing against the notion that women must depend on men for economic, legal, and social protection. At the end of these novels, domestic virtue and female chastity triumphed over evil, and all wrongs were righted. Grace Greenwood (aka Sara Lippincott) also trumpeted the belief that women should be self-reliant and clever. Libbie no doubt was comforted in her aloneness by the belief that she could succeed and prevail over her tragedies and present condition by her own talents and will, just like the heroines in her favorite novels.[14]

At one point, Libbie listed her favorite things as part of a parlor game. Her favorite color was rose. Her favorite season was autumn. Her favorite animals were horses and dogs. Her favorite perfume was English violet. Her favorite poet was Tennyson. And her favorite book other than the Bible was her photo album.[15]

As the years passed, Libbie began to wrestle with her faith, believing herself to be wicked and inadequate as a Christian. She constantly questioned her character, and agonized over her faults, whether it was poor progress in French, or being too lazy with piano practice, or her relationships with others. "How wild I am getting," she analyzed in her diary. "Oh! how discouraged I am with regard to doing right. God help me for I know I do wrong every day." She made a conscious effort to become a better person and be more considerate toward others. Her doubts can be dismissed as simply teenage angst, typical of passing from childhood into womanhood.[16]

By 1858, at the age of sixteen, Libbie desperately longed to move back with her father and keep house for him. She also dreamed of visiting Mary Case, her aunt, and being part of a family again. Even with all the special privileges afforded her at the seminary, Libbie could not come to terms with her fate. She confided to her diary, "No one knows how much I lost but myself, when mother died."[17]

In time, Daniel Bacon recognized his daughter's inner turmoil and removed her from the seminary before the semester had ended. He took her to his sister Mary's Onondaga, New York, farm, where she eventually boarded at the Young Ladies Institute in Auburn, New York. It was here that Libbie would come under the influence of the coprincipal, Reverend Mortimer L. Browne, who, along with his wife, would change her life forever.[18]

Libbie was not the only member of the Bacon family who had been lonely. Daniel had met a woman named Rhoda Wells Pitts, the widow of a former innkeeper from Canandaigua, New York. Mr. Pitts had been converted into the Presbyterian faith, left the inn business to become a minister in Tecumseh, Michigan, and had passed away in 1855.

Sixty-year-old Daniel courted Rhoda for a year and, after discussing the subject with Libbie, who approved, married his forty-eight-year-old bride in Orange, New Jersey, on February 23, 1859. Daniel and Rhoda boarded with friends while the Bacon home on South Monroe Street was repaired, refurbished, and repainted.[19]

In May 1859, Libbie left school and moved back in with her aunt at Howlett Hill. It was here where she reflected on her past, especially the kindness and counseling offered her by Mortimer Browne and his wife at the seminary. They had shown her that she was not wicked or worthless, that she had a place in the world and that her Christian faith was the basis for that place. Libbie would write that they had brought her to "the feet of the Savior," and this "Christian example" would "guide and save and keep me."

Libbie had undergone a conversion—she had been born again in both a spiritual and worldly sense—and was now confident that she was a person in her own right and could be of some benefit to society. The parental guidance shown by the Brownes had been the reason for her maturity as a person and in the Christian faith. "I went there a stranger—they took me into their hearts as if I were their child and ever *ever* will I thank them for it. I went there a *child,* but came away a *woman.* God be praised."[20]

Libbie returned to Monroe from New York in June, and she and her father and stepmother moved into their residence and became a family. Rhoda, a devout Presbyterian, quickly won the heart of her stepdaughter with her sense of humor and engaging personality. Libbie joked that "Mother and I laugh and grow fat." Cousin Rebecca Richmond visited her uncle's house, and observed that her Aunt Rhoda "thinks as much of Libbie as Libbie does of her." Libbie's wish to be part of a loving family again had finally come true.[21]

Libbie reenrolled in the Young Ladies' Seminary and Collegiate Institute, and would remain there for the next two years. She became lifelong friends with Annette "Nettie" Humphrey and Fanny Fifield, and the three of them moved easily within the upper social class of Monroe, each the subject of great interest by local young men.

At graduation, Libbie finished first in her class and delivered a speech as the valedictorian. Her speech, on a rather unusual subject, "crumbs," where she explained the essential greatness in little things, as in larger ones, was judged by the *Detroit Free Press* to be "one of the best."[22]

Monroe had been sending its share of young men off to war, which certainly limited the pool of eligible future husbands. These men would return on furlough wearing their uniforms and bragging about their exploits to impress the girls. Even Libbie Bacon had dreamed of marrying a soldier and running away with him. "We were obliged to hide from rebels in a pond of water," she wrote in her journal, "and go through many perils all of which I was willing to do for my spouse." Her dream continued the next night, until it "ended so beautifully, my cares and sorrows had vanished and I was walking with my arm in that of my dear man who forms the subject of the journal often."[23]

Although she did not know it at the time, her fantasy dream soldier entered her life on Thanksgiving Day, 1862, at a party given by the Boyds at the seminary. Conway Noble, the brother of one of Libbie's friends, introduced her to a young army officer with reddish-blond hair and intense blue eyes, who was named George Armstrong Custer. Noticing his captain's bars, Libbie remarked, "I believe your promotion has been very rapid." Custer replied, "Yes, I have been very fortunate." Those were the only words spoken between them that night.[24]

Armstrong Custer had been predictably discouraged about his military status. He had been trying to make the best of being without a duty station, however, by sleighing with the girls and partaking in all the social opportunities available to a young war hero home awaiting orders. But on that night, although a barbed-wire wind blew across the lake and snow fell, Custer's heart could not have been warmer. He had met a girl—not just any girl but literally the girl of his dreams. Armstrong was immediately smitten with Libbie Bacon, and swore that he dreamed about her that night—a classic case of love at first sight.

The Bacons, it must be remembered, were members of the upper class, and Custer was the son of the village smithy—and the two classes rarely socialized, much less courted and married. Not only that, but Libbie and her father had witnessed a drunken, boisterous Custer stagger past their house the previous year. Libbie had no way of knowing that Custer had reformed and had not tasted liquor since that night. Regardless, Daniel Bacon as a rule did not allow suitors in uniform to visit his daughter.[25]

Custer ignored this social disparity, and on the following day stood and watched as Libbie entered a seamstress shop. She noticed his attention, and later wrote, "Oh, how pleased I was." Armstrong relentlessly courted Libbie by showing up wherever she happened to be and continuously strolling past her home. He even began attending the local Presbyterian church, and sat where the two could exchange glances during the services. Libbie jokingly scolded him after one service, saying, "You looked *such things* at me." Custer would approach her after church or at her singing school and walk her home. On one cold night, they were walking, and "in spite of the rain and sleet he went solderlike without an umbrella, for which I admire him."[26]

Libbie admired his perseverance, but was not quite sure what to make of this handsome army officer and remained standoffish to his advances. She refused to see him when he called upon her at her house. Libbie also declined to attend a seminary concert with him in favor of being escorted by her father. After the performance, however, Custer appeared and opened a gate that had become stuck to allow Libbie and her father to leave the grounds, to which she replied, "Thank you, sir."[27]

Custer returned to Washington two weeks before Christmas. Libbie wrote in her journal, "I could almost have given way to the melting mood. I feel so sorry for him. I think I had something to do with his going." She also admitted that she would miss seeing him stroll slowly past her house "forty times a day."[28]

Custer had headed back to Washington to await orders. In the meantime, Ambrose Burnside had moved his Army of the Potomac to the outskirts of Fredericksburg, where he planned to cross the Rappahannock River, seize the town, and move on to attack Richmond. Bridges across the river had been destroyed, and it was seventeen days until pontoon bridges had been positioned to ferry his 120,000 men across the river. This delay afforded the Confederate army time to evacuate Fredericksburg and deploy seventy-eight thousand soldiers at strategic places in the surrounding hills.

Following two days of Union shelling, and despite the geographic disadvantage and the strength of the Confederate position, General Burnside attacked on the morning of December 13. The Union soldiers advanced twelve times, and each time the Confederates held their ground and inflicted catastrophic casualties on their exposed enemy. The battle, a monumental blunder by Burnside, was called a "tremendous slaughter," and cost the Union army approximately 12,653 men as opposed to 5,309 for the Confederates— another devastating defeat for the North.[29]

Back in Monroe just before Christmas, Armstrong Custer, in true cavalry fashion, was executing a frontal assault on two fronts. The first one was an attempt to secure the colonelcy of the Seventh Michigan Cavalry, an endeavor that had fared poorly. The appointment involved political patronage, and the Republican governor took a dim view of Custer's Democratic views and associations, such as his relationship with George McClellan. Apparently his Republican mentor from Ohio, Representative John A. Bingham, had not come to his aid in this case. Custer's pursuit of Libbie Bacon, on the other hand, showed some promise.[30]

Custer had pledged his undying love to Libbie, which she rebuffed. He had even proposed marriage and exclaimed his willingness to sacrifice every earthly hope to gain her love.

Libbie told her cousin Rebecca that she only cared for him as an escort, but his persistence had softened her heart to the extent that she wrote in her journal, "He is noble, brave and generous and he loves, I believe, with an intensity that few know of or as few ever can love. He tells me he would sacrifice every earthly hope to gain my love and I tell him if I could I would give it to him. I told him to forget me and he said he *never could* forget me and I told him I never should forget *him* and I wished to be his true friend through life but it is no use to offer myself as a friend for he will never think of me otherwise than his wife. Oh, *Love, love,* how many are made miserable as well as happy by the all powerful influence."[31]

Libbie became even more confused about this relationship when Custer began seeing Fanny Fifield, a friend from the seminary. Armstrong began escorting Fanny to parties and calling upon her at home. They were even seen strolling together in public. Fanny—which oddly enough happened to be one of Custer's nicknames at West Point—was openly attracted to the young army officer. Libbie brushed off the relations between Custer and Fanny to her friends, but there was no doubt it had a troubling effect on her.[32]

Judge Bacon, who had noticed Custer's interest in Libbie, did not fancy his only child married to a common military man—especially one whom he had witnessed in an intoxicated state the previous spring. The judge made Libbie promise to not see Custer again or write to him when he returned to duty. Libbie secretly gave Armstrong her ring at a party, but soon afterward informed him that she must abide by her father's wishes and never see him again. Judge Bacon might have thought that he had succeeded in saving his daughter, but had perhaps underestimated the determination of a young man in love—particularly a young man like Armstrong Custer, who relished a seemingly impossible challenge.[33]

Libbie went to visit friends in Toledo, twenty miles south of Monroe, and who appeared on the train platform to help with her bags but Armstrong Custer? It was a wonder that Custer did not accompany her on that train, but she had already warned him to forget that notion. Judge Bacon was furious about Custer's presence at the train station. He wrote to his daughter in Toledo, reminding her that she had promised not to see the army officer again.

Libbie replied, "Father, I told Mother to tell you of my interview with Captain Custer. I never had a trial that made me feel so badly. I did it *all for you*. I like him very well, and it is always pleasant to have an escort to depend on. But I am sorry I have been with him so much, and you will never see me in the street with him again, and never at the house except to say good-bye. I told him never to meet me, and he has the sense to understand. But I did not promise *never* to see him again . . . He has many fine traits, and Monroe will yet be proud of him . . . You have never been a girl, Father, and you cannot tell how hard a trial this was for me . . . And Monroe people will please mind their own business, and let me alone. I wish the gossipers sunk in the sea."[34]

On January 25, 1863, President Lincoln reacted to the debacle at Fredericksburg by replacing army commander Ambrose Burnside with Major General Joseph "Fighting Joe" Hooker. This new leader was a vain and assertive commander whose name made a contribution to the American vernacular with his policy of permitting "camp followers" into his soldiers' camps. He would spend the next few months reorganizing and equipping his troops in preparation for a spring campaign.

Custer and his West Point comrades suffered a painful loss in March 1863. On the morning of March 17, Union Brigadier General William W. Averell and 2,100 cavalrymen crossed the Rappahannock at Kelly's Ford and were advancing toward the Orange & Alexandria Railroad. Jeb Stuart's cavalry had rushed to confront Averell, and during the ensuing engagement an artillery shell burst near Major John Pelham. Fragments from the shell struck this gallant artillery commander in the back of the head, and he died the following afternoon without regaining consciousness.

The resolute Federals had been repulsed, but Stuart had lost his beloved subordinate, and Custer had lost his West Point friend. The Confederate cavalry commander wept over Pelham's body, then kissed his forehead and whispered an emotional "Farewell" before turning away in anguish. He ordered his troops to wear a black mourning cloth around their left arms, and renamed his headquarters Camp Pelham.[35]

"Gallant" John Pelham—as he would be referred to from then on—lay in state for several days in the Confederate Capitol Building in Richmond. Sallie Dandridge traveled from Martinsburg and kneeled at his coffin, spending one last moment with the man she so dearly loved and had planned to marry. Pelham would later be buried in Jacksonville, Alabama.

Found in John Pelham's personal effects was an undated note, "After long silence, I write. God bless you, dear Pelham; I am proud of your success. G. A. C."[36]

In addition to the loss of Pelham, Colonel Tom Rosser had been severely wounded on those sanguinary fields at Kelly's Ford. As the blue and gray riders had dueled with smoking pistols and scarlet-stained sabers, Rosser felt a minié ball slam through his boot and lodge in his foot. He refused to leave his regiment, however, and led them in several charges. Later, the bullet was removed from his foot, and in order to avoid infection, it was prescribed that he be temporarily relieved of duty to rest and recover.

During his recuperation, Rosser was a regular visitor at a house where earlier in the war he and several other officers had stopped for a drink of water. At that time, he had joked to the boy who accommodated them that he would return someday "and marry your sister." A year later, Rosser once again stopped at the house, this time to borrow a pen and ink. The door was opened by that same boy, who yelled back into the house, "Sis Betty! Sis Betty! Here's that man come to marry you!"

Nineteen-year-old beauty Betty Winston presented herself, and it was love at first sight. Rosser was seriously smitten. He began to court Betty, visiting when he could, and writing long letters when he was away.[37]

The former West Point roommates, Rosser and Custer, had each seemingly found the love of his life in the midst of a conflict that had torn the nation apart.

After Libbie Bacon returned from Toledo, Armstrong Custer's campaign to win her heart resumed with the stealth of a reconnaissance mission behind enemy lines. Custer would escort Fanny Fifield to various functions, but only to be able to gain admittance to Libbie's inner circle of friends without raising suspicions. Libbie and Armstrong would share private moments together at social gatherings or at church, and they had persuaded Libbie's friend, Nettie Humphrey, to serve as a go-between for messages. The two would pass notes back and forth, and Libbie gave him an ambrotype—a thin photographic negative made to serve as a positive picture—of herself. Wherever Libbie ventured, Custer was sure to follow. And he never minced words—always promising her his undying love and affection.

Libbie wrote, "He acts it, speaks it from his eyes, and tells me every way *I love you*." After he futilely attempted to kiss her, in her estimation for the four thousandth time, she confessed, "I long so to put my arms about his neck and kiss him and how often I lay my head on his breast—in my imagination— and feel how sweet it would be to make him entirely happy."[38]

Caught in a web of conflicting emotions, Libbie tried to convince herself that she could turn away from the affections of Armstrong Custer. She wrote in her journal, "I was not in love—yes, I was perhaps, but I am sure that the deep feelings which I know have not been stirred by anyone—the chords of my heart were not swept by him. Yes, I like him so much now—no one knows how much—but I feel that it is proof that I do not really love for how could I silence so soon feelings that are always so deep."[39]

By April 8—Libbie's twenty-first birthday—when Custer boarded a train to return to duty in Washington, love had blossomed between them, although she still refused to allow him to kiss her—even when he hinted that Fanny Fifield had kissed him. But the future of their relationship had not by any means been settled due to Judge Bacon's adamant opposition.[40]

First Lieutenant Custer arrived in Washington on April 10, and was informed that General George McClellan had requested his assistance in preparing the official reports of his tenure as commander. Custer traveled to New York, where he lived in the Metropolitan Hotel while working at McClellan's "magnificently furnished" home. The task was completed by the end of the month, and Custer was assigned temporary office duty at the War Department.[41]

Custer would have been yearning to get back into the fight, but likely not as bad as he yearned to be back in Monroe, Michigan, in the arms of Libbie Bacon. He must have been battling with doubts about her sincerity and whether she was ready for a serious relationship. Distance may make the heart grow fonder, but it can also create an obsession that could serve as a distraction—to the average young man. George Armstrong Custer, however, was too dedicated a soldier to allow the thought of Libbie to get in the way of his ambition. Libbie would have been on his mind, but the prospects of his next assignment would have burned deeper within him. Personal glory could go a long way toward reaching goals—both professional and personal. And his next assignment would bring him closer yet.

Eight

Pleasonton's Pet

By the end of April, Fighting Joe Hooker had planned an operation designed to outflank the Army of Northern Virginia. To that end, he marched his 75,000 troops across the Rappahannock River, through a second-growth forest known as the Wilderness, and established his headquarters near Chancellorsville. On April 28, Hooker sent three corps and cavalry to Kelly's Ford while General Stoneman's cavalry attempted to maneuver to the rear of the Confederate army.[1]

On May 1, General Robert E. Lee countered Hooker by sending his fifty-thousand-man Confederate infantry under Stonewall Jackson against Union forces in open country near Chancellorsville. The two armies sparred back and forth in a fiery duel of exploding ordnance and blazing firearms, with blood flowing freely on both sides. Although the battle was going well on the Federal side, Hooker inexplicably ordered his men to break contact and withdraw into the timber encircling the crossroads of Chancellorsville.[2]

That evening, Generals Lee and Jackson sat on cracker boxes while warming their hands over a campfire and discussed strategy. Jeb Stuart's cavalry had discovered that Hooker's right flank was unprotected. Lee decided to take advantage of that intelligence, and devised an extremely risky and daring plan to divide his force. Jackson's twenty-six thousand troops would march to the Union rear and attack, which in the meantime would leave only about seventeen thousand men at Lee's disposal to hold off an advance by Hooker. If successful, they could crush Hooker between them, but if Hooker detected the maneuver he could turn on either fragmented force and likely overpower them. Lee decided that it was worth the gamble.

At 5:00 A.M. on May 2, Stuart's cavalry led Jackson's corps on its fourteen-mile all-day march through the Wilderness, around the Union army's vulnerable right flank. From all indications, this bold movement had not been detected by the enemy.

At twilight, Stonewall Jackson's troops charged into their unsuspecting foe. The surprised Union infantrymen were quickly routed into a panicked retreat, and disappeared into the darkness before Jackson could overtake them. Lee's initial plan had worked, and now he must follow up on the day's success.

However, that evening in the faint light of dusk, while on a reconnaissance mission between lines, Stonewall Jackson was mistakenly shot and wounded by members of his own Eighteenth North Carolina. Jackson was taken to a nearby home, where, late that night, his left arm was amputated. General Jeb Stuart was summoned to take command of Jackson's corps.[3]

When the sun rose the following day, Stuart launched an attack into the dense undergrowth, where the entrenched Union soldiers waited. Each charge of the Southerners was met with fierce opposition, and repulsed. Finally, Hooker, who had been wounded in an artillery barrage, ordered his men to fall back toward the Rappahannock River. The South held the field and lost about thirteen thousand men while inflicting over seventeen thousand casualties on the Northerners.

The battle of Chancellorsville has been called Lee's greatest victory—a masterpiece of warfare perhaps unequalled by any other American general. He had gambled with the future of his army and executed a flawless offensive. On the other side of the lines, Hooker had demonstrated one of the worst decisions of the war when he abandoned his advance on the first of May—losing his nerve when facing Lee directly, becoming a "whipped man," as one of his subordinates described him.[4]

Jeb Stuart had distinguished himself once more—this time as an infantry commander. He was also confident in the supremacy of his cavalry, which had not as yet come within two whoops and a holler of being challenged by Union horsemen. In fact, his troopers were now known as the "Invincibles" to the frustrated enemy.

No doubt twenty-three-year-old George Armstrong Custer had viewed this Southern victory with a strong desire to be part of the army on the battle-field and make a difference. His participation in the war thus far had been that of a mere ambitious aide-de-camp to various generals—and presently an officer without permanent assignment. He had been away from the army for six months, and craved field action. The war was passing him by, and his opportunities for promotion, not to mention fame and glory, were vanishing with each day.

Custer did learn the inside story about how Lee had outgeneraled Hooker at Chancellorsville, and wrote about it to George McClellan on May 6, add-ing, "To say that everything is gloomy and discouraging does not express the state of affairs here. Hooker's career is well exemplified by that of a rocket, he went up like one and came down like a stick." Custer also related that rumors swirled about that Hooker may have been drunk during the cam-paign, "Even Hooker's best friends are clamoring for his removal. You will not be surprised when I inform you that the universal cry is 'Give us McClellan.'"[5]

On the same day that Custer wrote the letter to McClellan, he was offered the opportunity to be rescued from his dreary desk job at the War Depart-ment in Washington. An official invitation arrived from Brigadier General Alfred Pleasonton, commander of the First Cavalry Division of the newly organized Cavalry Corps, requesting that Custer serve as an aide-de-camp on his staff.

In early 1863, Fighting Joe Hooker had reorganized the Union cavalry and its purpose. George McClellan had previously assigned mounted regi-ments to infantry brigades, which greatly diminished their effectiveness in battle. Hooker had placed the cavalry under the command of Major General George Stoneman, and employed independent tactics patterned after those of Jeb Stuart's cavalry.

The cavalry corps at that time numbered about ten thousand officers and men and had been divided into three divisions of seven brigades. Division commanders included Brigadier Generals Davis Gregg and John Buford—both West Pointers—and Colonel Alfred Duffie, a Frenchman who had been decorated for his service in the Crimean War. Brigade commanders included Colonels Judson Kilpatrick, John Irvin Gregg, Thomas C. Devin, and Benjamin "Grimes" Davis, all of whom were rising stars in the Union cavalry.[6]

The reorganization experiment had not worked initially, as evidenced by actions during the Chancellorsville Campaign. The Federal horsemen had been dispatched on a raid against Lee's communication lines to Richmond, and their absence had contributed to the Union defeat.

General Pleasonton, however, had personally distinguished himself in that engagement by routing a small band of Confederate infantry, and was introduced several days later by Hooker to President Abraham Lincoln with the words, "Mr. President, this is General Pleasonton, who saved the Army of the Potomac the other night!" Soon after, when Stoneman journeyed to Washington to seek treatment for piles, Hooker seized the opportunity to replace his ineffective commander "temporarily" with the more aggressive Pleasonton.[7]

New Yorker Alfred Pleasonton, a West Pointer, class of 1844, and a veteran of the Mexican War and various frontier posts, had been promoted to brigadier general following the Seven Days' Campaign, and had led a division at Antietam, Fredericksburg, and Chancellorsville. In the tradition of a cavalryman, he was a self-confident man, a fastidious dresser, and, perhaps more importantly, had the advantage of being politically well-connected.

His ambition, a trait that compelled some to observe that he had already risen beyond the level of his field competency, was no secret to anyone. Rumors about his lack of bravery under fire were commonplace. He also became known for embellishing his own role in a battle or blatantly taking credit for actions in which he did not participate. Some called Pleasonton a bald-faced liar and a shameless bootlicker in his efforts to curry favor with superiors.

Massachusetts officer Charles Francis Adams, Jr., wrote to his mother, "He [Pleasonton] is pure and simple a newspaper humbug. You always see his name in the papers, but to us who have served under him he is notorious as a bully and a toady. Yet mean and contemptible as Pleasonton is, he is always *in* at Head Quarters." Postwar writers would dub him the "Knight of Romance," on account of his dispatches, which were said to be full of "sound and fury, signifying nothing."[8]

To be fair, if possible, some degree of the criticism of Pleasonton stemmed from the fact that General Winfield Scott Hancock had been the popular candidate for cavalry commander but had been passed over for the post. Hancock, as commander of II Corps, would in the near future win great acclaim at Gettysburg.

Pleasonton had become acquainted with George Armstrong Custer's impetuosity and ability to relate accurate reconnaissance reports when both served with McClellan, and for that reason had requested his service as an aide-de-camp.

In the words of Custer's future personal bugler, Joseph Fought: "Genl. Pleasonton, a very active officer, was always anxious to be posted about what was doing in front of him. He himself could not be in the front all the time, and in that respect his Trusties [aides] were more valuable to him than his brigade commanders. If Lt. Custer observed that it was important to make a movement or charge he would tell the commander to do it, would not dare question, because he knew Lt. Custer was working under Genl. Pleasonton who would confirm every one of his instructions and movements."[9]

Custer had at first declined the invitation by Pleasonton out of loyalty to McClellan. But, after reconsidering that decision—any position in the field was better than sitting at a desk—wholeheartedly transferred his fierce allegiance to his new commander. He termed Pleasonton "an excellent cavalry officer," and was quite pleased with his new status.

The thirty-nine-year-old Pleasonton responded to Custer's fidelity with what could be called a paternal affection. Custer emulated Pleasonton in dress and mannerisms—studying in particular the art of self-promotion—and soon became known as "Pleasonton's Pet."[10]

While Custer settled in on Pleasonton's staff, the South suffered a devastating blow to their leadership on May 10, when General Stonewall Jackson, whose wound from Chancellorsville was complicated by pneumonia, died. Twenty-five months into the war, Robert E. Lee would have to do without his most trusted military commander. The Army of Northern Virginia would never be the same without Stonewall.

General Pleasonton's confidence in Custer was quickly made evident on May 20, when he dispatched his aide under personal orders from General Hooker on a dangerous mission deep into enemy territory. Pleasonton was wary of the operation, believing it to be an impossible task, but, nonetheless, obeyed orders and mapped out the route, which extended almost as far south as Richmond and fifty miles to the east.

Custer was assigned to accompany a squadron, two companies of seventy-five men each from the Third Indiana Cavalry, under Captain George H. Thompson, in an effort to intercept a party of Southern civilians from Richmond who were said to be traveling down the Rappahannock River to Urbanna in possession of important Confederate mail and a large amount of money.

The Union detachment—men and horses—departed down the Potomac aboard two steamers after dark on the night of May 21. After navigating bothersome sand bars, they arrived at eleven o'clock the following morning at a cove called Moon's Landing on the banks of the Yeocomico River. The boats were hidden in the brush on the shoreline. The troops quickly mounted in a column of twos, and rode down a wagon-rutted road. The column passed through marshes and fields, aware that the clanking of saber chains, saddle squeaks, and rumble of horse hooves could give away their position at any moment. Although there were no large bodies of troops in the area, local militiamen were always a threat for an ambush.

At noon, Custer and his comrades passed through an expanse of fields, and emerged to observe a number of houses. They had arrived at Heathsville. After forming a column of fours, the horsemen raced through this tiny hamlet, leaving the shocked citizens behind to wonder what was happening. The cavalrymen then rode fifteen miles farther down the road, and tore through Lancaster Court House in the same manner.

After riding forty miles in a little more than five hours, they arrived in the vicinity of Urbanna. The column concealed itself in the woods, and the troops fed their horses and themselves, but lit no fires, and slept until the next morning.

At dawn, the column set out exploring the marshy shore of the lower Rappahannock, and located two weather-beaten boats that the troops quickly made serviceable. Captain Thompson sent out two crews of ten men each in these boats—with Armstrong Custer aboard one, and the captain the other—while the remainder of the squadron guarded their position. When an approaching Rebel sailing vessel was sighted, with perhaps ten people aboard, Custer and his crew set out in pursuit. There was a good chance that this was the party they had been dispatched to intercept.

The occupants of the sailboat had likely recognized the distant blue uniforms, and tacked for the southern shore in an attempt to escape. The chase was on for some ten miles, until the vessel was forced to run aground in a patch of tall grass. At that point three blacks, likely slaves, jumped overboard and were permitted to wade away.

Custer and company held their fire and captured the boat and the six passengers, who were in possession of a large sum of Confederate money. This group of people—which Custer later said included two attractive young Jewish ladies—tried to persuade the cavalrymen that they were refugees fleeing the Confederacy. The ruse did not work. Custer and Thompson were certain that these people were the ones that they had been sent to capture.

The prisoners were escorted to the bivouac area, while Custer's boat investigated the south shore of the Rappahannock Inlet. Before long, a plantation with lush fields and a mansion beyond came into view.

Custer, accompanied by four men, went ashore and cautiously approached the main house. He observed a Confederate artillery officer relaxing on the veranda engrossed in reading a copy of Shakespeare's *Hamlet*. This man was readily taken prisoner and, with apologies by Custer to the ladies of the house, removed to the boat as their captive.

Custer and twenty men in three small boats then visited Urbanna on the opposite bank. They burned two schooners and the bridge over Urbanna

Bay, finally returning to the north bank, where they captured twelve more prisoners, boxes of Confederate supplies, and thirty horses. Custer appropriated for himself one of the horses, a blooded iron-gray stallion that he named Roanoke. Another fine mount was brought along as a gift for General Pleasonton.

The ambitious raiding party departed Urbanna with their prisoners and booty, and rendezvoused with their comrades at the bivouac. At midnight, Custer and Thompson led their troops northward through enemy territory, and returned home on May 26 without incident and without suffering a casualty.[11]

In a letter dated on the day of his return to camp, Custer related his account of the raid to Annette Humphrey. He added, "General Hooker sent for me and complimented me very highly on the success of my expedition and the manner in which I had executed his orders. He said it could not have been better done and that he would have something more for me to do."[12]

It must be noted that there were occasionally differing versions of events on this expedition between Custer's account and that written by Captain George H. Thompson in his official report. Custer cannot be blamed for perhaps embellishing his role, however, given the fact that he knew that Nettie Humphrey would be relaying the thrilling exploit to the hungry ears of Libbie Bacon. And, after all, he had been tutored by Pleasonton, the master of writing reports to make himself look good.

Back in Monroe, with Custer out of the picture, former and new suitors appeared to try to win the affections of Libbie Bacon. Each one, however, failed to measure up to the audacious young army officer. "I like a man who is pleased with what I say as to listen and treasure my words but the Frank or France [two suitors] is either too conceited to wish to listen or isn't interested," Libbie wrote. "C—has quite spoiled me. Everything I said or did was remembered and treasured by him. He was more devoted than I ought to expect in any other man."[13]

And during those times of doubt and frustration over their estrangement, when Libbie vowed to forget Armstrong Custer, Nettie would receive a letter from him, and he would continue to dominate her thoughts and her heart. "I found myself suddenly matured from girlhood to womanhood, anxiously reading the paper, and no longer laughing and teasing those girls among us who had been watching the mail so intently for letters." She confessed "that the little God of Love worked charms in my heart."[14]

Custer's raid behind enemy lines once again fueled his ambition for a command of his own. He was aware that many of his West Point classmates, particularly on the Confederate side, had already risen to field-officer status. His pursuit of the colonelcy of the Seventh Michigan Cavalry that had commenced while on furlough in Monroe continued when he mailed another request to Republican Governor Austin Blair on May 31.

He had enclosed a letter of recommendation from General Pleasonton that read in part, "Captain Custer will make an excellent commander of a cavalry regiment and is entitled to such promotion for his gallant and efficient services in the present war of the rebellion. I do not know anyone that I could recommend to you with more confidence than Captain Custer." Pleasonton's letter included an endorsement from General Hooker, "I cheerfully concur in the recommendation of Brig Genl Pleasonton. He [Custer] is a young officer of great promise and of uncommon merit."[15]

With such powerful recommendations as the army commander and the cavalry commander, how could Governor Blair refuse?

It has been suggested that the venturous Armstrong Custer even went as far as to visit the camp of the Fifth Michigan while its commander, Colonel Russell A. Alger, was absent and sought support in the form of a petition requesting his appointment from the brigade's officers—to no avail. The officers presumably considered Custer too young for the command, and likely resented the brashness of someone who would seek to dispose of their commander in such an underhanded manner.[16]

Another stumbling block in Custer's pathway to command a Michigan unit was that he had been branded a "McClellan Man," which was the kiss of death for any request to a Republican governor. George B. McClellan, after all, had been rumored as the potential Democratic opponent to Lincoln in the next election.

Governor Blair predictably denied Custer's request on the grounds that the accepted custom was to award commissions to the men who had helped in the recruitment of the regiment. Privately, however, Blair informed Isaac Christiancy, founder of the state Republican party and a justice on the Michigan Supreme Court, that "His [Custer's] people are rebel Democrats. He himself is a McClellan man; indeed McClellan's fair-haired boy, I should say . . . I cannot place myself . . . whatever his qualifications."[17]

Custer, much like Democrat George McClellan, who had opposed policies of the Republican administration, had been a victim of politics. True, West Pointers his same age were colonels commanding Union regiments, but they were Republicans. He did not, however, intend to allow this minor setback to interfere with his pursuit of a command. Custer pledged to distinguish himself in such a manner that he could not be denied again. Little did he know that opportunity was within his reach just across the Rappahannock River.

Pleasonton reported to Hooker that Brigadier General David Gregg's division had been patrolling on May 28 within fifteen miles of Culpeper Court House, and had noted that three Confederate cavalry brigades under General Jeb Stuart had moved from Fredericksburg to that location. Pleasonton offered the opinion that Lee was assembling his troops for a major offensive in the North. Hooker was skeptical, but Pleasonton persisted.

Reconnaissance balloons and additional reports appeared to confirm Pleasonton's theory. By June 4, Hooker was convinced, and informed the president that he intended to engage those Confederates under Stuart that were believed to be camped along the Rappahannock.[18]

Hooker ordered Pleasonton to launch on June 9 a two-pronged surprise cavalry attack—at Beverly Ford and Kelly's Ford—comprised of eleven thousand men, a number that included about twenty-eight hundred infantrymen and twelve pieces of artillery.[19]

George Armstrong Custer would be in the saddle for what would be the largest true cavalry engagement of the war. Although he would not be in command of a unit, he would demonstrate his talent for field generalship and hope that his efforts would lead to a more active role. Custer would find a way in which to distinguish himself in this battle—and that action would once again see him cited for bravery.

Nine

<hr>

Brandy Station

O n the night of June 8, thirty-year-old Jeb Stuart went to sleep under only a tent fly on Fleetwood Hill with the satisfaction and confidence of a man who had advanced his claim to the title of the South's reigning knight in shining armor. The war was headed north, and final victory, or at the very least additional tributes, were in his future. He was on top of the world, and having the time of his life.

His petition, after Stonewall Jackson had died from his wounds, for the command of a corps and promotion to lieutenant general had been politely denied by General Robert E. Lee. Some measure of conciliation and recognition, however, came when Stuart was granted a larger force. Lee was aware that Hooker had consolidated his cavalry, and for that reason had decided to expand the role of his own horsemen. Lee added two cavalry brigades, which now gave Stuart 9,536 men, the largest number that he had ever commanded.

There was only one problem with that sense of comfort and contentment enjoyed by Stuart. While he soundly slept, the Union cavalry was on the move, and within hours would splash across the Rappahannock to temporarily douse the major general's aspirations.

On the night before the impending battle, General Alfred Pleasonton had

established his headquarters about a mile from Beverly Ford at a private residence. George Armstrong Custer, who was officer of the day, paused from
his rounds of the camp to write a letter to his sister stating that, "I never was
in better spirits than I am at this moment." But, with a flair for the dramatic,
he added that he could be killed the following day. "In case anything hap-
pens to me," he wrote, "my trunk is to go to you. Burn all my letters."[1]

The cavalrymen were already in place when Custer awoke General Pleas-
onton at 2:00 A.M. for the planned 4:00 A.M. crossing of the Rappahannock.
Brigadier General John Buford's First Division was poised to cross at Beverly
Ford while a combined force of the Third Division under Brigadier General
David Gregg and Colonel Alfred Duffie's Second Division would strike at
Kelly's Ford.

Buford and Gregg were respected by their peers and subordinates, and
both had the reputation of being tough as old boots. Duffie, on the other
hand, had been born in France and, perhaps due to his training in European
heavy-cavalry tactics, had been saddled with the tag of someone who had
been promoted beyond his capabilities. Pleasonton personally disliked foreigners, and Duffie in particular, and hoped that the colonel would eventually furnish a reason for replacement.[2]

First Lieutenant Custer, at the direction of Pleasonton, accompanied the
Eighth New York, a regiment of Buford's division commanded by Alabama-
born and Mississippi-reared Colonel Benjamin F. "Grimes" Davis, that
would lead the way across the foggy river near Beverly Ford at 5:00 A.M.
Davis, a West Pointer who had escaped the 1862 battle at Harpers Ferry before the Union had surrendered, solemnly passed the word, "Stand ready,
men, and begin firing as soon as you see anything!"

The blue-clad horsemen entered the water and proceeded across the
stream. Before long, a voice from the fog ahead sharply demanded, "Halt!
Who goes there?"

Davis and Custer answered the challenge with the first shots of the battle,
fired at startled Confederate pickets with Company A of the Sixth Virginia.
Davis, with Custer at his side, rode to the front of the Eighth New York,

unsheathed his saber, and charged to engage the enemy. The battle of Brandy Station had commenced.[3]

On Fleetwood Hill, Jeb Stuart was either asleep or had just awakened when he heard the distant sound of gunfire. Within moments, a courier reported with word of the attack at Beverly Ford, where his brigade under William E. "Grumble" Jones was camped. Stuart, without precise knowledge of the size of the force of Federal cavalry, was unable to formulate any specific strategy and simply ordered his men to fight. He did, to his credit, have the presence of mind to dispatch a courier directing General Beverly Robertson's brigade toward Kelly's Ford, which he had correctly assumed might be struck as well.

General Wade Hampton's brigade hurried from Brandy Station to reinforce Jones at the point of attack. Rooney Lee, Robert's second son, took a position on Buford's right flank behind a stone fence, and was supported by Colonel Thomas Munford commanding Fitz Lee's brigade. Stuart himself remained on Fleetwood Hill, and attempted to gather enough intelligence to adequately deploy his cavalry. But, he was dismayed to admit, the element of surprise by the Union had succeeded, and his men could be in for the fight of their lives.[4]

Buford's Union division, led by Grimes Davis and his brigade, with George Armstrong Custer riding with them, had charged into those Rebels camped at Beverly Ford and virtually trampled them beneath their horses' hooves while firing at will and slashing them apart with swinging sabers.

Stuart's shocked men, who had been sleeping or huddled in front of small fires, most in various stages of undress, were unable to offer much immediate resistance to the charging horsemen. They were far more concerned with mounting their own skittish horses or dashing on foot into the nearby timber to escape this unexpected tumult. A small number of Confederate cavalrymen paused at the tree line in an effort to provide a base of fire to assist their beleaguered comrades in this every-man-for-himself retreat.[5]

Joseph Fought, the young bugler-orderly on Pleasonton's staff, who at first meeting had felt an affinity between himself and Custer and had now attached himself to the lieutenant, wrote about this moment, "Lt. Custer and I crossed the Ford and took the inside of the field. There were two or three Rebels near the woods, but we clipped along towards them, and they fired at us, and we fired back. One kept on in the road, and the Lt. said I shot him, and I said he did. The others got back into the woods."[6]

The banks along the Rappahannock were the scene of mass chaos as thousands of unyielding Federal cavalrymen swooped down upon their unsuspecting prey. The early morning was ablaze with discharges of gunfire—the plumes of smoke and pungent odor of sulfur stinging eyes, irritating nostrils, causing voices to be harsh and barely audible above the din. Running men were cut down with savage saber strokes; others toppled from their horses in the same manner. The dewy ground was soon littered with writhing, torn bodies, wounded and dying. Cries of agony, terror, triumph, and surrender combined with bugle calls, urgently shouted orders, and the high-pitched whinnies of frightened, bolting horses to create a macabre quality that would forever be etched into the memories of the participants.

Colonel Davis directed his men into the woodlands to chase the fleeing Rebels. The Union horsemen dashed through the trees wreaking havoc upon their enemy as they passed, and emerged to view a cleared area several hundred yards in length that ran almost to St. James Church. At the far edge of this clearing, beyond the scrambling Confederates that had been overrun, several pieces of Rebel artillery could be observed.

It was well known that thus far during the course of the war Jeb Stuart had not lost even one cannon to his enemy. An exhilarated Grimes Davis immediately called for a charge of this emplacement. His troopers, including George Armstrong Custer, responded by pounding across the meadow to attack the seemingly exposed South Carolina battery.

The Yankee cavalrymen were nearing their objective when out of the woods on their flank burst a countercharge of at least 150 Rebel horsemen under Major Cabell E. Flourney. The surprised Union troops frantically yanked on their reins to restrain their mounts and abort the charge. Many were thrown from the saddle, scrambling to leap aboard a loose mount or escape on foot in order to avoid the resolute Confederate assault. Numerous casualties were inflicted as the Union force commenced a hasty retreat back to the relative safety of the timber.[7]

There was one exception to that sudden retreat. Colonel Benjamin Davis, defiant and gallant, stood his ground. After the colonel had emptied his pistol at his oncoming enemy, he resorted to the saber. It had been said of Grimes Davis by a member of the Eighth New York, "When Colonel Davis found the Rebels he did not stop at anything, but went for them heavy. I believe he liked to fight the Rebels as well as he liked to eat." In this case, however, his determination perhaps overruled prudence.[8]

Virginia cavalry Lieutenant R. O. Allen targeted Davis, and cautiously approached by hugging his horse's neck to evade the blade of the colonel's slashing saber. Allen closed the distance between them, raised his pistol, and fired three shots point blank at Grimes Davis. The third bullet struck Davis in the forehead, killing him instantly and knocking him from his horse to the ground.[9]

The withdrawal of the Eighth New York to the woods thwarted the advance of the Eighth Illinois, which had been following closely behind. The troopers dismounted at the tree line to fire their carbines, and were augmented by barrages from Captain James M. Robertson's artillery battery. This action eventually discouraged the Rebel counterattack, and exacted a toll of at least thirty men. The Union cavalrymen could not take advantage, however, because four Confederate brigades had assembled to keep them pinned in the timber with small arms fire.[10]

The role that George Armstrong Custer played in events that immediately followed the death of Grimes Davis could be called a matter of interpretation. Some biographers have related that Custer, in spite of being subordinate on the field to Major William McClure of the Third Indiana Cavalry, at that point assumed command of the three brigades. This may or may not be correct. No official documentation has been located to confirm or debunk the story.

There exists the distinct possibility, however, that Custer by virtue of his actions became de facto leader of the entire brigade or at least an individual detachment. It was well known that Custer had a zeal for active battlefield leadership, which had been demonstrated in past engagements, and he could conceivably have taken charge in this instance as well. He had, for example, displayed this tendency at Williamsburg in May 1862, when on impulse he spurred his horse and rallied hesitant Union troops against the enemy.[11]

By some accounts, Custer was said to have led a series of charges that day at Brandy Station, one of which caused his outnumbered force to be surrounded, a predicament that he remedied by eventually fighting his way through the enemy. During the action, Custer allegedly had two horses shot out from beneath him, and a bullet tore through his boot.[12]

At some point, however, Custer was prevented from leading anyone—his horse had bolted and slammed into a fence, where it huddled in fright and could not be coaxed to move. Custer dismounted, wrestled with the frightened animal, and finally managed to mount just as it raced away. To the immediate front loomed a stone wall, which the terrified horse maladroitly toppled over, tossing Custer boot heels over kepi. Custer was dazed but unhurt, and quickly remounted to dash away to take refuge with a friendly artillery battery.[13]

Custer would report back to Pleasonton while cavalrymen on both sides raced across fields and down roads to confront each other in duels to the death. Confederate and Union horsemen fought until sent tumbling from their mounts and resuming the battle on foot. The ground became littered with crippled horses struggling to rise and bodies of men dead, dying, and wounded sprawled along fences and in ditches. Remarkably, the Yankee cavalry held its own against this vaunted Rebel cavalry that had embarrassed them for the first two years of the war.

Jeb Stuart was livid. The Confederate cavalry commander could not fathom that his Invincibles were being contested by an enemy that he had without exception dominated. His cavalry was the eyes and ears of the army, yet they had been blindsided, surprised by the upstart Yankee horsemen. And, to add insult to injury, Stuart was now in the unaccustomed position of having to plot a *defensive* strategy.

The Union offensive might have been more effective had it not been for the unexplained delay by Colonel Alfred Duffie in crossing the Rappahan-nock at Kelly's Ford. Duffie's inexplicable tardiness had cost General Gregg four hours, and could have been disastrous had it not been for the question-able actions of Beverly Robertson, whose Rebel brigade Stuart had earlier dispatched to that location.

Robertson's position in the woods was noted by Gregg, who avoided di-rect conflict and simply bypassed the Confederate line by marching in a southerly direction down a road that led to Stevensburg. Robertson watched Gregg pass, but for reasons known only to him made no effort to attack or even to inform Stuart about the movement. Duffie then continued on to Ste-vensburg while Gregg took a circuitous route heading northwest back to-ward Brandy Station.[14]

It was about noon when a courier arrived to advise Stuart that a long col-umn of Federal cavalry was preparing to advance up Fleetwood Hill. Gregg, who had encountered no opposition, had targeted Fleetwood Hill as the place where he could command the entire field, and the likely position where the Rebels would make a stand. It would be devastating for the entire Confeder-ate command if Union troops supported by artillery succeeded in capturing that strategic position.

Stuart understood that he must respond quickly or all would be lost. He ordered an aide to ride to Culpeper and summon into the fray the infantry that was assembled there.[15]

Meanwhile, Stuart's adjutant, Henry McClellan, remained atop Fleetwood Hill with only several couriers and an artillery piece with little ammunition, and watched as the long line of Yankee cavalry advanced toward him. The courageous McClellan attempted to bluff Gregg into thinking that Fleet-wood Hill was adequately defended by ordering his men to commence firing the six-pounder at a slow rate. The ruse stopped Gregg in his tracks, and compelled him to return fire from below in order to prepare his horsemen for a major assault.

Shells rained down on McClellan, who had fired the last of his ammuni-tion and was forced to abandon the headquarters. Stuart's adjutant mounted and raced toward the Twelfth Virginia that, oddly enough, was approaching at a trot. McClellan prodded the troops forward, and the unit responded at the gallop.

Union troops under Colonel Percy Wyndham were only fifty feet away from the crest of Fleetwood Hill when the Twelfth Virginia reached the top. The Confederates crashed into Wyndham's men and, by sheer force of their momentum, passed right on through the Yankees and down the opposite slope. Wyndham, for the moment, had control of Fleetwood Hill, and set up a perimeter to wait for reinforcements.[16]

Possession of Fleetwood Hill changed numerous times in the ensuing battle as the opponents in units from company to regimental size charged and countercharged to gain the high ground. The issue was finally settled when Wade Hampton's brigade gradually drove the Union cavalrymen back to Brandy Station in a running battle fought for the most part hand to hand or with sabers. Stuart quickly took advantage of what he could presume would only be momentarily in his favor, and concentrated his command around Fleetwood Hill to strengthen his hold on that coveted position.

Sporadic fighting raged for some time on the flanks. Several miles north, Colonel Duffie had engaged the Second South Carolina and the Fourth Virginia. He had in some small measure redeemed himself by doing quite well, but the skirmish prevented him from assisting at Fleetwood Hill, which might have made a difference in the final outcome.[17]

General Robert E. Lee, whose headquarters were only about a half mile from the fighting, arrived on the field in time to observe his son, Rooney, being carried away on a stretcher. Rooney had suffered a bullet wound in the thigh while leading a charge against Captain Wesley Merritt's men, who were attempting to flank the Confederate line near the Cunningham farm.[18]

Custer acquaintance Wesley Merritt—West Point class of 1860—who had served mostly on staff duty in Washington or as an aide-de-camp, had returned to field duty with the Second Cavalry just in time for this engagement. At one point, Merritt and another man became separated from their unit and were confronted by a Confederate colonel or possibly a general. This man swung his saber at Merritt's head. Merritt managed to raise his own blade in time to partially parry the blow, but the enemy saber cut through his hat and sliced into his scalp. Nearby Rebel soldiers shot at the two lone Yankees, but Merritt and his companion burst through to ride for Union lines. Merritt's wound bled heavily, but he left the field only briefly while it was bandaged. He would be cited for bravery for his actions under fire.[19]

At about five o'clock, General Pleasonton determined that, with the loss of Fleetwood Hill, it was time to withdraw his weary troops back across the Rappahannock. Pleasonton had apparently caught the scent of the Confederate infantry's advance from Culpeper, and understood that after a day of fighting his troops were in no condition to continue the battle against greater odds. The Union cavalry, to their credit, had conducted themselves courageously and gathered vital intelligence, which had been a primary purpose of their mission.

Jeb Stuart, the consummate aggressor, did not press whatever advantage he might have gained by holding Fleetwood Hill; rather, he permitted his enemy to gradually withdraw without any pursuit. This had been a close call, and Stuart was wise enough to circle his wagons and assess the situation before rushing off into what could be another surprise.[20]

There can be no question that George Armstrong Custer in some manner distinguished himself during the charges and countercharges in the vicinity of St. James Church. General Pleasonton, who had established his headquarters at a nearby residence, had evidently observed or been informed about Custer's actions. Pleasonton singled out his aide for "gallantry throughout the fight" in his dispatches. Custer, who had reported back to Pleasonton before noon, was chosen to personally deliver to General Hooker those dispatches along with a list of prisoners and a battle flag captured from the Twelfth Virginia Cavalry.[21]

The battle at Brandy Station, also known as Fleetwood Hill or Beverly Ford, the greatest cavalry engagement of the century, had concluded. Both sides, as might be expected, claimed victory. In truth, the battle was tactically and statistically won by the Army of Northern Virginia. The Confederates had held the field at the end and sustained fewer casualties—estimates ranged up to 936 for the Union, although many were said to have later re-joined their units, and about 523 for the South.[22]

Victory, however, must at times be judged by elements that have little to do with field position or casualty estimates. In the case of the Union cavalry, Brandy Station had been a moral victory, and, at least in the minds of the troopers, a military one as well.

This shining success was an affirmation that Stuart's Invincibles were no longer quite as invincible. That in itself, after two years of devastating defeats and embarrassment at the hands of Rebel horsemen, was reason enough to celebrate. A Federal artillery officer summed up these sentiments when he said, "The affair at Brandy Station certainly did a great deal to improve the morale of our cavalry, so that they are not now afraid to meet the 'rebs' on equal terms."[23]

The Confederates, on the other hand, had reason to be concerned. And Jeb Stuart was the person on whose shoulders the heaviest burden of criticism was placed. The brother of one of Stuart's aides wrote, "The cavalry battle at Brandy Station can hardly be called a *victory*. Stuart was certainly surprised and but for the supreme gallantry of his subordinate officers and men in his command it would have been a day of disaster and disgrace. Stuart is blamed very much, but whether or not fairly I am not sufficiently well informed to say." A clerk in the Confederate War Department said, "The surprise of Stuart, on the Rappahannock, has chilled every heart."[24]

The *New-York Tribune* summarized the ecstatic reaction of the North when it wrote, "The Confederates begin to find that their boasted cavalry is being overmatched by the Union horsemen. Our troops will make as fine cavalry as can be found in the world."[25]

And from the arbitrament of the saber at Brandy Station a new hero was about to emerge to help lead that fine Union cavalry. Twenty-three-year-old George Armstrong Custer was on the verge of rising from relative obscurity into the spotlight of glory that he so coveted.

Ten

———◆———

Boy General

Neither army lingered for any length of time on the battlefield following hostilities at Brandy Station. On June 10, Robert E. Lee resumed his mission to invade the North and dispatched Richard Ewell down the Shenandoah, James Longstreet east of the Blue Ridge Mountains, and Ambrose Hill to trail Ewell.

On June 17, the two opposing cavalries would collide in the Virginia Piedmont at Aldie, which was strategically located at the western end of a gap in the Bull Run Mountains and at the fork of two roads leading to Winchester.[1]

Fitz Lee's brigade, commanded by Colonel Thomas Munford in Lee's absence, had been sent ahead to guard Aldie. Munford moved from Upperville through Middleburg, deployed pickets east of Aldie, and continued on to procure supplies at a local residence.

Jeb Stuart and his staff retired to the picturesque village of Middleburg to engage in what had become the cavalry commander's favorite pastime—entertaining young ladies, many of whom could be termed camp followers, with music and tales of daring. For the second time in just over a week, Stuart's cavalry, the eyes and ears of the Army of Northern Virginia, would be taken by surprise when Pleasonton and three brigades of David Gregg's Second Division arrived at Aldie about four o'clock that afternoon to attack Munford.[2]

Riding with Generals Pleasonton and Gregg was aide-de-camp George Armstrong Custer, who had made himself conspicuous just prior to the assault by soaking himself in a river after watering his horse. Custer had been urging his mount up a steep bank when the animal toppled over backward, spilling its rider into the water. One of Gregg's staff quipped that when Custer emerged from his impromptu bath the dust "settled on his wet clothes and wet hair, (and) Custer was an object that one can better imagine than I can describe." Fortunately for the embarrassed lieutenant, this incident would be a mere footnote to his actions that day.[3]

The battle commenced when Judson Kilpatrick's brigade stormed into Aldie and sent Munford's pickets reeling into a hasty retreat. Custer's West Point friend, Colonel Tom Rosser, rallied his Fifth Virginia with a bold saber charge, then posted sharpshooters behind haystacks on the right of the Snickersville Road and held firm against Kilpatrick's advance. The two cavalries charged and countercharged as the fighting raged west of Aldie with neither side gaining a clear advantage.[4]

Stuart's flirtatious dallying was abruptly interrupted when frantic pickets ran down the street yelling, "The Yankees are coming!" Stuart and his staff leaped astride their horses and raced away just as a regiment of Duffie's cavalry approached at the gallop. Stuart joined Beverly Robertson's brigade, and dispatched a message at about dusk calling for Munford to fall back to Middleburg. Munford complied with Stuart's order, and a running battle ensued as Kilpatrick chased the stubborn Confederates down the road leading into the village proper.[5]

First Lieutenant Custer had been occupied with carrying dispatches for General Pleasonton throughout the initial stages of the battle. Late in the day, he arrived at Kilpatrick's position. Kilpatrick was one of those officers who was the subject of Custer's envy. Kilpatrick had been only one year ahead of Custer at West Point, but already was in command of a brigade. Custer, who was always eager to trade his aide functions for combat experience, asked and received Kilpatrick's permission to enter the fray. An orderly on Pleasonton's staff wrote, "He was always in the fight no matter where he was."[6]

Custer would certainly have been anxious to impress Kilpatrick, not to mention Pleasonton, with his competence under fire. In this instance, however, it would not necessarily be the ability of Custer that would turn heads, but the initiative of a runaway horse that would gain its rider instant fame.[7]

Custer was becoming widely known, and likely ridiculed, for his skittish horses—first at Brandy Station, then earlier in the day when he had taken the dunking. These episodes in no way reflected a true picture of his skill in the saddle. As evidenced by his ability at West Point, he was a natural-born equestrian, and very few could compare to him when it came to horsemanship. Perhaps, it was poetic justice to compensate for the other mishaps that this occasion would provide more positive results. Custer was riding a black horse that he had named Harry in honor of his five-year-old nephew—who, incidentally, would be nicknamed Autie in honor of Custer and would die with his famous uncle at the Little Bighorn.[8]

Harry the horse became unnerved by the din of battle and bolted—straight toward the enemy. Custer fought to restrain his mount, but was unable to rein up the terrified animal. Before long, Harry had carried his hapless rider directly into the midst of Munford's cavalry.

Two Rebel cavalrymen quickly targeted Custer and closed in for the kill. Custer instinctively drew his Toledo blade. The Confederate horsemen were greeted with Custer's heavy saber, and one was cut from the saddle. Harry then treated Custer to a wild, harrowing ride for at least a mile through enemy lines. Finally, Custer managed to control his horse, escaped out a flank, and circled the entire field at a gallop to return safely to Kilpatrick's headquarters—no doubt with the cheers of the troops ringing in his ears.[9]

Custer claimed that his deliverance could be attributed to his soft, felt, Confederate-style hat, which best protected his fair skin from the sun. He wrote in a letter to his sister dated June 25, "I was surrounded by rebels, and cut off from my own men, but I had made my way out safely, and all owing to my *hat*, which is a large broad brim, exactly like that worn by rebels. Everyone tells me I look like a rebel more than our own men. The rebels at first thought I was one of their own men, and did not attack me, except one, who rushed at me with his sabre, but I struck him across the face with my sabre, knocking him off his horse. I then put the spurs to 'Harry' and made my escape."[10]

In spite of Custer's protestations to the contrary, which were a rarity for such a masterful self-promoter, many observers were of the opinion that he had intended to charge right through the whole Confederate army. Newspaper correspondents knew a good story when they saw one, and embellished the "charge" into enemy lines to depict Custer as the hero of the battle.[11]

One Michigan newspaper later reported, in part, "Outstripping his men in pursuit of the enemy, one of them turned, fired, but missed, his revolver being knocked by a sword blow that sent the rider toppling to the ground. Another enemy trooper tore alongside, but Custer, giving his horse a sudden check, let the man go shooting by. Then face to face they fought it out, gray going down before blue."[12]

Artist A. R. Waud of *Harper's Weekly* rendered a sketch of this valorous charge by Custer, which several months later would grace the cover of that prestigious national magazine.[13]

Perhaps more consequential to Custer at the time than his "charge" was the news that as a result of the successful battle at Aldie cavalry commander Alfred Pleasonton had been promoted to major general. This meant that Custer could once more assume the brevet rank of captain. But, unbeknownst to anyone at present, he would barely have time to get accustomed to his new rank before Dame Fortune would smile upon him with a much more significant promotion.[14]

Two days later, the Union cavalry struck Middleburg again. Duffie led the charge, which pushed the Confederate troops further west to near Upperville. The skirmishing between detachments of the two armies raged on in earnest, but Jeb Stuart had wisely positioned his men in a long line from Middleburg to Upperville, which maintained his ability to protect the gaps for Lee's advancing army.[15]

Pleasonton continued to sporadically probe Stuart's line, but remained contently settled in for the time being around Middleburg. The new major general was confident that his men were in the process of delivering a Union victory, but there was one exception. Alfred Duffie's regiment had been cut to ribbons—losing nearly two-thirds of its men. Duffie, likely over Pleasonton's objections, had been promoted to brigadier general a few days earlier. Now, Pleasonton finally had reason to remove the Frenchman. At his urging, Hooker reassigned Duffie to Washington.[16]

Union artillery shells were bombarding the streets, and Stuart decided out of regard for the women and children who resided there to withdraw to Ashley's Gap in the Blue Ridge Mountains. Soon after, Pleasonton fell back to Aldie. Stuart, satisfied that he had won a victory, returned to his position before Aldie.[17]

During the four days of skirmishing, the Union had suffered an estimated eight hundred casualties compared to five hundred to six hundred for the Confederate army—numbers comparable to those at Brandy Station.[18]

While Generals Longstreet and Hill advanced down the Valley and Ewell was on his way into Pennsylvania, Stuart sent proposals to General Lee pertaining to an independent cavalry reconnaissance intended to slow Hooker's movements by harassing him, confusing him as to the whereabouts of Lee's army, cutting communications, and providing vital intelligence. Lee recognized the value of Stuart's reasoning, and agreed with his request.[19]

These orders, with the implication that he would be required to ride around the enemy army or risk disclosing Lee's plans, were accepted by Stuart at the time as standard operating procedure. At one o'clock in the morning on June 25, his six-thousand-man column rode south and east to set the operation in motion. Two days later, after a march of only a disappointing thirty-five miles in forty-eight hours, Stuart continued his movement east and south toward Fairfax Court House while Fitz Lee detoured east to tear up railroad tracks and cut telegraph lines at Burke's Station. Fairfax Station was found to be held by eighty-six troops from the Eleventh New York Cavalry, who were on duty there for the purpose of guarding army stores. In the ensuing brief skirmish, the New Yorkers were able to inflict a number of casualties before twenty-six of them were either killed or taken prisoner while the others fled into the nearby timber.[20]

On June 28, Stuart crossed the Potomac and immediately put his men to work until dawn destroying property along the Chesapeake & Ohio Canal and capturing additional stores—including several barrels of whisky. The men were then rewarded by their commander with the opportunity to rest.[21]

Behind Union lines, Fighting Joe Hooker, who had been the subject of dissatisfaction since Chancellorsville, tendered his resignation as army commander. On June 28, President Lincoln, who had lost confidence in Hooker, readily accepted. The president subsequently appointed General George Gordon Meade to replace Hooker.

Forty-seven-year-old George Meade had been born in Cadiz, Spain, while his father had been stationed there as a naval agent. The family returned to Washington, where Meade's father died, and the family finances suffered to the point that George was forced to drop out of private school. He did, however, later secure an appointment to West Point, and graduated nineteenth out of fifty-six in 1835. Meade aided in the survey of the Long Island Railroad, served in Florida during the Great Seminole War, and eventually resigned from the army to work for the railroad as well as survey the Mississippi and Texas borders.

After marrying, Meade rejoined the army in 1842, and again was assigned to surveying and engineering projects until his transfer to Texas during the Mexican War, where he was cited for bravery at Monterrey. From the Mexican War to the Civil War, he was once more involved in engineering and surveying work.

In 1861, Meade was made a brigadier general of volunteers, and led a Pennsylvania brigade at Bull Run. He journeyed down the Peninsula with McClellan and fought in battles at Mechanicsville, Gaines' Mill, Second Bull Run, and Antietam. As a major general, Meade commanded troops at Chancellorsville, and was critical of Hooker's lack of aggressiveness. He was tracking Lee's troops as they made their way north when he received word of his appointment to the top army post. Meade was at first reluctant to take the job, and then accepted it as "God's will."[22]

Major General Alfred Pleasonton sought an audience with George Meade on the afternoon of the new army commander's first day at the office. The purpose of Pleasonton's visit was to recommend a reorganization of the cavalry corps. Meade had been authorized by the president to replace or promote any officer deemed necessary to improve the effectiveness of his army.[23]

Pleasonton had earlier sought the counsel of a political ally, Congressman John F. Farnsworth, whose nephew, Elon, served on the general's staff. Pleasonton vowed in a letter to the congressman to resign if rumors were true about Hungarian native Major General Julius Stahel being appointed commander of the cavalry corps. "I have no faith in foreigners saving our Government or country," Pleasonton professed. "Stahel has not shown himself a cavalry man."[24]

Pleasonton made the request directly to Meade that Major General Stahel, who outranked Pleasonton, be relieved of duty, in addition to replacing Brigadier General Joseph Copeland, commander of the Michigan Brigade. Meade granted the request.

The cavalry commander also recommended the promotions to brigadier general of three young officers whom he regarded as men "with the proper dash to command cavalry." Barely twelve hours after Meade had assumed command, he approved the promotions with an official date of rank of June 29 for Captain Elon Farnsworth, the capable Captain Wesley Merritt, and First Lieutenant, brevet captain, *George Armstrong Custer*.[25]

Various versions over the years about how Custer received and reacted to the astounding news of his promotion to brigadier general have created more legend than fact. In one of the more popular and amusing accounts, Custer had returned to his tent following an inspection tour of pickets while enduring the rain and mud. His tent-mates greeted his arrival by announcing, "Gentlemen, General Custer!" The banter continued with phrases such as, "You're looking well, General," and "How are you, General Custer?"

Custer was somewhat embarrassed, and rebutted with the promise that they may laugh now but someday he *would* be a general. He was then directed to an envelope addressed to "Brigadier General George Armstrong Custer, U. S. Vols." Custer was allegedly mortified, chagrined, and on the verge of tears.[26]

Whether or not the above account contains any truth would be a matter of conjecture. More than likely, Pleasonton, who regarded Custer as a surrogate son, would have desired to personally break the news. In a letter to Isaac Christiancy dated July 26, 1863, Custer wrote that he had been summoned to cavalry headquarters at three o'clock on the afternoon of Pleasonton's meeting with Meade. It was at that time that the announcement was made that would stun Custer and confound and infuriate veteran officers. "I had not the remote idea that the president would appoint me," Custer wrote, "because I considered my youth, my low rank and what is of great importance at times & recollected that I have not a single 'friend at court.' To say I was elated," he added, "would faintly express my feelings."[27]

At the tender age of twenty-three, Custer was now the youngest general in the Union army. Orderly Joseph Fought described the reaction to the promotion, "All the other officers were exceedingly jealous of him. Not one of them but would have thrown a stone his way to make him lose his prestige. He was way ahead of them as a soldier, and that made them angry." General Pleasonton would respond to any criticism of his choice by saying, "Custer is the best cavalry general in the world and I have given him the best brigade to command."[28]

Not only was the promotion itself remarkable, but the accompanying assignment was almost equally astonishing. Pleasonton had replaced General Stahel with Brigadier General Hugh Judson Kilpatrick as commander of the Third Cavalry Division, and placed Custer in command of that division's Second Brigade. This brigade, formerly commanded by General Copeland, who was recently relieved of duty, consisted of the First, Fifth, Sixth, and Seventh Michigan Volunteer Cavalry Regiments—known as the Wolverines. Custer had earlier exercised every possible act within his power—from upstanding to conniving—to be appointed colonel of any one of the Michigan regiments. Now, he commanded them all. The appointment certainly enabled Custer to exact some measure of sweet revenge on the Republicans in his home state.[29]

Apparently, not only fellow officers were surprised and baffled by Custer's promotion. The Monroe, Michigan, *Commercial*, Custer's hometown newspaper, was initially skeptical, "Upon the first appearance of the report that

Captain Custer had been made a brigadier general of Cavalry, we were in some doubt as to its genuineness: but it proved to be a bona-fide appointment. He had fairly earned his promotion to this position, and it is an honor which Monroe citizens should be proud of. He will no doubt prove fully capable and efficient."[30]

The first order of business for the fashion-conscious Custer was to properly display his new rank. He was in possession of a flashy uniform, but locating a pair of stars would be a challenge. He dispatched bugler Fought on a scavenger hunt, which, finally late into the night, was successful when two silver cloth stars were purchased from an army sutler.[31]

Joseph Fought sewed on the stars to complete the uniform that he described as "a velveteen jacket with five gold loops on each sleeve, and a sailor shirt with a very large collar that he got from a gunboat on the James. The shirt was dark blue, and with it he wore a conspicuous red tie—top boots, a soft hat, Confederate, that he had picked up on the field, and his hair was long and in curls almost to his shoulders."[32]

Not everyone was impressed with Custer's homemade costume. One of General Gregg's staff officers quipped that Custer looked like a "circus rider gone mad." This was the distinctive uniform, however, that Custer would be known by for the remainder of the war.[33]

While Custer was coming to terms with his promotion and preparing himself to ride out early the following morning and introduce himself to his new command, Jeb Stuart and his three brigades were riding and raiding through the lush Maryland countryside. Stuart had crossed the Potomac to arrive on the outskirts of Rockville at about noon on June 28, and was delighted to be welcomed by an adoring group of young ladies from a local female academy.[34]

The enjoyment of the company of these fair maidens was interrupted when Wade Hampton relayed word that he had spotted a Union wagon train. This supply train, which stretched for eight miles in length and was comprised of 150 wagons and 900 mules, had earlier departed Washington bound for Meade's army.[35]

Stuart and his troops swooped down on the unsuspecting wagons and captured 125 of them, and confiscated the generous load of supplies, which included delicacies such as ham, sugar, and whisky, and then paroled the four hundred teamsters. Perhaps more importantly, most of the wagons contained oats, a boon to the horses, which were in poor condition. The column re-formed at Cookeville to camp for the night.[36]

Brigadier General George Armstrong Custer rode out before dawn on June 29 to take command of his brigade, which was encamped forty-five miles away at Abbottstown, a few miles north of Hanover.[37]

One can only imagine the thoughts going through the mind of this twenty-three-year-old as he drew closer to his first command as a general—as if he could even come to terms with the suddenness of his promotion. There had to be some measure of apprehension about meeting his subordinates—most of whom would be older—and gaining the respect that he knew was necessary to effectively lead troops. But, then again, this was George Armstrong Custer, a young man who probably believed that he was predestined for greatness, and that fact alone gave him the confidence to meet any challenge—in camp or on the battlefield.

Eleven

East of Gettysburg

Upon reaching Abbottstown, Custer immediately assessed that his troops were poorly disciplined by officers who had been lax in enforcing regulations. Many of these subordinates had been field officers while Custer was a West Point cadet, but he refused to treat them ingratiatingly, which he considered would be a sign of weakness. Instead, he took a page from lessons learned from General Phil Kearney and acted cold and aloof while purposely issuing petty orders, from a regular army standpoint, to improve readiness—and to let everyone know who was now in charge.[1]

Custer summed up his sentiments by later writing, "From the very nature of the military rule which governs and directs the movements and operations of an army in time of war, it is essentially requisite to success that the will of the general in command shall be supreme, whether or not he possesses the confidence of his subordinates. To enforce obedience to his authority, no penalty should be deemed too severe, particularly in a country like this, where scheming ambitious men, lacking ability as well as patriotism, but believing that they combine within themselves the military qualifications enabling them to determine in a better manner than can officers placed over them the plans of the campaign, find it easy at times to not only create dissention and lack of confidence in the ranks of portions of the army, but to repeat the murmurs and grumblings to the executive of the nation. Such practices, if allowed to proceed, would render abortive the efforts of the ablest commander."[2]

Custer understood that his officers and troops might dislike him at first, but he pledged to change their minds when the opportunity to lead them into battle presented itself. "I should soon have them clapping me on the back and giving me advice," he wrote.[3]

The Fifth and Sixth Michigan earlier had been detailed on a scouting mission. The remainder of Custer's brigade, which included Battery M, Second United States Artillery, commanded by West Point friend Alexander C. M. Pennington, rode out later that day toward Littlestown to spearhead the main body of Meade's army across the Pennsylvania state line. Meade intended to remain between Lee and the city of Washington. Unknown at that time to either side was that Meade's objective would put his army on a collision course with Lee's army that would climax in a battle for the ages in the rolling hills of southern Pennsylvania near the town of Gettysburg.[4]

At the same time that Custer was assuming command for the first time, Jeb Stuart rode on a northerly route through Maryland toward Pennsylvania. Along the way, Stuart's men destroyed telegraph lines that effectively severed communication between Washington and points north and west, tore up track along the Baltimore & Ohio Railroad, and wrecked a bridge at Sykesville. Late in the afternoon, after attempting without success to intercept trains on the B&O, Stuart moved on and defeated two companies of the Delaware cavalry at Westminster.[5]

Stuart himself remained in Westminster, settled into a chair propped against a private residence, and slept without the knowledge that George Armstrong Custer and his troops were bivouacked less than eight miles away.[6]

General Custer's men were treated to an unaccustomed breakfast from sympathizers. His regiment had led the way for Kilpatrick on the ride that rainy morning that brought them to Hanover at about eight o'clock. Hanover was anticipating a siege by the enemy, and had taken appropriate precautions. According to the Reverend William K. Zieber, pastor of the Emmanuel

Reformed Church, "Bank deposits and valuable articles owned by private citizens were sent away. Some people concealed their treasures in their houses or buried them in their yards or gardens."[7]

For that reason, the Union cavalrymen were greeted like conquering heroes and lauded with hardy applause and cheering—as well as a serenade by young girls in front of the Lutheran church parsonage. Gifts of cigars, loose tobacco, and baskets of flowers were presented. Word was passed around town by Reverend Zieber that the troops were hungry and had little food. The locals responded with enthusiasm, and before long the men were enjoying a fine meal. Custer and his cavalrymen remained in town for almost two hours enjoying the hospitality before departing toward Abbottstown out the York Pike.[8]

Meanwhile, Jeb Stuart's men rode along a back road that would permit them to ride around Union forces. The column eventually crossed the Mason-Dixon Line into enemy territory, which evoked cheering throughout the ranks. Confederate troops had a habit of reacting in this manner whenever stepping onto enemy soil.[9]

The plan to dodge the enemy was dashed when Colonel Chambliss' brigade ventured into Hanover and stumbled upon elements of the Eighteenth Pennsylvania Cavalry. The Federals, under new general Elon Farnsworth, had followed Custer into town and had received the same gracious welcome.

Without waiting for orders, Chambliss' Second North Carolina Regiment charged into Farnsworth's troops, and drove the Pennsylvanians back through the town. Farnsworth and the Fifth New York mounted a counterattack, and quickly routed the Confederate troops.

Jeb Stuart rode to the sound of firing just as his Second North Carolina, the "Black Horse Cavalry," under Colonel W. H. Payne, was sent into a panicked retreat out the Littlestown Pike with Federal horsemen in hot pursuit, engaging in hand-to-hand combat and saber duels. Stuart assumed a position on a ridge southeast of Hanover, which afforded him a commanding position for his troops. He discouraged the enemy from advancing with accurate artillery barrages while waiting for Hampton's and Fitz Lee's brigades to move up.[10]

The arrival of those two capable units could place the Union soldiers in a desperate position. General Judson Kilpatrick, with Custer's Michigan brigade hot on his heels, raced back to Hanover to try to save the day.

General Kilpatrick, whose horse collapsed from exhaustion when he arrived, set up a command post on the square in the Central Hotel. The terrified citizens of Hanover had barricaded the streets to the south with store boxes, wagons, hay ladders, fence rails, barrels, bar irons, and anything else that would prevent the enemy from dashing into town.

General Custer tied his bay horse to a maple tree on the southwest corner of the square, which would become known to the townspeople as "Custer's Tree." Kilpatrick quickly dispatched Custer to deploy his regiments and two six-gun batteries on a ridge northwest of town known as Bunker Hill. Farnsworth would station his regiments along the eastern and southern approaches, directly opposite Stuart's cavalrymen. [11]

Custer's Fifth and Sixth Michigan, the regiments that had been out scouting, now approached Hanover from the south and the west, and stumbled into Fitz Lee's brigade on Stuart's left flank. Lee formed his men for an assault. Colonel George Gray of the Sixth Michigan realized that his men would be overwhelmed by the superior Rebel force. He deployed a line of skirmishers commanded by Major Peter Weber to hold Lee at bay, and escaped with his main body of troops by riding northwest. Weber withstood two determined attacks by the Confederates, largely due to their .56-caliber Spencer rifles with the seven-shot magazines. Just after noon, the two regiments were united with Custer on the Union right, which enlarged the Boy General's command to about twenty-three hundred men. [12]

The two sides engaged in dueling cannons for the better part of the afternoon. The scorched ground shook and debris rained down from the mighty onslaught as each side sought an advantage. Finally, Custer tired of this stalemate, and moved about six hundred of Colonel Gray's troopers west of Hanover to face the position occupied by Fitz Lee's artillery. Custer dismounted his men, and led them across the pasture of the Carl Forney farm, at times crawling on hands and knees, to a position within three hundred yards of the enemy. Custer then ordered a barrage of Spencer rifle and Colt pistols, which effectively rousted the Confederates from their cannons. Lee rushed up reinforcements in an effort to hold the position. Custer countered by calling for another barrage. It was evident that Custer's cavalrymen would be unable to seize the position, but they accomplished the next best thing by successfully assuming vantage points that discouraged Stuart from committing himself to an attack.[13]

George Armstrong Custer, on his second official day as a brigadier general, had proven himself an effective take-charge leader. In the words of cavalryman James H. Kidd of the Sixth Michigan, "It was here that the brigade first saw Custer. As the men of the 6th, armed with Spencer rifles, were deploying forward across the railroad into a wheatfield beyond, I heard a voice new to me, directly in the rear of the portion of the line where I was, giving directions for the movement, in clear resonant tones, and in a calm, confident manner, at once resolute and reassuring. Looking back to see whence it came, my eyes were instantly riveted upon a figure only a few feet distant, whose appearance amazed if it did not for the moment amuse me . . . an officer superbly mounted who sat his charger as if to the manor born. Tall, lithe, active, muscular, straight as an Indian and as quick in his movements, he had the fair complexion of a school girl . . . It was he who was giving the orders. At first, I thought he might be a staff officer, conveying the commands of his chief. But it was at once apparent that he was giving orders, not delivering them, and that he was in command of the line."[14]

Jeb Stuart bided his time until sundown, then commenced a quiet withdrawal heading eastward beyond the Union left flank, and then turning north. He would march his exhausted men and animals—along with the wagon train and about four hundred prisoners—throughout the night without any definite knowledge of the location of the Army of Northern Virginia.[15]

General Kilpatrick was quite pleased with the performance of his troops—Farnsworth and Custer, in particular, who had distinguished themselves by respectively driving Stuart's cavalry out of Hanover and crushing the Confederate left. His horsemen might have lost over two hundred men in the standoff—which was likely about fifty more than his enemy—but Jeb Stuart's withdrawal was sufficient evidence of another Union victory. For reasons known only to himself, however, Kilpatrick stepped out of character and decided not to initiate an aggressive pursuit. Instead, he sent out a few patrols and ordered his men into bivouac along the Abbottstown Pike.[16]

While Lee's and Meade's armies marched on a collision course that would rendezvous the next morning at Gettysburg, Jeb Stuart with his three brigades, prisoners, horse herd, and 125 wagons trudged along for twenty miles through the darkness. The troops were short on rations and battle weary.[17]

When the gray cavalry column reached Dover, the men were granted a well-deserved rest. Wade Hampton arrived by daylight on July 1, and Fitzhugh Lee followed, reporting that Jubal Early had marched west. Stuart, however, found recent newspapers at Dover that gave him the impression that the army he was seeking was concentrating around Shippensburg. Lee encouraged the cavalry commander to follow Early's trail, which should lead them to the as yet unknown position of the Confederate army. Instead, Jeb dispatched Major A. R. "Reid" Venable with orders to discern the exact location of General Early. Then, inexplicably, Stuart mounted his troops and resumed his march toward Carlisle Barracks with the hope of locating rations and fodder. This mistake would cost Stuart a full day's ride, further testing the endurance of his men and animals and resulting in serious consequences to his reputation.[18]

Kilpatrick had no knowledge of Stuart's ambitious ride toward Carlisle. He roused his division early on the morning of July 1, and marched back through Abbottstown and then north to East Berlin in a futile search for his elusive enemy around that area. Before long, barrages of rifle and artillery fire could be heard originating from the direction of Gettysburg, about nine miles to the west of Kilpatrick's position. It was evident that a serious firefight had ensued at that crossroads town.[19]

A Confederate division commanded by Major General Henry Heth, who was seeking boots and shoes for his men, had encountered Union cavalry under Brigadier General John Buford about four miles west of that strategically important town where nine roads converged. Heth's men mounted several charges on the dismounted cavalrymen, but were repulsed each time.

Both armies hurried to reinforce the field, and the ferocious battle for possession of Gettysburg commenced in earnest.[20]

Jeb Stuart's absence during this critical time was a source of great con-
sternation for his commander. General Lee had apparently expected the
arrival of his cavalry by then, and expressed his anxiety to Major General
Richard Anderson. "I cannot think what has become of Stuart," Lee pon-
dered. "I ought to have heard from him long before now. He may have met
with disaster, but I hope not. In the absence of reports from him, I am ignorant of what we have in front of us here. It may be the whole Federal army, or
it may be only a detachment."[21]

Major G. Campbell Brown, an aide to General Ewell, reported to Lee that
afternoon with dispatches confirming that Ewell's divisions were on their
way to Gettysburg. According to Brown, Lee asked him "with a peculiar
searching, almost querulous impatience, which I never saw in him before but
twice afterward" whether Ewell had heard from Stuart. There had been no
word for three days, Brown reported, although it was acknowledged that
Stuart's instructions would have placed him on Ewell's right. Lee then ordered that patrols be dispatched in an effort to contact Stuart. [22]

That morning's chance encounter between the blue and gray armies
would ignite an escalating firestorm of sound and fury on the field. Brigadier
General George Armstrong Custer and his comrades, who must have been
champing at the bit to enter the fight, would endure the uproar created by
this major engagement throughout the day without receiving orders to move.
While Kilpatrick's anxious men rested, Lee would successfully overwhelm
twenty-three thousand Union soldiers with his twenty-seven thousand Confederates, driving the Union troops through Gettysburg and onto Cemetery
Ridge and Culp's Hill on the high ground south of town, and celebrate a
temporary victory. Word passed through the ranks that only darkness had
saved Meade's army from being wiped out by the aggressive Rebels.[23]

By evening, Jeb Stuart, who was unaware of the monumental battle unfolding at Gettysburg—twenty-five miles to the south—had arrived on the
outskirts of Carlisle. Instead of finding easily attainable provisions that his

men so direly needed, he was informed that Carlisle had recently returned to Union hands. Brigadier General William F. "Baldy" Smith had cheered the local residents by retaking the town with two brigades of infantry, a detachment of cavalry, and some artillery support.[24]

Stuart could have chosen to bypass this moderately sized garrison, but his fatigued men and animals simply could not travel any farther without food, rest, and forage. Besides, giving quarter was not compatible with Stuart's combative style. To that end, Stuart ordered Fitz Lee to blast the Federals into submission with artillery. Lee approached close to the barracks, and commenced a highly ambitious but relatively inaccurate barrage.[25]

The attack was rapidly developing into a minor farce for Jeb Stuart. It had become apparent that the obstinate Baldy Smith did not intend to surrender under any circumstances less than total annihilation, which would require more than merely artillery on the part of the Rebel cavalry. An angry General Stuart ordered another round of shelling, this time setting fire to the town's lumber yard and gasworks and igniting several barns and at least one residence. A total of 134 shells had ripped into Carlisle Barracks, yet had resulted in only a dozen or so wounded.[26]

During the wee hours of July 2, Major Venable, who earlier had been sent to locate General Early, reported back with orders to Jeb Stuart from Robert E. Lee. Stuart was informed that his services and that of his cavalry were required at Gettysburg without delay. He finally had been provided directions to find his way back to the Army of Northern Virginia. Stuart mounted his exhausted troops, and lit out on a route that would pass through Heidlersburg and Hunterstown and on to Gettysburg. At dawn, Stuart dismounted, wrapped himself in his cape, and slept leaning against a tree. After two hours, he awoke and rode off alone to report to Robert E. Lee.[27]

Union cavalry General Kilpatrick also received orders during that night. His commander, General Pleasonton, had paid him a visit with instructions "to move as quickly as possible toward Gettysburg." At about 6:00 A.M.— with Lee and Meade already in position facing each other across the field— Kilpatrick moved his troops down the Baltimore Pike to the York Pike toward the sound of guns. In late morning, the column swung west through New

Oxford, then north in the direction of Hunterstown, five miles from Gettysburg. At about 2:00 P.M., the Third Division halted at the rear of Meade's army and awaited further orders. The troops were faced northwest in order to guard against the Rebel cavalry attacking from behind and turning the Union right flank.[28]

While George Armstrong Custer and his men remained formed in a column of fours, Jeb Stuart reported to Lee at Gettysburg. The Knight of the Golden Spurs, according to some estimates, was more than sixty hours late. Lee was said to have greeted Stuart by saying, "Well, General, you are here at last."[29]

Lee's statement cannot be properly interpreted without knowing its tone and intent but was in keeping with the commander's reserved character. Another reason for Lee's restraint could be attributed to the fact that the previous day had gone quite well for his army, and the prospects thus far that day were encouraging as well. Many of those present, however, suggested that Lee was piqued, perhaps even angered, by his headstrong subordinate's prolonged absence.

The meeting concluded when Lee ordered Stuart to gather whatever information he could about Union movements while guarding the Confederate left. Jeb rode off to establish his headquarters on the Heidlersburg road about a mile from Gettysburg.[30]

After a three-hour wait wilting under the hot sun, Judson Kilpatrick finally received orders in late afternoon. James Longstreet had maneuvered his two Rebel divisions beyond Meade's left and attacked. The Third Division was told to assume a position to the right of the main force to prevent that flank from being turned. The division, with Custer and the Sixth Michigan taking the lead, backtracked north to York Pike, then turned east toward Hunterstown—where, unbeknownst to Custer, Brigadier General Wade Hampton and six regiments—1,750 Rebel cavalrymen—had halted about a mile south.[31]

Custer had dispatched a detachment of the Sixth Michigan led by Lieutenant Charles E. Storrs forward to reconnoiter the area. At sundown, these troopers had dismounted to sneak through the woods along the Gettysburg road, and eventually happened upon Hampton's rear guard, which included the general himself. The two sides exchanged a series of volleys that sent Hampton's men scurrying for cover.

General Hampton, however, remained in place to engage in an impromptu duel with rifleman James C. Parsons of I Company. A bullet from Parson's Spencer grazed Hampton's chest. Hampton ignored the superficial wound, and was about to fire his revolver when he noticed that his adversary's rifle had fouled. In an act of chivalry, Hampton waited for Parsons to clean the bore, and then calmly shot the man in the wrist. Parsons fled to seek medical attention.

The duel with the trooper was over, but Hampton now faced another threat. Without warning, Lieutenant Storrs dashed from the woods to strike Hampton in the back of the head with his saber. Only the general's slouch hat and thick hair saved him from a serious wound or even death. Hampton aimed his revolver point blank at Storrs' face, but the percussion cap was faulty and failed to discharge. Storrs hastily retreated into the woods, and a disgusted Hampton retired to the rear to get patched up. While seeking medical attention, the general learned that Union cavalrymen were advancing, and received orders from Stuart to head up the road to meet them.[32]

After conferring with Lieutenant Storrs about the reconnaissance, General Custer moved forward to view a wooden house and a wooden barn, and beyond, perhaps a half mile wide, were fields with wheat and corn. Past the fields was a tree line, and within that thick cover Custer could observe through his field glasses elements of the Confederate cavalry positioned within those trees as well as behind rail fences and in the fields. The newly appointed general was anxious to fight, and quickly estimated that there could be no more than a couple of companies—two hundred or so dismounted enemy cavalrymen—to his front.[33]

Custer reported this information to Kilpatrick, and it was decided that the Boy General would challenge the enemy force on what was the John Felty farm. Custer deployed artillery on the knoll, sent the Sixth Michigan inside the barn and amongst the farm outbuildings facing the road, and formed Captain Henry E. Thompson's A Company of the Sixth—perhaps fifty men strong—across the road in fields of corn and wheat for the attack. Three other dismounted companies that would act as skirmishers were deployed to the right in the trees and bushes, the Seventh Michigan to the left, and the Fifth held in reserve. Alexander Pennington's six-gun artillery battery was also placed across the road near the wood line.[34]

When his units were in place, Custer astonished and delighted his men by riding to the front with the obvious intention of leading the charge. Generals rarely, if ever, led individual companies into battle, but this was Custer's first charge as a general and he was not about to be denied any glory associated with what he presumed would be a smashing victory.

The entrenched Confederates may have noticed some activity to their front, but given the lay of the land with the cornfield and a large barn obscuring their vision, they likely did not right away realize the number of troops forming in Custer's detachment. Custer's plan was to surprise the Rebels with his presence, and then pull back, luring the gray-clad horsemen out of their cover to chase him. These unwitting troopers would ride straight into the sights of his strategically deployed riflemen with their Spencers, and the devastating canister shot from Pennington's guns.

Custer drew his saber, sounded the charge, and galloped forward to lead Thompson's men directly, not into a couple of hundred, but into more than six hundred of Wade Hampton's troopers—under the command of Custer's West Point friend Colonel Pierce M. B. Young of Cobb's Legion.[35]

The result was inevitable. Company A was sliced to ribbons by volley after volley of carbine fire—some of it coming from the weapons of Union skirmishers that had been poorly deployed. Captain Thompson and more than thirty of his troopers were blasted from their saddles. Thompson's second-in-command, Lieutenant S. A. Ballard, was also shot and subsequently captured. Custer lost one killed, thirty-four wounded, and nine captured.[36]

Custer narrowly escaped death or capture when his horse was shot out from under him and he became a prime target for Rebel sharpshooters. He was fortunate that twenty-two-year-old Private Norvill F. Churchill of the First Michigan noticed the plight of his commander and rode through the fusillade to lift Custer onto his mount and gallop back to the Felty farm.[37]

The Rebels mounted a charge, but the day was saved from total disaster when riflemen from the Sixth and Seventh Michigan opened up on the pursuers from their positions on the side of the road. Pennington's and Elder's artillery batteries were brought into action, and that timely barrage, combined with small arms fire, succeeded in relieving the pressure and pushing Young's men back.

The surviving Yankees eventually hightailed it down the road toward the relative safety of Hunterstown. Wade Hampton brought up artillery that dueled with the Union batteries until after dark, when he chose to withdraw and return to Stuart, leaving behind twenty-two dead gray-clad cavalrymen.[38]

Custer, in his camp at Hunterstown, was predictably devastated by his failure, although his conduct had for the most part impressed his brigade and was the subject of lavish praise by his commander, who said he "fought most handsomely." He had pledged when he assumed command of the Michigan Brigade that he would instill a sense of confidence in his men with his ability under fire, but that notion had been temporarily dashed. That night, Custer analyzed his actions over and over, and realized that the lack of knowledge about the precise size of the enemy waiting in front of him had brought about his downfall. He vowed that he would not make that same mistake twice.[39]

At 11:00 P.M., Kilpatrick moved his exhausted troops out of Hunterstown to Two Taverns, five miles southeast of Gettysburg on the Baltimore Pike. The Third Division cavalrymen straggled down the road, arriving at their bivouacs anywhere between 3:00 A.M. and dawn to catch whatever amount of sleep was possible before the next march.[40]

The second day at Gettysburg had been another killing field for the two armies, a slaughterhouse of unimaginable proportion. Places assigned unofficial names such as the Peach Orchard, the Wheatfield, Devil's Den, Little Round Top, the Valley of Death, and Culp's Hill—the location of the final action of a day that ended with another abortive Rebel attack—would forever be inscribed on the pages of war annals as sites of some of the bloodiest engagements ever waged in this country.

Lee had mounted two attacks against Meade's army, with the main assault by General James Longstreet with two I Corps divisions, and by General

Richard Ewell with three brigades against Culp's Hill. The Union had been driven out of the Wheatfield and the Peach Orchard by Longstreet's two-hour bloody assault and back to Cemetery Ridge, where they frantically worked to shore up defenses from Cemetery Hill in the north and Little Round Top to the south.

Most of the dirty work to this point had been conducted between opposing infantry and artillery. The cavalries on both sides, however, had now arrived in force and were itching to pick a fight with each other.

Tomorrow would be July 3, 1863, the final day of the most monumental battle ever waged on American soil—and George Armstrong Custer and James Ewell Brown Stuart had an appointment with destiny. And it just could be that the youngster had a few tricks up his sleeve for the old master.

Twelve

─═══◉═══─

Custer vs. Stuart

Before dawn on July 3, Jeb Stuart led four brigades of his command—about five thousand mounted men reinforced with one thousand infantrymen—northeastward along the York Pike. His destination was a position around the far right of the Union line. Lee would be renewing his attack on Culp's Hill, and planned to later execute a bold move that would thrust a massive and powerful gray fist into the belly of the blue line. George Pickett and eleven infantry brigades from four divisions—over thirteen thousand men—were scheduled to mount a heroic frontal assault that afternoon on Cemetery Ridge, the center of the Union defense.

Jeb Stuart's cavalry was without question intended to play a vital role in Lee's daring strategy. It would be likely—in spite of the widespread disapproval of Stuart's recent actions—that the cavalry commander would have been briefed about the particulars of such an audacious undertaking. Stuart's part in this offensive would be to wade into the Union rear in coordination with Pickett's charge that afternoon and create mass confusion as well as weakening the line by killing as many as possible and drawing away the enemy to fight the cavalry.

The exact time of this mounted attack would be determined when circumstances warranted, and could be arranged by Lee dispatching a courier but, taking into consideration Stuart's subsequent actions, was more than likely worked out to in some manner coincide with the conclusion of an artillery barrage. If Pickett's charge was to be successful, Stuart must be in precisely the right position to discover it and improve the opportunity by hitting the Union rear. This one-two punch would, in Lee's estimation, ultimately result in an overwhelming Confederate victory. To prepare for this mission, Stuart had consulted his topographical maps in order to select the perfect location to embark on this surprise offensive strike.[1]

While Stuart rode down the York Pike, Judson Kilpatrick received orders from General Pleasonton at 8:00 A.M. to move his division in support of Meade's line at Little Round Top and Big Round Top. Kilpatrick had already departed with Farnsworth's First Brigade by the time George Armstrong Custer received orders for the movement and roused his troops.

Custer had just gotten under way when an aide from Brigadier General David Gregg, commander of the Second Division, brought word that Gregg wanted Custer to join him about three miles north on the Hanover Road. Gregg had been charged with protecting Meade's right flank and, given the amount of enemy cavalry activity operating in the area, feared that he lacked enough men to adequately defend that position. Gregg assumed responsibility for Custer's presence without clearing the order through proper channels, but did so with concern for protecting the Union rear.[2]

Custer joined Gregg and formed his twenty-three-hundred-man brigade in a line along the intersection of Hanover and Low Dutch roads facing Gettysburg, partially on a property of farmland and forest owned by a farmer named John Rummel. The lesson learned the previous evening about the importance of reconnaissance convinced Custer to immediately send out patrols in every direction. The general was not about to be caught unaware of enemy strength or movement on this day.[3]

At about 10:00 A.M., Jeb Stuart directed his troopers off York Pike at a crossroads two and a half miles beyond Gettysburg. The horsemen rode another mile along a country road to approach a lengthy ridge that ran upward from the south, with heavy timber on the northern end. Cress Ridge, Stuart judged, would be the ideal position.

The high ground of Cress Ridge fell away to a level valley, and commanded views of pastoral pastureland dotted with an occasional farmhouse and separated in places by stone and stake-and-rail fences. Three hundred yards from the foot of the ridge stood a large wooden barn owned by the Rummel family. Hanover Road was a mile and a quarter away, and, more importantly, the position afforded direct access to the Union line to the south. Stuart had made an effort to conceal his movement into the thick woods behind the ridge, but Wade Hampton's and Fitzhugh Lee's brigades happened to pass through open ground and unintentionally revealed their presence.[4]

Custer's vigilance about dispatching reconnaissance patrols had been rewarded. A patrol comprised of members of the Sixth Michigan had observed Stuart's cavalry. The patrol commander, Major Peter Weber, returned before midday to report that at least two brigades of Rebel cavalry and one artillery battery had been observed moving forward through the trees one mile to the west of Cress Ridge. "I have seen thousands of them over there," Weber related. "The country yonder is full of the enemy."[5]

It did not take Jeb Stuart long to confirm the major's report to his enemy. Shortly after noon, he ran out a section of Captain W. H. Griffin's Maryland Battery and personally ordered the firing of four shots—and only four shots. Jeb then dispatched a dismounted detachment of Brigadier General Albert G. Jenkins' Thirty-fourth Virginia to descend Cress Ridge and occupy some outbuildings on Rummel's farm.[6]

At the time, the reason for Stuart's impulsive artillery action befuddled not only the Union observers but his adjutant, Major Henry McClellan. Later, however, McClellan speculated that the firing of the four rounds may have been a prearranged signal to let General Lee know that Stuart had successfully reached his position at the Union rear and was prepared to carry out his mission.

McClellan's assumption rings true. Stuart, the master of stealth, would not have fired the cannons and compromised his position simply to determine the location of his enemy. He knew, after all, that he was at the rear of the Union line and that there was a detachment to his front. His actions therefore can be interpreted to mean that the cavalry indeed was an integral part of a plan to strike the rear in coordination with Pickett's frontal assault. Lee was now free to carry on with his bold strategy.[7]

Gregg held his own units in support, and assigned the front to the Michigan Brigade. Brigadier General Custer had studied the terrain with field glasses, and formulated his reply to Stuart. He ordered Battery M under Lieutenant Alexander C. M. Pennington, his West Point friend from the class of 1860, to return fire, and deployed the Sixth Michigan on the left, the Seventh on the right, and the First in the center. The Fifth was dismounted as skirmishers to the left and center.

The opposing riflemen exchanged fire for some time until Union artillery fire, or perhaps an order from Stuart, eventually succeeded in causing the Confederate troops and battery to withdraw. The fight at that point was reduced to long-distance sniping between the two sides into early afternoon.[8]

While Gregg and Custer anxiously waited for Stuart's next ploy, the brigade commanded by Colonel John McIntosh arrived and began to relieve Custer's men at the forward positions. The colonel reported to Custer, who explained the situation. McIntosh pointed toward the distant ridge, and jokingly said, "I think you will find the woods out there full of them." These fresh troopers spread onto the field and to some extent escalated the skirmishing.[9]

While Custer's men retired to the rear, a courier from General Kilpatrick reported to Gregg with orders for the Michigan Brigade to rejoin the Third Division. At about the same time, Gregg received orders from Pleasonton to release Custer, but also learned from Major General Oliver O. Howard, commander of the Sixth Corps atop Cemetery Hill—a former classmate and friend of Jeb Stuart at West Point—that a large number of enemy cavalry earlier had been observed moving to the right.

Gregg was faced with a predicament. He was already aware of Stuart's presence, but was now concerned about the strength of his enemy. He had been charged with protecting the Union rear, and could use all the troops he could muster. McIntosh would at some point require reinforcements. Custer was of the opinion that a fight was imminent, and volunteered to stay with Gregg. The general agreed that Custer and his brigade should remain at that location, and decided to countermand both Pleasonton and Kilpatrick and keep the Wolverines with him for the time being.

Custer deployed his regiments south of Hanover Road, and positioned the six artillery pieces of Pennington's battery and four guns commanded by Captain Alanson Randol nearby.[10]

At 1:00 P.M., the relative silence of the Cress Ridge and Rummel farm area was interrupted by the deafening roar of an artillery bombardment originating from the direction of Seminary Ridge, some four miles distant. The ensuing barrage was so heavy that it caused the ground to shake beneath the feet of the cavalry troops. Captain James Kidd later wrote, "The tremendous volume of sound volleyed and rolled across the intervening hills like reverberating thunder in a storm."[11]

Jeb Stuart would have been aware that the Confederates had opened fire with 150 artillery pieces in an effort to soften up the Federal line in prelude to Pickett's charge. This was his signal to ready his men for an attack on the Union rear. But first he must dispose of the blue cavalrymen who presently blocked his pathway.

Custer, on the other hand, would have been comforted to know that Federal guns had answered the challenge with seventy-two pieces of their own fired from behind the stone walls on Cemetery Ridge. But he would not have been fooled into thinking that this was exclusively an artillery duel at Gettysburg. He was savvy enough to recognize—as were many of his men—that such an ambitious Confederate bombardment had been initiated for a specific purpose. Everyone would have remained alert, wary of Stuart's role in this pending offensive.[12]

Stuart did not waste any time before attempting to remove the obstacle that stood between his cavalry and the Union rear. Shortly before 2:00 P.M., a skirmisher line of Virginia regiments under Brigadier General Micah

Jenkins—about fifteen hundred men—stepped from the woods on Cress Ridge and commenced a long-range engagement with the forward line of McIntosh's regiment that ran along a fence near Rummel's springhouse.

At the same time, Stuart ordered Griffin to open up with his cannons. The Rebel riflemen quickly gained the upper hand in what became a one-sided affair due to the fact that McIntosh's men were running low on ammunition. McIntosh made an effort to disengage, but encountered problems getting away through the intense fire and called for assistance.

Union general David M. Gregg was an "ambulance general," which was the term used for those generals who commanded from a safe place in the rear. He assigned the privilege of fighting Stuart's Rebels on the field to his subordinate, George Armstrong Custer.

The new general responded by ordering Russell Alger's Fifth Michigan to move forward on foot and deploying several companies of the Sixth on their left to relieve some of the pressure on McIntosh. Stuart countered by directing his artillery at the newcomers. The shells ripped into the midst of the Fifth Michigan to inflict numerous casualties. Custer quickly moved his men back to the shelter of a fence line where they could fire from cover.[13]

While the opposing artillery batteries engaged in a fierce duel, the dismounted Confederate Ninth Virginia cavalry broke into a charge. Alger's Fifth Michigan patiently waited until the Confederates were within 120 yards before firing a furious volley. The Rebels were urged by their officers to strike before the enemy could reload. Unknown to the gray-clad troops, however, was the fact that the Wolverines had been outfitted with Spencer carbines. The Spencer could fire seven cartridges without reloading, and the Yanks discharged four accurate and devastating volleys that effectively stopped the onrushing Rebs in their tracks.[14]

The tough Invincibles regrouped and returned with reinforcements from Hampton's and Lee's brigades. The Fifth Michigan held its ground and maintained the same fire discipline. The Union men, however, were dangerously low on ammunition and were forced to retreat.

The withdrawal of those Wolverines inspired the Confederates to press forward. Lieutenant Colonel Vincent Witcher, commander of the Thirty-fourth Virginia, described this charge, "With a wild yell the whole line dashed forward, retook the fence and swept the Federal men back." Stuart dispatched additional troopers, both on foot and mounted, to chase the retreating enemy. Relief was necessary at this point or the Fifth Michigan would be overrun.[15]

Captain Kidd noted what happened next, "Just then a column of mounted men was seen advancing from the right and rear of the Union line. Squadron succeeded squadron until an entire regiment came into view, with sabers gleaming and colors gaily fluttering in the breeze."

Without being ordered to do so, George Armstrong Custer had ridden to the front of the Seventh Michigan. He unsheathed his saber, and shouted, "Come on, you Wolverines!" He kicked his spurs into his horse's flanks and charged across the field at his enemy in front of his troops.[16]

As explosions ripped the earth, yelling and cheering at the top of their lungs, these troopers of the Seventh Michigan—their average age eighteen—followed Custer into the open field and slammed full force into the ranks of the Ninth and Thirteenth Virginia regiments. Stuart's men outnumbered Custer's men, but most of the Rebels were on foot and commenced a hasty retreat from the intent horsemen. Custer and his Wolverines pursued their panicked enemy and rode them down while rounding up small groups of prisoners.

To his dismay, however, Custer topped a rise to abruptly run into a stone wall with a rail fence on top. His troops bunched up at this barrier, which created a chaotic mass of rebelling horses and confused riders. The retreating Confederates noticed this turmoil, and turned about to fire at the trapped men from point-blank range.

One Union trooper who observed this action from a distance described that predicament, "To our astonishment and distress we saw that regiment, apparently without any attempt to change direction, dash itself upon a high stake and rider fence, squadron after squadron, breaking upon the struggling masses in front, like the waves of the sea upon a rocky shore until all were mixed in one confused and tangled mass."[17]

Troopers from the Seventh Michigan labored under heavy fire to tear down the wall. Colonel John McIntosh rode into the fray, shouting, "For God's sake, men, if you are ever going to stand, stand now, for you are on your free soil!"

They eventually succeeded in breaking through the stone wall. Custer skillfully directed them on a furious assault up the slope toward Rummel's farm with the objective being a Confederate artillery battery. Once there, they were met with another sort of wall—this one of the human variety. The opposing cavalries tore into each other in a life-or-death, every-man-for-himself struggle described as a "desperate, but unequal hand-to-hand conflict" that grew worse by the minute for the outnumbered Yankees.[18]

Stuart ordered reinforcements—the First North Carolina and the Jeff Davis Legion—forward to support the Virginians. These newcomers to the field waylaid Custer's move toward the battery, and in a running battle forced the Yankee horsemen southward across the farm.[19]

Custer had noticed that additional enemy cavalrymen were pounding toward the position from the flank, and wisely ordered his battered troops to retreat. The Rebels raced forward with intentions of cutting them off. Colonel Russell Alger was determined to ride to the rescue. While McIntosh's troopers laid down a steady base of fire, Alger mounted two squadrons of his Fifth Michigan and charged into the Rebels, which allowed the besieged Wolverines to retire and restored distinct battle lines on the field.

There was not any time to rest, however. Jeb Stuart had a mission of the utmost importance to reach the Union rear. He may have been thwarted once by this upstart Union cavalry, but he was steadfast in his belief that his Invincibles could and would prevail. After all, they had always responded magnificently to any of his requests.[20]

Less than half an hour later—presumably at the same instant that Pickett and thirteen thousand Confederate infantrymen were streaming across the field toward the center of the Union line at Gettysburg—Stuart gathered his horsemen for one final desperate charge. If there was any conceivable hope of supporting Pickett, he needed to reach the Union rear, three miles away, as soon as possible or the day could be lost for the Confederacy. Stuart had no choice but to initiate his own version of Pickett's charge on horseback and force the Yankees from the pathway to his objective.[21]

Stuart instructed Colonel John Chambliss to hastily organize eight regiments from Hampton's and Lee's brigades. The legendary cavalry commander had intended for this force to remain concealed in the timber until he gave the order to move, but his wishes were apparently misunderstood. This long gray line of mounted Southerners soon emerged from the woods on Cress Ridge and formed an impressive attack column.

The appearance of the Rebel horsemen was described by one awed Union participant, "In close columns of squadrons, advancing as if in review, with sabers drawn and glistening like silver in the bright sunlight, the spectacle called forth a murmur of admiration."[22]

Captain William Miller of the Third Pennsylvania wrote about the moment the Confederates started on the move toward the Union position, "A grander spectacle than their advance has rarely been beheld. They marched with well-aligned fronts and steady reins. Their polished saber-blades dazzled in the sun. Shell and shrapnel met the advancing Confederates, tore through their ranks. Closing the gaps as though nothing had happened, on they came."[23]

The Southern cavalry started at a trot, picked up speed to a canter, then galloped directly toward the center of the Union line.

Custer quickly sized up his situation as the Rebels steadily advanced— and it did not look good. The Seventh and Fifth Michigan were in the process of re-forming, and the Sixth was protecting Pennington's artillery battery, which was furiously firing at the approaching horsemen. Custer had only one option left. Colonel Charles H. Town's outnumbered First Michigan Regiment would have to ride out and meet this overwhelming threat. The First was a veteran, experienced unit, but with the odds greatly stacked against them, one officer summed up the feelings of his comrades by exclaiming, "Great heavens! We will all be swallowed up!"[24]

Colonel Town, who was ill and tired and rode strapped to the saddle, had never in his career shied away from a fight—no matter the odds. If he was to die, there was no better manner, to his chivalrous way of thinking, than during the execution of a heroic charge. He obediently ordered his troops forward with sabers drawn, and prepared to face the enemy on what could only be called a suicide mission.

At that moment, Brigadier General George Armstrong Custer, his long, yellow curls flowing behind him, galloped up to Colonel Town, saluted, and politely indicated that he would assume command. The young general, much to the surprise and admiration of his troops, had decided to lead the First Michigan on this dangerous charge. Custer rode to the front, where every eye could see him, unsheathed his heavy Toledo blade, and trotted forward with his customary bravado. He watched intently as his enemy approached down Cress Ridge.[25]

By this time, Colonel Chambliss' gray-clad horsemen had progressed halfway to their objective across the open field. Custer, hearing the cheers and yells of his inspired men behind him, confidently urged his mount forward to close the distance between the two cavalries. Perhaps glancing now and then at the faces of the awestruck spectators he passed along his lines, Custer carefully maneuvered around fences and other obstacles and aimed his outnumbered regiment directly at the head of the onrushing Confederate force. Pennington's battery had been blasting canister shot into the oncoming Confederates, but now ceased firing for fear of shelling their own men.

When the Rebels had advanced to within about one hundred yards away, Custer, from a position four lengths ahead of his troops, kicked his mount into a gallop, and shouted, "Come on, you Wolverines!" The blue column surged forward in what Colonel Alger would later call "the most gallant charge of the war."[26]

An eyewitness from McIntosh's brigade described the dramatic scene, "The two columns drew nearer and nearer, the Confederates outnumbering their opponents as three or four to one. The gait increased—first the trot, then the gallop. As the charge was ordered the speed increased, every horse on the jump, every man yelling like a demon. The columns of the Confederates blended, but the perfect alignment was maintained. As the opposing columns drew nearer and nearer, each with perfect alignment, every man gathered his horse well under him and gripped his weapon tighter."[27]

Captain William Miller recounted the meeting of the opposing cavalries from his position in reserve, "As the two columns approached each other the pace of each increased, when suddenly a crash, like the falling of timber, betokened the crisis. So sudden and violent was the collision that many of the horses were turned end over end and crushed their riders beneath them. The clashing of sabers, the demands for surrender, the firing of pistols and cries of the combatants now filled the air."[28]

Custer reported, "For a moment, but only for a moment, that long, heavy column stood its ground; then, unable to withstand the impetuosity of our attack, it gave way to a disorderly rout, leaving vast numbers of dead in our possession. I challenge the annals of warfare to produce a more brilliant or successful charge of cavalry."[29]

The fighting was so intense and at such close quarters that some of the killed were found in pairs of blue and gray, "pinned to each other by tightly-clenched sabers driven through their bodies." Another example of the intimacy of this battle was found by John Rummel when he later returned to his farm. In addition to thirty dead horses littering his lane, Rummel found the macabre sight of two opposing cavalrymen. "Their fingers, though stiff in death," the farmer recalled, "were so firmly imbedded in each other's flesh that they could not be removed without the aid of force."[30]

George Armstrong Custer, for the second time in twenty-four hours, was rudely thrown to the ground when his horse, Roanoke, the blooded iron-gray stallion he had appropriated on his Urbanna raid, was struck by a round in the foreleg and collapsed. The uninjured brigadier general quickly corralled a riderless mount and leaped into the saddle to direct his troops and wreak havoc with his own deadly saber.[31]

The sight of his undermanned comrades gradually driving back the enemy so affected and motivated Captain Miller that he said to Lieutenant William Brooke-Rawle, "I have been ordered to hold this position, but, if you will back me up in case I am court-martialed for disobedience, I will order a charge." Brooke-Rawle agreed, and the Third Pennsylvania Cavalry enthusiastically entered the fray. "The men fired a volley from their carbines, drew their sabers, sent up a shout, and 'sailed in,' striking the enemy's left flank about two-thirds down the column," Miller reported. Thirty-four years later, Captain Miller would be awarded the Medal of Honor for his courageous charge.[32]

Somewhere on that bloody field of battle rode Custer's friend Confederate Colonel Tom Rosser, who was participating in his first combat since returning to duty after recovering from the wound sustained at Kelly's Ford in March. With Custer leading those brazen charges of his troops, it was likely that Rosser knew who they were fighting—and may have learned right then about Custer's almost unimaginable promotion to brigadier general. The romantic view would be that the eyes of those two friends turned adversaries had briefly met at some point as they commanded their troops on the field.

While Jeb Stuart directed the fighting from the vicinity of Rummel's barn, additional Union units—remnants of the Fifth and Seventh Michigan, and the First New Jersey—slammed into the Rebels' flanks while Custer and the First Michigan gouged a gaping hole through the center. The reinforcements proved too much for the Confederates to withstand, and turned the tide in favor of the Federal horsemen. The Rebels grudgingly gave ground. A frantic Jeb Stuart now feared that his besieged Invincibles would become surrounded and decimated, and ordered his men to retreat all the way back to Cress Ridge.

Custer paused from the fray to watch this panicked retreat by the Rebels—while his cavalry held the field and chased the fleeing Rebels. With his enemy withdrawing to their original position, he realized that Stuart's threat to his troops—and to the Union rear—had been successfully repulsed. Any pursuit up Cress Ridge would be fruitless and only cost needless casualties. He prudently ordered a methodical withdrawal, all the while watching for any indication that Stuart might be only bluffing. It was no bluff—Stuart had quit.[33]

This skirmish had not only been perilous for the common Confederate cavalrymen who had made that final charge, but the lives of the cavalry hierarchy were also placed in jeopardy. According to John Esten Cooke, "We lost many good men. General Hampton was shot in the side and nearly cut out of the saddle by a saber stroke [to the head]. He was slowly being borne to the rear in his ambulance, bleeding from his dangerous wounds. General Stuart had a narrow escape in this charge, his pistol hung in his holster, and as he was trying to draw it, he received the fire of barrel after barrel from a Federal cavalryman within ten paces of him, but fortunately sustained no injury."[34]

The legendary Jeb Stuart had been soundly whipped—or at least fought to a draw and denied his objective. Just twenty-three years old and a general for less than a week, George Armstrong Custer had humiliated one of the greatest cavalry commanders in the world.

Three miles away, George Pickett and his eleven brigades—over thirteen thousand men—had charged the Union center with disastrous results for the South. Pickett and other officers gave speeches of encouragement as the men headed toward the "little clump of trees" at the Union center that was the objective of the attack. The mile-wide line, perfectly aligned, flags proudly waving, marched across the pasture at one hundred yards a minute. Halfway there, they executed a smart left oblique to close the gap between divisions.

Before long, enfilading sheets of canister artillery fire from Union guns on both Cemetery Hill and Little Round Top burst into their midst, shell after shell exploding to create gaping holes in the lines where men were blown apart. Union infantry riflemen saturated the field with a devastating fusillade of bullets, targeting officers and color-bearers, but making it a wonder that any living thing could survive such an onslaught.

Pickett's men broke into a run, yelling like demons, trying to reach their enemy in that clump of trees, but only a few Confederate warriors ever made it to the stone wall defense along the Union line. The gray-clad attackers quickly vanished within the sea of blue uniforms, while others were sent into a disorganized retreat, leaving behind great numbers of their comrades dead and wounded on the field. Fifty regimental colors had accompanied the Confederates across that field, and more than thirty of them would become trophies of war for the Union. Of the thirteen thousand men who started the march, perhaps five thousand returned. The battle at Gettysburg, for all intents and purposes, was over, and General Lee's grandiose strategy had failed.[35]

Although it was an utter failure, the plan for Pickett's charge as devised by Robert E. Lee was nothing short of brilliant. For unknown reasons, the attack on Culp's Hill that had been part of this three-pronged attack plan never occurred as scheduled, although there were two earlier probes. But the coordinated effort of Pickett and Stuart would have been devastating enough in its own right had it been executed.

It has always been assumed that the role of Jeb Stuart's cavalry on this final afternoon was to disrupt Union supply lines and chase fleeing Yankees after Pickett routed them from the lines. Although Lee never produced actual orders that confirmed his plan to send Stuart's cavalry against the Union rear, solid evidence exists that this was his intention. And that evidence comes from the official report written by Jeb Stuart himself.

Lee had reinforced Stuart's command with Jenkins' brigade of one thousand men, and dispatched them to that location on Cress Ridge. Stuart would not have been ordered to chase retreating Yankee soldiers after Pickett's charge with Jenkins' brigade attached. Pursuit would have been purely a cavalry operation. The foot soldiers were there to engage their Union infantry counterparts.

Consequently, Stuart's mission without a doubt was to descend Cress Ridge, cross the Hanover Road, turn southwest, and, as he wrote in his report, "to effect a surprise on the enemy's rear." Stuart *twice* stated that he had intended to make a mad dash for the Union rear. His mission had not been to chase fleeing troops but to charge into those that were entrenched at the Union rear in a coordinated effort with Pickett.[36]

It cannot be determined for certain what would have happened if Stuart's cavalry had been able to threaten or make contact with the Union rear. The Federals, however, would have been obliged to remove manpower from the line and send it against this formidable six-thousand-man cavalry/infantry detachment. Had that been the case, the Union center would have been much more vulnerable to the frontal assault headed its way and would have perhaps caved in as Lee had intended.

General Lee, to his credit, in keeping with his strong character, would have kept secret his plan now that it had failed. Exposure of the particulars could only embarrass his cavalry commander for its lack of success. Lee would not have been concerned about blame being placed on his own shoulders. He would protect his subordinate, and take his chances with his own reputation. Stuart, who had won the hearts of the Southern public, would be needed in the future if the Confederate forces were to prevail in this conflict. It would serve no purpose to demoralize the legendary cavalry commander.

Contrary to what some detractors would claim, Stuart had not shirked his duty. He had made every effort to fulfill Lee's orders. The legendary cavalry commander had encountered one problem, however—a newly minted brigadier general by the name of George Armstrong Custer. Technically, the ranking officer on the field was Brigadier General David Gregg, commander of the Second Division, who had persuaded Custer to remain at that location. But Custer was certainly the de facto commander on the field, and the strategies that countered Stuart's intentions were formulated and carried out by him.

The significance of the result of this battle east of Gettysburg, not to mention Custer's extraordinary personal bravery and tactical decisions, has been all but ignored by modern-day historians, likely due to prejudices and controversies from the Boy General's later career. Nonetheless, the actions of Custer that day are worthy of a prominent place in the history of the Gettysburg battle—perhaps even as the turning point—and in the history of the Civil War, as well as in the history of cavalry warfare throughout the ages.

Casualty totals for both sides in the cavalry skirmish east of Gettysburg have been a matter of contention. Stuart reported losses of 181 killed, wounded, or missing—excluding his artillery batteries and Jenkins' brigade. Gregg reported the loss of 35 from his Second Division. Custer's Wolverines had suffered 29 killed, 123 wounded, and 67 missing, which left no doubt about which unit had stymied Jeb Stuart's horsemen in this significant encounter.[37]

The last great cavalry saber battle of the war pitting Johnny Reb and Billy Yank against each other had ended with the Federals claiming victory and the Confederates contending that it had been a draw. One debate, however, that had originated at Brandy Station had been settled. Jeb Stuart's legendary Invincibles were no longer deemed invincible by the ecstatic Union cavalry.

This sentiment was echoed on the Confederate side of the lines by William Blackford. After calling the battle "about as bloody and hot an affair as any we had yet experienced," Blackford added, "The cavalry of the enemy were steadily improving and it was all we could do sometimes to manage them."[38]

The field east of Gettysburg was turned over to medical personnel, who tended to those combatants showing any sign of life while loading the unfortunate ones into creaky caissons that carried away the bodies from the carnage.[39]

Custer's Confederate friend, Tom Rosser, offered his reason as to why Stuart failed, "Stuart had been marching constantly almost day and night, on scant forage and little rest for man or horse, for eight days, within the enemy's lines, and while his conduct displayed a daring almost to recklessness, he accomplished little, save the wear and fatigue of long marches."[40]

At dusk, while Custer and the wary Union cavalry maintained a vigilant watch, Jeb Stuart abandoned Cress Ridge and withdrew his weary brigades down York Pike. Stuart displayed his own fatigue by leading his men in the wrong direction—directly toward enemy lines—until corrected by a staff officer. Stuart was good-natured about his error, and resumed his march in this new direction with only a courier at his side while his staff rode on ahead. At one point, the courier rode forward as Stuart slept in his saddle. His horse failed to recognize his rider's headquarters, and nearly carried Stuart into enemy cavalry pickets.

It had been an exhausting ten days for Stuart and his cavalry, but what lay ahead would perhaps be more personally demanding for the Beau Sabreur— the scrutiny of his actions by those seeking to place blame for this failure to defeat the enemy at Gettysburg.[41]

Somewhere along the Union cavalry lines, a jubilant George Armstrong Custer rested in the darkness. He had accomplished everything that General Gregg had expected of him—and, perhaps more importantly, everything he had expected of himself. His miscalculation of the previous night would now be relegated to a mere footnote or likely forgotten. He had gained redemption by meeting Jeb Stuart and emerging draped with glory.

Thirteen

———◆———

Withdrawal and Pursuit

On the morning of July 4—Independence Day—the green fields and rolling hills around the town of Gettysburg were colored bloodred and littered with spent shells, discarded equipment, damaged buildings, and ghastly, twisted human remains. The losses during this three-day affair were staggering. This battle had engaged over 170,000 Americans, and in the end nearly thirty percent of them—more than fifty thousand—had been killed, wounded, captured, or could be counted among the missing.

Over five hundred artillery pieces had roared over those seventy-two hours to gouge craters in the earth as they sent shards of shrapnel whistling through the air to tear into vulnerable human flesh. Both armies had not sought to renew the carnage of the past days—it had ended with Pickett's charge, although Alfred Pleasonton did attempt to persuade General Meade to allow the Union cavalry to assault the Confederate position one more time.[1]

Critics in the South might have considered the battle a loss—with casualties amounting to 3,903 killed, 18,735 wounded, and 5,425 missing—but the campaign had in many ways been successful. For instance, an abundance of supplies had been confiscated in the North, perhaps enough to last through the winter months. In addition, Robert E. Lee had demonstrated to the world and national observers that his army could hold its own against the Union on Northern soil. Had Lee gained a decisive victory at Gettysburg, the Army of the Potomac could have withdrawn to Washington and the Army of Northern Virginia would have resumed the invasion. In that case, the best that Lee could have hoped for would have been an opportunity to negotiate a peace agreement on a level playing field. Another scenario, however, shows that if Lee could have maneuvered his troops between the Union army and Washington, thereby cutting off his enemy's source of supplies, Lee would have had the upper hand in negotiations and the South might have ended the war as victors.[2]

On the night of July 3, Jeb Stuart had reported to General Robert E. Lee, and for the first time learned about the disastrous result of Pickett's charge. Lee's compassionate character would not permit him to condemn anyone else for actions he had directed as its commander. Other officers, however, had already begun dividing loyalties and pointing fingers. And Jeb Stuart, who had been occupied with riding around the Union army when the fighting had commenced, was their target.

The issue that has tarnished Stuart's reputation from that day forth focused solely on the conduct of his reconnaissance mission and the timing of his arrival at Gettysburg. Most officers, if any, would have been privy to the plan for Stuart to strike the Union rear at the same time as Pickett's charge— and its failure.

One can only imagine the reception Stuart received from other staff officers overlooking the bloody field at Gettysburg. Sides were being taken in the debate about whether or not Stuart had disobeyed orders and, if so, to what extent his actions had affected the outcome of the three-day battle.

The roster of officers who had harsh words for Stuart's alleged malfeasance that contributed to the loss at Gettysburg included James Longstreet, Henry Heth, Edward P. Alexander, Walter Taylor, and C. M. Wilcox. There was one officer, however, whose reaction was particularly blunt and condemning of Stuart. Lee's chief of staff, Colonel Charles Marshall, the officer who had prepared the orders issued for that questionable ride by Stuart around the Yankees, recommended that the cavalry commander should stand a court-martial.[3]

Stuart did not help matters when defending his actions in his official report, which was an astounding 14,300 words in length. The report, in essence, was a fictional account of Stuart's true mission. He recounted his success in "spreading terror to the very gates of the [Union] capital," and in a sense chided Lee by professing that enough cavalry had been left behind that, "properly handled, such a command should have done everything requisite." Jubal Early as well as A. P. Hill and James Longstreet came under Stuart's scrutiny for their alleged blunders for not finding him sooner or for advancing without better coordination with his cavalry.[4]

At the time Stuart delivered his report, he made an attempt to persuade Colonel Marshall to admit that the conduct of the cavalry had been justified. Marshall retorted that Stuart should have obeyed orders, and, predictably, an argument followed with neither man backing down.[5]

The last word belonged to Marshall, however. After reading Stuart's report, the colonel wrote a second report over the signature of Robert E. Lee in which he toughened his previous stance by adding that perhaps Stuart should have been shot. Lee later modified the report to exclude that severe and prejudiced opinion. He did note, however, that "the march toward Gettysburg was conducted more slowly than it would have been had the movements of the Federal army been known," and did not delete a statement that his army's operations were "much embarrassed by the absence of the cavalry."[6]

The question of whether or not Stuart disobeyed orders has been debated by battle participants and noted historians since that July day in 1863 when the battle of Gettysburg became a bitter disappointment for the South. Stuart has borne the brunt of the accusations likely because in death he was a convenient scapegoat to those contemporaries who fixed blame for the defeat on him in order to perhaps camouflage their own inadequacies during that battle.[7]

Outwardly, Stuart's apparent contempt for detractors and customary self-importance remained on display for all to observe—as evidenced by his arrival in Martinsburg, Virginia, during the withdrawal from Pennsylvania. Lee and his three corps commanders—Longstreet, Hill, and Ewell—rode along in a somber fashion befitting the mood after Gettysburg. Stuart, on the other hand, arrived in town with his typical flair of pounding hooves, announced by two buglers "blowing most furiously." The Beau Sabreur was not about to let anyone perceive that his spirit could be broken by rumors and innuendos that, in his mind, were totally baseless.[8]

However, another star that had brightly shone over Southern skies throughout the war was now rapidly becoming obscured by clouds of vilification.

Back at Confederate headquarters, confidants witnessed for the first time the stalwart commander Robert E. Lee briefly teeter near the emotional breaking point. Lee, who accepted personal blame for the defeat, had good reason to display his anguish. He quickly gathered himself, however, and tended to his soldiering responsibilities. His army remained entrenched in a defensive posture on Seminary Ridge, expecting an attack. But, as the hours passed, Lee correctly surmised that Meade was for the time being content to rest his battle-weary troops.[9]

Lee summoned his officers to a council of war, and arrived at the only logical conclusion under the circumstances—withdraw his army. The Confederate troops, who had expected to resume the fight, were disappointed by Lee's decision, which dispelled the rumor that the spirit of the rank and file had been broken. John Esten Cooke wrote, "Nothing is more erroneous than the idea that the Southern army was 'demoralized' by the results of the bloody action of these three memorable days. Their nerve was unshaken, their confidence in Lee and themselves unimpaired."[10]

Lee's first order of business would be the evacuation to Virginia of his wagons, supplies, and the ambulances that carried many of the wounded—including General Wade Hampton. Unfortunately, a great number of wounded would, out of necessity, be left behind with the hope that they would be treated with compassion by the enemy. Gettysburg, with a population of 2,400 civilians, would be overwhelmed when the swift-moving armies would leave behind 22,000 wounded men. The town would rally together to do its best to care for the wounded and bury the dead, while worried relatives of missing soldiers arrived in town to look for their loved ones.[11]

The safe passage of General Lee's wagon train, with its vital stores and equipment, was crucial to the survival of the Army of Northern Virginia. Therefore, the responsibility of guarding the extensive caravan could not be handed to just anyone, but Lee was confident in his selection of an escort.[12]

Brigadier General John Imboden had demonstrated skillful resourcefulness and the ability to act as a semi-independent command. His successful spring raid through western Virginia had cut the Baltimore & Ohio Railroad lines and captured a large amount of livestock. Imboden and his twenty-one hundred Virginia cavalrymen most recently had been acting as the army's rear guard, which had freed up Pickett for his fateful presence at Gettysburg. Lee now summoned Imboden, who reported just after midnight. Imboden greeted General Lee by saying, "General, this has been a hard day for you."[13]

Lee replied, "Yes, it has been a sad, sad day to us." He then told Imboden about Pickett's heroic charge, and commented, "I never saw troops behave more magnificently." After a moment of uncomfortable silence, Lee's emotions poured forth, and he said, "Too bad! Too bad! *Oh! Too bad!*" Lee composed himself, and issued orders for Imboden's unit to act as escort for the departing wagon train.[14]

While Imboden conferred with Lee, Brigadier General George Armstrong Custer was released by General Gregg and reported back to Judson Kilpatrick's Third Division. Certainly Gregg, as commander of the troops opposing Stuart, deserved some of the credit for the victory east of Gettysburg, but most of the glory was reserved for Custer, who had led the two daring cavalry charges and inspired and rallied his troops on the field by his courageous example. Perhaps more importantly to Custer than any official acclamation was that he had earned the utmost respect of his officers and troops. They had followed him into the depths of hell and emerged victorious. His courage and leadership skills on the field of battle were now unquestioned.[15]

On that night of July 3, Custer and his troops did not sleep, but rather maintained a vigilance, with one detachment waiting in ambush down the Baltimore Pike in case Stuart chose to attack. By 2:00 A.M., Custer was relatively certain that no attack was imminent, and bedded down his troops near the Rummel farmhouse. The men were weary but rejuvenated, and ready to resume the fight. A writer for the *Detroit Free Press* summed up the feelings of the Michigan Wolverines when he wrote, "The battle is fought, the victory is won, and Michigan troops are still ahead."[16]

The North, however, had little reason to celebrate, having suffered 3,155 killed, 14,529 wounded, and 5,365 missing. And, although losses from the Michigan Brigade in its significant role had contributed to that incredible casualty toll, Custer was saddened and troubled to learn upon reporting to Kilpatrick about one detachment of the Third Division that had fallen in a senseless slaughter.[17]

Kilpatrick's division had been skirmishing with the Confederates at the south end of the battlefield below Gettysburg late on the previous afternoon. The Yankee horsemen faced a well-entrenched line of Texas and Georgia infantry barricaded behind a stone wall and stake-and-rail fence. Attempts had been made to dislodge the Rebels, but the terrain, which was comprised of boulders, fences, and ditches, was unacceptable for effective cavalry maneuvers.

Regardless, Kilpatrick decided that, although this location held no significant strategic importance, he must take this Confederate position with an assault of his horsemen. Without Custer's brigade available, Kilpatrick had only the brigade commanded by Brigadier General Elon J. Farnsworth remaining to carry out the risky charge.[18]

Farnsworth, who had been promoted to general on the same day as Custer, opposed the action with the opinion that such a charge would be tantamount to suicide. Captain H. C. Parsons, who led one of Farnsworth's battalions, described his commander as "courage incarnate, but full of tender regard for his men, and his protest was manly and soldierly." Kilpatrick had responded by mocking Farnsworth's fortitude, and virtually goading him into agreeing to lead the charge.[19]

In an assault that was described by a Confederate eyewitness as wholesale slaughter, Farnsworth, who was shot at least five times, and sixty-six of his men were killed during the execution of this ill-conceived charge.

Kilpatrick's irrational act and its outcome would have likely chilled the blood of even George Armstrong Custer, who, as evidenced by his bravery at Cress Ridge, was no stranger to charging into the cannon's mouth. But there was a time to charge and a time not to charge. Kilpatrick had crossed that line. The men of the Third Division were angered by the general's reckless decision, which to them served as an example of their commander's disregard for lives when personal glory was at stake. The troopers began calling their commander "Kill-Cavalry" for the needless slaughter of Farnsworth and his men.[20]

Captain James Kidd wrote, "He [Kilpatrick] had begun to be a terror to foes, and there was a well-grounded fear that he might become a menace to friends as well. He was brave to rashness, capricious, ambitious, reckless in rushing into scrapes, and generally full of expedients in getting out, though at times he seemed to lose his head entirely when beset by perils which he himself, had invited."[21]

But there was no time to dwell on the past. Orders passed from General Pleasonton to Kilpatrick instructed that the Third Division would ride south and attempt to intercept the Confederate wagon train that was reportedly on the move.

While the great armies fought at Gettysburg, another major operation was concluding to the west. On May 19, General U. S. Grant had arrived with his Union forces on the outskirts of Vicksburg, Mississippi, with intentions of capturing that city, which would give the North complete control of the Mississippi River and split the Confederacy in half. Grant attacked Vicksburg from both above and below the port of entry, mainly with frontal assaults, but none were successful. The general was not to be denied, however, and commenced what would become one of the longest and most devastating sieges of the war.

Throughout May and June both armies maintained their positions in the trenches, while the city withstood barrages from over two hundred Union artillery pieces. It may have taken a while, but the cannons eventually yielded the desired effect. By the end of June, the defenders of Vicksburg—unable to receive provisions or reinforcements from the outside—were weary, starving, and dying in their trenches, and could no longer prolong the inevitable. On

July 3, the Confederates requested a peace treaty, and General Grant gave them his famous reply of "unconditional surrender" as his terms. There was no choice for the Southerners but to comply. The next day, July 4, Union soldiers entered Vicksburg and ended that long campaign.

Just after noon on that Independence Day, Brigadier General George Armstrong Custer and his Michigan Wolverines were back in the saddle, riding with General Kilpatrick's division, when the heavens opened up to soak them and add further misery to the march. Captain James Kidd wrote, "It seemed as if the firmament were an immense tank, the contents of which were spilled all at once. Such a drenching as we had! Even heavy gum coats and horsehide boots were hardly proof against it. It poured and poured, making every rivulet a river and of every river and mountain stream a raging flood."[22]

The downpour had an even worse effect on the Confederate wagon train commanded by John Imboden. The panicked mules rebelled in the blinding torrent, and the canvas covering the wagons could not adequately repel the rain, which added to the suffering of the wounded occupants. When the caravan neared Cashtown in late afternoon and commenced its climb over the mountains, Imboden rode toward the front and realized that his wagons stretched for seventeen miles along the muddy pathway.[23]

Imboden endured a personal nightmare as he traversed that lengthy line of wagons. "For four hours I hurried forward on my way to the front," he wrote, "and in all that time I was never out of hearing the groans and cries of the wounded and dying. Scarcely one in a hundred had received adequate surgical aid, owing to the demands on the hard-working surgeons from still worse cases that had been left behind. The jolting was enough to have killed strong men, if long exposed to it." A shaken General Imboden swore that "During this one night I realized more horrors of war than I had in all the preceding two years."[24]

General Kilpatrick reached Emmitsburg about 3:00 P.M., and rendezvoused as planned with Colonel Pennock Huey's brigade from Gregg's division, which brought his total strength to more than five thousand. By late afternoon, en route in a southwest direction toward Frederick, scouts delivered a civilian, C. H. Buhrman, to Kilpatrick. Buhrman reported that a huge Rebel wagon train had been observed moving south along Fairfield Gap in South Mountain toward Hagerstown, Maryland. This was not Imboden's train, rather one commanded by Richard Ewell that had departed Gettysburg several hours after the wounded and supply train.[25]

Kilpatrick viewed the capture of this wagon train as an opportunity to restore his somewhat tarnished image. With Buhrman guiding, Kilpatrick pushed his troops along the soggy earth in a driving rainstorm toward Fairfield.

At about 10:00 P.M., Custer's brigade, which led the march, arrived at a fork in the road—the northwest branch led to Fairfield Gap, the southwest to Monterey Pass—to learn that the Rebel wagons had passed onto the northern road within the past three hours. A Confederate cavalry picket line had been deployed near the fork, but withdrew toward Fairfield after only token resistance when the Yankees approached.

In an effort to head off the wagon train, Kilpatrick ordered Colonel Charles Town and the First Michigan along the Fairfield Road to attack the rear of the caravan while the main force moved toward Monterey.

One regiment of Colonel Town's battalion, commanded by Lieutenant Colonel Peter Stagg, approached its objective, but was repulsed after destroying several wagons. The Wolverines suffered a number of casualties, including Stagg, who was injured when his horse was shot out from under him.[26]

Kilpatrick's column also encountered opposition, and was stopped in its tracks inside Monterey Pass by a company from the First Maryland Cavalry reinforced by elements of the Fourth North Carolina and one artillery piece. In spite of being greatly outnumbered, the Rebels were aided by the rainy weather, the darkness, and terrain that afforded them a clear field of fire down the road from their positions behind rocks and trees. The narrow pass prevented an orderly retreat by the Yankees, and the Rebel sharpshooters effectively pinned them down with accurate fire.

General Armstrong Custer quickly deployed his troops near a once-popular health resort named Monterey Springs. Seven companies of the Fifth

Michigan dismounted and scrambled up the slopes to form a skirmish line on both sides of the mountain road. The Sixth was placed on the right, extending down to the road not far from a bridge across a stream that had supplied mineral water to the spa. The two remaining companies of the Fifth remained mounted and poised to charge, while the First and the Seventh were held in reserve.

Custer ordered the Wolverines forward in a series of attempts to mount an offensive and dislodge the Rebels, but the pitch-black darkness, nagging rain, and thick underbrush—not to mention the accurate fire of the hidden enemy—thwarted each effort. James Kidd, who more than once was sent sprawling by vines and briars, wrote, "One had to be guided by sound and not by sight."

Finally, just after midnight, Colonel Russell Alger of the Fifth Michigan returned from a reconnaissance and reported to Custer that the bridge remained intact and could be crossed. That was all the frustrated Custer needed to hear to formulate his strategy—an immediate charge was in order.

Custer dismounted the Sixth Michigan and seven squadrons of the Fifth, while the First and the Seventh were held in reserve. The Boy General then led Alger and the Wolverines of the Fifth Michigan on the assault, and rushed full tilt across the bridge into the midst of the enemy. It was difficult to maintain order on this charge due to the darkness, the rough terrain, and the stormy conditions. The position of the Confederate skirmishers could only be determined by spotting their muzzle flashes.

By sheer numbers, however, firing their Spencers at muzzle flashes, Custer's men cleared the way for the Seventh Michigan to follow them across the bridge. The small Confederate force understood that in the face of this resolute attack it was now time to break contact, and vanished into the dark countryside. During the brief fray, Custer's horse was shot dead—reportedly his seventh mount lost in the Gettysburg Campaign—but Custer was uninjured in the fall.[27]

The next order of business was to secure the wagon train, which was located a half mile away. Kilpatrick's men, embarrassed that only a handful of the enemy had stymied three brigades for several hours, swooped down with a vengeance on Ewell's wagons. The Rebel drivers viciously whipped their teams to urge them on, causing numerous wagons to overturn. The wounded inside, whose screams could be distinctly heard, were rudely thrown out onto the muddy ground. But it was too late to make a run for it—the Federal horsemen, with their sabers in hand, quickly halted and commandeered the wagon train.

The train, with its 400 vehicles, which reportedly extended for some ten miles, was easily captured, along with 1,360 prisoners, who were for the most part Gettysburg casualties. Supplies were confiscated, and most of the wagons were hacked apart or burned before an enemy brigade arrived to chase away the Yankee cavalry. Kilpatrick moved his troops, prisoners, and newfound riches to Ringgold, where at dawn a halt was ordered.[28]

The division, according to *New York Times* reporter E. A. Paul, was "tired, sleepy, wet, and covered with mud. Men and animals yielded to the demands of exhausted nature, and the column had not been at a halt many minutes before all fell asleep where they stood." Paul noted that the "gallant Brigadier" Custer found refuge under the eaves of a chapel, "enjoying in the mud one of those sound sleeps, his golden locks matted with the soil."[29]

This respite from the saddle was short-lived, however, when after two hours Kilpatrick roused his weary troops. He was determined to locate and engage Jeb Stuart's cavalry, and pushed onward in the direction of Smithstown (present-day Smithsburg), fifteen miles away. The dogged pursuit would continue.[30]

Fourteen

———◦◦◦———

Evasion

The entire Confederate army was on the move. Jeb Stuart's cavalrymen, who were guarding both of Lee's flanks, had no better time of it in the downpour and barely passable roads than did the Union cavalry. Stuart decided to detour around Kilpatrick, and with that in mind departed Emmitsburg at midmorning. When Stuart approached the outskirts of Smithstown, however, he was surprised to discover that Kilpatrick was lying in wait with skirmishers deployed on each side of the road and artillery positioned on three hills.

Colonel Huey and Colonel Nathaniel P. Richmond—now commanding Farnsworth's brigade—had been assigned the front; Custer's Wolverines remained in the rear. Federal guns pounded Stuart's advance units, and he was incapable of immediately counterattacking—his own artillery was far behind and inaccessible for the time being. Stuart quickly dismounted his troops to return fire, dispatched a courier to bring up the artillery, and summoned Colonel M. J. Ferguson, whose Jenkins Brigade was engaged with Richmond, to reinforce Chambliss.[1]

The Union cavalry held a major advantage, and threatened to trap Chambliss in the pass even with assistance from Ferguson. Stuart, however, was afforded a lucky break when Kilpatrick, who was informed of Ferguson's movement, committed a tactical blunder. Instead of pressing his advantage, Kilpatrick inexplicably disengaged his troops and ordered them to ride for Boonsboro, twenty miles to the south.

The Third Division commander later wrote in his report that he had broken off contact in order "to save my prisoners, animals, and wagons." Perhaps Kilpatrick had suffered a momentary bout of faintheartedness at the prospect of fighting Stuart's Invincibles. To be fair, however, Kilpatrick may have been uninformed about Stuart's true strength, and, although uncharacteristic for a man with a reputation for sending his men headlong into the face of danger, on this occasion chose to err on the side of prudence. Kilpatrick's troops reached Boonsboro at 10:00 P.M., and bivouacked for a well-deserved rest.[2]

Meanwhile, Stuart dutifully reported the movements of the Union cavalry to General Lee, and then led his column toward Leitersburg to rendezvous with Beverly Robertson. Stuart, who had been informed that Kilpatrick was in Boonsboro, had his four brigades in the saddle by daylight heading southward toward Hagerstown and the Potomac.[3]

Kilpatrick had caught wind of Stuart's movement, and was preparing to mount a pursuit when General John Buford arrived in Boonsboro. Buford had been on the trail of Imboden's wagon train, and was armed with the information that his quarry was presently stalled at Williamsport—thirteen miles to the northwest. The capture of this supply train could conceivably cripple the Army of Northern Virginia beyond recovery.

It was decided that Buford, supported by Custer's Michigan Wolverines—and personally accompanied by Kilpatrick—would attempt to surround the train at Williamsport. The other column would ride for Hagerstown and engage Stuart to try to prevent his cavalry from assisting Imboden.[4]

Colonel Richmond led the Union advance into Hagerstown, and encountered Chambliss and Robertson approaching from the northeast. The Confederates initially gained the upper hand and, fighting street to street, pushed Richmond's disorganized troops backward. Reinforcements were sent in to bolster the attack, and eventually succeeded in driving Chambliss' under-sized unit out of town.

Stuart was aware that Kilpatrick's ultimate objective would be Imboden's wagon train at Williamsport, and he must at all costs hold Hagerstown. Chambliss was ordered to charge directly down the road while Ferguson and two of Robertson's regiments would attempt to strike the Union flank.[5]

While the blue and the gray horsemen dueled on the streets of Hagerstown, Buford and Kilpatrick approached Williamsport at about 1:30 P.M. to discover a well-fortified enemy. General Imboden had deployed his two brigades of cavalry, two regiments of infantry, twenty-four pieces of light artillery, and even the teamsters armed with the weapons of the wounded, into a tight perimeter at the base of a hill below town to protect his immobile caravan. Ambulances had been unloaded and the wounded moved into nearby houses, and makeshift rafts had begun ferrying supplies across the swollen river. Imboden had prepared to hold the position until the remainder of Stuart's cavalry and Lee's infantry could arrive to reinforce the position and drive off any enemy.

Imboden greeted Buford with a barrage of small arms fire and artillery designed to impress upon the Yanks that they would pay dearly should they advance. Skirmishers were sent forward in various spots along the line to bluff an attack and keep Buford confused with respect to the size and position of his troops. Buford retaliated with a series of assaults, which were for the most part easily repulsed.[6]

At one point, Kilpatrick dispatched Custer and the Fifth Michigan to advance through town on a saber charge, but had second thoughts and rescinded the order. Colonel Alger's riflemen were then dismounted and sent forward, but were met with heavy resistance and, as one cavalryman described, "with shells bursting over our heads," and they could not get close enough to be effective.[7]

Back at Hagerstown, Stuart was supported by the head of Lee's infantry column and an artillery brigade from Ewell's corps, which supplied enough firepower to push the Union cavalrymen into a fighting retreat. The final blow was administered when the head of Longstreet's corps arrived to rein-force Stuart.

Colonel Richmond halted once to counterattack, but was quickly routed by the Fifth North Carolina and Eleventh Virginia, and this strategic posi-tion was in sole possession of the Army of Northern Virginia. By evicting the Union army from Hagerstown, Stuart was now free to concentrate on the threat by Buford and Kilpatrick to Williamsport.[8]

With darkness descending and Jeb Stuart and Fitz Lee approaching, General Buford made the decision to withdraw. Custer and his Wolverines accompanied Buford's First Division into camp at Jones's Crossroads, while Kilpatrick and Huey retired to Boonsboro. General Imboden summed up the sentiments on the Confederate side of the line at the sight of the retreating Yankees when he wrote, "The news was sent along our whole line, and was received with a wild and exultant yell. We knew then that the field was won."[9]

The actions by Jeb Stuart and his horsemen had saved the day for the Confederates. The loss of the supply wagons—gathering supplies, after all, had been the initial purpose of the campaign—would have been disastrous.

The reports written by both Buford and Kilpatrick grudgingly acknowl-edge their failure to seize this opportunity to possibly crush the Confeder-acy. Buford wrote, "The expedition had for its objective the destruction of the enemy's trains, supposed to be at Williamsport. This, I regret to say, was not accomplished. The enemy was too strong for me, but he was severely punished for his obstinacy. His casualties were more than quadruple to mine." Buford might have overestimated the losses suffered by his obstinate enemy. Union casualties in the engagement amounted to about four hundred; the Southerners reported 254.[10]

News traveled rather slowly throughout the country in time of war, and it was not until July 6 or thereabouts that Libbie Bacon heard about the promo-tion of Armstrong Custer to brigadier general. And she was informed of the news by none other than her rival, Fanny Fifield. Libbie tried to act apathetic to this startling revelation, but must have been overjoyed and proud. Her ela-tion was tempered at the time, however, by Fanny suggesting that Libbie and

Nettie Humphrey could serve as bridesmaids for the nuptials between Fanny and her beau. Libbie wondered if Armstrong was simply flirting with Fanny, or if he was serious about her in case his romance with Libbie would come to an end.[11]

Soon after, however, she became upset when she learned that Custer had shown her ambrotype to Fanny. She wrote, "He had no business to write the passionate messages he has about me & to me when he has been writing so constantly & lovelike to Fan. He is nothing to me. He never will be."[12]

Libbie was somewhat embarrassed when David Reed, Armstrong's brother-in-law, visited the Bacon household bearing a drawing that Al Waud of *Harper's Weekly* had rendered about Custer's dangerous ride into the Rebel lines on a runaway horse. Reed, who handed a letter to Libbie as well—that summarized the episode—explained that Armstrong had wanted him to show the picture to all of Fanny's friends. Reed also mentioned that he expected Armstrong to return in the fall and marry Fanny Fifield.

David Reed then oddly asked Libbie if that was what she thought would happen. Libbie was noncommittal, but later wrote, "By his manner his words & all, he knew C—loved me." Libbie begged her stepmother not to mention Reed's visit to her disapproving father.[13]

In the moonlight that night, Libbie wrote in her journal, "I love him still. I know it is love from fancy with no foundations, but I love him still and theory vanishes when practice comes into play. There is no similarity of tastes between us and I will never think of it, but I *love him*."[14]

Brigadier General George Armstrong Custer and his men remained in a rain-drenched camp to rest throughout the day on July 7, while Stuart deployed his troopers in strategic locations to enable General Lee to freely inspect approaches to the river that would afford a safe crossing for his army back into Virginia. Lee, whose army was now concentrated around Williamsport and Hagerstown, was in no hurry to test the flooded river. Before he would make a final decision, he would spend his time consulting with his subordinates and discussing the merits of various potential crossing areas designated on maps drawn by his engineers. [15]

The opposing cavalries engaged in a heated skirmish on July 8 when the wily Stuart, who intended to aggressively cover the presence of his army, executed a ploy designed to make his enemy think that he was heading for the South Mountain passes beyond Boonsboro.

General Pleasonton had issued orders for his cavalry to protect these mountain gaps in order to enable passage by Meade's infantry, which was on the far side of the mountain moving south. And Stuart intended to keep the cavalry confused with respect to specific movements and locations.

Stuart led four brigades—Lee, Jones, Chambliss, and Baker—down the Hagerstown Pike from Funkstown and met Union forces at about 5:00 A.M. near Jones's Crossroads and Boonsboro. The battle commenced when Stuart ordered McGregor's artillery battery to open up on Buford's right flank. This was followed by an attack by Grumble Jones's dismounted brigade—on foot due to the soft, saturated earth, which made it difficult for mounted troops to maneuver. Colonel Ferguson's brigade arrived from the northwest and was dispatched by Stuart to strike the Union left flank. The combination of smoking cannons and bold skirmishers was successful—Buford's men were compelled to withdraw up the mountain into Turner's Pass.[16]

Kilpatrick responded by stabilizing the center of Buford's line with Custer's brigade and the left flank with Richmond. The batteries commanded by Elder and Pennington, which were positioned on the hills behind Boonsboro, began having an effect on holding back the aggressive Confederate skirmishers. The horsemen of Custer and Richmond, supported by Colonel William Gamble's infantry, shored up defenses and in time gained the upper hand. Custer and his Wolverines forced the enemy back to Beaver Creek, three miles away.

The intense fighting continued throughout the afternoon, with casualties mounting on both sides—including Colonel Russell Alger of the Fifth Michigan, who was severely wounded when struck with a minié ball in the left thigh. The capable Alger would not return to action until September.

As five o'clock approached, Jeb Stuart was aware that he had accomplished his mission. Upon learning that his men were running low on ammunition, he ordered a gradual pull back in a northerly direction on the old National Road toward Funkstown. The Federal troops pursued, but Stuart deployed a strong line of defense four miles away below Funkstown, which effectively brought an end to hostilities.

Buford and Kilpatrick reasoned that their original role had been to guard the mountain passes, and that endeavor had been achieved by chasing away Stuart. They were now content to return south with their jubilant, albeit battle-weary troops, who to a man were certain that another victory had been won that day. One ecstatic Wolverine wrote, "This is the eighth fight we have had with the Rebs and have whipped them everry [sic] time."[17]

General George Meade had moved his army to within eight miles west of South Mountain, and issued orders for Pleasonton's cavalry to harass the enemy all they wanted but to avoid a major engagement. That reluctance to crush the Army of Northern Virginia, which was virtually trapped with its back to the river, did not particularly sit well with President Lincoln, Secretary of War Edwin Stanton, or Chief of Staff Major General Henry Halleck. But, taking into consideration the consolidated Confederate position, which extended in an almost uninterrupted line for eight miles and contained a six-foot-wide parapet dotted with frequent gun emplacements, Meade's decision in hindsight was appropriate.[18]

Meade's cautiousness afforded Custer and his Wolverines a couple of lazy days spent resting and refitting. The Union cavalrymen and horses had endured an extensive stretch of continuous battle in elements that would test even the hardiest person. The morale of the troops, however, was soaring, as evidenced by George R. Barse, who wrote, "Although much worn down by fatigue and need of rest, the cry is, 'No rest until the rebels are driven from the State.' We can whip them, and must do so, cost what it will." This welcome respite provided ample time to clean and repair mud-covered clothing and equipment, care for the horses, reflect on the victory at Gettysburg, and perhaps speculate about the victories that surely lay ahead.[19]

General Lee had selected a crossing point for his army at the village of Falling Waters, four miles below Williamsport, and his engineers toiled to construct pontoon bridges at that location. Jeb Stuart and his horsemen were kept busy in the saddle protecting the stranded army from the enemy, which would prove to be a constant chore.

At about 8:00 A.M. on July 10, Buford's foot soldiers waded Beaver Creek and advanced down the road from Boonsboro toward a line of Stuart's dismounted cavalry. The Federal attack pushed the Rebels north to Funkstown toward a Confederate infantry position above Antietam Creek. The engagement continued until about 3:00 P.M., when Buford's men ran out of ammunition and chose to withdraw and bivouac about four miles away. While directing the vicious fighting, Stuart had a horse shot out from under him but otherwise emerged unscathed.[20]

Early on July 12, with Meade's infantry arriving to darken the hills around them, General Custer and his Wolverines were roused from their inactivity. Custer's brigade, in advance of the Third Division, charged "screaming and yelling" into Hagerstown unopposed to grab fifty prisoners and occupy the town. Detachments of the First, Fifth, and Seventh Michigan advanced toward Williamsport, but ran into Rebel entrenchments and wisely decided to wait for reinforcements from Meade's infantrymen. The foot soldiers, who had not fought in ten days since Gettysburg, compared to Custer's men, who had seen battle every couple of days, soon appeared and enabled the cavalrymen to fall back.[21]

On that same Sunday that Custer's Wolverines had charged into Hagerstown, the names of the first draftees in New York City were published in accordance with the National Conscription Act, which declared that all able-bodied men between the ages of twenty and forty-five were liable for military service. The response to this unpopular act was four days of rioting on the streets as a mob of fifty thousand people roamed about the city lynching blacks, assaulting abolitionists, looting, and destroying property. Soldiers returning from the Gettysburg battle were called upon to reinforce the police to quell this violence, and were forced to fire upon the crowd. Order was maintained in this instance, but this would not be the last time or place that rallies were held to protest the draft. In reality, however, the draft ended up providing only about 46,000 men from the 775,000 names that were drawn—about 6 percent of the Union army.

On July 12, General Meade convened a council of war to relate his intention to thrust his massive army against Confederate fortifications at Williamsport in order to follow up on his success at Gettysburg. The majority of his infantry generals at the meeting, however, argued in opposition to an immediate attack. Meade, in another controversial decision, deferred to their wishes. The assault would be postponed. Instead, reconnaissance patrols would be dispatched in the morning to gather additional intelligence regarding the specific positions of his enemy.[22]

By that time, the water had receded to a level low enough to chance a crossing, and the Rebel engineers and sappers had completed their work placing the pontoons across the river. General Lee had hoped that his enemy would test the strength of his entrenched army. But, upon learning that the Federals had commenced digging fortifications, which indicated that an attack was not imminent, Lee decided that he could wait no longer to cross. He remarked, "They have but little courage."[23]

At 4:15 P.M., Jeb Stuart was summoned, and issued his orders by Lee. Stuart's cavalrymen would assume the positions of fifty thousand foot soldiers in an attempt to deceive the enemy into thinking that the trenches along the nearly eight-mile line remained occupied. After the entire army had crossed, Stuart and his men would ride to safety.[24]

On that dark, rainy night, with thunder rolling and lightning cracking, the Confederate army made its move. Longstreet's and Hill's corps began crossing at Falling Waters while Ewell's corps forded at Williamsport. By first light, in spite of losing a small number of men and wagons that had been swept away, Lee's army was well on its way of completing its mission with near flawlessness.[25]

At about 3:00 A.M., the first word of an enemy movement reached Kilpatrick's ears. Scouts informed him that Confederate pickets had retired from the works below Hagerstown. General Buford's reconnaissance reported at the same time that Confederate positions farther to the east were empty, and the enemy had been observed crossing the river. Both divisions advanced slowly forward. Buford indicated that he would attempt to maneuver between the river and Lee's rear guard, apparently expecting Kilpatrick to follow suit with his cavalry and assist by distracting the enemy.

Kilpatrick did not coordinate his efforts with Buford, and instead headed south, with Custer and the Fifth Michigan in the lead. At about 6:00 A.M., the Wolverines galloped up the hills overlooking Williamsport. Custer's troopers discovered only a few stragglers from Ewell's corps at that location, and chased those panicked men into the river with the support of Pennington's guns. Perhaps as many as fifty Rebels drowned and twenty-five wagons with their mule teams were swept away in the raging torrent. Other fleeing members of the Rebel rear guard were found along the road and gathered up as prisoners.

Local residents informed Kilpatrick that a large force of Confederate troops was presently crossing the river four miles downstream at Falling Waters. The Fifth Michigan remained at Williamsport to mop up while Custer and his three other Michigan regiments hastened toward Falling Waters.[26]

By now, most of the Confederate army, as well as Stuart's cavalry, had reached Virginia. Locals told Kilpatrick that two divisions of Henry Heth's and William Pender's infantry remained behind on the north bank at Falling Waters. Custer deployed the Fifth at Williamsport, and led the other three regiments in a dash to cut off the Southerners. Two miles from their objective, Custer and an advance detachment of the Sixth Michigan encountered the Rebel rear guard and drove them steadily south.[27]

At about 7:30 A.M., Custer and his Wolverines halted in a woodlot a mile and a half from the river, and from that point could view the enemy crossing point. Imposing breastworks and trenches had been constructed on a crescent-shaped knoll, and were manned by artillery and veteran troops of the Thirteenth Alabama and the First, Seventh, and Fourteenth Tennessee, veterans from Henry Heth's division. These men had been lazing around, waiting for Union soldiers to arrive. Their commander was Brigadier General J. Johnson Pettigrew, who had led these same men on the ill-fated Pickett's charge at Gettysburg. They were not about to be intimidated by the force of cavalry that approached.

At present, Custer had only two companies at his disposal—the others had been delayed with rounding up prisoners—and thought it prudent to probe the position with dismounted skirmishers while waiting for the main force to arrive. Companies B and F under Major Peter Weber were ordered forward on foot for that purpose. During this movement, Weber confided to Captain James Kidd that he desired one more chance to make a saber charge.

Judson Kilpatrick arrived on the scene, and afforded Weber that opportunity. The Third Division commander decided to countermand Custer's order. Without knowing what was in front of him, Kilpatrick directed Weber to mount about fifty-eight men and charge into what would amount to thousands of enemy occupying the hill.[28]

Major Weber must have been aware that this situation was strikingly similar to Elon Farnsworth's earlier ill-fated charge on the last day at Gettysburg. Regardless, he offered no objection, and obediently mounted his men and lit out at a trot across the open field and up the hill at a gallop. [29]

The advance of the Union horsemen was observed by Heth and his staff as soon as it had emerged from the woods. But the consensus opinion was that it must be the rear guard of Stuart's cavalry. No detachment of Federals this small would dare attack a Confederate infantry division. And it was believed that the cavalry—which, incidentally, had earlier crossed by mistake—was bringing up the rear.

The identity of Weber's cavalry unit remained a mystery to the Rebels until it was in their midst, unfurling a "Stars and Stripes" guidon and unleashing a murderous saber attack and yelling, "Surrender!"

The relaxed Confederates had stacked their weapons, and now resorted to using fence rails, axes, and rifles as clubs to fend off the surprise assault. Weber and his men hacked with their sabers and fired their pistols, exacting a toll that included General Pettigrew, who was mortally wounded.[30]

James Kidd, who was wounded in the foot by a bullet while in the rear of the charge, wrote about what happened next, "Weber, cutting right and left with his saber, and cheering on his men, pierced the first line, but there could be but one result. Recovering from their surprise, the Confederate infantry rallied, and seizing their arms, made short work of their daring assailants." The brave Wolverines never had a chance against the overwhelming force.[31]

The Confederate infantry blasted Weber's men with a point-blank volley. Weber and his executive officer, Lieutenant Charles E. Bolza, were cut from their saddles—along with at least thirty other Wolverines, more than half of the unit, who were killed, wounded, or captured. Captain David G. Royce of the Sixth Michigan was also killed when his dismounted squadron supported the initial charge. Lieutenant George Crawford would be struck by a bullet that shattered his leg, which would later require amputation. Kill-Cavalry had once again ordered a suicide charge that had resulted in mass slaughter.

The remnants of Weber's companies struggled to find refuge in the trees, while General Armstrong Custer dismounted what remained of the Sixth and, along with the First and Seventh, led a series of charges that kept the Confederates at bay until the rest of the brigade could reach the field.

Private Victor E. Comte of the Fifth Michigan, who had been chosen as personal escort to Custer and was at his side throughout the engagement, later wrote home, "I saw him [Custer] plunge his saber into the belly of a rebel who was trying to kill him. You can guess how bravely soldiers fight for such a general."[32]

After a couple of hours of fierce fighting, Custer's men overwhelmed their enemy, and either killed them or drove them across the pontoon bridge over the Potomac. The Wolverines captured about fifteen hundred prisoners, three battle flags, and a ten-pound Parrott gun. The Confederates had lost one hundred twenty-five killed and fifty wounded, compared to twenty-nine killed, thirty-six wounded, and forty missing for the Union.

General George Meade could not fathom that cavalry could have such success against an entrenched enemy, and had Kilpatrick's report read to him twice before he would approve it. Equally amazed was *New York Times* correspondent E. A. Paul, who witnessed the action, and wrote, "This is cavalry fighting the superior of which the world never saw."[33]

And it was Custer's Wolverines who had achieved this near impossible feat. Although marred by Kilpatrick's suicidal order for Major Weber and his men, the Michigan Brigade had risen to the occasion and brought glory upon themselves—and their commander.

Confederate General Henry Heth, who had fired the opening shots at

Gettysburg, now cut the ropes behind him on the pontoon bridges at Falling Waters to effectively end the campaign.[34]

That night, the Third Cavalry Division bivouacked near Boonsboro. In the morning, Judson Kilpatrick complained of a pain in his side that may have been an inflammation of the kidneys. He requested and was granted a temporary medical leave of absence.

In place of Kilpatrick, Alfred Pleasonton chose twenty-three-year-old Brigadier General George Armstrong Custer to command the division.[35]

Now that the dust—or rather the mud—of Gettysburg had settled, the Boy General was on the verge of becoming a national hero for his exploits during this significant campaign.

Fifteen

———◆———

Culpeper

Civil War officers were expected to motivate and inspire their troops under fire by example—bravery was contagious. George Armstrong Custer, however, elevated that responsibility to a higher level. While few cavalry generals, if any, would ever consider leading a charge into the enemy at the front of his troops, Custer had made it a practice—and a tactic of proven success.

And by his actions, Custer had proven during the Gettysburg Campaign that contrary to those who had questioned General Alfred Pleasonton's judgment in promoting the twenty-three-year-old to brigadier general, he was quite capable of commanding a brigade. In addition, he had gained the admiration of his men with his propensity for leading charges rather than simply directing movements from a safe position in the rear. This one distinct trait had instilled within his troops a confidence that if Custer, a general, had the nerve to charge into the blazing guns of the enemy, then there was no reason not to believe that if they followed, victory would be within their grasp.

Custer had demonstrated a special affinity for cavalry tactics. James Kidd told how this general reacted instinctively to the movements of the enemy and the terrain during a battle, and that "his perceptions were intuitions."

Custer had followed the textbook example of deploying his men and seeking intelligence with respect to his enemy's strength and capabilities before calling for a charge. He had not exhibited the rashness that was a trademark of Kilpatrick, whose disregard for the lives of his troops was well known; rather, he used a more calculated procedure, knowing that at some point in the battle there would likely be an opportunity to strike the enemy's weak underbelly—and once identified he would charge. Custer certainly believed that cavalry tactics required boldness, with flying horses' hooves, sabers gleaming in the sunlight, and a leader who was unafraid when charging and could encourage his men to follow with such cries as, "Come on, you Wolverines!"[1]

Edwin Havens of the Seventh Michigan described Custer in a letter dated July 9, 1863, "Gen. Custerd [*sic*]. He is a glorious fellow, full of energy, quick to plan and bold to execute, and with us has never failed in any attempt he has yet made." Another proud Wolverine offered praise, "Our boy-general never says, 'Go in, men!' HE says, with that whoop and yell of his, 'Come on, boys!' and in we go, you bet."

Captain S. H. Ballard of the Sixth Michigan remembered that "The command perfectly idolized Custer. The old Michigan Brigade adored its brigadier, and all felt as if he weighed about a ton." He added, "When Custer made a charge, he was the first sabre that struck for he was always ahead."

Another said that Custer "was not afraid to fight like a private soldier and that he was ever in front and would never ask them to go where he would not lead." Lieutenant James Christiancy wrote to Custer's future father-in-law, Daniel Bacon, "Through all that sharp and heavy firing the General gave his orders as though conducting a parade or review, so cool and indifferent that he inspired us all with something of his coolness and courage."[2]

The Michigan Brigade was so impressed that they had, in their opinion, whipped Jeb Stuart at Gettysburg that they began to emulate their commander by adopting Custer's trademark scarlet neckties, which he wore to make himself conspicuous to his troops during a battle. An artist for *Frank Leslie's Illustrated Newspaper* noted this gaudy feature of Custer's uniform, and described the necktie as "An emblem of bravado and challenge to combat—with the motion of the toreador flouting the Crimson cloth to infuriate and lure the bull to doom."[3]

That regard by his troops and the press for Custer's actions during the Gettysburg Campaign was echoed by his superior officers. General Kilpatrick wrote in his official report, "To General Custer all praise is due." Alfred Pleasonton stated in his report that Custer and Wesley Merritt "have increased the confidence entertained in their ability and gallantry to lead troops on the field of battle." The War Department rewarded Custer with a promotion to brevet major in the Regular Army, which dated from July 3, 1863.[4]

George Armstrong Custer, the obscure aide-de-camp who astonishingly had been promoted to brigadier general in command of a brigade, had suddenly captured the eye of the nation. The press had a fresh story, and a star had been born at Gettysburg that promised to rise higher with each ensuing engagement.

Custer's spirits were flying high. He was thrilled with his brigade command, and welcomed the opportunity to command a division, albeit temporarily. His troops were kept busy on patrol throughout the summer, but engaged in only a series of minor skirmishes that resulted in few casualties. His mind and heart, however, were never far from Monroe, Michigan.

On July 19, he wrote to Nettie Humphrey, "I was rejoiced to hear from you, Nettie, but I regret that Libbie should suppose I had violated my promise to her in regard to her ambrotype. I never showed it, nor even described it, to Fanny. How Fanny was able to describe it I cannot tell, unless she got the information from the picture gallery. You know her quickness in guessing. Tell Libbie that Fanny has nothing in her power to bestow that wd. induce me to show her that ambrotype. I know nothing of what representations of our intimacy she has made to Libbie. I believe more than ever in destiny."[5]

The behind-the-scenes maneuvering by Fanny Fifield to try to convince Libbie of Armstrong's affection toward her must have been quite annoying to Libbie, who had to know his true feelings. But it was evident that Fanny was not about to easily give up on a future with the young general, and made a concerted effort to discourage Libbie, who could not directly appeal to her suitor. Custer, on the other hand, may have had feelings for Fanny, and was hesitant to end the affair in case he would lose Libbie Bacon—as evidenced by a letter he received from Nettie.

At some point Nettie had apparently told Custer not to be overly optimistic about his relationship with Libbie. Custer replied, "When the time comes for me to give Her up I hope it will find me the same soldier I now try to be—capable of meeting the reverses of life as those of war. You know me well, yet you know little of my disposition. Do not fear for me. I may lose everything, yet there is a strange, indescribable something in me that would enable me to shape my course through life, cheerful, if not contented."[6]

Interestingly enough, at the time of this romantic drama Custer had shown General Pleasonton a picture of Fanny, to which the impressed general offered Custer a leave, if he would return home to marry her. Custer wrote to his sister, "Shall I come?"[7]

One important task that Custer accomplished that summer was assembling a brigade headquarters staff. Among those chosen to serve on the general's staff was Captain Jacob Greene, a flute-playing friend from Monroe, Michigan, who would be adjutant or chief of staff. Greene, whom Custer met while on leave, was the suitor of Nettie Humphrey, the trusted go-between for Armstrong and Libbie. Custer also added two other Monroe residents— George Yates, who would die with Custer at the Little Bighorn, and James Christiancy, the son of Judge Isaac Christiancy, who had a drinking problem. Bugler Joseph Fought was summoned, and a waif named Johnny Cisco, who washed clothes, waited tables, cared for the horses, and slept with Custer's dog, attached himself to the general.[8]

The staff was complete when a seventeen-year-old runaway slave named Eliza Denison Brown "jined up with the Ginnel." Eliza had fled a plantation in Virginia, because "everybody was excited over freedom, and I wanted to see how it was. Everybody keeps asking me why I left. I can't see why they can't recollect what war was for, and that we was all bound to try and see for ourselves how it was." Early on, Eliza had reservations about her move, "Oh, how awful lonesome I was at first, and I was afraid of everything in the shape of war. I used to wish myself back on the plantation with my mother."[9]

Eliza would soon become the trusted and dependable manager of Custer's headquarters, handling her duties and responsibilities with the same efficiency as the general would on the battlefield. She would praise or admonish when necessary, not tolerate people being late for meals, and hold valuables for staff members when they went out on patrols or missions. Her presence was so notable that she became known throughout the unit as "the Queen of Sheba."[10]

George Armstrong Custer was a great lover of music, and forming a brigade band became one of his passions. He quickly gathered about him the finest musicians available, and had them drill as hard as his cavalrymen. Custer believed that there was no better inspiration and comfort to men in combat than music.

Consequently, this band was not reserved for concerts back at camp or playing during ceremonies; rather, it would accompany the troops into battle. Custer would keep the brass section near him as the cannons roared and the bullets zipped past. The horn players would try to ignore the bedlam around them and concentrate on performing some up-tempo patriotic tune amid the barking of carbines and thunder of artillery. Custer believed that it "excited the enthusiasm of the entire command to the highest pitch, and made each individual member feel as if he were a host in himself."[11]

The favorite song of the Michigan Brigade was without question the patriotic Revolutionary War tune "Yankee Doodle." Custer chose this song for one special purpose, as explained by an officer from the Sixth Michigan, "Our old brigade band was always on the skirmish line, and at Yankee Doodle every man's hand went to his saber. It was always the signal for a charge."[12]

The lone military conflict with potential to be of any consequence during that summer of 1863 occurred on July 24, when General Custer's command of twelve hundred men had crossed the Rappahannock River and penetrated fifty miles into enemy-held territory. An informant told Custer that General Ambrose Hill's corps was moving toward Culpeper. Custer was aware that if he could reach Culpeper before Hill, he could create a wedge between

Hill and Longstreet. Should that be accomplished, it would enable Meade to send up reinforcements and attack each Confederate corps separately, which would greatly enhance the prospects of victory.

Custer's report, dated August 28, 1863, summarized this skirmish, "My advance guard came upon the skirmishers of the enemy when within a half mile of the road leading from Gaines' Cross-Roads to Culpeper, at a point called Battle Mountain. The force in my front proved to be the corps of A. P. Hill. I attacked with both cavalry and artillery, compelling the enemy to halt his column and form line of battle. Having done this much, and knowing the overwhelming force the enemy was bringing to bear against me, I prepared to withdraw my command. An unlooked-for delay occurring in relieving my skirmishers, the enemy succeeded in pushing two brigades of infantry to my left and rear. By this movement the Fifth and Sixth Michigan Cavalry (Colonel Gray) and two guns of Battery M, under command of Lieutenant Woodruff, were entirely cut off, but, by a display of great courage by both officers and men, Colonel Gray succeeded in extricating his command from this perilous position with but slight loss."[13]

Custer lost thirty men killed, wounded, or missing—reporting "that [losses] of the enemy was known to be much greater"—and withdrew to Amissville. He informed Pleasonton of the opportunity to strike a major blow to the Confederate army, but Meade refused to send reinforcements, and, on July 31, Custer was ordered to withdraw across the Rappahannock.[14]

On August 4, Custer relinquished command of the Third Division to Kilpatrick, who had returned from leave, and resumed his duty with the Michigan Brigade. With time on his hands, he turned his attention to refitting the men, gathering horses, and making sure the unit was properly trained. He spent long hours in the saddle, visiting picket posts with regularity, and always made sure that scouts had been dispatched to gather information to prevent a surprise attack. Custer did everything within his power to try to mold his command into the best in the army, and was quite satisfied with his efforts. He wrote to his sister, "I would not exchange it for any other brigade in the Army."[15]

In mid-August, General Custer was paid a surprise visit by Tully McCrea, a former West Point roommate who now served as a Union artillery officer. Custer was thrilled to see his old friend, and the feeling was mutual. McCrea wrote home, "He is the same careless fellow that he was. He is the most romantic of men and delights in something odd. Last summer when he was on the Peninsula, he vowed that he would not cut his hair until he entered Richmond. He has kept his vow and now his hair is about a foot long and hangs over his shoulders in curls just like a girl. But he is a gallant soldier, a whole-souled generous friend, and a mighty good fellow, and I like him and wish him every success in his new role of Brigadier."[16]

On August 20, the brigade had moved downstream to a location outside of Falmouth, across the river from Fredericksburg. At that time, the cavalry division was reorganized. The veteran First Vermont Cavalry joined the brigade, and Colonel Henry E. Davies took over command of the brigade once commanded by the late Elon Farnsworth.[17]

The Confederate cavalry also underwent reorganization that summer. Jeb Stuart had submitted recommendations that General Robert E. Lee now decided to entertain. There was an element of self-interest to Stuart's plan. If Lee enacted the plan as designed, Stuart would be in charge of a cavalry corps, and promoted to the rank of lieutenant general.[18]

On September 9, Lee unveiled his intentions, and the cavalry was rearranged into two divisions—the First Division commanded by newly appointed Major General Wade Hampton, the Second Division by newly appointed Major General Fitzhugh Lee. Brigade commanders, all brigadier generals, in Hampton's division would be William E. "Grumble" Jones, Laurence S. Baker (newly appointed), and M. C. Butler (newly appointed). Fitz Lee's brigade commanders, all brigadier generals, would be Rooney Lee, Lunsford L. Lomax (newly appointed), and Williams C. Wickham (newly appointed).[19]

Although the cavalry technically had been organized as a corps, which called for a lieutenant general in charge, Jeb Stuart, much to his disappointment, had been passed over for promotion. This omission by Lee was likely not intended as a personal affront directed at Stuart, but rather most likely reflected Lee's belief that a cavalry command was not equal in responsibility to that of an infantry corps.[20]

In addition to Stuart, another cavalry officer who had been passed over for promotion was sorely dissatisfied. Colonel Tom Rosser had expected to play a major role in the reorganized cavalry, but apparently General Lee and the War Department had not agreed.

Rosser had distinguished himself with his bravery, and had recovered from a serious foot wound sustained during the Peninsula Campaign. On May 28, 1863, Tom had married Betty Winston in a ceremony attended by generals Jeb Stuart and Fitzhugh Lee, along with many staff officers. The maid of honor had been Sallie Dandridge, the girl whom John Pelham had been courting at the time of his death. Rosser believed that his career was about to soar as high as his love life—but that was not the case.[21]

Stuart attempted to mollify Rosser by assuring him that he would be the next one promoted to brigadier general, and provided Rosser with a letter to that effect. Rosser, however, believed that he had been betrayed by Stuart. His venom spilled forth in letters to his wife, Betty, "Stuart has been false to *me* as he has ever been to his country and to his *wife*. I will never give him an opportunity of deceiving me again."[22]

Unknown to Tom Rosser was that it had not been Stuart who had betrayed him. The War Department had judged that Rosser's regiment had declined in efficiency, and that he personally had been affected by the separation from his wife, which had affected his morale and driven him to drink. He would have to win back the confidence of the administration before receiving a promotion.[23]

The newly reorganized Confederate cavalry barely had time to become accustomed to riding together before they had to fight together.

Meade's army remained above the Rappahannock, Lee's below the Rapidan, and Stuart's cavalry patrolled the middle ground. Public and political pressure in the North called for Meade to push onward toward Richmond. Meade had learned that Lee had detached thousands of troops to the western theater, and ordered Alfred Pleasonton to cross the Rappahannock and conduct a reconnaissance to confirm this information. The Union cavalry set out on September 12 to probe Lee's positions in Northern Virginia.[24]

At 6:00 A.M., on September 13, Kilpatrick's cavalry division splashed across the upper Rappahannock at Kelly's Ford, and rendezvoused with Buford and Gregg at Brandy Station. The combined units—ten thousand men strong—resumed the march following along the tracks of the Orange & Alexandria Railroad, and finally halted on the high ground about three-fourths of a mile north of Jeb Stuart's headquarters at Culpeper Court House.[25]

This time, due to an informant who had visited his headquarters during the previous night, Stuart was not caught unaware of the Union advance. Dr. Hudgin, a surgeon with the Ninth Virginia, had been home on leave following the death of his wife, who, according to Henry McClellan, "had recently died from fright caused by the conduct of some of Kilpatrick's men." Hudgin had observed the enemy movements, and reported that information to Stuart, which afforded the cavalry commander ample opportunity to prepare.[26]

Without knowing the size of his enemy, Stuart immediately dispatched the wagons and disabled horses toward Rapidan Station. He then deployed Brigadier General Lunsford Lomax, commanding Grumble Jones's brigade, supported by three artillery pieces, among the buildings and railroad station around the vicinity of Culpeper—hardly a large enough force to contend with three Yankee divisions.[27]

At about 1:00 P.M., Buford and Gregg attacked Lomax's position. The Union troops were met with a ferocious barrage that stopped them in their tracks. Pleasonton then ordered Kilpatrick to enter the fray.

Colonel Henry E. Davies and the Second New York Cavalry charged across the stream at the artillery battery, while the dismounted Sixth Michigan laid down a base of fire. Davies' troops, slashing with their sabers, captured two guns and drove Lomax's Virginia brigade through town, taking numerous prisoners and dealing severely with those who resisted.

Brigadier General Custer had been deployed at the extreme left of a semicircle on the Union line, with directions to pass around the Confederate flank, if possible, and strike from the rear. At the height of the fighting, Custer noticed a Rebel railroad train loaded with baggage and supplies chugging into town and stopping at the station. He mounted a battalion of the First Michigan and First Vermont at once, and led his men in a spirited charge after this prize.

Custer's troops were compelled to cross a swollen creek and pass through a marsh in order to reach Culpeper, and quickly became bogged down in the swollen, murky water and thick mud. While the troopers struggled through the morass, Pennington was ordered to open up with his artillery in an effort to stop the train. Custer rallied what troops he could muster from the swamp and led a charge. But, by that time, the train crew had reversed the engine and outraced the pursuit of the horsemen. Custer did, however, capture the remaining Rebel cannon, and chased the rest of the enemy troops out of town.

At one point, Custer had outstripped his men, and raced past a fence that was occupied by dismounted Rebel cavalrymen, who fired point blank at him as he tore over the muddy ground. These bullets never struck their target, but it had been another close call.[28]

At this point, Jeb Stuart, who was content to allow Lomax to command the field, sent forward additional artillery to support the Virginians, who had regrouped on Greenwood Hill, southwest of Culpeper. The Confederates lobbed canister shot with deadly accuracy at the attacking Fifth New York Cavalry.[29]

Custer reacted instantly to this threat, and rallied elements of the First Vermont and Seventh Michigan on a charge toward the enemy gun emplacement. The Virginians turned their attention to those Federal horsemen, and sent shells bursting into their midst—one exploding near Custer. Pieces of shrapnel struck and killed his white stallion while another shard tore through his boot to strike his foot, causing a painful wound. His command continued up the hill to capture the enemy battery as Custer proceeded to rise from the ground and assess the seriousness of his injury—amazingly, his lone wound of the war.[30]

Accounts exist that indicate Custer simply shrugged off his injury, mounted a loose horse, and rejoined his men to resume the charge through the streets of Culpeper to rout the Rebels. Although that would be a fitting addition to the Custer legend, it would be more likely that the wounded general was helped from the field while his men carried on to seize the artillery.[31]

Stuart had no choice but to withdraw from the overwhelming force of

Yankees, and reached Rapidan Court House after nightfall, leaving behind three artillery pieces. Tom Rosser wrote to his wife, "This I think is the finishing stroke to Stuart's declining reputation."[32]

Custer was escorted to the rear, where his wound was attended to by a surgeon. He was said to have then ridden up to Pleasonton and exclaimed, "How are you, fifteen-days' leave-of-absence? They have spoiled my boots but they didn't gain much there, for I stole them from a Reb." Pleasonton evidently enjoyed Custer's humor, and granted his brigade commander a twenty-day furlough.[33]

Custer had once again impressed observers with his battlefield generalship. A captain of the Second New York Cavalry wrote that "No soldier who saw him that day ever questioned his right to wear a star, or all the gold lace he felt inclined to wear." One cavalryman wrote to his wife, "He is a bully general and brave too. He is a very odd man but he understands his business."[34]

The business of war for George Armstrong Custer would be placed on a back burner for the next twenty days, however, while he visited Monroe, Michigan. It had been five months earlier when he had departed that town wearing the golden bars of a brevet captain, and he would now be making a triumphant return with a bright star on his collar.

He would be going home to his family, and to pursue the hand of Libbie Bacon. Or—would it be Fanny Fifield? It would become evident that there never was a question about which girl had captured his heart.

Sixteen

———◦◉◦———

The Bristoe Campaign

On September 16, Brigadier General George Armstrong Custer, the hometown boy made good, returned to Monroe, Michigan. He would put that town on the map nationally when the October 3, 1863, issue of *Harper's Weekly* depicted Custer, his saber drawn, charging into the midst of Confederate guns.

Prominent families, especially those with eligible daughters, competed to invite him to dinner, or parties, or other private and public affairs to show him off and be seen with him. The local celebrity was much in demand, particularly from the young ladies, who would stand outside the Reed home, twirling their parasols, hoping to catch the eye of the handsome young general. The son of the former town smithy, who previously had been looked down upon for his low station in the world, was now the toast of the upper crust of Monroe society.

But Armstrong only had eyes for Libbie Bacon. He was confused, however, about the mixed signals that Libbie had relayed through Nettie Humphrey's letters, and set out to "attack," as Libbie would later call it, this girl of his dreams.[1]

Custer executed a frontal assault that Jeb Stuart could not have withstood—calling on Libbie, strolling with her, and sitting beside her in church. When he first called on her, Libbie "saw him at once, because I could not avoid him. I tried to, but I did not succeed." But that would be the last of her deception. Libbie could not deny it to herself any longer. It was soon apparent to everyone—Libbie Bacon was madly in love with Armstrong Custer.[2]

On September 28, Armstrong escorted Libbie to a masquerade ball given in his honor. He attended dressed as Louis XVI, and she as a gypsy girl complete with tambourine. Later that night, under a tree in the Bacon garden, Armstrong proposed marriage.

Libbie recalled, "The General's proposal was as much a cavalry charge as any he ever took in the field. First on the astonished me who knew that in books lovers led up to proposals by slow careful approaches and chosen language, and so had some of the General's predecessors, quite living up to the poetic or romantic. But this vehement, stammery disclosure of years of purpose I had no breath to protest. (Sometimes when greatly excited he had a slight hesitation in speech, then out poured a torrent of words.) Proposing a second time I saw him as a violent contrast to the ambling ponies of my tranquil girlhood."[3]

Libbie readily accepted this proposal. The only drawback was that she insisted that the engagement not be announced until Custer had asked for and received her father's blessing—that would be the second cavalry charge, and must be calculated with the greatest of tact and sincerity. This proposition would test the mettle of the young cavalry officer.[4]

On October 5, with Libbie, Judge Bacon, and other friends seeing him off, Armstrong Custer boarded the train for his return to duty. The gallant field general who had time and again confronted his enemy with wild abandon had not been able to bring himself to ask for Libbie's hand from Judge Bacon. He did, however, promise to write the judge about a matter that concerned them both. "Very well," the judge responded, and Custer bid them farewell.

After Custer had departed, Libbie wrote in her journal, "I never was kissed so much before. I thought he would eat me. My forehead and my eyelids and cheeks and lips bear testimony—and his star scratched my face. I read him in all my books." She longed to "feel his strong arms around me and his dear lips to mine." Perhaps remembering those nights when she dreamed of being swept away by a military dream lover, she wrote, "When I take in the book heroes there comes dashing in with them my life hero my dear boy general. Yes, I love him devotedly. Every other man seems so ordinary beside my own particular *star*."[5]

While he traveled back to army life, Custer wrote a hopeful letter to Nettie Humphrey from Baltimore, "In every city I pass through I see something to admire, and am struck with wonder at man's art and ingenuity in improving that which Nature already has made beautiful. But my heart turns lovingly to our unassuming little town on the banks of the Raisin. I have thought much of my intended letter to Libbie's father, my mind alternating between hope and fear—fear that I may suffer from some unfounded prejudice. I feel that her father, valuing her happiness, would not refuse were he to learn from her own lips our real relation to one another."[6]

On October 8, Brigadier General George Armstrong Custer reported to his unit, which was camped southwest of Culpeper Court House, and received three cheers from the troopers as the band played "Hail to the Chief." In his absence, the men had bestowed upon him a new nickname. To honor the golden locks that he had vowed not to cut until he rode into Richmond, the troopers now affectionately called their brigadier "Old Curly."[7]

While Custer returned to the adulation of his men, General Robert E. Lee was in the process of implementing his latest strategy. Lee had never abandoned his ambitious plan to maneuver his army between Meade's army and Washington, and now commenced amassing his troops with the intention of marching west around Meade's right flank. Meade was unaware of the extent of Lee's plan, and chose to wait until further intelligence could be gathered before moving out to challenge his enemy.

Custer, whose men were prepared to move at a moment's notice, found the time to write a letter to Nettie Humphrey, "I arrived last evening and was welcomed in a style both flattering and gratifying," he told her. "I feel that here, surrounded by my little band of heroes, I am loved and respected. Often I think of the vast responsibility resting on me, of the many households depending on my discretion and judgment—and to think that I am just leaving my boyhood makes the responsibility appear greater. That is not due to egotism, self-conceit. I try to make no unjust pretensions. I assume nothing I know not to be true. It requires no extensive knowledge to inform me what is my duty to my country, my command . . . 'First be sure you're right, then go ahead!' I ask myself, 'Is that right?' Satisfied that it is so, I let nothing swerve me from my purpose." The charming and thoughtful suitor of Libbie Bacon enclosed some flowers for his fiancée that had been picked in front of Headquarters near the Rapidan.[8]

Custer's letter writing was interrupted when his pickets along the north bank of Robertson's River were attacked and a portion of the line was forced back upon the reserves. At the same time, heavy enemy columns moving toward Madison Court House had been sighted by scouts. Custer advised Meade about this Rebel movement, and the commanding general decided to dispatch two divisions of cavalry—Kilpatrick and Buford—across the Rapidan on a reconnaissance to determine precise enemy positions.[9]

On the morning of the tenth, Jeb Stuart sent Colonel O. R. Funsten, commanding Jones' brigade, as advance guard toward Woodville on the Sperryville Pike and led his remaining troops toward James City. Stuart drove enemy pickets at Russell's Ford back to Bethsaida Church, where the 120th New York Infantry waited. General James B. Gordon's brigade drew the attention of the New Yorkers from the front while Stuart led his detachment through the woods to the right and rear. The First South Carolina was ordered to charge, and quickly routed the whole line, capturing eighty-seven prisoners in the process. Stuart then led his troops to James City, a two-and-a-half-mile ride.[10]

At 1:00 P.M., Brigadier General George Armstrong Custer received orders to advance to James City, and arrived two hours later to discover Stuart already in possession of the town. Custer ordered Alexander Pennington to open up and shell the enemy position in the woods at the edge of the village, while Colonel Russell Alger and one battalion of the Fifth Michigan charged the artillery battery. Stuart met the advance of the Wolverines with sharp-shooters from the First South Carolina, and, in Custer's words, the charge "failed for want of sufficient support."[11]

The opposing cavalries traded sporadic fire throughout the remainder of the day, but for the most part were content to observe each other from parallel positions of high ground with James City located in the valley between.

Kilpatrick received urgent orders at about 3:00 A.M. to move his command across the Rappahannock toward Culpeper Court House to cover the withdrawal of the infantry. By seven o'clock, the Union cavalry was in the saddle, with Custer's brigade on the eastern flank. Stuart noticed this withdrawal, gathered his troops, and hurried down the Sperryville Pike toward Culpeper.[12]

Kilpatrick's division had passed through Culpeper, oblivious to the fact that Meade had already removed the infantry from the vicinity, virtually abandoning the cavalry in enemy-held territory. The horsemen were finally informed of Meade's action, and raced toward the Rappahannock to avoid being caught in an exposed position without infantry available for support.

Custer's brigade rode at the end of the column. The first word of the potential consequences of this predicament came from a young woman in Culpeper who informed the rear guard that "You will catch it if you don't hurry." Custer had departed town, following the tracks of the Orange & Alexandria Railroad, when his rear guard was struck by Stuart's cavalry. Kilpatrick was some distance ahead, and Custer would be on his own if the enemy chose to attack in force.[13]

Jeb Stuart, riding with his advance, the Twelfth Virginia, had ordered the charge. His men bravely responded, but encountered a wide ditch and a stone wall, which effectively aborted the advance and, for the time being, saved Custer.

Custer reacted to Stuart's initial charge by deploying his troops on the ridges north of Culpeper, and dug in to prepare for an attack.

Stuart at this time learned that the Union infantry had crossed the Rappahannock, and decided not to strike Custer's position. Instead, he devised a plan designed to trap the enemy cavalry between his division and that of

Fitz Lee's division, which was presently located north of Culpeper. Stuart left behind a detachment to harass Custer, withdrew the remainder of his troops, and led them along the back roads toward Brandy Station.[14]

When it became evident that an assault by Stuart was not forthcoming, Custer mounted his men and resumed his desperate ride toward the Rappahannock in an effort to rejoin Kilpatrick, Buford, and Pleasonton.[15]

The Wolverines had ventured only a short distance when Stuart's horsemen once again commenced nipping at the heels of the column. At the same time, Custer noticed a strong gray column—Fitz Lee's division—on his outer flank racing to intercept his line of march. Rather than halt and deploy, Custer pushed his men in the direction of Brandy Station—riding directly into Jeb Stuart's trap.[16]

Lieutenant George Briggs, the adjutant riding with Colonel William D. Mann's Seventh Michigan, described the action with the rear guard, "To unflinchingly face and hold in check the advancing enemy until the receding column of your comrades is out of sight; to then break to the rear a short distance and again face about to meet an on-coming and confident foe, is a duty that only brave and well disciplined troops can properly perform. Breaking to the rear only to repeatedly face about in a new position, which must be held as long as safety will permit, is one of the most trying services that a soldier is called upon to perform."[17]

Judson Kilpatrick, however, was not entirely fooled by Stuart's ploy, and ordered Buford's Second New York into the fray. Custer's men rode to save themselves from being cut off, while Fitz Lee encountered Buford's New Yorkers at the railroad tracks on the outskirts of Brandy Station and forced them into a fighting retreat across Raccoon Creek. Lee, expecting that Buford would make a stand at Brandy Station, chased his enemy in that direction.

Tom Rosser had something to celebrate and something to prove. He had been officially promoted to brigadier general and named in command of the Laurel Brigade that day. Rosser detached the First Maryland and Fifteenth Virginia from Fitz Lee and spurred ahead in an effort to maneuver in front of Custer at the river.[18]

Stuart, riding with Hampton's division, pressed forward, and encountered a battalion of the Fifth New York that had been separated from the main column. He ordered the Twelfth Virginia and the Fourth and Fifth North Carolina to charge. The Union troops held their ground by blockading the road and preparing to fight with drawn pistols. Stuart then dispatched the Seventh Virginia into the Union flank, killing and capturing many of them.

Stuart's vise was closing when, unexpectedly, he came under heavy artillery shelling—originating from the direction of Fitz Lee's guns. Stuart's advance had been so rapid that his horse artillery could not keep up, and he therefore had no way of notifying Lee of his arrival. Lee had mistaken Stuart's command for enemy cavalry. The only manner in which to reveal their identity was to attack the Yankees. The Twelfth Virginia was formed, and prepared to charge into the scattered enemy.[19]

When Custer and his Wolverines arrived at the depot, Rosser was in a position at his front, which cut him off from the river. Custer reported, "The heavy masses of the rebel cavalry could be seen covering the heights in front of my advance (where it is remembered that my rear guard was hotly engaged with a superior force), a heavy column was enveloping each flank, and my advance confronted by more than double my own number. The peril of my situation can be estimated."[20]

Jeb Stuart had successfully surrounded Custer's command. The only question was whether or not the Knight of the Golden Spurs could coordinate his various detachments effectively enough to deliver the killing blow before the Wolverines could escape.

Custer ordered Pennington's six-gun battery to blast their way through the impasse, but the Yanks were soon quieted by heavier Rebel shelling. At that point, Generals Pleasonton and Kilpatrick surprisingly braved the ride through the enemy to confer with Custer. There were few options, and, when Custer proposed "to cut through the force in my front, and thus open a way for the entire command to the river," Pleasonton approved, saying, "Do your best."[21]

Custer wasted little time mounting the Fifth Michigan on his right in a column of battalions, and the First on his left in a column of squadrons. The Sixth and Seventh would guard the flank, where Stuart's horsemen had been poised. The Boy General then scanned the enemy position with binoculars in an attempt to discern a weak point.

Moments later, satisfied that he had located a likely spot, Custer rode to the front of his men, and ordered, "Draw sabers!" He waited for the clanking of the heavy metal weapons to die down, and then informed them that they were surrounded, and all they had to do was open a way with their sabers. "I told them of the situation frankly of the great responsibility resting on them and how confident I was that they would respond nobly to the trust reposed in them. You should have heard the cheers they sent up."[22]

Custer, looking over that sea of sabers and anxious faces, called out, "'Boys of Michigan, there are some people between us and home; I'm going home, who else goes?' They showed their determination and purpose by giving three hearty cheers." The enthusiasm of the command was heightened when the bandmaster was ordered to play "Yankee Doodle"—the official song for a charge.

General Custer issued the order to move forward, and the command responded at the trot. "I never expect to see a prettier sight," he later wrote to Nettie Humphrey. "I frequently turned in my saddle to see the glittering sabres advance in the sunlight."[23]

At his chosen time, Custer rose in his stirrups, pointed his saber, and shouted "Charge!" The buglers echoed the call, and the Wolverines bolted toward the ranks of the Southerners. Captain William Glazier described the scene, "Custer, the daring, terrible demon that he is in battle, dashed madly forward in the charge, while his yellow locks floated like pennants in the breeze. Fired to an almost divine potency, and with a majestic madness, this band of heroic troopers shook the air with their battle cry."[24]

Within forty rods of Stuart's cavalry, Custer's opposition wilted away—but within moments wheeled around and charged his flank and rear. General Tom Rosser explained his actions, "I withdrew my regiment, and advised the other colonels to fall back so as to avoid the heavy blow in our rear. These troops were moving at a full gallop; they were not charging upon us, for we stood in line off to one side, and for a moment I looked on in amazement at the performance. I soon concluded that they were being pursued, and charged them in flank."[25]

Jeb Stuart supported his horsemen with a vicious artillery barrage. Custer was blown from his horse by a bursting shell, quickly scrambled to remount another, which was slain by a bullet, and he resumed the charge atop a third mount.[26]

The two cavalries charged and countercharged throughout the afternoon and into the evening—the Federals trying to fight their way through Confederates who were just as determined to stop them. Judson Kilpatrick rode into the fray to yell at Colonel Russell Alger of the Fifth Michigan, "You charge and give them hell, and I'll give them heller."

Stuart placed Lomax's and Chambliss' brigades on the right to pour a cross fire into the Union flank, while the main force attacked the front. At one point, Kilpatrick's wagons and ambulances were threatened, but the Sixth and Seventh Michigan thwarted Stuart's men long enough for most of the train to escape.[27]

Brandy Station, in the words of Confederate officer Henry McClellan, was once again the scene of a "sanguinary cavalry battle. [The Union cavalrymen] fought bravely, even desperately. Several times [our] dismounted men, while eagerly pressing forward, were surrounded by the enemy's cavalry, and either fought their way out with their carbines and revolvers or were rescued by charges of their mounted brigades. Five times did the 5th, 6th, and 15th Virginia Cavalry make distinct sabre charges." Tom Rosser added, "Never in my life did I reap such a rich harvest in horses and prisoners."[28]

However, Custer successfully punched a hole through his enemy, opening a route wide enough to allow the cavalry to commence withdrawing across the river to Brandy Station.

By the time Fitz Lee realized what was happening and joined Stuart, the beleaguered Yankees, supported by artillery, had managed to occupy Fleetwood Hill. A series of counterattacks failed to dislodge the resolute enemy, and Stuart eventually declined to send his troops against such a strong position.

Colonel Pierce M. B. Young arrived with his Georgian brigade just before nightfall. Young deployed his men as sharpshooters and commenced a determined barrage that deceived the Federals into believing that infantry support had arrived. As darkness descended, Confederate campfires were built along a two-mile line, and the brass band played "Bonnie Blue Flag" and "Dixie" while the Union cavalrymen quietly slipped away in the night.

By about eight o'clock, every able-bodied Yankee had crossed the pontoon bridge and reached the relative safety of the far side of the Rappahannock River—but had left over five hundred of their comrades behind as Jeb Stuart's prisoners.[29]

General Alfred Pleasonton had accompanied the Michigan Brigade throughout the battle, and had nothing but praise for Custer and his men. "Boys," he said, "I saw your flag far in advance among the rebels."[30]

Later, Lieutenant George Briggs would write, "The salvation of the Michigan Cavalry Brigade from capture or destruction at Brandy Station was little less than a miracle. That it was saved for its subsequent career of brilliant services was due to its fighting qualities, its confidence in the leadership of the beloved Custer, and the failure of the enemy to take advantage of a great opportunity."[31]

No one was more pleased about the performance of the Michigan Brigade than its commander, however, who wrote that night to Nettie Humphrey, "Oh, could you but have seen some of the charges that were made! While thinking of them I cannot but exclaim 'Glorious War!' "

On October 18, General Meade ordered Judson Kilpatrick to confirm reports that Robert E. Lee was withdrawing his army. At three o'clock that afternoon, the Third Division, with Custer's Michigan brigade in the van, crossed Bull Run and moved down the Warrenton Turnpike. Stuart was covering Lee's withdrawal, and his horsemen offered only token resistance at Gainesville before retiring when the First Vermont advanced. Kilpatrick's troops bivouacked at Gainesville for the night, while Stuart deployed Wade Hampton's division, which remained under his personal command, into a strong defensive position just three miles to the west at Buckland Mills.[32]

At daybreak on the cold, rainy morning of October 19, General Custer's brigade, with Major James Kidd's Sixth Michigan in the advance, moved down the Pike from Gainesville to Buckland, and encountered only light skirmishing. Shortly before noon, however, the Wolverines approached Broad Run and came under intense small arms and artillery fire from three cavalry brigades located on the southern bank. Custer quickly dismounted the Fifth, Sixth, and Seventh Michigan, and placed them on both sides of the Warrenton Turnpike. The mounted First Michigan and First Vermont were held in reserve. Custer understood that an assault under the circumstances would not be prudent, and therefore dispatched the Seventh to move through the woods downstream in an attempt to cross the creek below the Rebel right flank.[33]

Jeb Stuart was aware of Custer's intention to try to turn his flank. While contemplating a tactic to counter this threat, a courier from Fitz Lee arrived. Lee's division, he informed the cavalry commander, was approaching from the east. Lee suggested that Stuart withdraw toward Warrenton and lure the Yankees into pursuit, which would permit his division to strike from the flank while Stuart could turn around and hit them from the front. Lee would fire a cannon shot to indicate when he was in position. Stuart gladly accepted the plan, and commenced pulling back.[34]

Custer waited for the Seventh Michigan to engage the Rebels on the flank, and then sent Colonel Alger and the Fifth Michigan on a charge across the creek. *New York Times* reporter E. A. Paul wrote, "The skirmishers, not to be left behind, boldly waded the river, and not withstanding all the obstacles to such a movement, kept up an excellent line, the whole command pushing forward under a very heavy fire. The conflict, though comparatively brief here, was sharp, the enemy contending manfully for every foot of ground." The Confederates began to withdraw in the face of this assault.

Custer was of the opinion that he had forced Jeb Stuart's horsemen from their position, and halted after a mile or so of pursuit to allow his hungry men to prepare dinner.[35]

Judson Kilpatrick arrived with Davies' brigade and, after complimenting Custer on his actions, ordered him to mount up his troops. Custer protested that his men had not eaten since the previous evening, and Kilpatrick agreed that they should eat.

"It was characteristic of him to care studiously for the comfort of his men," explained James Kidd. But in this instance, Custer had apparently wanted a respite from the fight in order to assess the situation. Old Curly did not feel comfortable, and purposefully warned Kilpatrick that something was amiss, that his lone brigade should not have so easily dislodged an entrenched enemy division. In addition, his scouts had observed great numbers of Confederate infantry on both flanks that could have been merely stragglers without horses from Hampton's division.

Custer advised his commander to be wary and proceed with caution, that the wily Stuart might be attempting to cut the Third Division off from Broad Run. Kilpatrick scoffed at his subordinate's concern and ordered Custer to follow the last brigade that passed. Kilpatrick then rode off with Davies vowing to overtake Stuart's retreating troops.[36]

Stuart had hidden his division behind ridges at Chestnut Hill, two and a half miles northeast of Warrenton, and watched as Kilpatrick and Davies rode toward them along the turnpike. The Union cavalry was within two hundred yards of Stuart's position when Fitz Lee announced his presence with cannon fire. The Southerners attacked Kilpatrick's column from the front and flank, and the blue-clad cavalry had little choice but to flee for their lives.[37]

At about 3:00 P.M., Custer had just gotten under way when his Wolverines came under attack by a line of foot soldiers. General Fitz Lee had sent Colonel Thomas Owen's Virginia brigade up from Auburn as an advance unit to strike Kilpatrick's rear. Lee's entire division had followed, and two brigades of Kilpatrick's division were caught in dire circumstances, unable to retreat back to Broad Run.

Custer quickly discovered that, with Davies in retreat, he had been left on his own—abandoned by Kilpatrick. He posted the dismounted Fifth, Sixth, and Seventh in the woods, with the mounted First Vermont and First Michigan in reserve, and ordered Battery M to open up. The woods quavered with gunfire and were choked with plumes of white smoke as Major Kidd's Sixth Michigan fired into the long gray line of dismounted cavalry.[38]

Lee countered with his own artillery and an overwhelming number of troopers advancing on foot. The Rebels charged time and again, but the Wolverines made a series of valiant stands against this seemingly endless flood of aggressors. There were twelve enemy regiments against them, and only his posting of the skirmishers in the woods had averted disaster. Custer deployed one of Pennington's guns and the First Vermont to guard any attempt by the Confederates to take Broad Run bridge. He worried about the fate of Colonel Davies' brigade, but the enemy was simply too powerful. He must try to save his own men.

Confederate Major P. P. Johnston, who was commanding a section of the artillery, reported, "The battle was of the most obstinate character. Fitz Lee exerting himself to the utmost to push the enemy, and Custer seeming to have no thought of retiring. Suddenly, a cloud of dust arose on the road toward Warrenton, and as suddenly everything in our front gave way. The mounted cavalry was ordered forward, and I saw no more of the enemy."[39]

Custer had wisely perceived that he was in peril of being trapped between Lee and Stuart, and had no other choice but to order his men to withdraw across Broad Run and ride away to save themselves from certain annihilation.[40]

General Custer led his Wolverines toward Gainesville, where they found safety behind the pickets of the Sixth Corps. He would later call the episode "the most disastrous [day] this Division ever passed through." To add to Custer's anger and humiliation, his baggage and correspondence had been captured. Confederate William Blackford noted, "Some of the letters to a fair, but frail, friend of Custer's were published in the Richmond papers and afforded some spicy reading, though most of the spicy parts did not appear."[41]

Colonel Davies' brigade did not fare as well as the Michigan boys. They had passed through New Baltimore, four miles west of Buckland Mills, when Kilpatrick was informed that the enemy held the turnpike to their rear. Kilpatrick dispatched his wagons and two regiments on an alternate route, leaving Davies to engage the enemy. Eventually, Davies ordered an every-man-for-himself retreat, and the regiments dissolved as the horsemen raced to save themselves.

Jeb Stuart's cavalry chased the Union cavalrymen for five miles, and along the way captured about 250 prisoners and eight to ten ambulances. Kilpatrick and Davies were able to save themselves, but the episode was certainly not only costly in lives but an embarrassment for the Union. Stuart termed this hasty retreat by the Union the "Buckland Races," and boasted that he was "justified in declaring the rout of the enemy at Buckland the most signal and complete that any cavalry has suffered during the war."[42]

The Knight of the Golden Spurs and his Invincibles had regained, at least for the time being, a dominance over the enemy, which had been a matter of contention in recent days.

The Bristoe Campaign had come to an inglorious end with Robert E. Lee once again getting the better of Union forces. George Meade had been forced back forty miles from where the campaign had begun, and had been denied use of the railroad at Bristoe Station for over a month. The Yankee cavalry had performed in spectacular fashion, however, but had more than once been placed in peril without support and were fortunate to have been able to fight their way out of harm's way on their own.

Perhaps the most displeased—to put it kindly—officer on the Union side at the way the recent actions were conducted was George Armstrong Custer. And his wrath was directed at one man.

"Under very distressing circumstances," Custer wrote to Nettie Humphrey on October 20 from Gainesville, "I turn to you and *her* [Libbie Bacon] for consolation. It is for others that I feel. October 19th, was the most disastrous this division ever passed through . . . I was not responsible, but I cannot but regret the loss of so many brave men . . . all the more painful that it was not necessary."[43]

With those words, Custer for the first time displayed criticism of Judson Kilpatrick. The loss of 214 Wolverines killed, wounded, or captured in the previous ten days, combined with the previous day's debacle, compelled him to break his silence in correspondence, if not in private to confidants on his staff. Kill-Cavalry had ignored Custer's warning about a potential trap at Buckland, and only Custer's foresight had averted a worse disaster for his own men. The battered Michigan Brigade would require an extended recuperation, clothing to replace their "rags," and the replacement of hundreds of mounts lost in the fighting.

The relationship between Custer and Kilpatrick would never be the same, and it may have been on Custer's mind to confront his superior about his reckless disregard for the troops, but good judgment won out—at least for the time being.[44]

Seventeen

Marriage

T he one bright spot in Custer's life remained his relationship with Libbie, yet one major hurdle remained—the letter to Judge Bacon asking to marry his daughter. He had finally composed what he considered the most important letter of his life, which arrived at the Bacon residence on October 21.

"I had hoped for a personal interview," Custer told the judge, but obligations had prevented that while he had been in Monroe on furlough. Custer asked the judge for Libbie's hand in marriage, and then attempted to promote his worthiness and explain away any concerns by saying, "It is true that I have often committed errors of judgment, but as I grew older I learned the necessity of propriety. I am aware of your fear of intemperance, but surely my conduct for the past two years—during which I have not violated the solemn promise I made my sister, with God to witness, should dispel that fear. You may have thought my conduct trifling after my visits to Libbie ceased, last winter. It was to prevent gossip. I left home when but sixteen, and have been surrounded with temptation, but I have always had a purpose in life."[1]

The letter was received by Judge Bacon and his family with mixed emotions, and evoked considerable debate from the various members. The judge replied to Custer that his decision on the matter would require "weeks or even months before I can feel to give you a definite answer." He did compliment Custer at the end of the letter by writing, "Your ability, energy and force of character I have always admired, and no one can feel more gratified than myself at your well-earned reputation and your high and honorable position."[2]

Following a lengthy discussion with Libbie one evening that lasted until the fire had burned down to embers, however, the judge lifted his ban on her corresponding with Custer. Her father's "great soul," as Libbie put it, had opened the door for her marriage to Armstrong.[3]

Libbie opened her first letter to Armstrong with, "My more than friend—at last—Am I glad to write you some of the thoughts I cannot control? I have enjoyed your letters to Nettie, but am delighted to possess some of my own. I was surprised to hear how readily Father had consented to our correspondence. You have no idea how many dark hours your little girl has passed . . . I had no idea six weeks could go so slowly." [4]

She related her family's guarded blessing to their proposed union, and it was not Daniel who was the main stumbling block. The judge had lifted the ban on writing and receiving letters "because he feels how much harm has often been done by parents refusing." Libbie wrote that "Father is on my side," but it was Rhoda who argued that Custer would not make a good husband. She was joined in opposition by Daniel's brother, Albert Bacon, who agreed with Rhoda's assessment.[5]

At the moment, Libbie cared only about the opinion of her father, but openly admitted to her own apprehension. She wrote to Custer, "Ah, dear man, if I am worth having am I not worth waiting for? The very thought of marriage makes me tremble. Girls have so much fun. Marriage means trouble. If you tease me I will go into a convent for a year. The very thought of leaving my home, my family, is painful to me. I implore you not to mention it for at least a year." [6]

Custer did not relish hearing about a wait of a year. He immediately sought a furlough in order to travel to Monroe and claim his bribe-to-be. General Pleasonton agreed, but with one stipulation—Custer must first go out and capture Jeb Stuart.

West Point Cadet George Armstrong Custer, 1861

Union artillery Commander Alexander Pennington, 1862

Lieutenant James B. Washington, a Confederate prisoner and Custer's friend at West Point, with Custer in a photo *Harper's Weekly* captioned: "Both Sides, the Cause," 1862

Confederate General Thomas L. Rosser, Custer's closest friend at West Point; they would meet each other on the battlefield on numerous occasions.

Confederate artilleryman John Pelham, whose expertise earned him the sobriquet "The Gallant Pelham" from Jeb Stuart

Newlyweds George Armstrong and Elizabeth Bacon Custer, February 15, 1864

The depiction of a classic Custer charge from *Harper's Weekly*, March 19, 1864

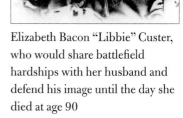

Elizabeth Bacon "Libbie" Custer, who would share battlefield hardships with her husband and defend his image until the day she died at age 90

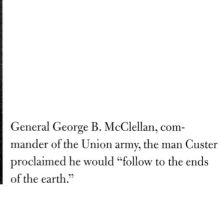

General George B. McClellan, commander of the Union army, the man Custer proclaimed he would "follow to the ends of the earth."

Brigadier General Custer and Major General Alfred Pleasonton, who was instrumental in Custer's promotion from captain to general, 1863

General Phillip "Little Phil" Sheridan, the cavalry commander who would become Custer's mentor for the remainder of his life

Future president of the
United States, General
Ulysses S. Grant, commander
of the Union army

General Phillip Sheridan
with his staff, 1864 (from left)
Sheridan, Generals James
Forsyth, Wesley Merritt,
Thomas C. Devon, and
George Armstrong Custer

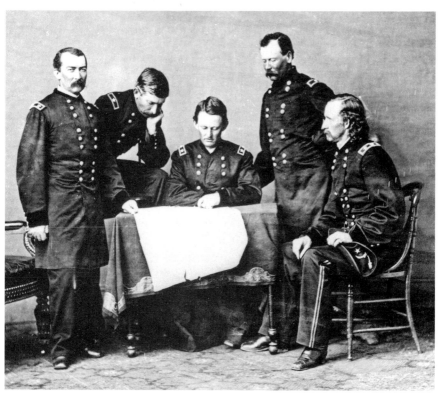

James Ewell Brown "Jeb" Stuart, the legendary Confederate cavalry commander who rode rings around the Union army in the early stages of the war

Confederate Colonel John Singleton Mosby would become a thorn in the side of Custer's cavalry in northern Virginia.

Confederate army Commander General Robert E. Lee, whose brilliant tactics and ability to motivate his troops nearly resulted in victory for the South

General William Henry Fitzhugh Lee, the second son of Robert E. Lee, became the youngest major general in the Confederate army in 1864.

Confederate General Wade Hampton, whose family owned one of the largest plantations with the greatest number of slaves in the South

Union General Hugh Judson Kilpatrick, who became known by his subordinates as "Kil-cavalry" for his recklessness with their lives in battle.

Thomas W. Custer, the brother of George Armstrong, wearing his two medals of honor

The classic Matthew Brady photograph of Major General George Armstrong Custer, May 1865

The general consoled himself by spending the evening singing songs around the campfire with Jacob Greene, Joseph Fought, and James Christiancy, who had just returned from Monroe. With guitar and violin accompaniment, they sang "Then You'll Remember Me," the song that Libbie had promised to sing for him when they were reunited. That same night, Libbie entered in her journal, "I love you Armstrong Custer. I love *you*. I love my love and my love loves me—and I am happy."[7]

Word of Custer's proposal to Libbie, which certainly became known within her circle of friends, did not set well with one young lady—Fanny Fifield. Fanny was angry over her rejection, and began spreading rumors that were "prejudicial" to Armstrong Custer. He heard about this gossip, and wrote to Nettie Humphrey, "I am not surprised at Fanny's telling that my likeness is in her locket. I would be surprised at nothing she chooses to do. For myself I am indifferent, but I hope she will not annoy Libbie."[8]

The gossip about Armstrong naturally did distress Libbie, but she dismissed any apprehensions by writing, "I love him though notwithstanding all." She could understand that a woman who perceived herself to be scorned might say anything, whether true or not, to soothe her heartbreak and humiliation. Libbie Bacon trusted her husband-to-be, and would not allow gossip to destroy their love for each other.[9]

Meanwhile, Brigadier General George Armstrong Custer became worried about his brigade's lack of adequate cavalry mounts. His Wolverines had lost a huge number of horses, and the replacements furnished by the government, in Custer's judgment, were less than satisfactory. Custer took up the matter with General Pleasonton, who forwarded his subordinate's letter to Major General George Stoneman. The chief of cavalry took a dim view of Custer's complaint, and wrote back his assurance that the Wolverines had been sufficiently remounted—with the opinion that "Custer's brigade are great horse killers."[10]

Indeed, one of the favorite pastimes around camp was horse racing. Generals Kilpatrick and Pleasonton both joined Custer in some friendly wagering on which of the brigade's horses was the fastest. Custer did mention this diversion to Libbie, along with poker games, and promised to abstain from them in the future because they were "wrong in principle." It would be a difficult promise for him to keep.[11]

On November 19, while Custer was settled into his winter quarters near Stevensburg, not far from Brandy Station and Culpeper Court House, perhaps the most powerful and enduring speech in American history was delivered by President Abraham Lincoln. The occasion was the dedication of a national cemetery for the Union dead at Gettysburg, Pennsylvania. The primary speaker that day was Edward Everett, one of the nation's greatest orators. As a courtesy, the president had been invited to "make a few remarks." Surprisingly, Lincoln had accepted, viewing the opportunity as his chance to convey the Union's purpose in the war. Everett spoke for two hours, and then Lincoln rose, delivered his speech from two sheets of paper—"Fourscore and seven years ago . . ."—and was finished before most of the audience even realized he had spoken.

Contrary to popular belief, Lincoln's words were enthusiastically received, and some reporters instantly recognized their significance. The president remarked that "the world will little note, nor long remember what we say here," which certainly proved to be false. The Gettysburg Address has become the conscience of the American people, with the resolve "that this nation, under God, shall have a new birth of freedom—and that government of the people, by the people, for the people, shall not perish from the earth."

While Lincoln was defining his vision of the United States and those states were in the midst of a great Civil War, the thoughts of the young General George Armstrong Custer never ventured far from his intention of marrying Libbie Bacon—and the timetable she had set did not sit well with him. He wanted them to marry during the winter of 1864, when the lack of field operations would allow him to receive a furlough. In other words, he wanted the wedding to happen as soon as possible in spite of her protestations.

On November 22, he wrote to Libbie, "I am sorry I cannot accede to almost the first *written* request my little Gypsie has made, but such unfortunately is the case. You bid me maintain strict silence upon a certain subject until next winter and then we are to discuss the subject of your becoming Mrs._____ and arrive at a conclusion the following winter. This like all other bargains requires two to complete it. Now had you presented a single, good reason why the course you make out should be adopted, I might have yielded assent, but you have not done so." Custer was not bashful about revealing his true intentions, and had initiated another frontal assault on Libbie worthy of his reputation as a bold and daring cavalry officer.[12]

There were also assaults on the battlefield at this time. In October, following his victory at Vicksburg, Major General Ulysses S. Grant was able to concentrate on eastern Tennessee. He had moved his seventy-thousand-man army from the west and the Mississippi River to lay siege to Chattanooga, where General Braxton Bragg's fifty thousand Confederates were entrenched on Missionary Ridge, northeast to southwest of town, and Lookout Mountain, on the southwest edge of town.

On November 23, Grant decided to break the siege, and ordered General William T. Sherman to cross the Tennessee River and assault the north end of Missionary Ridge at the enemy's right, while General Joseph Hooker would attack Lookout Mountain from the left, and General George H. Thomas would stand ready to hit the center or reinforce either flank. After three days of fighting, Bragg's Army of Tennessee was sent into full retreat, and the Union army was in complete control of the area around Chattanooga. It became apparent with this victory that complete domination of the South seemed imminent and the Confederacy could no longer take the offensive and attack the North but must worry about simply defending itself. Robert E. Lee would disagree with that premise, however, and did not allow this setback to shatter his confidence in his troops or purpose.

On November 26, General George Meade, prodded by the administration in Washington to undertake an offensive before winter, crossed the Rappahannock in a maneuver designed to turn Lee's right flank and force the Confederates toward Richmond. Meade's eighty-five thousand troops undertook this movement against Lee's forty-eight thousand in what would be called the Mine Run Campaign.[13]

A possible confrontation between George Armstrong Custer and Judson Kilpatrick had been avoided when the commander was called to Washington to appear as a witness in a court-martial. Custer would once again assume command of the Third Division. And his men were in the saddle, although Meade had slowed his advance at Brandy Station.

General Custer's mission would be to act as a diversionary force upriver from the Union crossing site. On November 15, Davies' brigade was deployed at Raccoon Ford; Colonel Town, commanding the Wolverines in place of Custer, was sent to Morton's Ford; and Major James Kidd led the Sixth Michigan upstream toward Somerville Ford.

When these units were in position, Custer ordered Pennington to open up with artillery while the troops feinted crossing the Rappahannock at four points. The Rebels answered with at least thirty-six guns of their own, and revealed that the trenches were occupied by infantry.

Custer had learned his artillery lessons well at West Point, and was anxious to test his skills. He found a target of ten Rebels in a rifle pit, dismounted, and fired two of Pennington's guns himself. His first shot was a direct hit, which killed six of the occupants. The other four men dashed for another pit, but Custer placed his second round so close that they fled for their lives.[14]

"I have been entirely successful in deceiving the enemy to-day as to my intention to effect a crossing," Custer reported to Meade late that afternoon. "I have compelled him to maintain a strong line of battle, extending without break from Morton's to above Raccoon. The enemy was massing his infantry and strengthening his artillery. He evidently expects us to attempt a passage at those points to-morrow morning." As darkness approached, Custer added to the ruse by ordering that a long line of campfires be built and having his band serenade the Confederates from several different places along the river.[15]

The following morning, however, the fortifications across the waterway were found to be empty. The enemy had vacated upon learning about Meade's actual movements. Colonel Town was sent to investigate, and happened upon a small force of cavalry, which he chased. He captured thirty-two prisoners while losing only one man.[16]

Meade's slow advance had permitted Lee to position his army in strong defensive fortifications along the west bank of Mine Run. When an assault by the Union had not materialized by November 30, Lee seriously considered attacking Meade. That night, Lee held a council of war to discuss the matter.

Lee and Stuart favored an immediate assault; Ewell and Hill were opposed. Lee decided to make a personal reconnaissance the following day.

In the meantime, Meade thought better of a frontal assault on Lee's position, and on December 1 wisely retired across the Rapidan. A disappointed Lee wrote, "After awaiting his advance until Tuesday evening, preparations were made to attack him on Wednesday morning. This was prevented by his retreat."[17]

Both armies prepared to settle into winter quarters with the Rappahannock and Rapidan rivers as barriers between them.

Custer and his Wolverines settled into the Third Cavalry winter quarters located in the vicinity of Stevensburg, near Brandy Station and Culpeper Court House. The men commenced constructing huts for the officers from a combination of fresh-cut logs as well as lumber, nails, bricks, and other materials scavenged from abandoned houses. These huts, which measured about twelve feet square, were furnished with fireplaces and windows, and situated on streets by company and regiment.[18]

Custer had been relentless in his frontal assault to convince Libbie to marry him as soon as possible. He even wrote to Nettie Humphrey, asking, "Cannot you *threaten* her, or use your influence to induce her to do as she *ought*?" He also wrote to the judge, stating that he was sending a large, colored photograph of himself—a Christmas present—and asked that it be placed in her room as a surprise. He penned another letter in which he promised that as a husband he would be "guided and activated by the principles of right" and that "an aim of my life" would be "to make myself deserving of the high and sacred trust you have reposed in me."[19]

Libbie had commenced her own assault on her father—and daughters have been known to have a spiritual and mystical effect upon their fathers.

On December 12, Custer received a letter from Judge Bacon that held the answer to his hopes that matrimony would be a part of his near future. It can only be imagined how much the battle-tested general's fingers trembled as he opened this letter.

"My Young Friend," Daniel Bacon began, and addressed the matter of marriage, "You cannot at your age realize the feelings of a parent when called upon to give up and give away an only offspring," the judge wrote. "I feel that I have kept you in suspense quite too long, and yet when you consider my affection and desire for her happiness you will pardon me for this unreasonable delay." Bacon acknowledged that he had no right to stand in the way of his daughter's wishes, and although he might have preferred that Custer had been "a professor of the Christian religion," affirmed that "you are the object of my choice." [20]

Judge Bacon added that "he was not a wealthy man." His holdings were in real estate, "with sale and price depending on unseen contingencies." Libbie would inherit the Bacon home, and would bring to the marriage a several-thousand-dollar trousseau, but she could not expect to have "a patrimony at my death exceeding $10,000." He ended his letter with, "May God in his kind providence favor the union."[21]

Five days later, Custer opened a letter from Libbie that compelled him to exclaim, "I am so supremely happy that I can scarcely write, my thoughts go wandering from one subject to another so rapidly that it is with difficulty that I return [to] one long enough to transfer it to paper. Am I not dreaming? Surely such unalloyed pleasure never before was enjoyed by mortal man."[22]

Libbie Bacon had surrendered to his aggressive advance, and agreed to marry him that winter.

While Libbie prepared for a February wedding—the exact date dependent upon Armstrong's ability to gain a furlough—Custer was informed by Pleasonton of a rumor that dampened a portion of his happiness. Pleasonton, who betrayed his own shock, had learned that Custer's official confirmation as brigadier general was being opposed by Republican Senator Jacob M. Howard of Michigan, who was a member of the Military Affairs Committee.

Howard had questioned Custer's youth, and the fact that the Ohio native was not a *Michigan Man.* More than likely, however, the real reason was that Custer was a "McClellan Man," who presumably was out to sabotage the policies of the present administration. Pleasonton told Custer that if he should be stripped of his promotion "it would be a lasting disgrace on the part of the government to allow such injustice." He advised Custer to exert whatever influence he could muster to fight this action by Howard and other unnamed political enemies. [23]

Custer speculated that Governor Austin Blair and the former commander of the Michigan Brigade, Joseph Copeland, were "at the bottom of this attempt." He took action that night by writing to Senators Jacob Howard and Zachariah Chandler, and Congressman F. W. Kellogg, requesting that they "look after my interests."

In a letter to Isaac Christiancy, Custer wrote, "I have addressed this letter to you with the hope that you could and would bring influence to bear with both Howard and Chandler which would carry their votes in my favor. If my confirmation was placed in the hands of the army I would not expect a single opposing vote." [24]

Christiancy replied with assurance that he would contact the senators on Custer's behalf. He added his opinion that Custer, as the son of a Democrat and former member of McClellan's staff—and now a general in the army— was subject to the bitter political infighting that ruled Washington. The views of a general about such matters as the Emancipation Proclamation could be as influential as his exploits in combat.

At the same time, Custer received a reply from Senator Howard, which requested answers to questions about whether or not the Boy General was indeed a "McClellan Man," or a "Copperhead."

Copperheads, of course, were those Democrats who were more conciliatory toward the South—Peace Democrats. They represented primarily Midwestern states; their leader, Clement L. Vallandigham, was from Ohio, Custer's native state. They wore a copper penny as an identification badge, hence the name. The Copperheads, a strong and vocal minority in Congress, accused the Republicans, who were mostly from the Northeast, of provoking the war for their own interests, and asserted that military means would fail to restore the Union. And George B. McClellan, whom Custer was known to worship, was being touted as their presidential candidate to oppose Lincoln in the next year's election.

Custer was pleased about the opportunity to state his case rather than being labeled by others without recourse. He wrote a letter to Senator Howard, and established his position as a loyal supporter for the policies of his commander in chief, Abraham Lincoln. "The president," Custer affirmed, "cannot issue any decree or order which will not receive my unqualified *support* . . . All his acts, proclamations and decisions embraced in his war policy have received not only my support, but my most hardy, earnest and cordial *approval*."

Custer addressed his position on the Emancipation Proclamation by declaring that his friends "can testify that I have insisted that so long as a single slave was held in bondage, I for one, was opposed to peace on any terms. I would *offer* no compromise except that which is offered at the point of the bayonet."[25]

Custer privately had blamed Lincoln and Secretary of War Stanton for the dismissal of George McClellan as commander of the Army of the Potomac, and had at that time shared the commanding general's opinion regarding the conduct of the war. The beliefs stated to Howard in this most important letter, however, can be judged sincere rather than simply a contrived, hypocritical performance presented in order to gain confirmation of his promotion.

Custer was no longer a wandering aide-de-camp but a brigadier general whose leadership had been tested under fire, and that in itself had a way of maturing and altering youthful impressions. To add further credence to the issue, Custer had previously pledged his loyalty to the Lincoln administration in a letter to Judge Bacon—and his future father-in-law was known to despise Lincoln.

Howard and his Republican colleagues were satisfied that Custer was a loyal "Lincoln Man," and the Senate readily confirmed his nomination to brigadier general. Custer was relieved that he had escaped becoming a victim of politics, and expressed his feelings to Judge Bacon, "The subject has caused me no little anxiety, but now my fears are at rest. I would have written you at once when I learned of the efforts made to injure me, but did not wish to trouble Libbie. You would be surprised at the pertinacity with which certain men labor to defame me. I have paid but little attention to them, trusting to time to vindicate me. And I do not fear the result." Custer would take pains in the future to curry favor with the power elite in Washington rather than rely merely on his battlefield prowess.[26]

While Custer fought for his promotion, Libbie had attended several Christmas parties. At one of these events, she happened upon Fanny Fifield, who wore expensive furs and displayed a huge diamond on her finger. Fanny would soon be marrying Charles Thomas, a wealthy merchant, and moving to Boston's fashionable Newbury Street.[27]

Now that the promotion obstacle was behind him, pressing family matters were foremost in the mind of George Armstrong Custer. He arranged for a furlough, and the wedding date with Libbie was set for February 9, 1864.

On January 27, Custer, Jacob Greene, George Yates, and James Christiancy boarded a train and, with a stopover in Washington, made the three-day trip to Monroe, Michigan. The Custer family, who with Armstrong's financial assistance had moved from Ohio to Monroe, welcomed the cavalry-men with a party. Private Tom Custer of the Twenty-first Ohio Infantry had also obtained a furlough, and the two brothers were reunited for the first time since Armstrong had visited home in 1859.

Incidentally, the Custer family was apprehensive about the marriage, and not because they in any way disapproved of Libbie. Armstrong had been helping to support them, and they worried that these funds might end, although he promised they would not. It would take over a year before Emanuel would be able to sell their Ohio farm and profit a thousand dollars.[28]

A series of teas and receptions fêted the couple in the days preceding the ceremony—including a large invitation-only party at the Humphrey House— and the wedding gifts were displayed in the Bacon parlor. The First Vermont Cavalry had sent a silver dinner service, engraved with "Custer"; the Seventh Michigan, a seven-piece silver tea set; Judge Bacon presented his daughter with a Bible; Mrs. Bacon gave Libbie a white parasol covered with black lace; and Armstrong bestowed upon his bride-to-be a gold watch engraved with the initials E. B. C. Dozens of other well-wishers had responded with items such as napkin rings with gold linings, two white silk fans, a knit breakfast shawl, a lavishly bound copy of Elizabeth Browning poems, and a book titled *Whisper to a Bride*, by Lydia Howard Sigourney, and a mosaic chess stand made of Grand Rapids marble.

The Bacons would stay awake all night for fear that burglars would pay them a visit. All the valuable gifts were packed up in the morning and taken to the bank for safekeeping.

At 8:00 P.M. on February 9, 1864, George Armstrong Custer and Elizabeth Clift Bacon were united in marriage at the First Presbyterian Church (which still stands) in a storybook wedding with a standing-room-only congregation of witnesses. Reverend Erasmus J. Boyd, who served as principal at the Young Ladies' Seminary and Collegiate Institute, where Libbie had attended primary school, performed the ceremony, assisted by Reverend D. C. Mattoon. Custer, with hair cut short—to the disappointment of some observers—and wearing his dress uniform, chose his adjutant Jacob Greene as his best man.

Libbie wore a traditional gown, described by her cousin Rebecca Richmond as "a rich white rep silk with deep points and extensive trail, bertha of point lace; veil floated back from a bunch of orange blossoms fixed above the brow." Libbie's long, dark hair had been pinned up under her veil. She was given away by her father, who later boasted, "It was said to be the most splendid wedding ever seen in the State."[29]

The wedding party was whisked away in sleighs with bells jingling for a reception in the Bacon parlor that was attended by more than three hundred guests. The judge provided a generous buffet of delicacies that featured tubs of ice cream. According to Rebecca Richmond, "The occasion was delightful, hilarious and social." She had never met Custer, and found him to be "a trump," a "right bower . . . he isn't one bit foppish or conceited. He does not put on airs. He is a simple, frank, manly fellow. And he fairly idolized Libbie. I am sure he will make her a true, noble husband. As for Libbie, she is the same gay, irrepressible spirit we found her a year ago. They cannot but be happy."[30]

At midnight, the bridal party—four couples—boarded a train, and arrived in Cleveland at 9:00 A.M. the following morning. After an afternoon reception and an evening party hosted by friends, Armstrong and Libbie traveled alone to Buffalo, then on to Rochester, where they attended a performance of *Uncle Tom's Cabin*. The honeymoon continued with the bride and groom calling on Libbie's upstate New York relatives, taking a trip down the Hudson River to visit West Point, and then going on to New York City.[31]

At West Point, Libbie was left in the care of several cadets while Armstrong visited his professors. She would later confess to him that the cadets had escorted her down what was known as "Lover's Walk," and that one of the faculty members had wanted to kiss the bride and had done so. On the train from the Point to New York City, Armstrong fumed in jealous silence with an expression that Libbie described as an "incarnated thundercloud." Reduced to tears, she argued that the professor had been "a veritable Methuselah." And the cadets were but harmless schoolboys. He was not moved. Finally, in exasperation, Libbie cried, "Well, you left me with them, Autie!" Libbie would find that this would not be the last of what she would refer to as his "silent seasons."

No clinical explanation has ever been given for the dark moments in Custer's life, but it can be speculated that he had advanced so far so early in life and was still immature enough to be occasionally affected by the immensity of his responsibilities. He had written that he was acutely aware that the lives of men—and their families—rested on the decisions he made. Perhaps at times he needed to escape within himself to deal with the stress of command. Whatever issue at present bothered him may have been used as an excuse for his behavior and more was made of it than under normal circumstances. [32]

Otherwise, the honeymoon was delightful for them both. Their final stop was Washington, D.C., where they roomed at a boardinghouse, attended church, went sightseeing, and dined with Michigan members of Congress and other dignitaries. One night, they visited the theater for a performance of the play *East Lynne*. Libbie was amused to notice that her Autie "laughed at the fun and cried at the pathos in the theatres with all the abandon of a boy unconscious of surroundings."

In spite of Armstrong's occasional moodiness, the love shared between the two of them from this point forth would endure as one of the great romances in American history.

The joyous Custer honeymoon came to an abrupt end, however, when Armstrong was ordered back to duty for the purpose of being a pawn in a dangerous scheme concocted by Judson Kilpatrick. This action was destined to bring great embarrassment upon the Union and place lives unnecessarily in harm's way.

Eighteen

The Kilpatrick-Dahlgren Raid

Brigadier General George Armstrong Custer and his bride were met at the train station by his staff members and escorted to brigade headquarters at Stevensburg. The newlyweds were taken to Clover Hill, the nearby residence of John S. "Jack" Barbour, president of the Orange & Alexandria Railroad. Custer had chosen this house as his brigade headquarters, and the Barbours had graciously moved out to accommodate this arrangement.

The first floor of the Barbour house served as brigade headquarters, while on the upper level were officers' quarters. The room that would be occupied by the Custers was sparsely decorated with what Libbie would term "rough furniture," including a four-poster bed with calico curtains made by officers' wives, but all in all she was pleased and thought their first home together "looked very homey."[1]

They would not share their new home for long, however. General Custer was almost immediately called away on a special mission. Libbie wrote, "I found myself in a few hours on the extreme wing of the Army of the Potomac, in an isolated Virginia farm-house, finishing my honeymoon alone."[2]

General Judson Kilpatrick had learned that Richmond was presently guarded by only about three thousand old and worn-out militia men, supported by young boys and administrative staff members. He proposed that he could lead a force of four thousand and six guns past Lee's right flank and free the fifteen thousand Union prisoners that were being held in the Confederate capital.

Cavalry commander Alfred Pleasonton objected to the plan, calling it "not feasible at this time," but Kilpatrick went over his head. Kilpatrick managed to gain the backing of President Lincoln and Secretary of War Stanton, which was all that was required to earn General George Meade's approval. Colonel Ulric Dahlgren, the twenty-one-year-old son of Admiral John Dahlgren, volunteered to accompany Kilpatrick. Dahlgren, who had lost a leg at Gettysburg and had been fitted with an artificial limb, was heartily welcomed.

To make this Kilpatrick-Dahlgren Raid, as it would be called, a success, a diversionary force of fifteen hundred horsemen would be required to draw away any interference from Jeb Stuart's cavalry. Armstrong Custer would command these cavalrymen, which many observers believed would be placed in great peril.[3]

Custer was instructed to ride around the Confederate left flank, and "attempt the destruction of the Lynchburg Railroad bridge over the Rivanna, near Charlottesville," a distance of fifty miles into enemy territory. Reports indicated that the bridge was heavily guarded by fortifications and an unknown number of infantrymen—and that at least five thousand cavalrymen were bivouacked in the area. These Confederate cavalrymen were commanded by Brigadier General Tom Rosser, who was quickly earning the reputation as one of the South's most competent leaders of mounted men. And if Rosser required any assistance, waiting down the road was Major General Jeb Stuart and the rest of his Invincibles.[4]

There can be no doubt that George Armstrong Custer viewed this operation as a suicide mission—another Kilpatrick blunder—and that he would have to call upon all his abilities to save the lives of his men. It was too soon, he would have vowed, to make Libbie a widow. He would, however, carry out his mission to the letter, no matter the risk.

General Custer departed headquarters on February 28 to rendezvous at Madison Court House with his ad hoc unit, which would consist of the First and Fifth New York, the Sixth Ohio, the Sixth Pennsylvania, and a battery of artillery. Support at the Madison Court House would be provided by the Sixth Corps, commanded by Major General John Sedgwick, which would wait at that location for the raiders to return.

To Custer's dismay, Kilpatrick had chosen to take with him most of the men from his Michigan Brigade, and he would be commanding troops who were competent but nonetheless a unit comprised of men he did not know. He would be unable to determine beforehand how they would react if he ordered them to charge the cannon's mouth—and vice versa. It was important that soldiers had confidence in their leader when facing combat, and only a small number of these men from Gregg's Second Division and Wesley Merritt's Reserve Brigade had ever served under Custer.

At 2:00 A.M., Custer's cavalrymen were in the saddle and on the move, and at daylight his decoy force crossed the Rapidan at Bank's Ford, where the Sixth Pennsylvania chased away a handful of Rebel pickets. They arrived three hours later at Stanardsville, where another enemy outpost was scattered, and curious townspeople watched the blue column pass through town. Custer had given orders to confiscate every horse and capture all adult men, which came as quite a shock to those in Stanardsville who lost their stock or became prisoners. The procession encountered another group of Rebels north of the Rivanna River, and the Sixth Pennsylvania again pushed them away with a saber charge.[5]

About a half mile across the river—three miles from Charlottesville—Custer ran into four batteries of Jeb Stuart's artillery, commanded by Captain Marcellus N. Moorman, which were resting in winter quarters. Captain Joseph P. Ash and a sixty-man detachment from the Fifth New York were sent to scout the position, and subsequently charged. Ash routed the Southerners, inflicted two casualties, and captured six caissons, nine mules or horses, and two forges, but the artillery pieces were removed to safety. The camp was burned, destroying the personal effects of the Confederate artillerymen.

Custer brought up the main body, but withdrew after receiving an erroneous report of the approach of enemy infantry. Train whistles from the direction of Charlottesville were said to have announced the arrival of Jubal Early's infantry division, but it was a false alarm. The raiders subsequently burned the Rio Bridge and stores of corn and meal at nearby Rio Mills.

At about 9:00 P.M., eight miles southwest of Stanardsville, Custer halted for one hour to rest the horses and allow the men time to eat.[6]

Jeb Stuart had been completely unaware of Custer's raiders until receiving information that afternoon about the enemy approaching Charlottesville. He gathered Brigadier General Williams C. Wickham's brigade, and set out in that direction. The distant sound of firing could be heard, but Stuart was informed that the enemy had withdrawn. He decided to turn his march northward with intentions of intercepting Custer's return at Stanardsville.[7]

General Custer dispatched Colonel William Stedman of the Sixth Ohio ahead with five hundred men as an advance guard, and resumed his march with the main force. Heavy rain and sleet plagued both columns, and the men strayed from the main road into a muddy ravine. The two Parrott guns could not traverse the sloppy ground, and Custer decided to bivouac for the night. Colonel Stedman, "through a misunderstanding," became separated from Custer and, unaware of the whereabouts of the main column, decided to continue on toward the Rapidan, which he reached at about 4:00 A.M.

Artist Alfred Waud of *Harper's Weekly* had accompanied Custer, and commented about enduring the night under such miserable conditions. "The night was rainy, and all had to lie upon the ground and get wet through. It was difficult to get fires to burn, and the rain began to freeze upon the limbs of the trees, so that by morning everything appeared to be cased in crystal."[8]

Stuart's troops also suffered through the freezing night, but reached their destination at about daylight to learn that one detachment had already passed on toward Madison Court House. Stuart would lie in wait for the arrival of Custer. Adjutant Henry McClellan wrote, "For two or three hours his men sat on their horses or on the ground, exhausted, wet, and shivering. They had no food, and no fires can be built. Under such circumstances men cannot fight."[9]

Custer roused his troops into the saddle at daylight on March 1, and rode through Stanardsville toward the Rapidan, destroying everything in their path that belonged to the Confederate government, including weapons and ammunition, food stores, and whisky. The raiders then headed along the road leading toward Madison Court House. About two miles outside of town, scouts informed Custer that Stuart's cavalry had been sighted across a fork in the road that led to nearby fords—Bank's Mills on the Rapidan, and Burton's on the Rappahannock. Custer dispatched a squadron of the Fifth Cavalry to draw out the enemy to determine their strength. The Yankee detail approached, and suddenly the woods were alive with Rebels—two entire regiments—that charged the small party.[10]

Jeb Stuart, aware of Custer's approach, had chosen not to wait for the main body of Union cavalrymen. He personally led this charge with elements of the First and Fifth Virginia into Custer's advance guard. The Union cavalrymen were for the moment forced back to the ravine.

Lieutenant George Yates related what happened next, "General Custer, having made adequate preparations ordered a charge of his entire force. Officers and men moved forward in magnificent style, charging desperately upon the enemy, driving them back in confusion. We captured about half a dozen prisoners, and learned from them that we were fighting General Stuart with two brigades of cavalry, one commanded by General Wickham."[11]

Custer's subordinates were wary about fighting Jeb Stuart, and suggested that they fire the Parrott guns while the rest of the command ran for their lives. Custer naturally scoffed at this idea of sacrificing his artillery and running away. He ordered his guns to open fire, and made a show of forming his troops for what would be a magnificent charge into the jaws of death.[12]

Stuart assumed that his enemy was going to attack in order to push across the Rappahannock. He concentrated his troops at Burton's Ford and prepared for an assault.

Custer, however, was not reckless enough to pick a fight. He had accomplished his mission of diverting the Confederate cavalry, and decided to simply outsmart Stuart.

Custer wrote, "The enemy, mistaking my real intentions, concentrated all his forces at the ford, for this purpose withdrawing them entirely from Banks' and the upper fords. Before he could detect my movement I faced my command and moved rapidly to the road leading to Banks' Ford, at which point I cross the river without molestation."[13]

By the time Stuart realized his enemy's intentions, the Yankees were out of reach. The five hundred cavalrymen that the Rebel cavalry commander dispatched to chase Custer watched as the rear guard of blue cavalrymen crossed the river. The missing Colonel Stedman and the Sixth Ohio had heard the sound of firing, and rushed to safely rejoin Custer's men on the Union side of the river.

Brigadier General George Armstrong Custer and his relieved and joyous command arrived back at Madison Court House and the protection of the Sixth Corps just before darkness fell.

Custer reported marching 150 miles in forty-eight hours, and capturing over fifty prisoners, about five hundred horses, and a Virginia state flag, without suffering any casualties. In addition to destroying a substantial amount of supplies, a bridge, six artillery caissons, and three large mills, Custer also returned with about a hundred runaway slaves who had fled local plantations.[14]

General Meade called Custer's raid "perfectly successful," and Alfred Pleasonton's assistant adjutant general sent a note that read, "The major-general commanding desires me to express his entire satisfaction at the result of your expedition, and the gratification he has felt at the prompt manner in which the duties assigned to you have been performed." *The New York Times* reported that "The diversion created in favor of Gen. Kilpatrick could not have been greater."[15]

Custer gained further tribute when the March 19 issue of *Harper's Weekly* featured one of his classic charges on the front cover, and a week later a double-page spread in the center of the magazine displayed drawings of his raid. Custer's lauded diversionary action, however, could not assure that Kilpatrick would be capable of duplicating that success in Richmond.[16]

In truth, the Kilpatrick-Dahlgren raid on Richmond was an embarrassing utter failure. Kilpatrick, leading one column of three thousand cavalrymen against only five hundred defenders with six pieces of artillery, lost his nerve on the outskirts of Richmond and pulled back to the safety of Union lines on the Lower Peninsula. A second column under Ulrich Dahlgren was ambushed, and every one of its hundred men was either killed or captured. Dahlgren, who was killed, was found to be carrying documents instructing his raiders to burn the city and kill President Davis. The contents of Dahlgren's papers incensed the Southerners, and inspired within them a renewed fighting spirit. [17]

This folly by Kilpatrick, who was described by one staff member at army headquarters as "a frothy braggart without brains and not overstocked with desire to fall on the field," cost the Union 340 men killed, wounded, or captured, and over 500 horses lost. To Custer's great personal distress, 176 of those casualties were members of the Michigan Brigade.[18]

Major James Kidd, who had led a detachment of the Sixth Michigan during the Richmond raid, observed, "It was a fatal mistake to leave Custer behind. There were others who could have made the feint which he so brilliantly executed, but in a movement requiring perfect poise, the rarest judgment and the most undoubted courage, Kilpatrick could illy spare his gifted and daring subordinate; and it is no disparagement to the officer who took his place at the time to say that the Michigan brigade without Custer at that time, was like the play of Hamlet with the melancholy Dane left out. With him the expedition as devised might have well been successful; without him it was foredoomed to failure."[19]

On March 2, Custer returned to his winter headquarters at Clover Hill near Stevensburg—and to the arms of wife Libbie. While waiting for Armstrong to return, Libbie had been well cared for by Chief of Staff Jacob Greene, and former slave Eliza, who had assumed "sole control" of the household chores—as cook, laundress, and domestic overseer—with limited assistance from Johnny Cisco, who Libbie called "Eliza's special henchman about the kitchen." Libbie, who was warmly welcomed by Eliza, described treatment by their servant being "as if you were a child and had a nurse."[20]

Libbie had been especially taken by Eliza, writing, "Eliza awaited me with motherliness and beaming face. She was young though with mature ways. She had taken care of her invalid master and mistress and had that rock-a-bye tone and coddling way that I fell victim to very soon."[21]

Libbie's introduction to military life—especially as the wife of a general—was an eye-opening experience. "All the new life was in the way of surprise," she wrote. "If I had been transported to Mars it could not have been greater." She was most impressed by the respect afforded her husband by "so many observances that go to enhance that dignity that hinges around a King." While other officers and their wives rode about in army ambulances, "my general has a carriage with silver harness that he captured last summer, and two magnificent matched horses (not captures). We have an escort of four or six soldiers riding behind. Such style we go in!"[22]

With minimal duties for Custer to perform, he and Libbie were free to spend their days getting to know each other, dining with other generals—including Alfred Pleasonton, who invited them to a six-course dinner—and on sunny days taking the occasional carriage or horseback ride, escorted by a handful of troopers.

During this time, Libbie also set her sights on the reformation of her husband. She knew that he no longer drank, but had heard that "General Kilpatrick used an oath with every sentence he uttered, and that General Custer was not better. I know this is exaggerated. But . . . God cure you of it." She also despaired that while she was trying to live a Christian life, Autie apparently had a lack of faith. Another "stain" on his character was his propensity for gambling.[23]

Armstrong readily admitted that he certainly had faults, but to his credit had overcome temperance. His profanity, which he regarded as a minor vice, was considered too satisfying to give up. He did, however, pledge to quit gambling—but would in the future have problems keeping this promise.[24]

The attempts by Libbie to improve her husband could not be called nagging, only a wife trying to help him become as good a person as he could be, and did not come between them whatsoever. She had written to him, "I tremble at the responsibility; I am but a little girl—not of course in years, but being an only child . . . It is a solemn thought to become a wife." [25]

On March 14, the couple was involved in a carriage accident when the team bolted. Libbie was unharmed, but Armstrong suffered a concussion when he was thrown from the carriage. "Everybody seems to think it is a miracle I was not killed," he remarked.[26]

To add to the pain of his head injury, Custer was about to become entangled in an espionage investigation.

A young lady who had been accused of espionage claimed that in the summer of 1863 she had been with the Union cavalry "as the friend and companion of Genl. Custer." Anna E. "Annie" Jones testified that General Judson Kilpatrick had become jealous of her relationship with Custer, and, in retaliation, alleged that she was a Confederate spy. She was subsequently arrested and incarcerated in Washington for three months. Pleasonton requested that both Kilpatrick and Custer explain their relationships with the woman.[27]

Allegations of womanizing were the last thing that the newlywed Custer needed at the moment—or at any time for that matter—but in keeping with his style on the battlefield, he faced them head-on. Kilpatrick refused to respond, but Custer prepared an official statement, which was submitted on March 22. He admitted that the woman in question had visited his camp on two occasions—the second time arriving in an ambulance furnished by Major General Gouverneur Warren. "Her whole object and purpose in being with the army," Custer speculated, "seemed to be to distinguish herself by some deed or daring . . . In this respect alone, she seemed to be insane . . . So far as her statement in relation to Gen. Kilpatrick and myself goes, it is simply not true. I do not believe," he added, "that she is or ever was a spy." [28]

Not surprisingly, evidence does not exist to substantiate or debunk the allegations directed at Custer or Kilpatrick by Miss Jones. Whether either man engaged in a relationship with her would be mere conjecture, a minor footnote of inconsequential nature that apparently was not worthy of documenting by those who shared campfires with the two generals. Perhaps desperation compelled the accused spy to prove her credibility in defense of the espionage charges by implicating these officers. Regardless, Annie Jones eventually received a parole, and vanished from the public record.

On March 24, Custer, still recuperating from his concussion, and his wife resumed their extended honeymoon with a twenty-day furlough that began when they boarded a train to Washington, where they would dine with Congressmen and dignitaries—and even saw President Abraham Lincoln at the theater when they attended a performance of *Rip Van Winkle*. Custer hobnobbed with Congressmen on the house floor, while Libbie watched from the balcony. The couple was recognized on the street, and Libbie vowed to start a scrapbook and collect clippings of her Autie.[29]

Libbie wrote to Daniel and Sophia, "None of the other generals received half the attention, and their arrivals are scarcely noticed in the papers. I am so amazed at his reputation I cannot but write you about it. I wonder his head is not turned. Tho not disposed to put on airs, I find it agreeable to be the wife of a man so generally known and respected."[30]

When Armstrong returned to duty at the front, Libbie took a room at Hyatt's Sixth Street Washington boardinghouse. The general would be taking along with him Eliza, Johnny Cisco, and his headquarters staff members, all of whom would normally be available to satisfy Libbie's every whim.

Before long, Libbie found herself inundated with invitations to socialize with Washington dignitaries and politicians. Michigan representatives F. W. Kellogg and Senators Zachariah Chandler and Morton Wilkinson were eager to take Libbie under their wings and make sure she did not become bored. At times, these older men would imbibe to excess and become lecherous, but Libbie was always able to delicately fend off their advances without hurting their feelings. She made it a point to tell Autie about these advances, perhaps to remind him that other men found her attractive. Armstrong had learned his lessons well, and would never think of confronting these powerful men who would be allies at promotion time.[31]

The highlight of her social life without question was a visit to the White House with Representative and Mrs. Kellogg. They arrived at 10:00 A.M., and were engulfed in a huge crowd that pushed off the porch and into "the holy of Holies, the Blue Room." This group was met there by a tall, gaunt man who appeared to be aging as each day passed, who stood beside his "short, squatty, and plain" wife.

In turn, Libbie Bacon Custer was introduced to Abraham Lincoln, the

President of the United States. Lincoln briefly shook her hand, and as she moved away he quickly reached to hold her hand once more, and said, "So this is the young woman whose husband goes into a charge with a whoop and a shout. Well, I'm told he won't do it any more"—an implication that marriage might have made him soft. When Libbie disagreed, the president replied, "Oh, then you want to be a widow, I see." Libbie and Abe Lincoln shared a laugh—perhaps enjoying a moment of gallows humor. Upon leaving the White House, Libbie mentioned to a secretary, "to tell Mr. Lincoln he would have gained a vote, if soldiers' wives were allowed one."[32]

Libbie must have once again gone through a private giddy spell when she returned to her room. She had met and had a conversation with the President of the United States, and he had actually known about the exploits of her husband.

Back at the war, the Union high command was about to undergo drastic changes, and the future of the cavalry—and George Armstrong Custer—would be greatly affected. There would be a new commander, a reorganization, and eventually a new mission that would alter the course of the war. The Union cavalry was about to be unleashed on its enemy.

Nineteen

———◆———

Change of Command

O ne of the officers on that train that Armstrong and Libbie Custer had
taken to Washington was a man whom Libbie described in a letter to
her parents, "Sandy hair and mustache; eyes greenish-blue. Short, and Mother,
not 'tasty' but very ordinary-looking. No show-off but quite unassuming,
talked all the time and was funny."[1]

This particular general happened to be Ulysses S. "Sam" Grant, who had
been summoned east to become general-in-chief of the army. Meade remained
in command of the Army of the Potomac, but Grant, the hero of Shiloh,
Vicksburg, and Chattanooga, had been handed authority no other military
man had wielded since George Washington, and would command Meade.

Grant had been born on April 27, 1822, at Point Pleasant, Ohio, the son
of a tanner who was descended from Puritans who immigrated to New En-
gland in the early seventeenth century. His father worried that Sam was too
lazy to make anything of himself in life, and managed to secure the boy an
appointment to West Point in 1839. Grant was not the most attentive student—
preferring romantic novels to studying tactics—but graduated in 1843 ranked
twenty-first out of thirty-nine cadets.

Grant was commissioned a lieutenant in the Fourth U.S. Infantry, and four years later fought in Mexico, winning brevets for gallantry at Molino del Rey and Chapultepec. His service after the war included a series of remote garrisons, where he could not bring his wife, Julia, and his two current children (he would have two more). This boredom and loneliness led to his drinking in excess, a habit that he continued at times throughout later years. In July 1854, he resigned his newly appointed captaincy, and returned home to his family in Missouri.

Grant had a difficult time making a living as a civilian, resorting at one point to peddling wood on the street, and grudgingly relied on charity from his father. The family moved into his parents' home, and Grant worked at a number of menial and low-paying jobs. Then came the outbreak of the Civil War.

With the assistance of a patronage-minded congressman named Elihu B. Washburne and Governor Richard Yates, Sam Grant was appointed colonel of the Twenty-first Illinois Infantry in June 1861. Two months later, while training his troops, Grant was promoted to brigadier general of volunteers.

In November 1861, Grant engaged Confederates near Belmont, Missouri, but fared poorly and was relegated to an administrative post. He escaped his desk job in February 1862, and served under Major General Henry Halleck, and brilliantly commanded troops that captured Forts Henry and Donelson on the Tennessee and Cumberland rivers. Two months later, he was routed near Pittsburg Landing and Shiloh Church, but rallied the next day to repulse the enemy. He went on with an attempt to seize Vicksburg, Mississippi, that December, but was unable to secure the city.

Grant did not give up on Vicksburg, and devised hard-hitting tactics that led to the fall of that city in July 1863. This victory earned him a promotion to major general. He followed up his successes with victories in Chattanooga, Lookout Mountain, and Missionary Ridge, and was lauded as the top general in that theater. President Lincoln rewarded him with the three-star rank and made him general-in-chief.[2]

This shakeup at the top would also be of interest to Brigadier General George Armstrong Custer, who would soon find himself without the comfortable and protective relationship he had enjoyed with General Alfred Pleasonton.

One of General Grant's first decisions was to relieve Major General Alfred Pleasonton as commander of the Cavalry Corps and replace him with a thirty-three-year-old West Pointer named Philip H. Sheridan.[3]

Although the date and place of his birth is uncertain, Phil Sheridan claimed to have been born in Albany, New York, in 1831. He was the third child of six born to immigrants from County Cavan, Ireland, and was raised in Somerset, Ohio. As a boy, Sheridan worked in a dry goods store, eventually rising to head clerk and bookkeeper. In 1848—full grown at five feet, five inches tall—he falsified his birth certificate and received an appointment to West Point, where he was suspended for a year for fighting with a classmate, future Civil War general William R. Terrill. Finally, in 1853, he graduated thirty-fourth in his class of forty-nine cadets.

Sheridan served in various posts throughout Texas, California, and the Pacific Northwest, fighting in the Yakima and Rogue River wars and being wounded by a bullet grazing his nose in 1857 in Oregon Territory. During his duty in Oregon, he lived with a Native American mistress, the daughter of the chief of the Klickitat tribe, and learned skills necessary for negotiating with the various tribes. He was promoted to first lieutenant in March 1861 and captain in May, just prior to the Civil War.

In the early stages of the war, Sheridan served with the Thirteenth Infantry in southwest Missouri, and then moved on to become quartermaster and commissary for the regiment. Seeking field action, Sheridan managed to be appointed colonel of the Second Michigan Cavalry in May 1862. One month later, he distinguished himself in a victory at Booneville, Mississippi, and was rewarded with the rank of brigadier general. He continued to impress his superiors in actions at Perryville while commanding an infantry division and at Stone's River when he was credited with saving Rosecran's army. In March 1863, he was promoted to the rank of major general.

The new major general distinguished himself once again at Chickamauga as commander of the Army of the Cumberland, and caught General Grant's eye at Chattanooga while leading a brilliant charge up Missionary Ridge.[4]

In appearance, "Little Phil," as he was nicknamed, did not by any means portray the prototype image of a cavalryman. He was "a small, broad-shouldered, squat man, with black hair and a square head." Lincoln wryly described him as "a brown, chunky little chap, with a long body, short legs, not enough neck to hang him, and such long arms that if his ankles itch he can scratch them without stooping." But what the Irishman lacked in physical presence was offset by his demeanor on the field of battle. "In action," one officer noted, "or when specially interested in any subject, his eyes fairly blazed and the whole man seemed to expand mentally and physically. His influence on his men was like an electric shock."[5]

Grant gave Phil Sheridan command of the Union cavalry—three divisions totaling about ten thousand men. Little Phil wasted no time reshaping the Union cavalry corps to suit his own taste in fighting men. The first move came when Wesley Merritt, who was thought by most observers to be in line as Buford's successor, was passed over for command of the First Division in favor of Brigadier General Alfred T. A. Torbert, a thirty-three-year-old West Pointer from Delaware. Surprisingly, Torbert, who had led a brigade in the Sixth Corps, had no experience in the cavalry. He had been, however, a schoolmate of Phil Sheridan.[6]

Command of the Second Division remained in the capable hands of General David Gregg, and—to the relief of the officers and troops—Judson Kilpatrick was relieved of his command and assigned, or banished, to the Western Theater. Custer believed that he was a worthy successor, and had been told as much by Kilpatrick. Instead, command of the Third Division was given to Brigadier General James H. Wilson. Wilson, who had been a classmate of Wesley Merritt at West Point, was an engineering officer and had never served in the cavalry. But the twenty-six-year-old had one major advantage over other qualified candidates. He had formed a friendship with U.S. Grant in the West, and it was Grant who had personally handpicked him for the command.[7]

There was one problem in this chain of command, however. Wilson had received his promotion to brigadier general on October 30, 1863, which made him junior in rank to Custer, Merritt, and Henry Davies. Regulations stated that Wilson could not command senior officers. To remedy the situation, Custer's brigade—the First, Fifth, Sixth, and Seventh Michigan—was transferred to the senior one-star position in the cavalry—the First Brigade of Torbert's First Division. Henry Davies' brigade was assigned to Gregg's Second Division. Custer was pleased with the new assignment, and with Torbert, whom he called "an old and intimate friend of mine and a very worthy gentleman."[8]

Despite George Armstrong Custer's father-son relationship with Pleasonton, whose removal must have saddened him, he professed an agreeable initial opinion of Phil Sheridan. This view was the result of a "get acquainted" meeting between Little Phil and Old Curly on the evening of April 15. "I remained at Genl. Sheridan's headquarters last night and to-day until nearly four o'clock," Custer wrote to Libbie. "[He] impresses me very favorably." He also mentioned his new cavalry commander to his sister, "Gen Sheridan from what I learn and see is an able and good commander and I like him very much."[9]

General Grant was anxious to test the resolve of Lee's Army of Northern Virginia—and Sheridan was equally as eager to pit his horsemen against Jeb Stuart. And now that the winter cold had given way to spring, it was time to heat up the action on the field of battle.

Phil Sheridan had ambitious plans for his ten-thousand-man cavalry, and sought a meeting to present them to Meade. He envisioned his horsemen as an independent unit with the freedom "to march where we pleased, for the purpose of breaking down General Lee's communications and destroying the resources from which his army was supplied." Sheridan also proposed that he draw Stuart's cavalry away from the protection of the infantry, where he could destroy it.

Meade denied Sheridan's requests, and insisted that the cavalry perform the traditional role of subservience to the infantry and screen and protect its movements. The decision did not set well with Sheridan, but the temperamental Irishman had no choice but to bow to Meade's wishes—for the time being at least.[10]

General Grant was anxious to take the offensive, and devised a strategy that called for his army to cross the Rapidan and Rappahannock rivers at various points—up the James; south of Richmond; up the Shenandoah to threaten the South's granary; and a march by Sherman on Atlanta. The main body would pass through the Wilderness toward Richmond, a movement that would assuredly draw the Army of Northern Virginia from winter quarters to engage the superior Union force. It would then become a war of attrition, with the numerical odds favoring Grant's army.[11]

At daylight on May 4, the Union cavalry departed winter quarters in the vicinity of Culpeper-Stevensburg and rode south. General Custer was disappointed to learn that his Wolverines had been assigned Torbert's rear—to guard the supply train—while the Second and Third Divisions led the infantry into the dense, second-growth timber known as the Wilderness. Grant had intended to pass beyond Lee's right flank and traverse this brambly arborous maze, where Fighting Joe Hooker had been defeated the previous year, before engaging the Confederates, rather than under conditions that would obstruct his artillery and impede cavalry movements.[12]

At about 2:00 A.M. on May 6, Custer's brigade with the cumbersome wagon train was on the move in the direction of Ely's Ford, trailing by some miles the main army. The column arrived at its destination by mid-morning, and the tedious task of crossing to the south bank was executed. The cracking of distant firing from the west could be distinctly heard as the wagon train rolled along, finally reaching Chancellorsville at noon and camping about a mile beyond on the slope of a plateau overlooking the Wilderness.[13]

The nearby thick woods produced an eerie, confounding acoustic effect, which compelled staff member George B. Sanford to remark, "The sound of musketry exceeded in intensity anything to which I have ever listened before or since." Custer could only anxiously gaze into that dark wall of timber, listen to the roar of gunfire, and imagine the battle that was unfolding without him.[14]

That battle was Tom Rosser's brigade confronting Wilson's cavalry and driving them back toward the vicinity of Todd's Tavern. Grant's intention to clear the confines of the Wilderness before Lee could react had failed. Rosser's initial engagement had triggered a firestorm of conflict that escalated into full-scale, continuous skirmishing between the two armies, which for the most part took place along roads and around the few clearings. It was virtually impossible to maintain military formations within the tangled undergrowth, which caused mass confusion on both sides and neutralized the numerical superiority of Grant's force.[15]

At Confederate field headquarters, a temporary command post off Plank Road in a small field hidden by dense foliage, General Lee was holding a conference with Generals Stuart, Pendleton, and Hill and other staff members. Within moments, this meeting was abruptly interrupted by the unexpected appearance of a small group of the enemy who had emerged from the woods within point-blank range. Lee hurriedly leaped onto his horse and galloped to safety, Hill ran on foot into the woods, and the others scattered for their lives. The Union intruders, who had mistakenly wandered ahead of their lines, were just as surprised as the Confederate officers and vanished in the woods just as quickly as they had appeared. The Confederacy had escaped what could have been a disastrous day had just one volley been fired by the Federals.[16]

The line of battle extended for six miles through the Wilderness. All afternoon, the men from both sides fought their way through thorny thickets while under constant fire from their enemy. They emerged from this prickly jungle late in the afternoon with ripped uniforms and faces scratched and bleeding.[17]

General Custer's ears had been filled with the sounds of distant fury all day, and now as nighttime silence settled around the Wilderness, the orders that he had been waiting for finally arrived. The Wolverines would move out at 2:00 A.M. and reinforce David Gregg's division, which was positioned south of Todd's Tavern. Wilson's division had been bested all afternoon by Stuart's cavalry, and had been saved from total disaster only by the timely arrival of Gregg. Custer had been relieved of the frustrating duty of dragging along the supply train at the rear, and was elated that he would have the opportunity to participate in tomorrow's struggle for control of the Wilderness.[18]

Several days before embarking on this operation, Custer had written to Libbie (from Camp Libbie, Virginia), and professed his most intimate preparations when a battle was imminent. "On the eve of every battle in which I have been engaged," he wrote, "I have never omitted to pray inwardly, devoutly.

Never have I failed to commend myself to God's keeping, asking Him to forgive my past sins, and to watch over me while in danger . . . and to receive me if I fell, while caring for those near and dear to me. After having done so all anxiety for myself, here or hereafter, is dispelled. I feel that my destiny is in the hands of the Almighty. This belief, more than any other fact or reason, makes me brave and fearless as I am."[19]

Custer arrived before daylight, and deployed his troops at the intersection of Furnace Road and Brock Pike. Pickets from the First and Sixth Michigan were posted around a five-hundred-yard-wide field—which was cut in half by a sloping ravine—while the remainder of the men were hidden in the woods. Custer received an order from Gregg to move down Brock Pike with two brigades and harass Longstreet, who was moving on the left flank. But before the order could be executed, the Thirty-fifth Virginia Cavalry, one of the regiments in Tom Rosser's brigade, burst from the trees to assail Custer's picket line, their Rebel yells splitting the stillness.

Custer immediately sprang into action. As Rosser's men streamed from the trees to drive back the Federal pickets, Custer rode to the front of his brigade and ordered the band to play "Yankee Doodle," which signaled to every Wolverine to form for a charge. Custer rode to the front, drew his saber and extended it toward the enemy, and shouted, "Forward, by divisions!"[20]

Major James Kidd described the charge, "The two regiments (the First and Sixth) charged with a yell through the thick underbrush out into open ground, just as the rebel troopers emerged from the woods on the opposite side. Both commands kept on in full career until they reached the edge of the ravine, when they stopped, the rebels apparently surprised by our sudden appearance and audacity, Custer well content with checking the vicious advance."[21]

Rosser rolled out a section of artillery, and reinforced his attack with another brigade on foot that threatened the right flank. Custer countered by deploying the Fifth Michigan to meet that rush and moved the Seventh beside the First. Rosser launched a series of frontal assaults, bolstered by part of Fitz Lee's division, but the Wolverines held firm. Gregg sent up eight artillery pieces, which Custer quickly brought into play and silenced the enemy's guns. Finally, Colonel Thomas Devin's brigade arrived, and Custer struck the Confederate left with the Fifth and Sixth Michigan as the Seventeenth Pennsylvania and the First and Seventh Michigan charged from the ravine.[22]

James Kidd wrote how his commander made an inviting target for enemy sharpshooters, "Custer was always on horseback. He was never seen on foot in battle, even when every other officer and man in his command was dismounted. And he rode close to the very front line, fearless and resolute."[23]

Custer reported, "The enemy, after contesting the ground obstinately, was driven from the field in great disorder, leaving his dead and many of his wounded upon the ground. We also captured a considerable number of prisoners, who informed us that we had been engaged with Fitzhugh Lee's division of cavalry. Orders having been received not to pursue the enemy beyond this point, we remained on the field until near night."[24]

Since daylight, Jeb Stuart's cavalrymen had been patrolling Plank Road in support of Longstreet. The day ended with Stuart halting a retreat, caused by a furious Federal charge, by placing his staff officers across Plank Road to restore order to the lines. At nightfall, neither side had asserted domination over the other, but the South had gained one strategic advantage by securing the area around Todd's Tavern.[25]

The Confederate army, however, did suffer one significant loss that can be attributed to the difficulty of fighting in such dense foliage. Reminiscent of the blunder that took the life of Stonewall Jackson, General James Longstreet was mistaken for the enemy by his own men, who fired a volley at him from point-blank range. Longstreet was struck by a bullet that entered near his throat and passed into his right shoulder. He was carried from the field with a serious wound that would incapacitate him for some months.[26]

An earlier incident that day demonstrated the aggressive nature of Robert E. Lee. At one point in the battle, Lee happened upon a brigade of Texans who were preparing to charge the enemy. He impulsively decided to lead this charge, but the Texans refused to move until Lee removed himself to a place of safety. The bridle of his horse was grabbed by some of the men, with calls for "Lee to the rear!" The commanding general grudgingly complied, and it became Longstreet's duty to tactfully inform Lee that he was much too valuable to be leading charges.[27]

On the morning of May 7, neither side resumed the infantry battle, but Custer and his Wolverines pushed two miles down Brock Pike to connect with Gregg. Custer encountered Fitz Lee's brigade three-fourths of a mile beyond the crossroads of the Pike and Furnace Road, and engaged in a fierce engagement. With assistance from Gregg, the combined force successfully drove the Confederates out of the area. The Wolverines settled in on Gregg's right flank, and were not challenged for the remainder of the day.[28]

The Confederates, however, had withdrawn from Todd's Tavern. Wilson's Third Division, supported by infantry, had advanced toward the crucial road juncture of New Spotsylvania Court House. By evening, Wilson was tangling with Fitz Lee's troops, while Stuart guided the approach of infantry reinforcements. The Union cavalrymen had managed to push Rosser's brigade from Spotsylvania, but Sheridan suddenly recalled Wilson to Fredericksburg, and any pursuit was abandoned. The opposing infantries were involved in a heated battle until the Union troops withdrew, and quiet once again settled over the Wilderness.[29]

The battle to occupy Spotsylvania resumed on the following day, May 8. Not more than a few miles away from the scene of the action at Spotsylvania, the name of Jeb Stuart was being bandied about in a heated discussion between Generals Sheridan and Meade.

Meade had made a habit of issuing orders for the cavalry without bothering to consult or inform Sheridan. This incessant meddling had provoked Little Phil's fiery Irish temper, which boiled over during a confrontation between the two strong-willed men.

"Meade was very much irritated," Sheridan later wrote, "and I was none the less so. One word led to another until, finally, I told him that I could whip Stuart if he would only let me, but since he insisted on giving the cavalry directions without consulting or even notifying me, he could henceforth command the Cavalry Corps himself—I would not give it another order." Little

Phil added, "If I am permitted to cut loose from this army I'll draw Stuart after me, and whip him, too."[30]

Meade reported this incidence of insubordination by Sheridan to Grant, likely with the prospect of being backed up in his handling of the cavalry and its commander. Instead, Grant replied, "Did Sheridan say that? Then let him go out and do it."

Meade might not have agreed with Grant, but dutifully issued orders for Sheridan "to proceed against the enemy's cavalry." For the first time in the war, the Union cavalry had been cut loose from the infantry, and was authorized to operate as an independent unit.

Sheridan summoned without delay his three division commanders— Wesley Merritt temporarily replacing Torbert, who was sidelined by an abscess at the base of his spine—to relate his plans and expectations. The cavalry would prepare to depart in the morning, and would at that time assume a route around Lee's flank in the direction of Richmond, a movement that would assuredly draw Stuart and his horsemen in hot pursuit. "We are going out to fight Stuart's cavalry in consequence of a suggestion from me," Sheridan told them. "We will give him a fair, square fight; we are strong, and I know we can beat him, and in view of my recent representations to General Meade I shall expect nothing but success."[31]

Each man present understood that the only hope the Union cavalry had of ever reaching Richmond would be over the dead body of Jeb Stuart. And there may have been an anticipation that the end could be in sight now that tactics had changed and they had a specific target to eliminate. No doubt many of them thought with confidence that if they were Jeb Stuart they would be very afraid right now—and for good reason.

Twenty

---◆◎◆---

Jeb Stuart

A t daylight on May 9, Sheridan's cavalry—seven brigades, six batteries,
and a wagon train—ten thousand men strong—saddled up and rode
out in a column of fours that stretched for thirteen miles and required four
hours to pass any given point.

Custer's Michigan Brigade led the impressive procession, which proceeded east of the infantry battle raging at Spotsylvania, then south on the
Telegraph Road. Sheridan moved them at an easy pace that would conserve
both man and horse in the event of an engagement, and, perhaps more importantly, would make them quite conspicuous to Jeb Stuart's scouts.[1]

This bold move by the Union cavalry to pass around the farthest of Stu-
art's outposts was immediately detected by Williams Wickham's brigade.
Wickham dispatched a courier to inform Stuart, and then dashed off in pursuit. The Confederate cavalry reached the Union rear guard, the Sixth Ohio
Cavalry, and engaged in a running battle. The Sixth Ohio was quickly reinforced by the First New Jersey, and made a determined stand near Mitchell's
Shop, which succeeded in temporarily fighting off the Rebels. By this time,
Stuart had mounted three brigades (Fitz Lee, Lomax, and Gordon)—about
forty-five hundred men—and took up the chase.[2]

Sheridan turned his column and took the route toward Beaver Dam Station on the Virginia Central Railroad. With so many troops on the move, this would indicate to Stuart that Beaver Dam was not his enemy's final destination, but the march would proceed toward Richmond. Stuart had to interpose his cavalry between Sheridan and the capital. Another factor, however, likely affected Jeb Stuart. His family had established a residence in Beaver Dam Station, and were now placed in imminent danger.[3]

Sheridan did not intend to ignore the railroad town. Shortly before sunset, Custer's Wolverines approached Beaver Dam Station to observe a detachment of the enemy escorting about four hundred Union prisoners, captured in the Wilderness battle, toward the railroad depot for transport to Richmond. One battalion of the First Michigan was ordered to charge the Rebels, and succeeded in liberating the prisoners as well as capturing a number of the enemy. The freed soldiers included one colonel, two lieutenant colonels, and many other officers, who were most grateful to their rescuers.

That fortuitous timing was further evidenced when the piercing shriek of locomotive whistles reached their ears from the direction of the depot. The impatient engineers were waiting for delivery of their human cargo, but were also there to restock Lee's advance supply base.[4]

Custer's First and Sixth Michigan dashed into town and easily seized two locomotives and three trains laden with several million dollars' worth of supplies that had been destined for the Confederate army. Custer reported that the boxcars were full of "bacon (200,000 pounds), flour, meal, sugar, molasses, liquor (confiscated by provost guards), and medical stores; also several hundred stand of arms, a large number of hospital tents." In all, supplies composing 1,500,000 rations had been waylaid.[5]

Custer distributed all the rations that his men could carry, and then burned what remained. He also ordered the one hundred railroad cars and depot put to the torch, disabled the locomotives by firing artillery shells through the boilers, tore up the tracks in the vicinity, and cut ten miles of telegraph line. The Wolverines then departed to bivouac south of the South Anna River.[6]

Jeb Stuart rode through the night, crossed the North Anna at Davenport's

Bridge, and reached Beaver Dam Station on the morning of May 10. He must have approached with some anxiousness, which heightened as he viewed the destruction that Custer's troops had left in their wake. His wife and children were staying at Beaver Dam, the town's namesake plantation, owned by Colonel Edmund Fontaine, located a mile and a half outside of town. To his profound relief, his family had not been harmed. Without taking the time to dismount, Jeb visited briefly in private with Flora, affectionately kissed her good-bye, and rode off with one of his staff, Major Reid Venable.

Stuart was strangely somber upon departing, and rode for some distance in contemplation before speaking. In a step out of character, he confided to Venable that he never expected to outlive the war and, further, that he did not want to survive if the South was defeated.[7]

Sheridan had roused his men early on May 10, and angled toward Hanover Junction on a pace more leisurely than on the previous day. Several miles before reaching that depot, the column crossed the South Anna River and headed northeastward toward Ashland Station. Sheridan's troops would cover eighteen miles to Ground-Squirrel Bridge before resting for the night.[8]

Stuart, however, could not afford to tarry in his pursuit of the Union cavalry. It would be far more advantageous for his troops to fight with their backs to the home front than it would be if Sheridan succeeded in threatening Richmond before Stuart could interpose his cavalry between the enemy and the capital. He dispatched Gordon's brigade to nip at Sheridan's heels, and led the three other brigades (Fitz Lee, Lomax, and Wickham) on an alternate route in an effort to get ahead of the Yankees.

Stuart reached Hanover Junction after dark and, at the request of Fitz Lee, reluctantly agreed to rest the weary men. Adjutant Henry McClellan was directed to remain awake, and ascertain that Lee's troops were back in the saddle by 1:00 A.M. Stuart rode ahead to Taylorsville, two and a half miles south, where he and Venable slept for several hours.[9]

At the same hour that Fitz Lee resumed the march, Sheridan had his cavalrymen, with Merritt's division in front, on the move down Mountain Road toward its junction with Telegraph Road. Sheridan was confident that this was the area where Jeb Stuart would make his stand.[10]

Stuart led his cavalrymen down the Telegraph Road through familiar country. On the left side of the road they passed the Winston farm, the place where Jeb had camped twenty-three months earlier on the night before his ride around the Army of the Potomac. Stuart came upon the road that led to Ashland—the area where he had met Stonewall Jackson at the beginning of the Seven Days' Campaign—and learned that a squadron of the Second Virginia had earlier driven part of the First Massachusetts out of town, but not before the enemy had destroyed a train and a storehouse of supplies. McClellan reported that as they rode along Stuart "conversed on many matters of personal interest. He was more quiet than usual, softer, and more communicative."[11]

At 10:00 A.M., after nine hours of steady riding, Stuart and his troopers arrived at the intersection of Telegraph and Old Mountain roads. These two roads merged into Brook Turnpike, which led to Richmond—only six miles beyond. The place was known as the Yellow Tavern, named for a nearby abandoned, ramshackle inn whose bright color had by now faded to gray.

Stuart had succeeded in placing his men ahead of the Union cavalry's drive toward Richmond, and mulled his defensive options. He could assume a position directly in front of Sheridan's approach, or remain on the flank, where he could attack his enemy as they rode toward the capital. With the numerical odds stacked against him by at least three to one—ten thousand Yanks as opposed to three thousand Rebs—he decided that it would be more prudent to strike the enemy's flanks rather than attempt to absorb a frontal assault.

With that in mind, Jeb dispatched Henry McClellan to Richmond to inform General Braxton Bragg, who commanded the city's defense force, about his disposition. The eventual strategy would depend on Bragg's ability to defend the capital. Stuart, however, was unaware that Sheridan's primary objective was not Richmond but to destroy once and for all the legend of invincibility possessed by the Confederate cavalry and its bold commander.[12]

Without knowing Sheridan's intentions or how many troops were at Bragg's disposal—and with Gordon's brigade at the enemy's rear—Stuart finally compromised between his two defensive options. He deployed Wickham's brigade along a ridge line on the right, parallel to Telegraph Road facing south-southwest. Lomax was placed on the left along another ridge at right angles to the road. Stuart's dismounted cavalrymen maintained an excellent defensive position, supported by several artillery pieces, but nonetheless were greatly outnumbered.[13]

Within an hour, the Union cavalry had advanced to the vicinity of the Yellow Tavern and observed the line of gray-clad defenders. One detachment was dispatched across country to seize the Brook Turnpike and effectively cut off Stuart from Richmond. Merritt sent Gibbs and Devin to feel out Stuart's lines, while General Custer's Wolverines waited in reserve. The Union troops were met with intense fire from the woods where Lomax's right connected with Wickham's left. This threat compelled the entire Confederate line to open up, and the Federals answered in kind. Full-scale combat ensued, much of it hand to hand at close quarters, as the Union force attempted to assert its will upon its unyielding opponent.

Custer's brigade was finally ordered to the front, and at once came under blistering fire from the woods directly ahead. Old Curly ordered the Fifth and Sixth Michigan forward to silence the Rebel riflemen. Before the Sixth could dismount, an eager Colonel Alger led his Fifth ahead on foot into an open field that stretched for some four hundred yards to a ridge where Lomax's men waited. Alger's troops immediately came under a vicious cross fire as scores of Southerners materialized from the timber to draw a bead on the exposed Yankees. In the words of Sergeant E. L. Tripp, "We were trying to return the fire, shooting in three directions."

Custer galloped up in clear view of enemy sharpshooters, and shouted to Alger's men, "Lie down, men—lie down! We'll fix them!" He ordered Major Kidd's Sixth Michigan to contend with the flank and, joining that unit with the Fifth, formed a skirmisher line and moved steadily forward. Custer's brazen maneuver—not to mention the firepower produced by the seven-shot Spencer repeaters—drove the surprised Virginians up the slope to their original position. The Wolverines remained in a swale, and exchanged fire with the enemy for about two hours while Custer went off to reconnoiter and consult with Merritt.[14]

Stuart was not concerned for the moment with the fact that his enemy had gained a position between his troops and Richmond. More significant was holding the flank on Telegraph Road, and his troops had responded to the initial Union challenge with unflinching determination. He was most impressed with the grit displayed by the Fifth Virginia, whose position was crucial to the overall defense of the line. This unit was commanded by Colonel Henry C. Pate, an officer whom Stuart had assisted in freeing from John Brown in Kansas. That good relationship, however, had deteriorated into a bitter feud when Stuart had sided with Tom Rosser rather than Pate in a dispute that had led to Pate standing a court-martial.

Now, during the heat of the battle, Stuart rode over to Colonel Pate and told him how much he was needed, asking him to hold off the enemy at all costs. Pate regarded Stuart, and then firmly said, "I will do it." Stuart thanked him for his resoluteness. After a moment, the colonel extended his hand, and Stuart warmly accepted this gesture of conciliation.

Stuart returned to his headquarters, and resumed the direction of his men as Sheridan's cavalry pressed the issue. Casualties on both sides mounted as the Yankees probed every inch of the line in an effort to detect any vulnerability. One of the areas most contended was the position of Colonel Pate's Fifth Virginia, which time and again repelled the earnest assailment. Although the Virginians had thus far successfully held their ground, word reached Stuart that their commander, Henry Pate, was killed in the process.[15]

At about 2:00 P.M., Henry McClellan returned from Richmond. Due to the presence of the enemy, the adjutant had been obliged to detour across fields adjacent to Brook Turnpike in order to avoid capture. McClellan's message from General Bragg, however, greatly relieved Stuart's concern for the security of the capital. Richmond was defended by four thousand irregular troops supported by artillery, and three brigades from Petersburg were presently en route to bolster the fortifications. Bragg was confident that his force could withstand an enemy assault.

During a lull in the fighting, Stuart relaxed near one of the batteries on the right of his line and conversed for more than an hour with McClellan, Venable, and other staff members. He expressed his intention to maintain his present position, and speculated that if reinforced by infantry coming up from Richmond he could assume the offensive and cripple the Yankee cavalry. "I cannot see how they can escape," he observed.

Perhaps that was wishful thinking, but certainly in keeping with Stuart's usual optimism. Apparently Jeb had not as yet arrived at the realization that Sheridan's true mission was annihilation of the Confederate cavalry. Stuart, in Sheridan's position, without question would have deployed a rear guard to occupy his enemy, then made a mad dash for the capital with his main force. For that reason, Stuart was of the opinion that the worst was over, and that Sheridan would at some point break contact and head south. [16]

The idea of withdrawing when his quarry was at bay never entered Phil Sheridan's mind. In fact, Little Phil was in the process of finalizing a plan designed to strike the entire length of the Confederate line with one massive assault. This concentrated thrust would deny Stuart the opportunity to shore up his defenses in any one place by moving reinforcements from another. But, at about four o'clock, before Sheridan could launch the attack, Stuart opened up with an artillery barrage from the south end of his line that wreaked havoc on Custer's horse holders and the ranks of the First and Seventh Michigan.[17]

"From a personal examination of the ground," Custer wrote in his official report, "I discovered that a successful charge might be made upon the battery of the enemy by keeping well to the right." Custer informed Merritt that he had detected a weakness that he could exploit with a mounted charge. Merritt approved, saying, "Go in, General. I will give you all the support in my power." Custer rode off to form his command as Sheridan joined Merritt and was briefed about the plan. "Bully for Custer!" Sheridan exclaimed. "I'll wait and see it."[18]

Custer formed Lieutenant Colonel Peter Stagg's veteran First Michigan in a mounted column of squadrons out of sight in the trees, and ordered Russell Alger's Fifth Michigan and James Kidd's Sixth Michigan to move forward on foot as a diversion to confuse the enemy. He was concerned about his left, and borrowed—with Sheridan's permission over the objections of the brigade commander—the First Vermont from Wilson's Third Division to guard that flank.[19]

Lieutenant Asa B. Isham of the Seventh Michigan, who had been nicked by a shell fragment from the offending Rebel battery, described the appearance of his comrades, "My attention was diverted by what appeared to be a tornado sweeping in the rear. It was the First Michigan Cavalry, in a column of squadrons, moving at the trot. It wheeled upon my flank as a pivot with beautiful precision, and it came to a halt a little in advance of me, squarely in front and in full view of the Rebel guns. This splendid body of horsemen was halted but for a moment, when General Custer reined in at the head of it with an order to 'charge,' and away it went toward the guns. It was swallowed up in dust and smoke, a volume of exulting shouts smote the air, the earth shook and it was evident that a besom of destruction was sweeping over the face of nature."[20]

One of Merritt's staff remembered, "His [Custer's] headquarters flag—of the gayest colors—was flying in advance of the moving mass of glittering blades. The shrill blast of one hundred bugles and the familiar air of 'Yankee Doodle' rang out upon the battlefield while brave men of the Michigan brigade rode boot to boot into what seemed the very jaws of death."[21]

The Confederate battery intensified its shell and canister barrage directed at both the diversionary force and the riders as they entered the clearing. To make matters worse, the terrain that Custer and the First Michigan would be required to traverse was rife with obstacles. The horsemen anxiously waited while five fences were opened to permit passage, and temporarily broke formation to cross a narrow bridge that only three at a time could pass over. Advancing to within two hundred yards of the battery on the bluff, the troopers dug their spurs into their horses' flanks and charged with what Custer termed "a yell that spread terror before them."

The Rebel battery was obliged to contend with the carbine and cannon fire from the advancing Fifth and Sixth Michigan, which enabled the charging horsemen to gain momentum and sweep into the position before any effective resistance against them could be mounted. The Confederate gunners were overwhelmed. Many fell under the sabers of the Wolverines, while two cannon, two limbers of ammunition, and a large number of prisoners were captured.[22]

Jeb Stuart mounted, and hurried with his staff to the scene of this breach in his line to encourage Lomax's regiments, which had fallen back about four hundred yards to a ravine and re-formed at right angles with Wickham to halt the Yankee advance for the time being. Stuart sat in the saddle, exposed to the enemy fire as he directed his men. Reid Venable was concerned for Jeb's safety, and remarked that men behind trees and other cover were being hit, perhaps Stuart should be more cautious. The Knight of the Golden Spurs, who had managed to elude enemy bullets during countless battles, laughingly replied, "I don't reckon there is any danger!"[23]

General Phil Sheridan was elated by Custer's audacious actions, and jubilantly ordered Merritt to "send a staff officer to General Custer and give him my compliments. The conduct of himself and his brigade deserves the most honorable mention."[24]

But Custer's job was far from finished. The First Michigan was exhausted and required reinforcement to dislodge the Rebels who had withdrawn to the ravine. He dispatched the mounted Seventh Michigan toward the enemy line, but the terrain impeded progress and the troopers became bunched up and easy targets for Rebel sharpshooters.[25]

Stuart decided that the best defense was an offensive. To that end, he ordered Venable to prepare Lomax's brigade for a counterattack. Meanwhile, Jeb rode to the left flank to join the First Virginia just as a combined force of blue-clad cavalrymen assailed that position.

To relieve the pressure on the First Michigan, Custer had assembled every available man from his four brigades of Wolverines and, reinforced by the First Vermont, threw them all at once against the tenuous Confederate position.

Stuart calmly advised, "Steady, men, steady; give it to them!" He emptied his pistol at the onrushing Union troopers, but his line virtually dissolved from the might of Custer's charge. Stuart shouted for them to rally, but the retreat was in full stride.[26]

Nearby, forty-four-year-old Private John A. Huff of Company E, Fifth Michigan, a veteran of the Second U.S. Sharpshooters, steadied his .44-caliber Colt pistol upon a fence rail. He peered through the sights to observe an officer wearing a plumed hat who sat astride his horse—only ten to fifteen yards distant—while firing his own pistol in the midst of the confusion. Huff took careful aim, and squeezed the trigger.[27]

Jeb Stuart was about to shout a command when a sudden, stabbing pain in his right side knocked him off balance. He reeled in the saddle, his head dropping, his hat tumbling to the ground, but remained astride his horse. Concerned troopers noticed, and rushed to Stuart's side to inquire about the seriousness of his wound. "Go tell General (Fitzhugh) Lee and Doctor Fontaine to come here," Jeb rasped.[28]

Captain Gus W. Dorsey, who commanded Company K, understood the danger of an incapacitated Jeb Stuart lingering in the line of fire. He led Jeb's horse toward the rear, but the animal resisted and became unmanageable. Stuart was incapable of controlling his mount, and asked Dorsey to help him down. Although fearing that the enemy would appear at any moment, Dorsey grudgingly obliged. The fierce battle still raged, and Stuart ordered Dorsey to gather his men and engage the enemy, but the captain refused to leave until Stuart was safely aboard another horse and headed for the rear.

Private Fred Pitts soon arrived with his horse, and Jeb was helped into the saddle. At about this time, a greatly distressed Fitz Lee, upon hearing the news, had raced along the entire length of the line to reach Stuart. Lee was the senior officer on the field now that Stuart was out of action, and was told by his commander, "Go ahead, Fitz, old fellow. I know you will do what is right!"[29]

Dorsey, Pitts, and others helped balance Stuart atop this mount and led him beyond the limits of another Union charge. All the while, Stuart implored that his men must repel the enemy and protect Richmond from Sheridan. An ambulance was provided, and Jeb was placed in the bed. Major Venable ordered the vehicle moved to the low land near the bridge, which would assure that they were completely out of range.

During this short jaunt, Stuart noticed numbers of his cavalrymen running away in a disorganized retreat. The angry commander shouted as loudly as possible in his condition, "Go back, go back and do your duty, as I have done mine, and our country will be safe. Go back, go back! I had rather die than be whipped!"[30]

Dr. John B. Fontaine and a staff member, Lieutenant W. Q. Hullihen, turned Stuart over on his side to allow the doctor to examine the wound.

Fontaine could not readily determine the extent of the wound, only that Stuart had a bullet lodged in his lower abdomen, which, if it had pierced the liver, would be fatal. Stuart's immediate danger, however, was going into shock, and the doctor prescribed whisky as a stimulant. Stuart at first declined, citing the pledge of abstinence that he had made to his mother. After some coaxing by Venable, Stuart reluctantly consented. By this time a large number of men had gathered around their commander. Stuart noticed them, and said, "Go back to the front, I will be well taken care of. I want you to do your duty to your country as I always have through my life."[31]

The next order of business would be to transport Stuart to Richmond. Union cavalry held Brook Pike, which compelled the ambulance and escort to make a series of wide detours. Jeb Stuart would endure great pain, apparently caused by peritonitis—an abdominal inflammation—on this jostling journey over seven miles of unfamiliar, winding, and bumpy roads before reaching his destination.[32]

Phil Sheridan permitted his men several hours of rest and celebration before resuming his march down Brook Pike toward Richmond. The Rebels had mined the road, and Sheridan ordered twenty-five prisoners to crawl on hands and knees in front of the column to alleviate this threat. But that was not the end of Sheridan's obstacles to taking Richmond. A Rebel spy had managed to appoint himself guide for the march into Richmond, and led Wilson's division directly into the city's defenses. Wilson's troops were taking a beating from the Home Guard, and were pinned down. Sheridan wisely called a halt to bivouac for the night and assess his situation in the daylight.[33]

Long after dark, Jeb Stuart arrived at the home of his brother-in-law, Dr. Charles Brewer, on Grace Street in Richmond. Word of his wounding had spread, and the foremost medical men of the city were waiting to attend to the famous cavalry general. After examinations had concluded, however, the consensus opinion was that nothing could be done but apply ice to the wound. Stuart would remain in intense pain, his disposition in the hands of the Almighty.

Major Heros Von Borcke, who was convalescing in the city, attempted to telegraph Stuart's wife, but the wires had been cut by the Union cavalry. The message was finally relayed by a circuitous route, and would not reach his wife until about noon on the following day. According to Von Borcke, after he left the telegraph office the operator heard that Stuart was getting better, and changed the wording of his message from "the General is dangerously wounded" to "slightly wounded."[34]

May 12 dawned with rain pouring down, and Phil Sheridan could now fully comprehend the ticklishness of his situation on the outskirts of Richmond. His cavalry was caught between the enemy earthworks and the swollen Chickahominy. The Confederates gave every indication that rather than remaining in a defensive posture they would mount an attack.

In addition, Stuart's cavalry under Fitz Lee were engaged with Gregg in the rear. Sheridan remained confident that, in spite of his present circumstances, he could take Richmond, but realized that he could not hold it. Therefore, he must fight his way out before becoming trapped by Rebel reinforcements. He ordered George Armstrong Custer to secure a crossing for his command five miles above the city on the north side of the Chickahominy River at Meadow Bridge.[35]

Custer reached the swollen river to discover that the planks had been removed from the bridge, which made it impassable. The only other way across was a railroad trestle that was too hazardous for horses to cross. On the north bank, Confederate cavalrymen lay in wait with artillery and rifles at the ready. Custer dismounted Alger's and Kidd's regiments, and ordered them to move across the railroad trestle as quickly as possible. The Rebels instantly opened up with artillery in an effort to destroy the trestle.[36]

Major James Kidd described the precarious crossing, "One man, or at the most two or three, at a time, they tiptoed from tie to tie, watching the chance to make it in the intervals between the shells."

Alger's men were the first across, and fanned out toward the left to lay down a base of fire to cover the movement of the Sixth. Custer was observing the crossing when a shell exploded in a ditch near him, splattering him with mud. He remarked to Major Charles Deane, "Well, that is pretty hot for us, Major, but we will get them out of that pretty soon."

True to his word, before long, Kidd's Sixth Michigan had joined Alger on the other side, and they successfully kept the Rebels at bay while engineer and pioneer teams laid a floor across the rails utilizing cut timber and lumber from nearby houses.[37]

By mid-morning, the trestle was deemed negotiable. Custer led the Seventh Michigan and elements of the Fifth and Sixth across, while the First Michigan was dispatched to rout the Rebels. The Wolverines chased their enemy for two miles, capturing several prisoners.

General Sheridan was so impressed with Custer's initiative that he remarked to Colonel Alger, "Custer is the ablest man in the Cavalry Corps." The actions of Brigadier General James H. Wilson, however, were less than acceptable. His blunder the previous evening had nearly cost Sheridan the Cavalry Corps. The First Vermont, which had been on detached duty with Custer and now returned to Wilson, sent a message to the Michigan Brigade requesting "a pair of Custer's old boots" to lead their division.[38]

While the Union cavalry crossed the Chickahominy, Jeb Stuart's wife, Flora, was receiving the first word of her husband's wounding. The telegram finally arrived in Beaver Dam Station while she was at the station assisting wounded troops sent from the fighting at Spotsylvania. Edmund Fontaine had accepted the message, but inexplicably neglected to show it to Flora until they had returned home.

Fontaine, president of the Virginia Central Railroad, secured a locomotive and car for Flora and her children, which took them as far as Ashland before they were compelled to transfer to an ambulance because the tracks between that point and Richmond had been destroyed. The party traveled on their difficult journey through a blinding thunderstorm along treacherous roads. Each time soldiers were encountered, Flora would inquire about her husband's condition. At one point, she was informed that the wound had not been that serious, which raised her hopes of finding him alive when she arrived.[39]

An alert Jeb Stuart was visited by Von Borcke in the morning; later Henry McClellan, who had delivered messages from Fitz Lee to General Bragg, arrived at his bedside. Between spasms of pain, Stuart dictated his final wishes to his trusted adjutant. Personal effects would go to his wife. Venable was to receive his gray horse, McClellan the bay. "You will find in my hat a small Confederate flag," Stuart related, "which a lady of Columbia, South Carolina, sent me, with the request that I would wear it upon my horse in a battle and return it to her. Send it to her. My spurs, which I have always worn in battle, I promised to give to Mrs. Lilly Lee of Shepherdstown, Virginia. My sword I leave to my son."[40]

Stuart was interrupted by the sound of distant artillery fire, and inquired about its origin. McClellan explained that Fitz Lee was attempting to trap Sheridan down the Chickahominy. "God grant that he be successful," Jeb fervently answered; then, with a sigh, "But I must be prepared for another world." After a moment, Stuart said, "Major, Fitz Lee may need you." McClellan understood that it was time for him to leave. He pressed his commander's hand before heading to the door, where he encountered President Jefferson Davis, who had entered.[41]

"General," Davis asked, taking Stuart's hand, "how do you feel?"

"Easy, but willing to die, if God and my country think I have fulfilled my destiny and done my duty."

The president departed after a brief visit. Stuart's condition worsened throughout the afternoon. He suffered painful seizures, and passed in and out of consciousness, occasionally shouting orders, and often asking about Flora. According to Von Borcke, Stuart's final connected words were spoken to him. "My dear Von," Stuart said, "I am sinking fast now, but before I die I want you to know that I never loved a man as much as yourself. I pray your life may be long and happy; look after my family after I'm gone, and be the same true friend to my wife and children that you have been to me."

He asked Dr. Brewer whether he might survive the night. When told that death was near, Jeb nodded, and said, "I am resigned if it be God's will; but I would like to see my wife . . . But God's will be done."[42]

At seven o'clock, everyone in the house gathered around Jeb's bed. Reverend Joshua Peterkin, an Episcopal minister, led them in prayers and the singing of "Rock of Ages," Stuart's favorite hymn. Jeb made a feeble effort to sing along, then turned to Brewer, and said, "I am going fast now. I am resigned; God's will be done." He then drifted into unconsciousness.[43]

At 7:38 P.M., James Ewell Brown Stuart passed into the hands of his God, whom he had trusted throughout his life.[44]

Jeb Stuart, the Knight of the Golden Spurs, a true Southern patriot who had given the Southern people hope and pride when he had ridden around McClellan's army and when he made his forays into the North to wreak havoc on the infrastructure, was not invincible after all. Few officers in either army were as capable in the role of leadership, as he had proved when he assumed command at Chancellorsville, but a chance encounter with a random bullet had cut short a brilliant career. His death was quite a shock, not only to his cavalry and every soldier in the Confederate army but to every Southerner—man, woman, and child—each of whom must have experienced a dark shroud of doom gradually descending over their prospects for a positive outcome of the war.

Twenty-one

---◆◉◆---

Trevilian Station

James Ewell Brown Stuart, the heart and soul of the Confederate cavalry, was dead. Robert E. Lee was devastated by the loss of his trusted cavalry commander. He mourned, "I can scarcely think of him without weeping."[1]

But the war went on, and the question regarding Stuart's successor was one that greatly troubled General Lee—Wade Hampton and Fitzhugh Lee were the candidates.

Hampton was older than Lee and possessed more prestige within the army than did Fitz. Hampton also had been promoted to brigadier general more than two months before Lee, although both had been made major general on the same date. They were basically equals when it came to field command. Fitz Lee, however, embodied more of Stuart's personality and joy of battle.

General Lee's difficulty in choosing between them stemmed from the fact that the two men, who were outwardly cordial to each other, were secret rivals. Virginian Lee represented the domination of the cavalry—and indeed the army—by his home state; Hampton was a South Carolinian who likely resented Virginia's domination of the army.[2]

Lee judged that appointing one over the other at this critical time might be demoralizing. With the wisdom of Solomon, the Confederate commander decided that each would command a division on equal terms and report directly to and receive separate orders from headquarters.[3]

General Custer's Wolverines enjoyed a period of "placid contentment" during the week following the battle at Yellow Tavern. The cavalry had moved to Haxall's Landing on the James River, where they refitted from quartermaster and commissary stores. According to Major Kidd, "The soldiers smoked their pipes, cooked their meals, read the papers, wrote letters to their homes, sang their songs and, around the evening camp fires, recalled incidents, humorous, thrilling or pathetic, of the march and battle-field. There was not a shadow on the scene."[4]

One of those who wrote home was George Armstrong Custer. "We have passed through days of carnage and have lost heavily," he told Libbie. "We have been successful . . . The Michigan Brigade has covered itself with undying glory . . . Genl. Sheridan sent an aide on the battlefield with his congratulations. So did Genl. Merritt: 'The Michigan Brigade is at the top of the ladder.'"[5]

But this period of rest and refitting could not last forever. After all, there was a war to be waged.

On May 21, General Grant ordered Meade south with intentions of placing the Union between Lee's army and Richmond. General Lee was aware of this ploy, and hurried his troops to assume a strong defensive position south of the North Anna River. Grant dispatched three of his four corps across the waterway to engage his enemy, but the Rebels effectively held their own for three days to thwart any passage. During this time, Sheridan's cavalry corps had ridden up the Peninsula to rendezvous with the main force on May 24 near Hanover Court House.[6]

Grant was not about to relinquish his initiative and abort his thrust toward Richmond on account of this stalemate at the North Anna. He decided on May 26 to send his reunited army in a southeasterly direction with the objective of skirting Lee's right flank. Wilson's division feinted toward the Confederate left in hopes of confusing Lee, while the remainder of the army headed toward the designated crossing point, which would be the Pamunkey River at Hanoverstown.

Sheridan's two divisions rode through the night in a driving rainstorm with orders to secure the crossing position. At daylight on May 27, Custer's brigade was sent to cover the construction by a New York engineer regiment of a pontoon bridge over the Pamunkey. His men soon came under fire, and Custer ordered the First Michigan across the river to rout the Rebels and clear the pathway.

Custer, incidentally, suffered another dunking when his horse faltered and he was compelled to dismount in midstream and swim to shore. He good-naturedly endured the hoots and cheers of his troops.

By 10:00 A.M., however, Old Curly was back in the saddle at the front of the column as Sheridan's men, whose mission it would be to draw Wade Hampton's cavalry away from the main force, led the way when the Union army marched safely across the Pamunkey.[7]

It was not long before David Gregg's Second Cavalry Division approached Haw's Shop, a blacksmith establishment located three miles from Hanovers-town, where he encountered two divisions of Hampton's cavalry. The Rebels were secured in the woods behind a swamp, protected by sturdy breastworks and supported by artillery. Gregg ordered a frontal assault. The Union troops determinedly advanced, but in a series of attacks and counterattacks that would last six hours, sustained severe casualties and found themselves pinned down. By early afternoon, the Confederate cavalrymen had taken the upper hand and were gradually penetrating the center of Gregg's line.[8]

Custer's troopers had skirmished with a Rebel detachment that morning in a three-mile running battle that had resulted in the capture of forty gray-clad prisoners. The triumphant Union cavalrymen were resting and water-ing their mounts along Crump's Creek when at two o'clock Sheridan ordered Custer to reinforce Gregg's beleaguered command.

The Michigan Brigade immediately mounted and set off on an arduous ride through the thick trees and underbrush west of Haw's Shop. It was not until about 4:00 P.M. that Custer arrived at Gregg's rear to discover that the

Union troops were barely managing to hang on to their position at the tree line facing their enemy. The field was being hammered with the impact of bursting artillery shells, and the fire from the Rebel sharpshooters was said to sound "like that of hot flames crackling through dry timber."[9]

Custer dismounted his men and formed them into two skirmisher lines—the First and Sixth Michigan on the right side of the road leading to the enemy entrenchments, the Fifth and Seventh on the left. At about this time, Wade Hampton learned that the Union army had already crossed the Pamunkey, which had been his original reconnaissance mission, and commenced a withdrawal.

Custer noticed this retreat. True to form, he rode to the front of his men, exposed to enemy fire, waved his hat, called for three cheers, and ordered a charge into what one observer called "that sanguinary hell of fire."

In spite of the gradual withdrawal of Confederate forces, several regiments of South Carolinians armed with Enfield rifles had remained at their fortifications to initiate a cross fire that made them the most stubborn foe Michigan ever had met in battle. Custer's Wolverines, however, were resolute and eventually convinced their enemy to flee.

The Michigan Brigade lost forty-one, killed in what was called by a Union soldier "one of the most gallant charges of the war." Burial and stretcher details combed the battlefield to attend to the "bleeding, mangled multitude [who] covered the surrounding grounds."

Custer's aide Jacob Greene had been hit in the head by a spent bullet that knocked him from his mount but only stunned him. Lieutenant James Christiancy had ridden to the front in the thickest of the fighting to encourage the troops. He was struck by two bullets—one inflicting a dangerous wound in the thigh, the other clipping off the tip of his thumb—while another round killed his horse. Christiancy was sent to Washington to be nursed by Libbie Custer, and later would be awarded the Medal of Honor for his actions.[10]

One other notable casualty was Private John A. Huff of Company E of the Fifth Michigan—the man credited with killing Jeb Stuart at the Yellow Tavern. Huff was reportedly struck in the head by a rifle ball, and died three weeks later.[11]

Much praise for the battle at Haw's Shop was reserved for George Armstrong Custer, who had a horse shot out from under him during the fray. Typical of the accolades from witnesses was the letter written to his parents by Major James Kidd, who described Custer as, "So brave a man I never saw and as competent as brave. Under him a man is ashamed to be cowardly. Under *him* our men can achieve wonders."[12]

After dark, Meade's infantry relieved Custer's exhausted cavalry, which then marched five miles southeast to Old Church and camped a mile or so from the mouth of Totopotomy Creek. They would remain at this position until the thirtieth, when Sheridan ordered them toward Cold Harbor.[13]

Grant had recognized the futility of charging Lee's fortified positions, and decided to return his attention to the strategy of attempting to cut off his enemy's main supply routes. Sheridan would lead his two cavalry divisions—Torbert's First and Gregg's Second—about six thousand strong—in an attempt to flank Lee to the far west.

On the afternoon of May 30 near Cold Harbor, Torbert's division came under heavy Confederate fire from Fitz Lee's horsemen. Custer's Michigan Brigade had been held in reserve, but on orders from Torbert dismounted and rushed forward to engage the enemy. The Confederates were quickly pushed back, and, as Custer readied a saber charge, the Rebels fled en masse to escape the wrath of the Union cavalrymen. After dark, with Cold Harbor thought to be relatively secure, Sheridan pulled out—only to be halted in his tracks when ordered by Meade to hold the place at all hazards. The troops spent the night fortifying the breastworks and waiting for an attack.[14]

The efforts of the Union cavalrymen served them well. At dawn on June 1, one division of Confederate infantry supported by artillery burst from the woods and stormed across the field to attack the entrenched Union troops. The bravery of the Rebels cannot be overstated as they charged, were forced back by barrages of withering fire from Union Spencer repeaters, and charged again, only to be ripped apart and regroup to assault the position once more.

Custer distinguished himself by riding along the lines—the only blue-clad horseman exposed to the enemy—while exhorting his men to maintain their positions and practice fire discipline. The ferocious battle continued for Custer and his Wolverines until about noon, when they were relieved by the Sixth Corps, commanded by Major General Horatio G. Wright. The cavalry mounted to the sound of the brigade band's rendition of "Hail Columbia," and rode to White House, where they camped for five restful days while the fighting at Cold Harbor raged on without them.[15]

The outcome of that battle would be disastrous for the Union. At dawn on June 3, General Grant, in a move that he would live to regret, ordered forty thousand soldiers in double lines along a six-mile front to execute a frontal assault against the well-entrenched Confederate positions. When the bloodletting had ended, nearly seven thousand Union soldiers had been killed while the Rebels lost less than fifteen hundred.[16]

While the two bloodied armies faced each other across the battlefield, Grant formulated an alternate strategy to avoid the folly of assaulting Lee's fortified positions. The plan called for Union forces to once again make an effort to cut off main supply routes from Richmond, this time by crossing the James River.

To that end, two divisions of Sheridan's cavalry were dispatched to ride seventy miles to the west with orders to destroy the Virginia Central Railroad and the James River Canal. They would then capture the town of Charlottesville and, if possible, link up with Major General David Hunter's forces, which were advancing on Lynchburg. The cavalry strike force rendezvoused at New Castle Ferry on June 6, were issued three days' rations and two days' forage, and set out the following morning.

Part of Grant's strategy was to draw the Confederate cavalry away in pursuit, thereby clearing the path for his own movement to Petersburg, the main supply depot twenty-two miles from Richmond. Grant was not disappointed; Wade Hampton's and Fitz Lee's divisions—about five thousand men—raced to intercept Sheridan.[17]

By the time Sheridan's cavalry bivouacked, at nightfall on June 10 near Clayton's Store, Hampton was in possession of Trevilian Station, three miles to the north on the Virginia Central. Fitz Lee was camped about four miles southeast of Hampton at Louisa Court House, three miles from the position of Custer's brigade.

Both commanders planned to attack without delay. Hampton believed that Sheridan would remain at Clayton's Store, and devised a two-prong offensive. His own division would charge into the enemy head-on while Lee's men would hammer them on the flank. It was Sheridan, however, who seized the initiative.[18]

Merritt's and Devin's brigades were in position just after sunrise to greet and surprise two Confederate lead brigades only several hundred yards from Trevilian Station as they moved down the road. The troopers dismounted and engaged in a furious battle from opposite stands of timber.

Custer had been assigned the task of protecting the left flank and, if possible, attacking the enemy from the rear. He led his troopers southwestward through growth so thick that his column of fours was reduced to double or single file. At about 8:00 A.M., Captain Hastings of the advance unit reported to Custer that he had emerged from the woods to observe hundreds of Rebel supply wagons, pack mules, and ambulances moving down the road.

One can only imagine Custer's ecstatic reaction to this news. The caravan, which he deduced was Wade Hampton's personal baggage train, was a prize that he could not resist attempting to capture. Custer immediately dispatched an aide to order Colonel Alger and the Fifth Michigan to charge the wagon train. Major Kidd's Sixth Michigan and Pennington's Battery M would support the charge.

Alger dashed from the woods in a hastily formed line, and quickly overwhelmed the defenseless string of wagons. The Fifth scattered the frightened teamsters and animals, and captured six caissons, forty ambulances, and fifty wagons. But, instead of being content with his booty, Alger, a man whom Custer later graciously described as being motivated by "the impulses of a pardonable zeal," noticed that up ahead waited the horse holders who were tending mounts belonging to Hampton's dismounted division, which was engaged with Merritt and Devin. Alger, contrary to Custer's orders, raced past Trevilian Station depot and gathered up some fifteen hundred horses and eight hundred prisoners.[19]

This bold act was met by a swift response when a wave of dismounted Confederates disengaged from fighting Merritt to arrive and effectively cut off Alger from Custer and the trailing Sixth Michigan. To make matters worse, Custer learned that additional Confederate troops were closing in on him—his rear was under attack by Fitz Lee's brigade, and the brigade commanded by Brigadier General Tom Rosser was presently routing the Fifth Michigan. The Wolverines would soon find themselves surrounded.

Custer, who was alone except for his staff, orderlies, and Pennington's battery, was determined to fight his way out. He relayed urgent orders for Kidd's Sixth to "take a gallop and pass the battery."

The Sixth Michigan regiment was strung out through the thick woods, and only four companies were able to respond to the order. Kidd located Custer, who with his staff was returning close-range Rebel fire. The general, according to Kidd, "never lost his nerve under any circumstances" but was "unmistakably excited" at that moment, and simply shouted, "Charge!"

Kidd's troopers drew sabers and galloped forward into the enemy, which, to their surprise, permitted the Union horsemen to pass through their ranks. Then, mounting a pursuit, the Rebels chased the disorganized Sixth Michigan directly into the retreat of the Fifth, which was being pressed by Rosser. Kidd's men bore the brunt of the charge. Many of them, including Major James Kidd, were captured by the swarming Confederates.[20]

Although Custer was decidedly on the defensive, he counterattacked with four companies of the Sixth Michigan commanded by Captain Manning D. Birge. Rosser could not withstand this added pressure, and Major Kidd and many of his men were rescued. In the meantime, the First and Seventh Michigan had arrived, and Custer barricaded the road and deployed those troops in a field southwest of the station.[21]

The Michigan Brigade, however, remained trapped and outnumbered—"caught on the inside of a living triangle," one participant wrote in his diary. Lee attacked from the east, Rosser from the west, and Hampton advanced from the north. The officer in charge of Custer's baggage train approached and asked if the wagons should be moved to the rear. Custer agreed, and then wondered aloud, "Where the hell is the rear?" The answer to that question was quite obvious—there was no rear.

The Rebels were relentless, gleefully taking advantage of their superiority over their beleaguered enemy. Custer formed his men into a circle for a last stand, and prayed that Merritt and Devin could fight their way through Hampton and arrive in time to save them.

Rosser blasted into Alger's command to liberate many of the wagons and men that the Fifth had recently captured, and rounded up about 150 prisoners. Lee's men crashed through to recover all their lost horses and wagons, and also captured the wagons and records at Custer's headquarters.

The Rebels had seized Custer's personal papers, love letters from Libbie, an ambrotype of Libbie, his commission to general, inscribed field glasses, dress uniform—even his underclothing. In addition to his possessions, Custer's cook, Eliza, was taken, but escaped later that day. His chief of staff, Jacob Greene, and orderly Johnny Cisco were not so lucky, and remained prisoners at Wade Hampton's headquarters. In Custer's words to his wife, "Would you like to know what they have captured from me? Everything except my toothbrush. I regret the loss of your letters more than all else." The letters were later published in a Richmond newspaper, much to the delight of its readers.[22]

Throughout this ordeal, however, Custer added to his growing legend as a cool and calculating tactician under the direst of circumstances. "Custer was everywhere present giving instructions to his subordinate commanders," Kidd later wrote.

He courageously rode around his lines to deploy and encourage his men, and in the process had three horses shot out from underneath him. When any part of the line was breached, Custer would quickly dispatch troops to reinforce that position. When one of Pennington's guns was captured, Custer personally led thirty men to retake the piece in a vicious hand-to-hand fight.

At one point, Custer ventured alone onto the field and, although struck and stunned by a spent bullet, carried to safety a wounded trooper. When the brigade's color bearer was mortally wounded, it was Custer who grabbed the flag, ripped it from the staff, and draped it over his shoulder for safekeeping.[23]

Custer's prayers were finally answered when Sheridan led an assault with

Merritt's and Devin's brigades into Hampton's line north of Trevilian Station to relieve the pressure. Custer formed the Seventh Michigan and pursued the retreating Rebels that had captured his headquarters wagon train. He managed to recover a few wagons—but none of his personal belongings.

Both exhausted armies camped for the night—the Confederates withdrawing south and west while the Federals remained in the fields around Trevilian Station. Custer's Wolverines had suffered one of the darkest days in their history with 41 killed, 375 wounded, and 242 captured—including nearly half of the Fifth Michigan.[24]

Sheridan was determined to continue the offensive, and at mid-afternoon the following day, Custer was assigned the task of engaging Fitz Lee while Merritt attacked Hampton's flank. The widespread fighting—which featured seven dismounted assaults by the Union cavalry, each repulsed—raged well into the evening, and exacted a toll nearly as large as the previous day.

At ten o'clock, Sheridan disengaged his troops, bivouacked, and then commenced a difficult march to reunite with the main force near Petersburg on June 25.[25]

Sheridan may have failed to severely damage the Virginia Central Railroad or rendezvous with Hunter, but he had nonetheless succeeded in proving once again superiority over his enemy.

In the two-day battle of Trevilian Station, the Union lost a reported 1,007 killed, wounded, and captured. Although exact figures are not available, Confederate losses likely were slightly higher, which was more devastating to the South than the North due to its dwindling supply of men available as replacements.[26]

Custer was afforded a respite from war when, on June 28, he greeted his wife, who had arrived aboard the steamer *River Queen* at City Point, Virginia. The couple then retired to Washington, where, on July 11, Custer requested and was granted a twenty-day furlough. Armstrong and Libbie traveled to Monroe, Michigan, to visit family and friends, and returned to the capital on July 29. Custer reported back to duty the following morning, on a day that would change the course of the war.[27]

Twenty-two

———◦◦◦———

The Shenandoah

On July 29, the Union army detonated four tons of gunpowder that had been stored within a mine chamber situated under Confederate lines at Petersburg. The explosion created a huge crater and killed or maimed about three hundred Southerners, but the ensuing Union assault resulted in a wholesale slaughter of Yankee troops.

In another stunning blow to the Union, Confederate cavalry burned the community of Chambersburg, Pennsylvania, to the ground, destroying over four hundred buildings. This brazen raid struck fear into the hearts of Northerners, who feared that the Rebels' next stop would be Washington.[1]

At the same time, Union cavalry troops under General George Stoneman failed in an attempt to liberate prisoners at Andersonville Prison in southwest Georgia. This notorious hellhole held about thirty-two thousand Union enlisted men, who were crowded into a stockade with inadequate shelter, poor sanitation, and a lack of food and medicine, making for miserable conditions. The impoverished South could not afford to feed and care for these captives, and General Grant contributed to the suffering by refusing to exchange Confederate for Union prisoners. News of Andersonville Prison—which would have thirteen thousand graves by the end of the war—greatly affected the conscience of the public in the North.

These embarrassing events, coupled with Grant's inability to clear the Shenandoah Valley of Confederate troops, threatened Lincoln's reelection chances, and the president demanded that Grant find a solution. Grant, whose own reputation had been severely tarnished, decided to consolidate his forces for the purpose of sweeping through the valley.

To the surprise of most observers, who thought he was too young, the leadership of what was called the Middle Military Division—fifty thousand troops—was bestowed on Little Phil Sheridan. Grant ordered Sheridan's force, which would include the First Cavalry Division with Custer's Michigan Brigade, to advance south up the valley and engage in total war—annihilate the enemy, capture stores for army use, and destroy any provisions that could aid the enemy. In other words, demolish the Confederacy.[2]

On August 10, Sheridan marched from Harpers Ferry. Torbert had assumed the position of chief of cavalry, and Merritt succeeded him as commander of the division. Holding a position of tremendous influence as Torbert's chief of staff was none other than Brevet Major Marcus Reno, the man who would disobey Custer's orders on June 25, 1876, and contribute greatly to the debacle at the Little Bighorn.[3]

The following month in the Shenandoah could not by any stretch of the imagination be considered a success for the Union cause. Sheridan, perhaps overly cautious due to fears that another defeat would be detrimental to Lincoln's reelection, spent the month maneuvering and skirmishing against Jubal Early's army with little to show for the effort. Confederate opposition became more intense the deeper Sheridan ventured into the valley. Finally, after fifty miles, he began a withdrawal in order to protect supply routes that he feared could be cut off.

Custer was involved in many of these running battles with the elusive enemy. In one early engagement, he was riding along his lines when a bullet grazed his head, clipping off some hair. His most nagging opponent, however, was Lieutenant Colonel John Singleton Mosby, the "Gray Ghost," legendary leader of an elusive band of guerillas. Mosby, the man who had originated the idea for Jeb Stuart's initial ride around McClellan's army, responded to the Valley invasion by leading his band of guerillas on a series of retaliatory acts.[4]

On August 18, a group of Mosby's men, who were dressed in common farmer clothing or blue uniforms, rode up to Custer's pickets and cold-bloodedly killed and wounded several Wolverines. Soon after that, a number of sentinels were bushwhacked by sharpshooters in the night. A cook and an orderly from the Seventh Michigan who had visited a nearby farm to obtain provisions were found hanging from a tree. Three companies of the Fifth Michigan were attacked and routed by a superior force of Confederates—many of them dressed in Union blue. Ten Michigan troopers surrendered, only to be murdered by Mosby's men.

Custer vowed revenge, and gained some measure of retribution by burning a few houses and barns, and managed to capture and hang a number of those deemed spies who had been caught while wearing Union blue. But Mosby, the master of hit-and-run tactics, frustrated Custer at every turn in this escalating blood feud between the two determined warriors.[5]

Sheridan's withdrawal was treated by Northern newspapers as another failure. An element of pressure on Lincoln had been alleviated with Sherman's capture of Atlanta on September 2, but the Shenandoah Valley remained a major problem. On September 16, Grant met with Sheridan, and the two men devised an offensive strategy designed to crush the enemy once and for all by riding down the Shenandoah and destroying the South's granary and main source of horses and supplies.[6]

The initial objective would be the town of Winchester, where General Jubal Early's men were entrenched. At 2:00 A.M. on September 19, Custer and his Wolverines, reinforced by the Twenty-fifth New York Cavalry, moved out into the darkness. As the tip of Sheridan's right flank, Custer and the dismounted Sixth Michigan came under intense fire at Locke's Ford along Opequon Creek.

Custer had his men lay down a base of fire, and formed the Twenty-fifth New York, supported by the Seventh Michigan, for an attempt to cross the waterway. Rebel riflemen and gunners opened up with a furious barrage, and Custer's men floundered. In a surprise bold move—charges were not normally executed across waterways—Custer ordered a charge across the stream by the First Michigan. The Confederate soldiers—under Custer's West Point friend, General Stephen Ramseur—were forced into a hasty retreat by Custer's aggressive maneuver.

Custer secured the ford, and then began chasing the retreating Rebels in the direction of Winchester. His men engaged in a series of minor skirmishes until mid-afternoon before eventually happening upon a Union division under General William Averell, which was engaged with a line of Rebels under Fitz Lee. Custer's appearance and subsequent saber charge drove the graycoats into the woods with Yankee horsemen in hot pursuit. Lee managed to form his men behind a stone wall and wide ditch. Custer never paused, and ordered a charge over the obstacles that sent the Confederates reeling once again. Lee, who had his third horse of the day shot out from beneath him, received a wound that would incapacitate him until the following year.[7]

Custer halted to await further orders. Word came that the battle in the center of the town was not going well for the Union. Sheridan, in a bold move, ordered his beleaguered men to charge. Custer, alone except for the sergeant carrying his personal guidon, rode well ahead of his troops as they galloped directly toward an enemy artillery battery. Suddenly, a bullet struck his color bearer, knocking him from his horse. A horde of Rebels raced to close in and finish off the downed man, and Custer as well.

Instead of prudently running for his life, Custer leaped from the saddle, grabbed his sergeant by the jacket collar, and pulled him to safety. Custer galloped away with the wounded man—all the while engaged in a saber and bayonet duel with the enemy—until a detachment of the Sixth Michigan under Major Charles Deane came to his rescue. Deane later called his commander's actions "as brave a thing as I ever saw Custer do." The Rebel battery had escaped, much to Custer's ire, but the general and his color bearer had been saved.[8]

Custer regrouped his men and moved them to a small crest within five hundred yards of the enemy line. The order came from Sheridan, "Tell

General Custer that now is the time to strike. Give him my compliments, and order him not to spare one damned ounce of horse-flesh."[9]

Custer, however, was of the opinion that a frontal assault at that time would be suicidal. He requested that his orders be amended to permit him to choose the timing of his charge. Questioning a direct order was just not done, and could result in severe punishment. Had most field commanders made that request, it would have been considered insubordination, and they likely would have been relieved of duty on the spot. Sheridan, however, apparently trusted Custer's assessment of the situation, and agreed to allow his subordinate to decide when to strike.[10]

In time, Custer determined that the right moment to attack had arrived. He ordered "Yankee Doodle," his song for the charge, be played, and off they went at a trot, then a gallop.

Harris Beecher, assistant surgeon of the 114th New York, described the scene, "Away to the right a dull thunder arose. Looking in the direction of the setting sun, our men saw the most impressive and soul-stirring sight it was ever their lot to witness. Custar's [*sic*] cavalry was making a charge. Ten thousand [actually only about five hundred] horsemen were pouring down at a keen gallop, upon the already discomfited enemy. Ten thousand sabers glistened and quivered over their heads. Ten thousand chargers threw up a great cloud of dust that obscured the sun . . . Oh! it was glorious to see how terror-stricken the rebels were, at the discovery of this impetuous charge."[11]

Brigadier General George Armstrong Custer's five hundred Union horsemen slammed headlong into about seventeen hundred infantrymen. After the first volley from these entrenched riflemen had been fired, Custer rallied his Wolverines forward before the enemy could reload. The well-timed charge, with sabers decimating the ranks, routed the Confederate boys.

"But see the gallant Custer!" one member of the band noted. "He is in the midst of a throng of the enemy, slashing right and left. A Confederate infantryman presents his musket full at Custer's heart and is about to pull the trigger. Quick as lightning the general detects the movement. With a sharp pull he causes his horse to rear upon its haunches, and the ball passes, just grazing the General's leg below the thigh. Then a terrible stroke descends upon the infantryman's head, and he sinks to the ground a lifeless corpse." [12]

The shattered Rebel army fled from Winchester down the road toward Strasburg. Custer's victorious Wolverines had captured more than seven hundred prisoners, including fifty-two officers, along with seven battle flags. Custer modestly wrote in his official report, "It is confidently believed that, considering the relative numbers engaged and the comparative advantage held on each side, the charge just described, stands unequaled, valued according to its daring and success, in the history of this war."[13]

The Rebels withdrew to Fisher's Hill, where on September 22 the Federals attacked Early's lines and once more routed the Confederates. Custer and his comrades chased the retreating enemy for more than twenty miles without success.[14]

Sheridan blamed the lackadaisical actions of Generals Averell and Torbert for the Union's inability to corral and destroy Early. On September 23, Averell was removed; then, three days later, Sheridan had the opportunity of ridding himself of Torbert. Grant had requested either Torbert or James Wilson, commander of the Third Division, for assignment in Georgia.

Sheridan, however, selected Wilson for this duty, and wasted little time naming a successor. Brigadier General George Armstrong Custer was Sheridan's choice as division commander.[15]

Custer, who at first had been assigned the Second Division, would as of September 30, 1864, be in command of the Third Division, which included the First Brigade, under Colonel Alexander C. M. Pennington, consisting of the Second New York Cavalry, Second Ohio Cavalry, Third New Jersey Cavalry, Fifth New York Cavalry, and the Eighteenth Pennsylvania and the Second Brigade, under Colonel William Wells, consisting of the First Vermont Cavalry, two companies of the Third Indiana Cavalry, Eighth New York Cavalry, Twenty-second New York Cavalry, and one battalion of the First New Hampshire Cavalry.[16]

The only downside to this promotion was that Custer would be leaving behind the Michigan Brigade, the unit that he had molded into the most celebrated cavalrymen in the Army of the Potomac.

Hundreds of Wolverine troopers, to no avail, signed petitions requesting transfer to the Third Division. Custer summed up the emotion of the separation in a letter to Libbie, "You would be surprised at the feeling shown," he wrote. "Some of the officers said they would resign if the exchange (an assignment of the Michigan Brigade to the Third Division) were not made. Major Drew said some actually cried. Axell, the band leader, wept. Some of the band threatened to break their horns." The Wolverines would continue to wear their red neckties out of respect and loyalty to their beloved leader.[17]

Meanwhile, six of Mosby's rangers had been hanged on September 23 at Fort Royal. Mosby was infuriated by the act and, believing that Custer was the culprit, requested permission from General Robert E. Lee to hang an equal number of Custer's men for each that Mosby lost. Permission was granted.

After one such lynching party, Mosby pinned a note to one of Custer's dangling troopers, "These men have been hung in retaliation for an equal number of Colonel Mosby's men, hung by order of Gen'l Custer at Fort Royal. Measure for measure."

The men hanged at Fort Royal, however, had not been executed by Custer, who had in fact taken a ten-mile detour around that particular city. Regardless, Mosby's brutal actions served to add fuel to the fire of this escalating personal feud between the two adversaries. And it was now Custer's turn to strike back.[18]

Custer's first assignment as commander of the Third Division would be a nasty, distasteful bit of business prompted by Mosby's executions. Three guerillas wearing Union uniforms had shot dead Sheridan's chief engineer not far from headquarters near Dayton, Virginia. Little Phil was outraged, and, as punishment for this cowardly act, ordered Custer to burn every house within five miles of the incident.[19]

This policy of Total War (a reign of terror on the civilian populace) would in years later be taken West and employed effectively against the Plains Indians, such as at the Battle of Washita in November 1868, which embroiled Custer in controversy for his actions under orders.[20]

Custer rode out on October 4, and in what one New Yorker called "the most heart-sickening duty we had ever performed," torched seventeen houses, five barns, and assorted outbuildings. Ironically, the "Burnt District," as it came to be known, was populated for the most part by pacifist Mennonites.[21]

Evidently Phil Sheridan was pleased with the results of Custer's burning foray, and received permission from Grant to continue the destruction. The Federals set out on October 5 to sweep across the countryside from the Alleghenies to the Blue Ridge, and commenced a systematic reign of terror. Barns, haystacks, mills, and grain fields were indiscriminately torched while livestock was either slaughtered or rounded up and taken along to feed the army.[22]

The infuriated Confederates responded to this affront by pursuing and skirmishing with elements of Sheridan's force, which delayed movement and hampered the burning. Much of this harassment was initiated by Tom Rosser, who was now being called the "Savior of the Valley." Rosser was in charge of all mounted troops attached to Jubal Early, and many of his men were natives of the Valley who sought revenge for the destruction caused by the Northerners.

Sheridan vowed to put a stop once and for all to Rosser's aggressive nature. And George Armstrong Custer was assigned the task of eliminating his West Point friend.[23]

Custer led his twenty-five-hundred-man Third Division out of camp on the morning of October 9, and halted on a ridge overlooking Tom's Brook. Rosser's thirty-five hundred men were securely dug into defensive positions behind stone walls on the south side of the brook, which in itself did not present an obstacle for horsemen.

Custer surveyed the scene, then, in an act of bravado of which legends are made, trotted out in front of his command, where he could be observed by every man on both sides of the field.

In a chivalrous gesture, Custer swept his broad-brimmed hat to his knee in a salute to his old friend—as if to say, "Let's have a fair fight. May the best man win."

Rosser was not particularly amused by Custer's showmanship. "You see that officer down there?" he said to his staff. "That's General Custer, the Yanks are so proud of, and I intend to give him the best whipping today that he ever got!"[24]

Confederate artillery, which was positioned on a higher elevation on the bluffs, opened up to pummel the Union lines. While the artillery dueled, Custer's skirmishers probed Rosser's defenses without success until mid-morning. At that point, Custer decided to take matters into his own hands and try to outflank the entrenched Rebels. Three regiments were dispatched toward the enemy's left, while another brigade was readied for a charge. When the flanking troops hit Rosser's left, Custer led the charge across Tom's Brook into the heart of the enemy line.

Rosser's troops wavered, then broke under the bold attack by the Yankee horsemen, and fled to the south. The Rebels engaged in a brief running battle, but in the end ran for their lives. Custer chased his fleeing enemy some ten to twelve miles, in the process capturing six cannon and the ambulance train, which included Rosser's headquarters wagon. Confederate Thomas Munford said of the shameful defeat, "[We] lost more in that one fight than we had ever done before, in all our fights together." The Federals, remembering Stuart's "Buckland Races," jokingly referred to the battle as the "Woodstock Races."[25]

An elated Custer wrote to his wife, "Darling little one, Yesterday, the 9th, was a glorious day for your Boy! I attacked Genl. Rosser's Division of 3 Brigades with my Division of 2, and gained the most glorious victory . . . I am now arrayed in Gen'l Rosser's coat."

Custer also got back the ambrotype of Libbie that had been captured at Trevilian Station, and appropriated a pet squirrel that had belonged to Rosser. That night in camp, he adorned himself in Rosser's baggy, ill-fitting uniform and treated his men to a good laugh. He later added to Rosser's humiliation by writing to ask that his old friend advise his tailor to shorten the coattails for a better fit. [26]

Perhaps more importantly, Custer had without question impressed his new command. One officer wrote in his journal that, "With Custer as leader we are all heroes and hankering for a fight." An Ohio cavalryman wrote, "We never began but we felt sure of victory. Custar [*sic*] always used to say that he could tell in 20 minutes after opening a fight if we could beat the enemy." After only one battle, Custer had instilled confidence in his new command— and in his leadership.[27]

Sheridan's army, with Custer's division, retired to camp along Cedar Creek in a line stretching a full five miles, with Custer's headquarters at the western end. The men were content to rest, recuperate, and brag about their recent victories. Jubal Early, however, was plotting an assault on the unsuspecting Federal troops.

On the morning of October 19, "Old Jube" launched his surprise attack of five divisions against the eastern tip of the encampment. His audacious action had been perfectly executed, and the Union defenders were being overrun and scattered from their camps, many taken prisoners by the determined Confederates.

Custer sprang into action and set out to protect the right flank. His action slowed the attack and forced a stalemate face-off against a superior force of enemy soldiers commanded by Tom Rosser.[28]

Early's exhausted troops had paused in their attack when an event occurred that would rally Union forces. Phil Sheridan, who had been visiting Washington, was halted up the road in Winchester. He heard about the battle, and galloped to Cedar Creek. At the suggestion of a staff officer, Sheridan rode up and down the lines, assuring his men that they would prevail. The nearly whipped Union troops responded to "Sheridan's Ride" with cheers and renewed faith.[29]

Late in the afternoon, Sheridan noticed a gap in the Rebel lines, and quickly notified Custer to prepare to charge the right flank. The two-thousand-man-strong Third Division, led by their commander, advanced from the west to crash into the gap with sabers flashing. The daring charge of Union horsemen split the enemy in half. "Regiment after regiment, brigade after brigade, in rapid succession was crushed," recalled Confederate General John Gordon.[30]

The Rebels commenced a hasty retreat, with Custer's command nipping at their heels. The Union cavalrymen inflicted heavy casualties while capturing vital Confederate equipment, including forty-five artillery pieces, dozens of wagons, and scores of prisoners—as well as five battle flags. One severely wounded captive was Custer's West Point friend, Stephen Ramseur, whom Custer rushed to Sheridan's headquarters for medical attention. Ramseur, the youngest West Pointer to attain the rank of major general in the Confederate army, died the next morning.[31]

That night, a jubilant Custer hugged his diminutive commanding officer, Phil Sheridan, and danced him around the campfire. "By God, Phil," Custer emotionally cried, "We've cleaned them out of their guns and got ours back!" An equally excited Sheridan proclaimed, "There, there old fellow; don't capture me!"[32]

The following day, Custer was dispatched by Sheridan aboard a special train to Washington to present thirteen Rebel battle flags to Secretary of War Stanton. At the same time, Sheridan recommended to Grant that "the brave boys Merritt and Custer" be promoted to brevet major generals.[33]

The ceremony at Stanton's office was postponed until the twenty-fifth, which allowed Custer time to fetch Libbie from Newark, New Jersey, where she had been visiting friends. With Libbie at his side, Custer formally presented the battle flags to the secretary of war. Stanton shook Custer's hand, and said, "General, a gallant officer always makes gallant soldiers." He then announced that the army had a new major general in its ranks. Custer's promotion would date from October 19.[34]

Typical of the public accolades bestowed upon Custer was the observation of *New York Times* reporter E. A. Paul, who described Custer's actions at Cedar Creek, "Here Gen. Custer, young as he is, displayed judgment worthy of Napoleon."[35]

Once again, Custer had been compared to Napoleon. And, hard as it may be to believe, the new major general was only getting warmed up for what lay ahead. As the war heated up, Custer's intensity and boldness would rise to match and even exceed the challenge.

Twenty-three

---◦◉◦---

Five Forks

Sheridan's Shenandoah campaign had effectively ended the war in the Valley, with much of the credit showered on the cavalry. Battle after battle had been won, which all but guaranteed Lincoln's reelection and made a national hero out of Phil Sheridan.[1]

George Armstrong Custer had proved himself to be an extraordinarily effective commander, who had made the transition from a brigade to a division without missing a beat. He had also demonstrated that he was not an impetuous loose cannon, but a man with an inherent talent and skill for sizing up the weaknesses of his enemy and exploiting it for his benefit. And, as had been his custom throughout the war, Custer showed that he was not an ambulance officer who viewed his troops in battle from some rear echelon position; rather, he was a fearless leader who chose to ride at the front of his men as they charged into the enemy's line of fire.[2]

Colonel Henry Capehart, a member of the Third Cavalry Division and future Medal of Honor winner, summed up Custer's actions by later writing, "I have seen him under the most varying and critical circumstances, and never without ample resources of mind and body to meet the most trying contingency. He was counted by some rash; it was because he dared while they dared not . . . If I were to begin giving instances of his daring, brilliancy, and skill, I should never stop."[3]

In spite of recent successes, the war was not by any means won. Skirmishes with Jubal Early and the torching of the Shenandoah continued for several more weeks until both armies more or less settled in for the winter. [4]

Custer sent for Libbie, who arrived on November 6, and the couple took up residence in a mansion called Long Meadow located four miles south of Winchester, the town where Phil Sheridan had moved his headquarters. Shortly after Libbie's arrival, another family member joined them.[5]

Thomas Ward Custer, a wild and adventurous youth six years younger than brother Armstrong, had made an attempt to enlist in Monroe, Michigan, at the outbreak of the war. His father had spoiled those plans by alerting the recruiter that Tom was only sixteen years old—too young by two years. Tom was not to be denied. On September 2, 1861, he had snuck across the border to New Rumley, Ohio, and been sworn in as a private in the Twenty-first Ohio Infantry.

Tom had fought as a common foot soldier for the next three years in such battles as Shiloh, Stones River, Chickamauga, Missionary Ridge, Chattanooga, and the Atlanta Campaign. He had distinguished himself enough to be promoted to corporal and orderly to Brigadier General James Scott Negley, and escort for Ulysses S. Grant, George Thomas, and James Palmer. He had been promoted to corporal on January 1, 1864.

Tom, however, craved the excitement and notoriety that the cavalry had provided for his famous brother. He recognized where real glory could be attained. After all, Autie had become a general at age twenty-three.

On October 23, 1864, Tom Custer received his commission as a second lieutenant from Colonel James Kidd of the Sixth Michigan, and, by virtue of Armstrong's influence with Phil Sheridan, was assigned to his brother's staff.[6]

The brothers were extremely close—Autie was the protector, and Tom worshiped his brother. This reunion was cause for elation and celebration. "We could not help spoiling him owing to his charm and our deep affection," Libbie wrote of her and Armstrong's conduct toward Tom.

On the other hand, Tom was not treated like a kid brother when on duty, and more than once complained that Armstrong yelled at him for "every little darned thing just because I happen to be his brother. If anyone thinks that it is a soft thing to be a commanding officer's brother, he misses his guess." Any charges of nepotism or doubt about Tom's worthiness would be replaced with widespread admiration for his actions during the upcoming spring offensive.[7]

On November 8, while Armstrong and Tom caught up on the past several years of separation, President Abraham Lincoln was reelected, primarily due to the success of General Sheridan's Shenandoah Campaign. His opponent was the still-popular former general George B. McClellan, who ran on a "Peace Platform," arguing that Lincoln had needlessly prolonged the war. McClellan won only three states, and lost in electoral votes 212 to 12. One can only imagine the bittersweet taste in Custer's mouth at the realization that his courageous actions had contributed to the defeat of McClellan, the man whom Custer had idolized like a father.

The Custer brothers were in the saddle on December 19 when Sheridan ordered a cavalry raid on the Orange & Alexandria Railroad at Gordonsville. At sundown on the twentieth, in the midst of a miserable sleet, Custer's cavalry bivouacked at Lacy Springs, nine miles north of Harrisonburg and thirty miles north of Staunton.

Custer had been informed by residents when passing through New Market that Confederate cavalry had been observed in the area. He posted pickets and set reveille at 4:00 A.M. for a 6:30 march. The morning arrived with about five inches of fresh snow—accompanied by "sharp, short, fierce, bark like yells" followed by "a dull thunderous sound." The Rebel cavalry commanded by Tom Rosser had ridden throughout the inclement night to attack the unsuspecting Federals.[8]

Brigadier General George Chapman's brigade was scattered by the action. Custer bolted from his tent into the saddle without his coat, hat, or boots, and encouraged his men to charge. The action allowed Chapman's brigade to regroup with enough strength to counterattack, which forced Rosser to withdraw. Custer set his losses at two dead, twenty-two wounded, and ten to twenty captured. He estimated that Rosser had lost from fifty to eighty killed or wounded and thirty captured.

Rosser's daring attack, however, compelled Sheridan to call an end to the raid. The cavalrymen were ordered to return to Winchester and construct permanent winter quarters.[9]

The end of December also concluded Major General William T. Sherman's "March to the Sea." Sherman had taken Atlanta, Georgia, on September 2, which resulted in his being hailed a hero in the North, and he occupied that city for ten weeks while he rested his army. On November 15, Sherman departed Atlanta, and advanced through Georgia—wrecking supply depots and railroads, sacking government buildings, and destroying property. In addition to his army's actions, he permitted marauding groups of men, called Bummers, to torch a pathway through the countryside up to sixty miles wide, leaving behind little more than debris and desolation, an excessive practice that earned lasting condemnation for Sherman and the Union in that state. On December 21—after 250 miles—Sherman completed his march by occupying the coastal city of Savannah.

Throughout that winter, Armstrong Custer and wife Libbie hosted and attended parties and dinners, and entertained and visited relatives. The "Michigan Brigade Ball" in early February reunited Custer with the officers and ladies of his former unit, who danced to the music of the Michigan Brigade band. Custer was observed by a fellow passenger on a train ride to visit Libbie's family in Grand Rapids, "Genl Custer reminded me of Tennyson's description of King Arthur . . . He is tall straight with light complexion, clear blue eyes, golden hair which hangs in curls on his shoulders."[10]

One notable event in Custer's spiritual life occurred on Sunday evening, February 5. The Custers attended a Week of Prayer service at the Monroe Presbyterian Church, and while Armstrong bowed in prayer, he underwent a conversion and became a born-again Christian. He penned a letter dated February 19 to Reverend D. C. Mattoon that read in part, "It was about this very hour two weeks ago tonight that I knelt with you and your family circle in Monroe. In your presence I accepted Christ as my Savior. I feel somewhat like the pilot of a vessel; who has been steering his ship upon familiar and safe waters but has been called upon to make a voyage fraught with danger. Having in safety and with success completed one voyage, he is imbued with confidence and renewed courage, and the second voyage is robbed of half its terror. So it is with me."[11]

The pleasant winter respite ended on February 27 when Sheridan's rejuvenated ten-thousand-man cavalry marched. Custer's Third Cavalry Division had been dispatched ahead of the column to reconnoiter the area around Waynesborough. Freezing rain pelted the troopers, and the road was transformed into a muddy mire. Horses wallowed almost to their bellies, and wagons became stuck. Regardless, a determined Custer kept his men struggling forward.

At about three o'clock on March 2, Custer spied exactly what he had been seeking. Two thousand Confederates under Jubal Early—two infantry brigades, artillery, and Tom Rosser's cavalry—were entrenched on a bend of the swollen South River.[12]

This position at first glance appeared insurmountable. Custer, however, eventually noticed one chink in Early's armor—a gap between his left flank and the river. He ordered three regiments from Pennington's First Brigade to dismount and sneak through the cover of thick timber to flank the Confederates on the left near the waterway. This detachment, armed with Spencer carbines, successfully moved to that position unseen by the enemy. Horse artillery was brought up to soften the lines. Custer then ordered his bugler, Joseph Fought, to sound the charge.

The flankers leaped from the timber to send a murderous volley into the rear of the startled enemy, while the other brigades followed the lead of their commander and tore across the muddy terrain directly toward Early's positions. The Rebel line wavered and collapsed under the weight of Custer's charge. Early's men broke and ran, with Custer's cavalrymen in hot pursuit.

"So sudden was our attack," Custer wrote in his official report, "that but little time was offered for resistance." Many battle-weary Rebels simply threw down their weapons and awaited the inevitable. Generals Early and Rosser narrowly escaped Custer's well-executed attack.[13]

Within three hours' time, the Third Cavalry Division had captured eighteen hundred prisoners, fourteen artillery pieces, nearly two hundred supply wagons, and seventeen battle flags. Amazingly, only nine Union cavalrymen had been killed or wounded in what Sheridan termed "this brilliant fight."[14]

It was a crushing defeat for the Army of Northern Virginia, and another colorful feather in Custer's overflowing war bonnet. Sheridan's aide, Captain George B. Sanford, was present when Custer reported to his commander. "Up came Custer himself with his following," Sanford later recalled. "And in the hands of his orderlies, one to each, were the seventeen battle flags streaming in the wind. It was a great spectacle and the sort of thing which Custer thoroughly enjoyed."[15]

Sheridan's troops then embarked upon an operation into the heart of Virginia. The men endured rainy weather, muddy roads, swollen waterways, and minor skirmishes with their enemy to tear through the countryside like a swarm of vengeful locusts—leaving behind a landscape of devastation and despair. Every vital piece of the Southern infrastructure or element of economic necessity in their pathway was either confiscated or reduced to smoldering ruins.

Railroad tracks were ripped up and cars demolished. Telegraph lines were cut. Bridges were blown up. Water tanks were drained. Boats and barges were sunk. Locks on the James River were wrecked. Cotton mills, foundries, lumber yards, great stores of tobacco, wheat, livestock, and any other source of income or sustenance were seized or burned to ashes. The mayor of Charlottesville turned over that town to Custer while the faculty of the University of Virginia stood nearby on their campus under a white flag.[16]

On March 18, the cavalry bivouacked at White House Landing on the Pamunkey River for a week of rest and recuperation spent mending equipment and readying the horses for the spring campaign.

Custer wrote to Libbie, "Our raid has been a chain of successes, and the 3rd Division has done all the fighting. I wish you could see your boy's headquarters now. My flag is floating over the gate, and near it, ranged along the fences are 16 battle-flags, captured by the 3rd Division. Neither Genl.

Sheridan nor Genl. Merritt within 10 miles when these captures are made. Nor did they know what I was doing. The 3rd stands higher than ever, in advance all the time."[17]

After the battle at Waynesborough, Custer had knelt in prayer with Chaplain Theodore J. Holmes. Now, Holmes was leaving the service, and wrote a letter to Custer that was forwarded to Libbie. The chaplain wanted to thank Custer for "the privilege of the relation to you afforded the past few weeks, as it has enabled me to know you better, and has made me respect you even more heartily than before. I cannot express my gratefulness to the Almighty that He should have made you such a general and such a man. I rejoice with the 3rd Division, with the army, with the whole country in the splendid military genius that has your name glorious in the history of the war. But even more I rejoice in the position you have taken deliberately, and, I believe, finally, in regard to moral and religious life."[18]

Libbie remained in Washington, where she enjoyed the companionship of Rebecca Richmond. On March 4, the two ladies were honored to stand near President Abraham Lincoln when he took the oath of office for his second term and delivered his address. Later, Libbie attended the inaugural ball at the patent office, escorted by Senator Zachariah Chandler.

But her husband was rarely out of her mind, especially the dangers he faced. She pled with him to be careful. "Don't expose yourself so much in battle. Just do your duty, and don't rush out so daringly. Oh, Autie, we must die together."[19]

Phil Sheridan had sent to Washington the seventeen battle flags captured at Waynesborough. Libbie Custer attended the flag presentation ceremony held in the office of Secretary of War Stanton, and later wrote to her husband, "Oh, what a happy day that was—the proudest of my life. The room was full, but Mr. Stanton perceived me and extended his hand most cordially . . . he introduced me as 'the wife of the gallant general.' As every flag was presented General Townsend read at the end, 'Brevet Major-General Custer commanding . . .' every time from the first to the seventeenth. I could hardly keep from crying out my praise of my boy. Before leaving I told the

Secretary I had waited a long time for a letter from you, but was more than repaid by having witnessed this. Mr. Stanton replied, 'General Custer is writing lasting letters on the pages of his country's history.' "[20]

Sheridan's command headed south across the James River on March 25, and rejoined the army two days later at City Point. Sherman had returned to Virginia from North Carolina for a brief visit to assist Grant in formulating a strategy designed to once and for all crush Lee's battered and weary army. Now was the ideal time to strike. Battle losses and desertions had compelled the desperate Confederates to conscript boys from ages fourteen to eighteen as well as older men up to age sixty. And it was Grant's intention to destroy Lee before he could gather strength or make a move to North Carolina to battle Sherman, which would prolong the war.[21]

Custer's Third Division was reorganized into three brigades on March 29. Pennington's First Brigade would now consist of the First Connecticut, Third New Jersey, Second New York, and Second Ohio; Wells' Second Brigade had the Eighth New York, Fifteenth New York, and First Vermont; and the Third Brigade, commanded by Henry Capehart, consisted of the First New York, First West Virginia, Second West Virginia, and Third West Virginia.[22]

When Sheridan's cavalry rode out on the morning of March 29, Merritt, not Custer, led the column. Merritt, who was often openly jealous of Custer, assigned his nemesis the undesirable and frustrating duty of escorting the wagon train. A torrential downpour the night before had created a quagmire that hindered progress to barely a frog's pace. Mules sank to their haunches in the muck, and it became necessary to unload wagons to free them from the saturated ground. Custer battled this stubborn natural enemy and slogged through along the road for three days.

On March 31, Sheridan's advance near Dinwiddie Court House came under a vicious attack by Confederate infantry commanded by General George E. Pickett of Gettysburg fame. Custer and two brigades were summoned to the front; the other brigade would remain behind to guard the wagon train.[23]

Custer and his aides raced ahead of the column, one of them unfurling Custer's new personal guidon, which had been made by Libbie and delivered the night before. They arrived at about four in the afternoon to find Dinwiddie Court House in turmoil. The Rebels may have been outnumbered two to one, but nonetheless Pickett had taken the offensive and presently held the upper hand. The Union troops had been driven back by the brutal onslaught but eventually managed to maintain a secure line.

Major General Custer received orders from Sheridan to deploy his troops behind hastily constructed barricades along the road to Five Forks. In the ensuing skirmish, one of his orderlies was killed beside him and his wife's name, which she had sewn on the guidon, was blasted off in the heavy gunfire.

As the battle intensified, Custer rode along the line exposed to enemy fire in an effort to encourage his men. The resolute Confederate infantry attacked, and briefly forced the Yankees back. Custer rallied the troops, imploring them to remain behind rail barricades and hold their position. At sundown, the Rebels were repulsed in one final desperate assault, and withdrew toward Five Forks. Custer counterattacked, but darkness impeded progress and the chase was called off.[24]

Lieutenant Colonel Horace Potter, Grant's aide-de-camp, mentioned to Sheridan that "We at last have drawn the enemy's infantry out of its fortifications, and this is our chance to attack it."[25]

Sheridan had intended to follow Potter's suggestion at dawn on the following morning. Infantry reinforcements, however, did not arrive by daylight, and it was four o'clock in the afternoon before the twelve-thousand-man Fifth Corps, commanded by Major General Gouveneur Warren, finally made its appearance at Dinwiddie Court House. Sheridan ordered an immediate attack on the Confederate position at Five Forks, where Pickett and about ten thousand troops had been positioned and told by Lee to hold "at all hazards."[26]

Custer had been skirmishing with the enemy throughout the day in an effort to determine its size and location. Now, as the Union column proceeded from Dinwiddie Court House, Custer's division led the cavalry. Custer and Devin would act as a diversionary force to distract Pickett while Warren's infantry stormed into the Rebels. The cavalry skirmishers pressed through the timber to probe the enemy lines, but Warren had miscalculated the extent of the Confederate line, charged into a gap, and was caught in a devastating cross fire.

Phil Sheridan was infuriated by Warren's bungled assault, and personally rode into the midst of the Fifth Corps to re-form and rally the troops. Warren's men responded with renewed fury, and crushed into the Confederate left. Sheridan would later that day relieve Warren of his command.[27]

Custer mounted two brigades, signaled the band to play "Hail Columbia," and, accompanied by his staff, led the charge into blazing Rebel fire. The bold thrust was met by stiff resistance as Rooney Lee's cavalry division appeared on the left flank to tear into the Yankees. The opponents fought hand to hand until Sheridan and Devin overpowered Pickett's line and began sweeping westward. At that point, Confederate forces executed a hasty withdrawal.

George Armstrong Custer and his red ties chased the Rebels for six miles, rounding up prisoners until darkness descended. Custer reported, "The retreat of over 5,000 of the rebels was then cut off, and this number was secured as prisoners of war. Besides these the loss in killed and wounded was very heavy." Thirteen battle flags and six artillery pieces were also captured. The end was now very near.[28]

Twenty-four

———◦◉◦———

Appomattox

General U.S. Grant had intended to immediately resume his attack on Petersburg, but reconnaissance revealed that Confederate trenches were empty. Lee's beleaguered army had stolen away in the night and evacuated Petersburg as well as Richmond. Union forces moved in the following day to occupy those strategic locations. Grant feared, however, that Lee was on his way to North Carolina by way of Lynchburg to rendezvous with his forces in that state. If the Federals could intercept the Army of Northern Virginia along the way, there was little doubt that the Confederacy would be doomed.[1]

Sheridan's four cavalry divisions—Devin, Crook, Custer, and Mackenzie—were dispatched at 9:00 A.M. on April 3 with the mission of hunting down and engaging the fleeing Rebels. Custer led the advance, anxious to be the first to locate the enemy and gain additional glory. His Third Division followed Lee west along the Appomattox River Valley until reaching Namozine Creek.

The bridge had been destroyed, and Rebel fortifications were observed on the distant bank. Custer was unaware of it at the time, but his men were greatly outnumbered. That small factor likely would not have deterred him had he known. He dispatched one troop to outflank the enemy position while other men with axes were detailed to remove fallen trees from the stream to clear the path for the main force.

An impatient Tom Custer, however, took a page from his older brother's book and spurred his horse to gallop across the waterway toward the enemy trenches. His act of bravado inspired the troops to follow. The Rebels fired volleys at the onrushing horsemen, but soon broke and fled to form a line at Namozine Church. Tom Custer led the charge that overcame that brief stand, and the battle became a running fight as the Rebels endeavored to elude their dogged pursuers. When hostilities had cooled, Tom presented his proud brother with a battle flag along with fourteen prisoners, including three officers. Phil Sheridan recommended that Tom receive the Medal of Honor for his actions.[2]

Robert E. Lee's retreating army was exhausted and in dire need of provisions. The Confederate commander believed that if his troops could reach the railroad at Appomattox Station, they would have a chance to resupply and elude the Union troops. Early on April 6, General Lee changed his order of march for the purpose of expediting their movement and escaping the pursuing Union horsemen. Lee rode ahead of the column with Lieutenant General James Longstreet and the infantry. They were followed by a lengthy line of supply wagons, and then Major General John Gordon's Second Corps acting as rear guard. Lee was approaching Farmville, where he hoped to procure provisions, when the column inadvertently split into two detachments. Lee continued on as planned, but the wagon train and Gordon veered to the north, where they came under Federal attack at a place called Sayler's Creek.

Custer had been trailing that enemy column, and his opportunistic cavalrymen plunged into the hottest of the engagement. The hastily entrenched Rebels put up an admirable fight, which kept the enemy at bay for some time. During the fray, Custer had his horse shot out from beneath him, and his color bearer was killed. The infantry finally arrived, and Custer led the charge against enemy lines.

The Rebels held their fire until the last moment, and then unleashed a vicious barrage. The assaulting cavalrymen were undaunted and soared over the fortifications with hooves flying, sabers slashing, and pistols smoking. Within a matter of minutes, the gray line was sent scattering in the wake of the surging Federals. The Rebels continued to fight as they withdrew to the north. Custer formed his division and gave chase to put the finishing touches on their day's work.[3]

Now that the most serious fighting was over, Tom Custer was intent upon distinguishing himself. He swooped down on a Rebel color bearer, who fired his pistol point blank at Tom. The bullet struck young Custer in the cheek and exited behind his ear. Blood spurted from the wound and his face was blackened with powder. The force of the blast had thrown him backward against his horse's rump, but he quickly righted himself in the saddle. He drew his own pistol, and coolly shot and killed the standard bearer. Tom then grabbed the coveted battle flag, wheeled his horse, and galloped through the chaotic battlefield to show off the trophy to his brother. The general ordered Tom to seek medical attention for his wound, but Tom was determined to return to the battle. As a result, Armstrong placed Tom under arrest and had him forcibly escorted to the surgeon. Colonel Capehart had witnessed Tom's heroic action, and later said, "for intrepidity I never saw this incident surpassed."

Tom Custer's demonstration of courage was rewarded with a brevet promotion to lieutenant colonel and the awarding of his second Medal of Honor—becoming the first man in history to receive two, and the only double recipient during the Civil War.

George Armstrong Custer was thrilled about his brother's brave exploits, and later wrote to Libbie saying, "I am as proud of him as I can be, as soldier, brother."[4]

Sayler's Creek had been a smashing victory for the Union. Over nine thousand Confederates—including Lee's son Custis and six other generals—had been taken prisoner, along with thirty-six battle flags. This amounted to the greatest number of American troops ever captured at one time on this continent, before the Civil War or after. Nearly one-third of the total force of the once-invincible Army of Virginia had been lost on an afternoon that would forever be remembered by the South as "Black Thursday."[5]

Custer formed his division the following morning for the march just as a long line of Confederate prisoners straggled past on their way to the rear. In a show of respect for his vanquished enemy, Custer ordered the band to play "Dixie" for these brave men, which evoked cheers from the Southern boys.

Custer's division, which had been leading the Union cavalry, had gone into bivouac some two miles from Appomattox Station in the early evening of April 8, when word was received that four trains full of Confederate munitions and supplies were presently unloading at the station. At the same time, a courier from Wesley Merritt delivered the order that Custer should rest his troops.

The prospect of capturing these trains naturally took precedence in Custer's way of thinking. He craftily dispatched a courier to inform Merritt about the trains and that he would attack unless receiving orders to the contrary. Custer then quickly roused his brigades and rode out for Appomattox Station before Merritt could respond.[6]

Custer's troops swooped down on the station, and easily overpowered the guards to capture the four trains—except for one engine that was uncoupled and steamed away. Within moments of the seizure, a torrent of Rebel artillery shells rained down on the Federals.

Confederate Brigadier General R. Lindsay Walker, who commanded a small brigade of cavalry, a wagon train, and around one hundred guns, had opened up from a ridge about a half mile from the station. Custer detailed former engineers and stokers to move the trains to safety, then formed his men for a charge on the enemy cannon.[7]

Without bothering to wait for his trailing brigades, Custer sent Pennington's New Yorkers and Ohioans toward the location of the bright flashes of artillery. The Union horsemen charged the cannon's mouth, but were shredded by close range volleys and small arms fire, and were forced to fall back. By that time, Wells' and Capehart's regiments had come up.

Custer rode along the line of blue-clad horsemen, and shouted, "Boys, the Third Division must have those guns! I'm going to charge if I go alone!" Custer then grabbed his guidon, lifted it high, and confidently called out, "I go; who will follow?" Custer had successfully whipped his weary men into an inspired, battle-hungry group of proud cavalrymen who would accept any challenge that their heroic commander presented. His words were affirmed by a deafening chorus of cheers.[8]

Old Curly, true to custom, personally led the mounted assault on the stubborn Confederate position. The Yankees swiftly closed on the artillery battery in the darkness, and braved the initial storm of fire to crush their enemy. The Rebels were forced to abandon their position, and left behind twenty-four pieces of artillery, seven battle flags, two hundred wagons, and a thousand prisoners—not to mention the four trainloads of supplies at the station. More importantly, the quick action on Custer's part had cut off Lee's retreat.[9]

Custer pushed on to Appomattox Court House, where his men encountered enough resistance from Lee's infantry that after an hour or so he ordered them to withdraw to the station. Phil Sheridan had arrived, and dispatched a message to Grant requesting that the infantry be brought up in prelude to a morning attack that he was confident would bring Lee to his knees.[10]

Robert E. Lee was desperate to seek an escape route through the blue line. At daybreak on April 9, Palm Sunday, Rebel cannons commenced firing volleys and gray-clad cavalry appeared from the dense fog to attack Custer's dismounted troopers. This last-ditch effort by Lee was thwarted when the Yankee infantry roared forward to reinforce the position and push the Rebels back. Custer mounted his men and moved them south with the intention of striking the Confederate flank.[11]

"Custer took the road at a gallop," recalled a member of the First New York Cavalry. "It was a glorious sight to see that division as it dashed along, with sabres drawn, the gallant Custer leading, and the Confederate army on a parallel road, only three hundred yards distant, vainly endeavoring to escape." Custer was readying his regiment for a charge, when a lone Confederate staff officer rode forward carrying a stick with a white towel attached.[12]

Major Robert Sims of General Longstreet's staff was received by Custer, and stated that General Lee requested that hostilities be suspended. Custer admitted that he was not the commander on the field, and would attack unless Lee agreed to an unconditional surrender. He then sent word back to

Sheridan and dispatched his chief of staff, Lieutenant Colonel Edward W. Whitaker, to accompany Major Sims to obtain an answer to his surrender demand.[13]

The Civil War was about to end on Custer's doorstep—that can be documented. The exact circumstances surrounding Custer's role in this surrender entreaty, however, has become a matter of controversy.

Eyewitness accounts—primarily a questionable remembrance by James Longstreet written thirty-one years after the incident—suggest that after dispatching Whitaker, Custer crossed the Confederate line and was presented to Longstreet. Custer demanded that Longstreet surrender the army. Longstreet allegedly was irritated by the brash young general, and refused—citing the fact that he was not the commander. In addition, Longstreet was said to have taunted Custer by boldly professing that the Rebs were not beaten and that Custer could attack if he damn well pleased. He then ordered Custer out of his lines. Longstreet claimed that Custer meekly retired, asking for an escort to safely return to friendly lines.[14]

In another account, Major Sims confirmed Longstreet's basic version. Sims entered Union lines carrying a flag that he said was "a new and clean white crash towel, one of a lot for which I had paid $20 or $40 apiece in Richmond a few days before." He had braved Federal pickets that fired upon him, and requested to see Sheridan but was told that only Custer was available. Sims relayed his message to Custer, who replied that nothing less than an unconditional surrender would be accepted. Sims departed with Whitaker to report back to Longstreet. When he arrived at Longstreet's headquarters, Custer was already there. Sims wrote, "I found General Custer and he [Longstreet] talking together at a short distance from the position occupied by the staff. Custer said he would proceed to attack at once and Longstreet replied: 'As soon as you please,' but he did not attack. Just after I left Custer came in sight of our lines. He halted his troops and, taking a handkerchief from his orderly, displayed it as a flag and rode into our lines. He was surrounded by some of our people and was being handled a little roughly when an old classmate of his recognized him and rescued him."[15]

Although Custer without question would have relished the glory associated with being the officer who accepted the Confederate surrender, he was West Point–educated and would have understood protocol in such matters. If he had indeed crossed the lines, it was perhaps out of concern for Whitaker's well-being. Longstreet's challenge to attack would not have been taken seriously. The Rebels were whipped, and Custer, though a man of action, would never have welcomed another slaughter.

Regardless of Custer's participation in prelude to the actual surrender, that afternoon Lee presented himself to Grant at the home of Wilmer McLean. "General Grant was standing beneath an apple tree when General Lee approached," remembered saddler Charles H. Crocker of the First New York Cavalry. "After a hand clasp, Lee removed his side arms and handed them to Grant who, after holding them for a moment, returned them to Lee." The two commanders then retired inside to McLean's parlor, and signed the surrender document.[16]

Custer was not present inside the McLean home during the signing; rather, he had been placed on the porch or in the yard renewing acquaintances with Southern friends from his days at West Point.

The small oval-shaped pine table upon which the surrender document had been signed was purchased for twenty dollars by Phil Sheridan. The next day, the cavalry commander handed the table to Custer as a gift to Libbie Custer. Sheridan enclosed a note, which read, "My dear Madam, I respectfully present to you the small writing table on which the conditions for the surrender of the Army of Northern Virginia were written by Lt. General Grant—and permit me to say, Madam, that there is scarcely an individual in our service who has contributed more to bring about this desirable result than your gallant husband." Libbie Custer treasured the table for the remainder of her life. After her death, the surrender table was added to the collection of the Smithsonian Institution.[17]

Edward W. Whitaker, chief of staff of the Third Division, summed up George Armstrong Custer's importance in the closing days of the war, "The country will never know the whole truth, or how much it owes to General Custer for turning the tide of battle to victory in the three last decisive engagements, Waynesboro, Five Forks and Appomattox Station. Failure in either one of these would have resulted in the prolongation of the war indefinitely."[18]

Custer, never one to ignore or take for granted that his achievements depended on the fidelity of his troops, penned a classic tribute on April 9 to the achievements of the cavalrymen of his Third Division:

> With profound gratitude toward the God of battles, by whose blessings our enemies have been humbled and our arms rendered triumphant, your commanding general avails himself of this his first opportunity to express to you the admiration of the heroic manner in which you have passed through the series of battles which to-day resulted in the surrender of the enemy's entire army. The record established by your indomitable courage is unparalleled in the annals of war. Your prowess won for you even the respect and admiration of your enemies. During the past six months, although in most instances confronted by superior numbers, you have captured from the enemy in open battle 111 pieces of field artillery, 65 battle-flags, and upward of 10,000 prisoners of war, including 7 general officers. Within the past ten days, and included in the above, you have captured 46 pieces of field artillery and 37 battle-flags. You have never lost a gun, never lost a color, and have never been defeated, and notwithstanding the numerous engagements in which you have borne a prominent part, including those memorable battles of the Shenandoah, you have captured every piece of artillery which the enemy has dared to open upon you. The near approach of peace renders it improbable that you will again be called upon to undergo the fatigues of toilsome march, or the exposure of the battle-field, but should the assistance of keen blades, wielded by your sturdy arms, be required to hasten the coming of that glorious peace for which we have been so long contending, the general commanding is proudly confident that in the future, as in the past, every demand will meet with a hearty and willing response. Let us hope that our work is done, and that, blessed with the comforts of home and friends.

For our comrades who have fallen, let us ever cherish a grateful remembrance. To the wounded and to those who languish in Southern prisons, let our heartfelt sympathies be tendered.

And now, speaking for myself alone, when the war is ended and the task of the historian begins; when those deeds of daring which have rendered the name and fame of the Third Cavalry Division imperishable, are inscribed upon the bright pages of our country's history, I only ask that my name be written as that of the commander of the Third Cavalry Division.[19]

The Army of the Potomac was honored by the country on May 23 with a parade in the nation's capital. Crowds of cheering admirers packed the route from the Capitol to the White House, where a reviewing stand had been erected. The cavalry led the procession: first Merritt—in place of Sheridan, who was in Louisiana—and then Custer's Third Division, each man adorned in a bright red necktie.[20]

General Horace Porter later wrote, "Conspicuous among the division leaders was Custer, his long golden curls floating in the wind, his low-cut collar, crimson neck-tie, buckskin breeches—half General, half scout, daredevil in appearance."[21]

Major General Custer proudly led his men down the street seated upon Don Juan, his favorite mount. The reviewing stand was in sight when—by most accounts—a group of young ladies rose to their feet and began to sing while showering Custer with flowers. Don Juan became spooked by this unexpected disturbance, and bolted in the direction of the reviewing stand.[22]

General Porter described the scene, "Within 200 yards of the President's stand his spirited horse took the bit in its teeth, and made a dash past the troops like a tornado. But Custer was more than a match for him. When the Cavalry-man, covered with flowers, afterwards rode by the officials the people screamed with delight." Detractors accused Custer of orchestrating the display simply to show off.[23]

Whatever the circumstances, George Armstrong Custer had made his final charge of the Civil War.

Epilogue

The historic image and reputation of George Armstrong Custer as a battlefield commander has been unfairly established from the events of one day in his life—the day he died at Little Bighorn—which has branded him to this day as the poster boy for military defeat. Every other aspect of his career has been overshadowed by perceptions about that lone, misunderstood fight against the Sioux and Cheyenne on the Western frontier.

In his time, however, Custer was not a symbol of defeat but a national hero on a grand scale due to his amazing achievements in the Civil War. If nothing else, the fact that he had a hand in turning the tide at Gettysburg should make him a legendary figure in the history of this country. But he accomplished so much more than success in just that one battle.

George Armstrong Custer rode the sanguinary battlefields of saber strokes and pistol fire with the utmost of distinction. He captured the first enemy battle flag taken by the Union army and he accepted the Confederate white flag of surrender at Appomattox. In between those notable events exists a series of intrepid acts of almost unimaginable proportion that earned him the admiration of his troops and the respect of his superiors, captured the fancy of newspaper correspondents, and gained him the adoration of the public.

It goes without saying that he also had the adoration of his widow, Libbie. She had been a model army wife, and had faithfully followed him to his duty stations whenever possible. She endured sacrifices and hardships on the frontier without complaint—satisfied to be at the side of the man she loved.

Libbie was thirty-four years old when Armstrong was killed at the Little Bighorn. At that time, she left Fort Abraham Lincoln in Dakota Territory and returned to Monroe to contemplate her future. Her mission in life was soon decided when a debate ensued over Custer's actions during that battle. Libbie worked tirelessly to protect the image of her late husband and vigorously defended him against those who brought criticism. Her first act was to assist Frederick Whittaker in his writing of the 1876 *A Complete Life of Gen. George A. Custer.* This favorable portrayal of Custer would be the predominant view of him for many years to come.

Libbie moved to New York City in the summer of 1877, and began supporting herself by writing. Her books include three excellent memoirs—each of which became quite popular with the public. She related her frontier adventures with detail and insight, which have helped countless researchers understand the rigors of army life and also serve to further shape the heroic image of her husband. Her stories recount how her marriage survived, and indeed flourished, in spite of the frustrations, dangers, and hardships of living on desolate posts, and they refute criticism of various mistakes Custer was alleged to have made. These fascinating books stand out as several of the best ever written about that period in history.

Custer's widow remained unmarried for the remainder of her life and lived most of the time in a Park Avenue apartment. She traveled the world and was much in demand as a public speaker—embracing issues that ranged beyond her husband's image to include the women's suffrage movement and other feminist causes.

Elizabeth Bacon Custer, the prettiest girl in Monroe, Michigan, died of a heart attack on April 4, 1933—four days short of her ninety-first birthday—and was buried beside her beloved Armstrong at the U.S. Military Academy at West Point, New York.

The bibliography of George Armstrong Custer and the Battle of the

Little Bighorn is one of the most voluminous in American history. Armchair generals, professional strategists, and learned historians have outlined their cases in excruciating detail to make their points about how this battle unfolded and why Custer made his tactical decisions.

Plenty of evidence exists that Custer's plan of attack was nothing less than brilliant, especially given the terrain. And with all due respect, the Native Americans on the frontier were no more ferocious, skillful, or cunning than the Confederate officers and men that he had engaged—and more often than not defeated even when outnumbered—on the battlefield time and time again.

There was one difference, however. Custer's skill as a battlefield strategist had not changed. But the makeup and mind-set of the cavalry had indeed changed in the ensuing decade, and in 1876 the men would not follow their commander blindly—as had Brigadier General Elon Farnsworth at Gettysburg, or Major Peter Weber at Falling Waters, or Custer on a number of occasions during the Civil War, regardless of risk. Nor were these soldiers fighting for the glory Custer had always believed men should attain in battle. Consequently, it was during that War of the Rebellion that the true picture of this extraordinary field commander emerges.

Horace Greeley, in the *New-York Tribune*, perhaps best summed up the Civil War legacy of George Armstrong Custer when he wrote, "Future writers of fiction will find in Brig. Gen. Custer most of the qualities which go to make up a first-class hero, and stories of his daring will be told around many a hearth stone long after the old flag again kisses the breeze from Maine to the Gulf. Gen. Custer is as gallant a cavalier as one would wish to see. Always circumspect, never rash, and viewing the circumstances under which he is placed as coolly as a chess player observes his game, Gen. Custer always sees 'the vantage of the ground' at a glance, and, like the eagle watching his prey from some mountain crag, sweeps down upon his adversary, and seldom fails in achieving a signal success. Frank and independent in his demeanor, Gen. C unites the qualities of the true gentleman with that of the accomplished and fearless soldier."

High praise, indeed.

Regardless of the outcome or our opinion about Little Bighorn, it must be examined whether or not historians have been wrong to condemn so severely a soldier who helped preserve the Union and was always prepared to defend his country against whatever foe he was ordered to fight. He did not choose his enemies. He simply obeyed orders and marched off to war to carry out his mission to the best of his ability, just like every other officer and enlisted man who served at the pleasure of their country has done to this day.

Should all those spectacular, meaningful charges, daring strategies, and intrepid deeds be ignored? Can the willingness of this officer to accept any assignment no matter how dangerous or distasteful be set aside? Should the injustice perpetrated on Native Americans by the United States of America be transferred to a man who publicly stated on more than one occasion that he respected his Native American enemies and did not blame them for their rebellion?

With this book as a testament, George Armstrong Custer's entire military career should be reassessed by fair-minded historians under a more favorable light and found to have been commendable. Few officers before or after have served with such honor and distinction.

In the end, he should receive praise rather than vilification for his patriotic service to America and be awarded his rightful place in history books alongside the greatest of cavalry commanders. After all, he not only proved himself time and time again on the field of battle but gave the ultimate sacrifice while wearing his country's uniform.

Notes

———◆———

One

West Point Cadet

1. Monaghan, *Custer*, 12; Schaff, *Spirit of Old West Point*, 2.
2. Wallace, *Custer's Ohio Boyhood*, 19.
3. Merington, *The Custer Story*, 7; Wallace, *Custer's Ohio Boyhood*, 19.
4. Wallace, *Custer's Ohio Boyhood*, 18, 21, 23, 24; Monaghan, *Custer*, 10–12.
5. Monaghan, *Custer*, 22.
6. Reynolds, *Civil War Memories*, 16.
7. The most entertaining and informative book about Custer's West Point years is Schaff, *The Spirit of Old West Point*.
8. Dupuy, *Men of West Point*, 13–14.
9. Schaff, *The Spirit of Old West Point*, 37 ff., 40, 68; J. P. Farley, *West Point in the Early Sixties*, 78.
10. *Register of Delinquencies*, 192; Horn, *"Skinned."* 1, 2; Frost, *Custer Legends*, 45.
11. Horn, *"Skinned,"* passim.
12. Sergent, *They Lie Forgotten*, 23, 24, 55.
13. Carroll, *Custer and His Times*, 9; Carroll, *Four on Custer*, 26–28. (Schaff, *The Spirit of Old West Point*, 159.)
14. *Regulations for the U. S. Military Academy*, 12.

15. *Register of Merit*, 104, 108, 113; *Register of Delinquencies*, 193.

16. GAC to brother and sister, June 30, 1858, George Armstrong Custer Collection, Monroe County Library System. Hereinafter referred to as GAC Collection, MCLS.

17. Monaghan, *Custer*, 29; Reynolds, *Civil War Memories*, 39.

18. Frost, *Custer Legends*, 136; Schaff, *The Spirit of Old West Point*, 194; Hutton, *Custer Reader*, 9.

19. Carroll, *Custer in the Civil War*, 87.

20. Sergent, *They Lie Forgotten*, 23–24.

21. Frost, *Custer Legends*, 137; Reynolds, *Civil War Memories*, 20; Schaff, *The Spirit of Old West Point*, 26, 193–95.

22. *Register of Delinquencies*, 342; Horn, "Skinned," 7–10.

23. O'Neil, "Custer's First Romance Revealed," 28.

24. *Record of Delinquencies*, 343; *Register of Merit*, 133, 139, 146, USMAA; Horn, "Skinned," 11–14.

Two

Rumors of War

1. Sergent, *They Lie Forgotten*, 86.

2. Pappas, *To the Point*, 310–11.

3. Monaghan, *Custer*, 35, 83.

4. Ibid., 37.

5. Ibid., 36, 37.

6. Carroll, *Custer in the Civil War*, 79–80; Monaghan, *Custer*, 35.

7. GAC to sister, November 10, 1860, GAC Collection, MCLS.

8. Oliver Otis Howard, *Autobiography*, I: 99.

9. Carroll, *Custer in the Civil War*, 84.

10. Schaff, *The Spirit of West Point*, 193–94.

11. Schaff, *The Spirit of West Point*, 207–208; Pappas, *To the Point*, 327–28.

12. Carroll, *Custer in the Civil War*, 81.

13. G. A. Custer, "War Memoirs: From West Point," *Galaxy*, 22, No. 3 (September 1876), 450–451.

14. GAC to sister, April 10, 1861, GAC collection, MCLS.

15. GAC to sister, April 22, 1861; GAC Collection, MCLS; Monaghan, *Custer*, 40–41.

16. Monaghan, *Custer*, 42.

17. *Record of Delinquencies*, 448, 449; *Register of Merit*, 150, 151, 158.

18. Carroll, *Custer in the Civil War*, 86.

19. Schaff, *The Spirit of West Point*, 260; Hatch, *Custer Companion*, 11–12.

20. Schaff, *The Spirit of West Point*, 260; Carroll, *Custer in the Civil War*, 87, 88; Special Orders, no. 21, U.S. Military Academy Archives (USMAA), 8.

21. Special orders, no. 21, USMAA, 8.

22. Special orders, no. 21, USMAA, 8, 9; Frost, *Custer Legends*, 76.

23. Special orders, no. 21, USMAA, 8, 9; Frost, *Custer Legends*, 76, 77.

24. Carroll, *Custer in the Civil War*, 88–89.

25. Ibid., 89.

Three

Bull Run

1. Carroll, *Custer in the Civil War*, 89; Monaghan, *Custer*, 43–44.

2. Ibid., 89.

3. Ibid., 90, 91.

4. Hatch, *Osceola*, 131.

5. Carroll, *Custer in the Civil War*, 90, 91.

6. Ibid., 91.

7. Ibid., 92–93; Monaghan, *Custer*, 47.

8. Carroll, *Custer in the Civil War*, 92–94, 96.

9. Ibid., 101, 102.

10. The best biography is Bushong and Bushong's *Fightin' Tom Rosser*.

11. Carroll, *Custer in the Civil War*, 103.

12. Ibid., 103–04; Whittaker, *Custer*, 67–68.

13. Carroll, *Custer in the Civil War*, 100.

14. Faust, *Historical Times Encyclopedia*, 90–92.

15. Davis, *Bull Run*, passim; Freeman, *Lee's Lieutenants*, I: 73–74; Merington, *Custer Story*, 12.

16. Carroll, *Custer in the Civil War*, 103, 105; Whittaker, *Custer*, 72–73.

17. Faust, *Historical Times Encyclopedia*, 92.

18. Davis, *Bull Run*, passim.

19. Merington, *Custer Story*, 12–13; Monaghan, *Custer*, 56.

20. Carroll, *Custer in the Civil War*, 105.

Four

The Cavalry Charge

1. Warner, *Generals in Blue*, 290–91; Sears, *George B. McClellan*, 95–101, 110, 111.

2. Warner, *Generals in Blue*, 290–91; Starr, *Union Cavalry*, I, 234–38.

3. Starr, Union Cavalry, I: 58–59; Warner, *Generals in Blue*, 258–59.

4. Carroll, *Custer in the Civil War*, 113–114.

5. Monaghan, *Custer*, 58–59.

6. Carroll, *Custer in the Civil War*, 115; Merington, *Custer Story*, 25.

7. Carroll, *Custer in the Civil War*, 118.

8. Hatch, *Custer Companion*, 10; Wallace, *Custer's Ohio Boyhood*, 25, 27.

9. Wallace, *Custer's Ohio Boyhood*, 25, 27; Hatch, *Custer Companion*, 19.

10. Frost, *General Custer's Libbie*, 14–17.

11. Whittaker, *Custer*, 89–90.

12. "Genealogical Information from the Emanuel Custer Bible," George Armstrong Custer Papers, Monroe County Historical Museum Association, hereinafter referred to as GAC Papers, MCHMA; Wallace, *Custer's Ohio Boyhood*, 6, 7.

13. Wallace, *Custer's Ohio Boyhood*, 5, 6, 7.

14. Ibid., 7.

15. Merington, *Custer Story*, 6.

16. Reynolds, *Civil War Memories*, 9.

17. Frost, *Custer Legends*, 101.

18. Wallace, *Custer's Ohio Boyhood*, 15, 16, 18; Merington, *Custer Story*, 7.

19. Wallace, *Custer's Ohio Boyhood*, 11.

20. Ibid., 17.

21. Frost, *General Custer's Libbie*, 13, 14, 19, 22.

22. Quaife, "Some Monroe Memories," 9–12; Reynolds, *Civil War Memories*, 4.

23. Monaghan, *Custer*, 61.

24. Sears, *George B. McClellan*, 108–116.

25. Whittaker, *Custer*, 93–94.

26. Carroll, *Custer in the Civil War*, 128–129.

27. Ibid., 129, 130; Monaghan, *Custer*, 62, 63.

28. Carroll, *Custer in the Civil War*, 129–30.

29. Carroll, *Custer in the Civil War*, 130; GAC to parents, March 17, 1862, GAC Collection, MCLS.

Five

Balloons and Battle Flags

1. Sears, *George B. McClellan*, 168.

2. GAC to parents, March 17, 1862, GAC Collection, MCLS.

3. GAC to parents, March 26, 1862; GAC to sister, March 28, 1862, GAC Collection, MCLS.

4. Carroll, *Custer in the Civil War*, 134.

5. McClellan, *Stuart*, 47; Blackford, *War Years*, 60–62.

6. Blackford, *War Years*, 60.

7. Merington, *Custer Story*, 29.

8. GAC to My Dear Sister, April 11, 1862, GAC Collection, MCLS.

9. E. H. Custer to GAC, April 18, 1862, Frost Collection, MCHMA; O'Neil, "Sister's Letter," *NLBHA* 27 (2):6–7.

10. Carroll, *Custer in the Civil War*, 146; Sears, *To the Gates*, 41, 54.

11. Carroll, *Custer in the Civil War*, 146.

12. Carroll, *Custer in the Civil War*, 147; GAC to sister, May 15, 1862, GAC Collection, MCLS.

13. Carroll, *Custer in the Civil War*, 146–149.

14. U.S. War Department, *The War of the Rebellion: A Compilation of the Official Records of the Union and Confederate Armies*. Hereinafter referred to as "*O. R.*," series 1, 11, pt. 1, 534; Carroll, *Custer in the Civil War*, 149–50.

15. *O. R.*, series 1, vol. 11, pt. 1, 526.

16. McClellan, *Stuart*, 48–50; Carroll, *Custer in the Civil War*, 150.

17. *O. R.*, series 1, vol. 11, pt. 3, 526.

18. *O. R.*, series 1, vol. 11, pt. 1, 273.

19. *O. R.*, series 1, vol. 11, pt. 1, 570–75.

20. *O. R.*, series 1, vol. 11, pt. 1, 535; Stephen W. Sears, *To the Gates*, 73–74.

21. *O. R.*, series 1, vol. 11, pt. 1, 536, 543, 608–13; Carroll, *Custer in the Civil War*, 154–58.

22. *O. R.*, series 1, vol. 11, pt. 1, pp. 536–543.

23. *O. R.*, series 1, vol. 11, pt. 1, pp. 536–543, 608–13; Carroll, *Custer in the Civil War*, 154–58; Sears, *To the Gates*, 78–81.

24. GAC to sister, May 15, 1862, GAC Collection, MCLS.

25. Starr, *Union Cavalry*, I: 268; GAC to sister, May 15, 1862, GAC Collection, MCLS.

26. *O. R.*, series 1, vol. 11, pt. 1, 111, 651; *National Tribune*, May 7, 1903.

27. *O. R.*, series 1, vol. 11, pt. 1, 651, 652, 653, 654; *National Tribune*, May 7, 1903; Reynolds, *Civil War*, 75.

28. *O. R.*, series 1, 11, pt. 1, 651; McClellan, *McClellan's Own Story*, 364; Merington, *Custer Story*, 31.

Six

Aide-de-Camp

1. McClellan, *McClellan's Own Story*, 365.

2. Sears, *To the Gates*, 103–112.

3. Sears, *To the Gates*, chapter 6; Faust, *Historical Times Encyclopedia*, 668.

4. Eicher, *The Longest Night*, 279.

5. Monaghan, *Custer*, 83; Katz, *Custer in Photographs*, 6–7.

6. Sears, *To the Gates*, chap. 6.

7. The best biography is Thomas, *Bold Dragoon*. For Stuart's adventurous tangle with the Cheyenne, see Hatch, *Black Kettle*, 61, 81.

8. Nesbitt, *Saber and Scapegoat*, 109.

9. Mosby, "The Ride Around McClellan," 246–48; *O. R.*, series 1, 11, pt. 1, 1038; Dowdey, *Wartime Papers of R. E. Lee*, 192; Freeman, *Lee's Lieutenants*, I: 277–78.

10. *O. R.*, 11, pt. 1, 1036; Von Borcke, *Memoirs*, I, 37; Freeman, *Lee's Lieutenants*, I: 282.

11. *O. R.*, 11, pt. 1, 1037–39; McClellan, *Stuart*, 54–57, 60–66; Freeman, *Lee's Lieutenants*, I: 282–83, 286, 288, 292–298, 300; Campbell, "Stuart's Ride," 86–89; Cooke, *Wearing of the Gray*, 175–181.

12. *Richmond Enquirer*, June 16 and June 18, 1862; *Richmond Examiner*, June 16, 1862; *O. R.*, 11, pt. 1, 1042; Dowdey, *Wartime Papers of Lee*, 197–98; Hatch, "Custer vs. Stuart," 45–47.

13. *O. R.*, 11, pt. 1, 1042; Dowdey, *Wartime Papers of Lee*, 198–200.

14. *O. R.*, 11, pt. 1, 117, pt. 2, 75; Sears, *George B. McClellan Papers*, 320; GAC to brother and sister, July 13, 1862, GAC Collection, MCLS.

15. *O. R.*, vol. 11, pt. 1, 574–75.

16. *O. R.*, vol. 11, pt. 2, 521.

17. Bushong and Bushong, *Fighting Tom Rosser*, 20.

18. GAC to brother and sister, July 13, 1862, GAC Collection, MCLS.

19. Monaghan, *Custer*, 87.

20. *O. R.*, 11, pt. 2, 954, 955; Merington, *Custer Story*, 32–33.

21. Sears, *George B. McClellan*, 240–45.

22. McClellan, *Stuart*, 86, 91; Freeman, *Lee's Lieutenants*, I: 643, II: 4–5; Bushong and Bushong, *Fighting Tom Rosser*, 20.

23. Schaff, *The Spirit of Old West Point*, 180–183; Merington, *Custer Story*, 34–35.

24. Merington, *Custer Story*, 35.

25. Tom Carhart, *Sacred Ties*, 138–139.

26. Faust, *Historical Times Encyclopedia*, 92–93.

27. Sears, *George B. McClellan*, 247; Murfin, *The Gleam of Bayonets*, passim.

28. Stackpole, *From Cedar Mountain to Antietam*, 301, 303, 314–15.

29. Monaghan, *Custer*, 103.

30. Stackpole, *From Cedar Mountain to Antietam*, passim; Murfin, *The Gleam of Bayonets*, passim; Long, *The Civil War*, 268–81.

31. Foner, *The Fiery Trial*, 239–42; Nevins, *Ordeal of the Union*, vol. 6: 231–41, 273.

32. Monaghan, *Custer*, 99–100.

33. Merington, *Custer Story*, 35.

34. GAC to Augusta Ward, October 3, 1862, typescript, GAC Letters, Rochester Public Library.

35. *O. R.*, 19, pt. 2, 52–56; Blackford, *War Years*, 164; Freeman, *Lee's Lieutenants*, II, 284–85.

36. *O. R.*, 12, pt. 2, 52–56; Blackford, *War Years*, 165–78; McClellan, *Stuart*, 140–41, 148–49, 163–64.

37. *Richmond Examiner*, October 15, 1862; *O. R.*, 19, pt. 2, 51.

38. Sears, *George B. McClellan*, 340–44.

Seven

Libbie

1. Leckie, *Elizabeth Bacon Custer*, 11–12.

2. Frost, *General Custer's Libbie*, 14, 15; Merington, *Custer Story*, 14–16.

3. Frost, *General Custer's Libbie*, 14–17.

4. Merington, *Custer Story*, 18–19.

5. Merington, *Custer Story*, 20–21.

6. Frost, *General Custer's Libbie*, 16.

7. Frost, *General Custer's Libbie*, 17, 18; Leckie, *Elizabeth Bacon Custer*, 5–7.

8. Leckie, *Elizabeth Bacon Custer*, 8; Elizabeth Clift Bacon Journal, 8 April 1852 to 31 December 1860. Gift of Marguerite Merington to Western Americana Collection, Beinecke Rare Book and Manuscript Library, Yale University, New Haven, CT (hereafter referred to as EBCJ), 9, 10, 11, 12, 18 April, 1852.

9. Leckie, *Elizabeth Bacon Custer*, 7, 8; EBCJ, 16, 19 April, 1852 and 5, 20 August, 1852 and 8 September, 1852.

10. EBCJ, 27 August, 1854.

11. EBCJ, 27 August, 1854; Frost, *General Custer's Libbie*, 25.

12. Leckie, *Elizabeth Bacon Custer*, 10, 11; EBCJ, 12 November, 1854.

13. Frost, *General Custer's Libbie*, 28–30.

14. Leckie, *Elizabeth Bacon Custer*, 12–13.

15. Kines, *A Life Within a Life*, 8.

16. Leckie, *Elizabeth Bacon Custer*, 14–15; EBCJ, 15 January 1858.

17. EBCJ, 15 January 1858.

18. Frost, *General Custer's Libbie*, 29–31.

19. Frost, *General Custer's Libbie*, 32, 33.

20. EBCJ, 18 May, 1859.

21. Frost, *General Custer's Libbie*, 32, 33; Merington, *Custer Story*, 42, 43.

22. *Detroit Free Press*, 20 June, 1862.

23. Libbie (Elizabeth Clift) Bacon's Journal, 1861–1863, Brice C. W. Custer Collection, a private collection, (BCWCC), hereinafter cited as LBJ, 28 February, 1862.

24. Merington, *Custer Story*, 46–47.

25. Merington, *Custer Story*, 48.

26. Merington, *Custer Story*, 47; LBJ, 17 December, 1862.

27. LBJ, 17 December, 1862.

28. Leckie, *Elizabeth Bacon Custer*, 24; LBJ, 17 December, 1862.

29. Blackford, *War Years*, 189; Von Borcke, *Memories*, II: 112–34; Faust, *Civil War Encyclopedia*, 287, 289.

30. Leckie, *Elizabeth Bacon Custer*, 24.

31. Merington, *Custer Story*, 50; Leckie, *Elizabeth Bacon Custer*, 25; Frost, *General Custer's Libbie*, 58.

32. Merington, *Custer Story*, 50.

33. Merington, *Custer Story*, 50; Frost, *General Custer's Libbie*, 58, 59.

34. Merington, *Custer Story*, 50–51.

35. *O. R.*, 25, pt. 1, 58–60; Blackford, *War Years*, 200–01.

36. Cooke, *Wearing of the Gray*, 116–129; Schaff, *The Spirit of Old West Point*, 133.

37. Bushong and Bushong, *Fighting Tom Rosser*, 42–43.

38. Frost, *General Custer's Libbie*, 33, 60, 61.

39. Frost, *General Custer's Libbie*, 60.

40. Leckie, *Elizabeth Bacon Custer*, 25; Frost, *General Custer's Libbie*, 59–63.

41. Monaghan, *Custer*, 115.

Eight

Pleasonton's Pet

1. Stackpole, *Chancellorsville*, passim; McClellan, *Stuart*, 218–24.
2. *O. R.*, 25, pt. 1, 1045–48.
3. Ibid., 886–89.
4. Ibid., 886–89.
5. Furgurson, *Chancellorsville*, 333.
6. Longacre, *Cavalry at Gettysburg*, 49.
7. Ibid., 46–47; Starr, *Union Cavalry*, I, 363, 367.
8. Ibid., 48–49; Starr, *Union Cavalry*, 1, 314n, 315.
9. Merington, *Custer Story*, 50–51.
10. Ibid., 53; Longacre, *Cavalry at Gettysburg*, 56; Carter, *Last Cavaliers*, 189.
11. *O. R.*, 25, pt. 1, 1116; Monaghan, *Custer*, 117–122.
12. Merington, *Custer Story*, 53–54.
13. LBJ, 26 April 1863; Leckie, *Elizabeth Bacon Custer*, 27.
14. Reynolds, *Civil War Memories*, 5.
15. A. Pleasonton to Austin Blair, May 30, 1863. Pleasonton Papers, Library of Congress.
16. Harris, *Personal Reminiscences*, 17, 23.
17. O'Neil, "Two Men of Ohio: Custer & Bingham," 33.
18. *O. R.*, pt. 3, 5–8; Longacre, *Cavalry at Gettysburg*, 61–62; Coddington, *Gettysburg Campaign*, 49–53.
19. *O. R.*, 27, pt. 1, 906; Longacre, *Cavalry at Gettysburg*, 62; Nye, *Here Come the Rebels!*, 30–32.

Nine

Brandy Station

1. GAC to sister, June 8, 1863, GAC Collection, MCLS.
2. *O. R.*, 25, pt. 2, 574; Carter, *Last Cavaliers*, 152.
3. Coddington, *Gettysburg Campaign*, 56; Longacre, *Cavalry at Gettysburg*, 66.
4. *O. R.*, 27, pt. 2, 679–85; Longacre, *Cavalry at Gettysburg*, 70; Starr, *Union Cavalry*, I, 366–73; McClellan, *Stuart*, 264–69.
5. Coddington, *Gettysburg Campaign*, 56.
6. Merington, *Custer Story*, 57, 58.
7. *O. R.*, 27, pt. 2, 754–55; Downey, *Clash of Cavalry*, 94.
8. Longacre, *Cavalry at Gettysburg*, 51, 67.

9. *O. R.*, 27, pt. 1, 1046; Merington, *Custer Story*, 58, 59.

10. *O. R.*, 27, pt. 1, 1047–48; Longacre, *Cavalry at Gettysburg*, 67.

11. *O. R.*, 27, pt. 1, 1047–48.

12. Monaghan, *Custer*, 127.

13. Merington, *Custer Story*, 58–59; Longacre, *Cavalry at Gettysburg*, 69.

14. Carter, *Last Cavaliers*, 154; Starr, *Union Cavalry*, I: 380–83.

15. Carter, *Last Cavaliers*, 154; Longacre, *Cavalry at Gettysburg*, 70.

16. *O. R.*, 27, pt. 2, 729, 772.

17. Downey, *Clash of Cavalry*, 123–24; Carter, *Last Cavaliers*, 159.

18. Longacre, *Cavalry at Gettysburg*, 84–85; Thomas, *Robert E. Lee*, 291.

19. Alberts, *General Wesley Merritt*, 58–59.

20. *O. R.*, pt. 3, 39–40; McClellan, *Stuart*, 294–95.

21. *O. R.*, 27, pt. 1, 905, 1046; Monaghan, *Custer*, 128.

22. *O. R.*, 27, pt. 1, 168–169, 904 and pt. 2, 719, 768; Faust, *Civil War Encyclopedia*, 76.

23. Longacre, *Cavalry at Gettysburg*, 90.

24. *O. R.*, 27, pt. 2, 687.

25. *New-York Tribune*, June 13, 1863.

Ten

Boy General

1. Long, *The Civil War*, 364–69; Carter, *Last Cavaliers*, 160–61.

2. McClellan, *Stuart*, 296–97; Longacre, *Cavalry at Gettysburg*, 102–04.

3. O'Neill, *Cavalry Battles*, 39; Meyer, *Civil War Experiences*, 33, 34.

4. *O. R.*, 27, pt. 2, 687–710.

5. *O. R.*, 27, pt. 2, 741.

6. O'Neill, *Cavalry Battles*, 60, 182n.

7. Longacre, *Cavalry at Gettysburg*, 108; Merington, *Custer Story*, 55–56.

8. Merington, *Custer Story*, 55–56.

9. Longacre, *Cavalry at Gettysburg*, 108; Merington, *Custer Story*, 55–56.

10. Merington, *Custer Story*, 55.

11. *The New York Times*, June 20, 1863; Longacre, *Cavalry at Gettysburg*, 108; Merington, *Custer Story*, 54–55.

12. Merington, *Custer Story*, 55.

13. *Harper's Weekly*, October 3, 1863.

14. Merington, *Custer Story*, 56.

15. *O. R.*, 27, pt. 1, 289, 908–10, 953–54.

16. *O. R.*, 27, pt. 3, 193, 210–11, 482.

17. McClellan, *Stuart*, 307–08, 312–13; Starr, *Union Cavalry*, 1: 411–12.

18. *O. R.*, 27, pt. 2, 687–710.

19. Longacre, *Cavalry at Gettysburg*, 148–49; Freeman, *Lee's Lieutenants*, III, 41.

20. *O. R.*, 27, pt. 3, 358, 430, 913, 915, 923; Gallagher, *First Day at Gettysburg*, 16–17; Nesbitt, *Saber and Scapegoat*, 57–67.

21. *O. R.*, 27, pt. 2, 693; Blackford, *War Years*, 223.

22. Faust, *Historical Times Encyclopedia*, 482; *O. R.*, pt. 3, 315, 334–36.

23. *O. R.*, 27; pt. 3, 373–74.

24. Alfred Pleasonton to John F. Farnsworth, June 23, 1863. Pleasonton Papers, Library of Congress.

25. *O. R.*, 27, pt. 1, 61, pt. 3, 373, 376.

26. Monaghan, *Custer*, 133.

27. Custer to Judge Christiancy, July 26, 1863. Christiancy-Pickett Papers, United States Army Military History Institute.

28. Merington, *Custer Story*, 60.

29. *O. R.*, 27, pt. 1, 167 and pt. 3, 376.

30. *Monroe Commercial*, July 28, 1863.

31. Monaghan, *Custer*, 134–35; Longacre, *Custer and His Wolverines*, 131.

32. Merington, *Custer Story*, 60.

33. Monaghan, *Custer*, 134–35; Longacre, *Custer and His Wolverines*, 131.

34. *O. R.*, 27, pt. 2, 687–710; Blackford, *War Years*, 224–25; Freeman, *Lee's Lieutenants*, III: 65–67.

35. *O. R.*, 27, pt. 2, 687–710; Coddington, *Gettysburg Campaign*, 198–99.

36. *O. R.*, 27, pt. 2, 687–710; Blackford, *War Years*, 224–25.

37. Monaghan, *Custer*, 134–35.

Eleven

East of Gettysburg

1. Longacre, *Custer and His Wolverines*, 131–32.

2. Carroll, *Custer in the Civil War*, 73–74.

3. Whittaker, *Custer*, 171.

4. *O. R.*, 27; pt. 1, 991, 992; Kidd, *Personal Recollections*, 124, 125.

5. *O. R.*, 27, pt. 2, 694–95; McClellan, *Stuart*, 325; Longacre, *Cavalry at Gettysburg*, 157–58.

6. McClellan, *Stuart*, 326–27; Nye, *Here Come the Rebels!*, 319–20; *O. R.*, 27, pt. 2, 694.

7. *O. R.*, 27, pt. 1, 992.

8. Longacre, *Custer and His Wolverines*, 132.

9. McClellan, *Stuart*, 327; Shriver, "My Father," 3.

10. *O. R.*, 27, pt. 2, 687–710; McClellan, *Stuart*, 327–28; Nye, *Here Come the Rebels!*, 322–25.

11. *O. R.*, 27, pt. 1, 992, 1000; Alexander, "Gettysburg," 26.

12. *O. R.*, 27, pt. 1, 992, 997; Kidd, *Personal Recollections*, 128.

13. Kidd, *Personal Recollections*, 127, 128; Alexander, "Gettysburg," 27.

14. Kidd, *Personal Recollections*, 125–29.

15. *O. R.*, 27, pt. 2, 696; McClellan, *Stuart*, 329–30.

16. *O. R.*, 27, pt. 1, 193, 924, 987–88, 992 and pt. 2, 713–14.

17. *O. R.*, 27, pt. 2, 696; Blackford, *War Years*, 228.

18. McClellan, *Stuart*, 329–30; Blackford, *War Years*, 228; Coddington, *Gettysburg Campaign*, 201; Freeman, *Lee's Lieutenants*, III, 136–37.

19. Longacre, *Custer and His Wolverines*, 38–39.

20. *O. R.*, 27, pt. 1, 927, 934, 939 and pt. 2, 637, 642–43, 646, 648–49.

21. *O. R.*, 27, pt. 1, 992; Carter, *Last Cavaliers*, 165.

22. Tucker, *Lee and Longstreet at Gettysburg*, 205.

23. *O. R.*, 27, pt. 2, 318.

24. Longacre, *Cavalry at Gettysburg*, 194–95; Coddington, *Gettysburg Campaign*, 201.

25. Longacre, *Cavalry at Gettysburg*, 194–95, 196; Cooke, *Wearing of the Gray*, 245; *The New York Times*, July 3, 1863.

26. *O. R.*, 27, pt. 2, 221; Longacre, *Cavalry at Gettysburg*, 196–97; Cooke, *Wearing of the Gray*, 245.

27. *O. R.*, 27, pt. 2, 221, 697; McClellan, *Stuart*, 330–31; Coddington, *Gettysburg Campaign*, 202.

28. *O. R.*, 27, pt. 1, 145, 992.

29. Freeman, *Lee's Lieutenants*, III: 139; Nesbitt, *Saber and Scapegoat*, 89–90.

30. Nesbitt, *Saber and Scapegoat*, 91; Thomas, *Bold Dragoon*, 247.

31. *O. R.*, 27, pt. 1, 992.

32. Mackey, "Duel of General Wade Hampton," 122–26; Nye, "Affair at Hunterstown," 29–30.

33. Shevchuk, "Battle of Hunterstown," 99.

34. *O. R.*, 27, pt. 1, 999; Nye, "Affair at Hunterstown," 33.

35. *O. R.*, 27, pt. 1, 992.

36. *O. R.*, 27, pt. 1, 992, 998–1000; Shevchuk, "Battle of Hunterstown," 99, 100; Kidd, *Personal Recollections*, 134.

37. Shevchuk, "Battle of Hunterstown," 100.

38. *O. R.*, 27, pt. 1, 992; Kidd, *Personal Recollections*, 134; Nye, "Affair at Hunterstown," 33; Shevchuk, "Battle of Hunterstown," 102, 103.

39. *O. R.*, 27, pt. 1, 992.

40. Kidd, *Personal Recollections*, 135.

Twelve

Custer vs. Stuart

1. *O. R.*, 27, pt. 2, 697, 699, 724; McClellan, *Stuart*, 337; Coddington, *Gettysburg Campaign*, 520–21.

2. *O. R.*, 27, pt. 1, 956; Trowbridge, *Operations of the Cavalry*, 9–12; Kidd, *Personal Recollections*, 136–42.

3. Alexander, "Gettysburg," 37; Longacre, *Cavalry at Gettysburg*, 223.

4. *O. R.*, 27, pt. 2, 697; Coddington, *Gettysburg Campaign*, 520–21.

5. Kidd, *Personal Recollections*, 139–44; Trowbridge, *Operations of the Cavalry*, 10–12.

6. Kidd, *Personal Recollections*, 139–44; Trowbridge, *Operations of the Cavalry*, 10–13.

7. McClellan, *Stuart*, 338–39; Coddington, *Gettysburg Campaign*, 521.

8. Kidd, *Personal Recollections*, 141–44; Robertson, *Michigan in the War*, 582–83; Harris, *Personal Reminiscences*, 29–30.

9. Alexander, "Gettysburg," 32.

10. *O. R.*, 27, pt. 1, 956; Coddington, *Gettysburg Campaign*, 521–22.

11. Kidd, *Personal Recollections*, 145.

12. Longacre, *Cavalry at Gettysburg*, 225; Longacre, *Custer and His Wolverines*, 148; Carter, *Last Cavaliers*, 169.

13. Krolick, "Forgotten Field," 84.

14. Longacre, *Cavalry at Gettysburg*, 228; Longacre, *Custer and His Wolverines*, 148–49; Nesbitt, *Saber and Scapegoat*, 100.

15. Harris, *Personal Reminiscences*, 31–32; Kidd, *Personal Recollections*, 148–49.

16. Kidd, *Personal Recollections*, 147–49.

17. Nesbitt, *Saber and Scapegoat*, 101; Longacre, *Custer and His Wolverines*, 150.

18. Lee, "Personal and Historical Sketches," 148–49; Trowbridge, *Operations of the Cavalry*, 13.

19. Brooke-Rawle, "The Right Flank," 480; Kidd, *Personal Recollections*, 148–52.

20. Kidd, *Personal Recollections*, 151–52; Longacre, *Cavalry at Gettysburg*, 231.

21. *O. R.*, 27, pt. 2, 687–710; McClellan, *Stuart*, 337–40; Kidd, *Personal Recollections*, 152.

22. *O. R.*, 27, pt. 2, 687–710; McClellan, *Stuart*, 337–40; Brooke-Rawle, "The Right Flank," 481; Kidd, *Personal Recollections*, 152–53.

23. Miller, "The Cavalry Battle Near Gettysburg," 404.

24. *O. R.*, 27, pt. 2, 687–710; Brooke-Rawle, "The Right Flank," 481.

25. Harris, *Personal Reminiscences*, 34; Kidd, *Personal Recollections*, 153–54.

26. Harris, *Personal Reminiscences*, 34; Brooke-Rawle, "The Right Flank," 481–82.

27. Brooke-Rawle, "The Right Flank," 481.

28. Miller, "The Cavalry Battle Near Gettysburg," 404.

29. Trowbridge, *Operations of the Cavalry*, 14–15; Miller, "The Cavalry Battle Near Gettysburg," 404–05.

30. Starr, *Union Cavalry*, I: 436; Miller, "The Cavalry Battle Near Gettysburg," 404–05; Carter, *Last Cavaliers*, 171.

31. Custer to his sister, July 26, 1863, U.S. Military Academy Library; Kidd, *Personal Recollections*, 154–55.

32. Miller, "The Cavalry Battle Near Gettysburg," 404–05.

33. McClellan, *Stuart*, 344; Nesbitt, *Saber and Scapegoat*, 105; Longacre, *Custer and His Wolverines*, 153.

34. Cooke, *Wearing of the Gray*, 247; *O. R.*, 27, pt. 3, 1001.

35. Miller, "The Cavalry Battle Near Gettysburg," 405.

36. *O. R.*, vol. 27, pt. 2, 697, 698.

37. *O. R.*, 27, pt. 2, 687–710; Riggs, *East of Gettysburg*, 49.

38. Blackford, *War Years*, 233.

39. Longacre, *Cavalry at Gettysburg*, 244.

40. Rosser, *Addresses*, 41.

41. Cooke, *Wearing of the Gray*, 248.

Thirteen
Withdrawal and Pursuit

1. *O. R.*, 27, pt. 1, 993.

2. Faust, *Historical Times Encyclopedia*, 307.

3. Tucker, *High Tide at Gettysburg*, 406–07; Tucker, *Lee and Longstreet*, 8, 205; Freeman, *Lee's Lieutenants*, III: 207.

4. *O. R.*, 27, pt. 2, 687–710.

5. Freeman, *Lee's Lieutenants*, III: 207.

6. *O. R.*, 27, pt. 2, 321; Nesbitt, *Saber and Scapegoat*, 132–33; Tucker, *High Tide at Gettysburg*, 406–07; Freeman, *Lee's Lieutenants*, III: 208.

7. The best source for debate about this controversy is Nesbitt, *Saber and Scapegoat*.

8. Blackford, *Letters from Lee's Army*, 195–96.

9. Coddington, *Gettysburg Campaign*, 535–37.

10. Blackford, *War Years*, 234; Cooke, *Wearing of the Gray*, 248–49.

11. A great book on the aftermath of the battle in Gettysburg is *Days of Darkness: Gettysburg Civilians* by William G. Williams. Shippensburg, PA: White Mane Publishing Co., 1986.

12. Coddington, *Gettysburg Campaign*, 535–37.

13. Longacre, *Cavalry at Gettysburg*, 245–46.

14. Carter, *Last Cavaliers*, 175.

15. Longacre, *Custer and His Wolverines*, 154.

16. *Detroit Free Press*, 15 July, 1863.

17. Faust, *Historical Times Encyclopedia*, 307.

18. *O. R.*, 27, pt. 1, 1018–19.

19. Carter, *Last Cavaliers*, 174.

20. *O. R.*, 27, pt. 1, 1018–19; Kidd, *Personal Recollections*, 161–65.

21. Kidd, *Personal Recollections*, 164, 165.

22. *O. R.*, 27, pt. 1, 993.

23. Longacre, *Cavalry at Gettysburg*, 246.

24. Imboden, "The Confederate Retreat," 424.

25. *O. R.*, 27, pt. 1, 993–94.

26. Ibid., 998.

27. Ibid., 994.

28. *O. R.*, 27, pt. 1, 994, 1000, 1019; Kidd, *Personal Recollections*, 168–71; Coddington, *Gettysburg Campaign*, 549.

29. *The New York Times*, 21 July, 1863.

30. Longacre, *Custer and His Wolverines*, 158.

Fourteen

Evasion

1. *O. R.*, 27, pt. 1, 994–95, 1006, 1014 and pt. 2, 700.

2. *O. R.*, 27, pt. 1, 994–95.

3. *O. R.*, 27, pt. 2, 700–01.

4. Longacre, *Cavalry at Gettysburg*, 254; Coddington, *Gettysburg Campaign*, 553.

5. *O. R.*, 27, pt. 1, 995, 998–1000; McClellan, *Stuart*, 357.

6. Kidd, *Personal Recollections*, 174–77.

7. Ibid., 174–77; Longacre, *Custer and His Wolverines*, 159.

8. McClellan, *Stuart*, 358–59; Coddington, *Gettysburg Campaign*, 553.

9. *O. R.*, 27, pt. 1, 928; Imboden, "The Confederate Retreat," 314.

10. McClellan, *Stuart*, 361.

11. LBJ, 6 July, 1863.

12. Ibid.

13. Ibid.

14. Frost, *General Custer's Libbie*, 75.

15. Coddington, *Gettysburg Campaign*, 565.

16. *O. R.*, 27, pt. 2, 703.

17. *O. R.*, 27, pt. 1, 999.

18. Coddington, *Gettysburg Campaign*, 365–67.

19. Longacre, *Custer and His Wolverines*, 161.

20. *O. R.*, 27, pt. 1, 663–64, 925–26, 929, 936, 941–42, 1033 and pt. 2, 398–99.

21. *O. R.*, 27, pt. 1, 988–89, 99 and pt. 2, 704–05; Kidd, *Personal Recollections*, 181.

22. Coddington, *Gettysburg Campaign*, 567–68.

23. Ibid., 569–70.

24. Heth, *Memoirs of Henry Heth*, 173; McClellan, *Stuart*, 366.

25. *O. R.*, 27, pt. 2, 327.

26. *O. R.*, 27, pt. 1, 929, 990; Kidd, *Personal Recollections*, 183–84.

27. *O. R.*, 27, pt. 2, 639–40, 705.

28. *O. R.*, 1, 27, pt. 1, 990.

29. *O. R.*, 27, pt. 1, 990, 1000 and pt. 2, 640–42.

30. *O. R.*, 27, pt. 2, 640–41, 648, 705.

31. Kidd, *Personal Recollections*, 185.

32. *O. R.*, 27, pt. 1, 990, 1000 and pt. 2, 640–41.

33. *O. R.*, 1, 27, pt. 1, 990; *The New York Times*, 21 July 1863.

34. Coddington, *Gettysburg Campaign*, 571–72.

35. Pohanka, "Letters," 6.

Fifteen

Culpeper

1. Kidd, *Personal Recollections*, 130, 131.
2. Custer, *"Boots and Saddles,"* 9–10; *Grand Rapids Daily Eagle*, July 8, 1876; *Chicago Tribune*, July 7, 1876.
3. Taylor, *With Sheridan up the Shenandoah Valley*, 30.
4. *O. R.*, 27, pt. 1, 918, 992–96.
5. Merington, *Custer Story*, 62.
6. Ibid., 62–63.
7. Leckie, *Elizabeth Bacon Custer*, 32.
8. Merington, *Custer Story*, 61; Frost, *General Custer's Libbie*, 95.
9. Custer, *Tenting*, 40, 41.
10. Frost, *General Custer's Libbie*, 95.
11. Wiley, *The Life of Billy Yank*, 157–58.
12. *Grand Rapids Daily Eagle*, 8 July 1876.
13. *O. R.*, 27, pt. 1, 999, 1001–04 and pt. 3, 753–54.
14. Ibid.
15. GAC to sister, July 26, 1863, GAC Collection, MCLS.
16. McCrea, *Dear Belle*, 146, 214–15.
17. *O. R.*, 29, pt. 2, 128.
18. Freeman, *Lee's Lieutenants*, III, 211.
19. Army of Northern Virginia, Special Orders, no. 226, September 9, 1863: McClellan, *Stuart*, 371–72.
20. Freeman, *Lee's Lieutenants*, III, 211–212.
21. Bushong and Bushong, *Fightin' Tom Rosser*, 43.
22. Freeman, *Lee's Lieutenants*, III, 212–13; Thomas, *Bold Dragoon*, 261–62.
23. Freeman, *Lee's Lieutenants*, III, 212–213.
24. *O. R.*, 29, pt. 1, 111; Henderson, *Road to Bristoe Station*, 36.
25. *O. R.*, 29, pt. 1, 111, 112; Henderson, *Road to Bristoe Station*, 32, 33; *The New York Times*, September 17, 1863.
26. McClellan, *Stuart*, 372–73.
27. Henderson, *Road to Bristoe Station*, 36, 38; *The New York Times*, September 28, October 21, 1863; McClellan, *Stuart*, 372–373.
28. *O. R.*, 29, pt. 1, 118, 119; Henderson, *Road to Bristoe Station*, 38, 39; *The New York Times*, September 28, 1863.
29. McClellan, *Stuart*, 373; Henderson, *Road to Bristoe Station*, 40.

30. Henderson, *Road to Bristoe Station*, 40, 39; *The New York Times*, September 17, 28, 1863.

31. Whittaker, *Custer*, 193–96; Monaghan, *Custer*, 161; McClellan, *Stuart*, 373–74.

32. McClellan, *Stuart*, 374.

33. *O. R.*, 29, pt. 1, 126–28; *Grand Rapids Daily Eagle*, September 25, 1863; Agassiz, *Meade's Headquarters*, 17.

34. Frost, *General Custer's Libbie*, 70.

Sixteen

The Bristoe Campaign

1. Frost, *General Custer's Libbie*, 75.

2. Ibid.

3. Reynolds, *Civil War Memories*, 6.

4. Frost, *General Custer's Libbie*, 75; Merington, *Custer Story*, 64.

5. LBJ, 18 and 25 October, 1863.

6. Merington, *Custer Story*, 65.

7. Frost, *General Custer's Libbie*, 75.

8. Merington, *Custer Story*, 65.

9. *O. R.*, 29, pt. 1, 389, pt. 2, 270; Carroll, *Custer in the Civil War*, 10; Henderson, *Road to Bristoe Station*, 70–72.

10. McClellan, *Stuart*, 377; Freeman, *Lee's Lieutenants*, III, 249.

11. *O. R.*, 29, pt. 1, 230, 374, 381, 389; McClellan, *Stuart*, 377–78; Carroll, *Custer in the Civil War*, 10; Henderson, *Road to Bristoe Station*, 78–81, 84, 86.

12. *O. R.*, 29, pt. 1, 230, 374, 381, 389.

13. *O. R.*, 29, pt. 1, 381, 390; *Grand Rapids Daily Eagle*, October 28, 1863.

14. McClellan, *Stuart*, 379; Cooke, *Wearing of the Gray*, 257.

15. Carroll, *Custer in the Civil War*, 10.

16. *O. R.*, 29, pt. 1, 381, 390, 393, 443.

17. Lee, *Personal and Historical Sketches*, 36–37.

18. *O. R.*, 29, pt. 1, 390 and pt. 2, 771–72, 779, 788.

19. *O. R.*, 29, pt. 1, 443.

20. Ibid., 390.

21. Ibid., 390; Carroll, *Custer in the Civil War*, 11; Merington, *Custer Story*, 66.

22. Merington, *Custer Story*, 66.

23. *O. R.*, 29, pt. 1, 390; Carroll, *Custer in the Civil War*, 11; Merington, *Custer Story*, 66.

24. Longacre, *Custer and His Wolverines*, 188; Carter, *Last Cavaliers*, 193.

25. McClellan, *Stuart*, 381–82; Freeman, *Lee's Lieutenants*, III: 251.

26. Longacre, *Custer and His Wolverines*, 188; Carter, *Last Cavaliers*, 193.

27. *O. R.*, 29, pt. 1, 387, 390.

28. McClellan, *Stuart*, 382–83.

29. *O. R.*, 29, pt. 1, 381, 390–91, 393–95; McClellan, *Stuart*, 383; Kidd, *Personal Recollections*, 205–09.

30. Merington, *Custer Story*, 67.

31. Lee, *History of the 7th Michigan Cavalry*, 38–39.

32. *O. R.*, 29, pt. 1, 382, 391, 451.

33. Ibid., 391, 397.

34. Ibid., 451, 464.

35. Kidd, *Personal Recollections*, 216–17; *The New York Times*, October 23, 1863.

36. Kidd, *Personal Recollections*, 216; Merington, *Custer Story*, 68.

37. Blackford, *War Years*, 241; McClellan, *Stuart*, 394–95.

38. *O. R.*, 29, pt. 1, 391; Kidd, *Personal Recollections*, 213–220.

39. Blackford, *War Years*, 241–42.

40. *O. R.*, 29, pt. 1, 391, 392.

41. Ibid., 383, 387–88, 391–92; Merington, *Custer Story*, 68; Kidd, *Personal Recollections*, 215–216; Henderson, *Road to Bristoe Station*, 204, 205.

42. *O. R.*, 29, pt. 1, 391, 392, 438–54; McClellan, *Stuart*, 394–95; *The New York Times*, October 23, 1863.

43. Merington, *Custer Story*, 68–69.

44. *O. R.*, 29, pt. 1, 392; Carroll, *Custer in the Civil War*, 10–13.

Seventeen

Marriage

1. Merington, *Custer Story*, 67; Frost, *General Custer's Libbie*, 77.

2. Frost, *General Custer's Libbie*, 78, 79.

3. Merington, *Custer Story*, 73, 74; Frost, *General Custer's Libbie*, 80.

4. Merington, *Custer Story*, 737.

5. LBJ, 18 and 25 October, 1863.

6. Merington, *Custer Story*, 74.

7. Ibid., 71, 72; Frost, *General Custer's Libbie*, 81.

8. Merington, *Custer Story*, 70.

9. LBJ, 19 October, 1863.

10. *O. R.*, 29, pt. 2, 448.

11. Frost, *General Custer's Libbie*, 84, 85.

12. Ibid., 83–85.

13. *O. R.*, *29*, pt. 1, 811; Long, *Civil War*, 439.

14. *The New York Times*, 18 November 1863.

15. *O. R.*, 29, pt. 1, 811, 815–16.

16. *O. R.*, 29, pt. 1, 811, 815–16.

17. *O. R.*, 29, pt. 1, 812–13, 816.

18. *O. R.*, 29, pt. 2, 555.

19. Merington, *Custer Story*, 76; Frost, *General Custer's Libbie*, 86.

20. Frost, *General Custer's Libbie*, 86.

21. Frost, *General Custer's Libbie*, 86; D. S. Bacon to My Young Friend, December 12, 1863, Frost Collection, MCHCA.

22. Frost, *General Custer's Libbie*, 87.

23. GAC to My Dear Friend, n.d. [two letters of January 7, 1864], GAC Papers, United States Military Academy Library (USMAL); Hutton, *Custer Reader*, 18.

24. GAC to My Dear Friend, n.d. [two letters of January 7, 1864], GAC Papers, US-MAL.

25. Hutton, *Custer Reader*, 18–19.

26. Merington, *Custer Story*, 80; GAC to My Dear Friend, January 20, 1864, GAC Papers, USMAL.

27. Libbie to Autie, 26 December 1863, BCWCC.

28. Frost, *General Custer's Libbie*, 90, 91; Monaghan, *Custer Story*, 177, 178.

29. Frost, *General Custer's Libbie*, 92, Merington, *Custer Story*, 82.

30. Ibid., 92, Merington, *Custer Story*, 82.

31. Ibid., 92–94, Merington, *Custer Story*, 82–84.

32. Merington, *Custer Story*, 84–85.

Eighteen

The Kilpatrick-Dahlgren Raid

1. Custer, *Boots*, 1; Reynolds, *Civil War*, 44, 45.

2. Custer, *Boots and Saddles*, 1–2.

3. *O. R.*, 33, 172–73; Thomas, "Kilpatrick-Dahlgren Raid," 4–6; Starr, *Union Cavalry*, II: 57–61.

4. *O. R.*, 33, 163, 169; Starr, *Union Cavalry*, II: 60; O'Neil, *Custer Chronicles*, I, 2.

5. *O. R.*, 33, 162, 164; Moore, "Custer's Raid," 340, 342, 344, 345.

6. Moore, "Custer's Raid," 340, 342, 344, 345; McClellan, *Stuart*, 399–401.

7. McClellan, *Stuart*, 401.

8. *O. R.*, series 1, 33, 161–65; *Harper's Weekly*, 26 March 1864, 193.

9. McClellan, *Stuart*, 401.

10. *O. R.*, 33, 162, 165; Carroll, *Custer in the Civil War*, 19; Moore, "Custer's Raid," 346, 347.

11. *O. R.*, series 1, 33, 165.

12. *The New York Times*, March 3, 1864.

13. *O. R.*, 1, 33, 163.

14. *O. R.*, 33, 162–63, 165–66; Moore, "Custer's Raid," 347, 348.

15. *O. R.*, 1, 33, 163, 166; *The New York Times*, March 3, 1864.

16. *O. R.*, 33, 163, 171; Frost, *General Custer's Libbie*, 103; *Harper's Weekly*, March 19, 26, 1864.

17. *O. R.*, 33, 174, 179, 188; Starr, *Union Cavalry*, II, 66, 67; Thomas, "Kilpatrick-Dahlgren Raid," passim.

18. *O. R.*, 1, 33, 174, 188.

19. Kidd, *Personal Recollections*, 235–36.

20. Frost, *General Custer's Libbie*, 96.

21. Reynolds, *Civil War Memories*, 43.

22. Custer, *"Boots and Saddles,"* 1–2, 10; Frost, *General Custer's Libbie*, 96; Merington, *Custer Story*, 86–87.

23. Merington, *Custer Story*, 76–77.

24. Leckie, *Elizabeth Bacon Custer*, 36.

25. Merington, *Custer Story*, 78.

26. Ibid., 86, 87.

27. McCann, "Anna E. Jones," 16, 18, 20; Frost, *Custer Legends*, 70, 71.

28. McCann, "Anna E. Jones," 18–23.

29. Monaghan, *Custer*, 187.

30. Merington, *Custer Story*, 87–89.

31. Ibid., 112–13.

32. Ibid., 90–92.

Nineteen

Change of Command

1. Merington, *Custer Story*, 87.

2. The best book for Grant is Grant, *Personal Memoirs*.

3. Starr, *Union Cavalry*, II: 68–80; Kidd, *Recollections*, 261–63.

4. The best book for Sheridan is Sheridan, *Personal Memoirs*.

5. Kidd, *Personal Recollections*, 299.

6. Starr, *Union Cavalry*, II: 77; Warner, *Generals in Blue*, 508.

7. *O. R.*, 33, 893; Starr, *Union Cavalry*, II, 75; Warner, *Generals in Blue*, 566–67.

8. Starr, *Union Cavalry*, II, 75, 76.

9. Merington, *Custer Story*, 89.

10. Starr, *Union Cavalry*, II, 80–82; Carter, *Last Cavaliers*, 206.

11. Long, *Civil War*, 492.

12. *O. R.*, 33, pt. 1, 815.

13. *O. R.*, 36, pt. 1, 816.

14. Sanford, *Fighting Rebels and Redskins*, 227–28.

15. McClellan, *Stuart*, 406; Trout, *With Pen and Saber*, 242, 244.

16. Trout, *With Pen and Saber*, 245–46.

17. Trout, *With Pen and Saber*, 246.

18. Carroll, *Custer in the Civil War*, 21; Kidd, *Personal Recollections*, 264.

19. Merington, *Custer Story*, 95.

20. *O. R.*, 36, pt. 2, 466; Steere, *Wilderness Campaign*, 379, 381.

21. Kidd, "The Michigan Cavalry Brigade in the Wilderness," I: 12–13.

22. *O. R.*, 36, pt. 1, 815–16; Carroll, *Custer in the Civil War*, 22; Steere, *Wilderness Campaign*, 381–83.

23. Kidd, *Personal Recollections*, 268–70.

24. Carroll, *Custer in the Civil War*, 22.

25. Trout, *With Pen and Saber*, 247

26. Freeman, *Lee's Lieutenants*, III: 365–66; 372.

27. Freeman, *Lee's Lieutenants*, III: 357–58.

28. *O. R.*, 36, pt. 1, 774.

29. *O. R.*, 36, pt. 1, 798.

30. Starr, *Union Cavalry*, II, 94–96; Sheridan, *Personal Memoirs*, I, 354–56, 367–70.

31. Sheridan, *Personal Memoirs*, I: 354–56, 367–70.

Twenty
Jeb Stuart

1. Longacre, *Custer and His Wolverines*, 209; McClellan, *Stuart*, 408.

2. McClellan, *Stuart*, 409–10; Freeman, *Lee's Lieutenants*, III: 413.

3. Freeman, *Lee's Lieutenants*, III, 414.

4. *O. R.*, 36, pt. 1, 817, 826, 828.

5. Ibid., 777, 812, 817, 828.

6. Kidd, *Personal Recollections*, 293–94; King and Derby, *Camp-Fire Sketches*, 249.

7. McClellan, *Stuart*, 410; Freeman, *Lee's Lieutenants*, III: 416.

8. Kidd, *Personal Recollections*, 294, 295; Starr, *Union Cavalry*, II: 99, 100.

9. McClellan, *Stuart*, 410–11.

10. Kidd, *Personal Recollections*, 295; Starr, *Union Cavalry*, II, 99, 100.

11. McClellan, *Stuart*, 411.

12. McClellan, *Stuart*, 412.

13. Freeman, *Lee's Lieutenants*, III: 420.

14. *O. R.*, 36, pt. 1, 817–18, 828, 834.

15. Freeman, *Lee's Lieutenants*, III: 421.

16. McClellan, *Stuart*, 412.

17. *O. R.*, 36, pt. 1, 818; King and Derby, *Camp-Fire Sketches*, 408.

18. Carroll, *Custer in the Civil War*, 23.

19. *O. R.*, 36, pt. 1, 818; Kidd, *Personal Recollections*, 302.

20. Lee, *Personal and Historical Sketches*, 224–25.

21. King and Derby, *Camp-Fire Sketches*, 408.

22. *O. R.*, 36, pt. 1, 818, 826.

23. Freeman, *Lee's Lieutenants*, III: 423.

24. King and Derby, *Camp-Fire Sketches*, 408–09.

25. *O. R.*, 36, pt. 1, 818; King and Derby, *Camp-Fire Sketches*, 408–09.

26. *The New York Times*, May 26, 1864; Freeman, *Lee's Lieutenants*, III: 424.

27. *O. R.*, 36, pt. 1, 819.

28. Ibid., 828–29.

29. McClellan, *Stuart*, 414–15; Oliver, "J. E. B. Stuart's Fate at Yellow Tavern," 531; Dorsey, "Gen. J. E. B. Stuart's Last Battle," 76–77.

30. Dorsey, "Gen. J. E. B. Stuart's Last Battle," 76–77.

31. Freeman, *Lee's Lieutenants*, III, 426–27.

32. McClellan, *Stuart*, 415–16.

33. King and Derby, *Camp-Fire Sketches*, 409.

34. McClellan, *Stuart*, 415; Von Borcke, *Memoirs*, II, 314.

35. King and Derby, *Camp-Fire Sketches*, 409–10; Sheridan, *Memoirs*, I: 384–87.

36. *O. R.*, 36, pt. 1, 819.

37. Ibid.

38. Ibid.

39. "The Wounding and Death of General J. E. B. Stuart," *Southern Historical Society Papers* 7 (1879), 140–41.

40. McClellan, *Stuart*, 416; Freeman, *Lee's Lieutenants*, III: 428–30.

41. McClellan, *Stuart*, 416.

42. McClellan, *Stuart*, 417; Von Borcke, *Memoirs*, II: 313–14.

43. McClellan, *Stuart*, 417; Freeman, *Lee's Lieutenants*, III: 431.

44. McClellan, *Stuart*, 417.

Twenty-one

Trevilian Station

1. Freeman, *Lee's Lieutenants*, III, 432.

2. Ibid., 436.

3. *O. R.*, 36, pt. 2, 1001.

4. Kidd, *Personal Recollections*, 314.

5. Merington, *Custer Story*, 97.

6. Long, *Civil War*, 506–09; *O. R.*, series 1, vol. 36, pt. 1, 792, 819.

7. Starr, *Union Cavalry*, II: 116–17; Sheridan, *Memoirs*, I: 394.

8. Kidd, *Personal Recollections*, 318–19, 325, 326; *O. R.*, 36, pt. 1, 820; Williams, "Haw's Shop," 13–14.

9. Kidd, *Personal Recollections*, 325, 326; Longacre, *Custer and His Wolverines*, 222–223.

10. Williams, "Haw's Shop," 16–18; Carroll, *Custer in the Civil War*, 27–28.

11. Carroll, *Custer in the Civil War*, 24.

12. James H. Kidd to parents, June 3, 1864, Kidd Papers, University of Michigan.

13. Starr, *Union Cavalry*, II: 119–20.

14. Starr, *Union Cavalry*, II: 119–20; Kidd, *Personal Recollections*, 329–32.

15. Baltz, *Battle of Cold Harbor*, 84; Starr, *Union Cavalry*, II: 119.

16. Baltz, *Battle of Cold Harbor*, passim; *O. R.*, 36, pt. 1, 822.

17. Kidd, *Personal Recollections*, 342; Sheridan, *Memoirs*, I, 413–17.

18. Longacre, "Long Run for Trevilian Station," 32–34.

19. *O. R.*, 36, pt. 1, 823, 830.

20. Carroll, *Custer in the Civil War*, 30; Kidd, *Personal Recollections*, 351–52; Freeman, *Lee's Lieutenants*, III: 521.

21. Carroll, *Custer in the Civil War*, 30–31.

22. Kidd, *Personal Recollections*, 357, 359, 360; Lee, *Personal and Historical Sketches*, 53; Merington, *Custer Story*, 104–105; Frost, *General Custer's Libbie*, 108.

23. Lee, *Personal and Historical Sketches*, 231; Pyne, *History of the First New Jersey Cavalry*, 263; Merington, *Custer Story*, 104–105.

24. *O. R.*, 36, pt. 1, 824, 832.

25. Carroll, *Custer in the Civil War*, 31; Morris, Jr., *Sheridan*, 175–76; Swank, *Trevilian Station*, 19–25.

26. Swank, *Trevilian Station*, 27, 31, 32.

27. Merington, *Custer Story*, 113–14; Frost, *General Custer's Libbie*, 111.

Twenty-two

The Shenandoah

1. *O. R.*, 18, pt. 1, 722, 730.

2. *O. R.*, 43, pt. 1, 698.

3. Monaghan, *Custer*, 203.

4. Monaghan, *Custer*, 203; Longacre, *Custer and His Wolverines*, 260–62.

5. *The New York Times*, August 21 and 25, 1864; Wert, *Mosby's Rangers*, 187–97; Taylor, *With Sheridan*, 523–27, 536–38.

6. Wert, *From Winchester to Cedar Creek*, 40–43; Sheridan, *Memoirs*, II: 8–9.

7. *O. R.*, 43, pt. 1, 454; Wert, *From Winchester to Cedar Creek*, 47–52, 71–73.

8. *O. R.*, 43, pt. 1, 457; Taylor, *With Sheridan up the Shenandoah*, 345; *Grand Rapids Daily Eagle*, July 8, 1876.

9. *O. R.*, 43, pt. 1, 457–58.

10. Ibid., 457–58.

11. Beecher, *Record of the 114th Regiment N. Y. S. V.*, 427–28.

12. King and Derby, *Camp-Fire Sketches*, 77.

13. *O. R.*, 43, pt. 1, 458.

14. Wert, *From Winchester to Cedar Creek*, chap. 6–7.

15. *O. R.*, 43, pt. 2, 158, 177, 218; Merington, *Custer Story*, 110–111.

16. *O. R.*, 46, pt. 1, 575.

17. Merington, *Custer Story*, 119–20.

18. Wert, *Mosby's Rangers*, 187–97; Taylor, *With Sheridan up the Shenandoah*, 523–27, 536–38.

19. Sheridan, *Memoirs*, II: 50–52; Taylor, *With Sheridan up the Shenandoah*, 434–35.

20. Hatch, *Custer Companion*, 83–84.

21. Monaghan, *Custer*, 210.

22. Sheridan, *Memoirs*, II: 53–56; Wert, *From Winchester to Cedar Creek*, 157–60.

23. King and Derby, *Camp-Fire Sketches*, 365–66.

24. Whittaker, *Custer*, 258; Merington, *Custer Story*, 121.

25. *O. R.*, 43, pt. 1, 521.

26. Merington, *Custer Story*, 122.

27. Rodenbough, Potter, and Seal, *History*, 60; Hannaford, "Reminiscences," 317-4, 318-1, Cincinnati Historical Society.

28. Freeman, *Lee's Lieutenants*, III: 598–603.

29. Sheridan, *Memoirs*, II: 66–81.

30. Freeman, *Lee's Lieutenants*, III: 607–08.

31. *O. R.*, 43, pt. 1, 53, 59, 435, 547, 582; Freeman, *Lee's Lieutenants*, III: 607–08.

32. Taylor, *With Sheridan up the Shenandoah*, 496; *Harper's Weekly*, November 5, 1864.

33. Merington, *Custer Story*, 126–27.

34. Ibid.

35. *The New York Times*, October 27, 1864.

Twenty-three
Five Forks

1. Starr, *Union Cavalry*, II: 256–58.

2. Kidd, *Personal Recollections*, 131.

3. Charles Capehart to Captain Charles King, August 16, 1890, E. B. Custer Collection, Little Bighorn National Battlefield.

4. Longacre, *Custer and His Wolverines*, 263.

5. Frost, *General Custer's Libbie*, 121–22.

6. Hatch, *Custer Companion*, 10.

7. Custer, *"A Beau Sabreur,"* 226.

8. *O. R.*, 43, pt. 1, 674–75; Starr, *Union Cavalry*, II, 339; Sheridan, *Memoirs*, II, 102.

9. *O. R.*, 43, pt. 1, 675–76.

10. Longacre, *Custer and His Wolverines*, 263.

11. Frost, *General Custer's Libbie*, 124.

12. *O. R.*, 46, pt. 1, 502.

13. Ibid.

14. Ibid., 476, 502–03, 505; Carroll, *Custer in the Civil War*, 57–58; Early, *War Memoirs*, 463–64.

15. Sanford, *Fighting Rebels and Redskins*, 316.

16. *O. R.*, 46, pt. 1, 818, 833–34, 848.

17. Merington, *Custer Story*, 140–41.

18. Ibid., 143.

19. Ibid., 136, 144.

20. Ibid., 145.

21. Grant, *Personal Memoirs*, 525–30; Bearss and Calkins, *Battle of Five Forks*, 2–3.

22. *O. R.*, 46, pt. 1, 575.

23. Ibid., 1130.

24. Ibid., 1103; Sheridan, *Memoirs*, II: 153.

25. Sheridan, *Memoirs*, II: 153.

26. Sheridan, *Memoirs*, II: 153, 154–59; Bearss and Calkins, *Battle of Five Forks*, 73–77.

27. *O. R.*, 46, pt. 1, 1130–31; Sheridan, *Memoirs*, II, 162–63; Bearss and Calkins, *Battle of Five Forks*, 83–85.

28. *O. R.*, 46, pt. 1, 1131; Bearss and Calkins, *Battle of Five Forks*, 108, 109.

Twenty-four

Appomattox

1. Grant, *Personal Memoirs*, 532–35.

2. *O. R.*, 46, pt. 1, 1131–32.

3. Ibid., 1125, 1132, 1136.

4. Merington, *Custer Story*, 150–51.

5. *O. R.*, 46, pt. 1, 1132, 1136.

6. Whittaker, *Custer*, 305; Bearss and Calkins, "Battle of Five Forks," 28.

7. Bearss and Calkins, "Battle of Five Forks," 30, 32–33.

8. Tenney, *War Diary*, 158.

9. *O. R.*, 46, pt. 1, 1109, 1132.

10. Reynolds, *Civil War Memories*, 142–43.

11. *O. R.*, 46, pt. 1, 1109.

12. Stevenson, *"Boots and Saddles,"* 349.

13. *O. R.*, 46, pt. 1, 1132–33; *The New York Times*, April 10, 1865; *National Tribune*, June 25, 1896.

14. Longstreet, *From Manassas to Appomattox*, 627; Burke Davis, *To Appomattox*, 360–63.

15. Botkin, *Civil War Treasury*, 484–86.

16. Private Collection of John Merritt, Colorado Springs, Colorado.

17. Cauble, *Surrender Proceedings*, 112–13; Merington, *Custer Story*, 165.

18. E. W. Whitaker to Charles E. Green, 4 February 1907.

19. *O. R.*, 46, pt. 1, 1133–34.

20. Ibid., 1191; Frost, *General Custer's Libbie*, 133.

21. Merington, *Custer Story*, 166.

22. *The New York Times*, May 24, 1865.

23. Frost, *Custer Legends*, 124–25.

Bibliography

———◆———

NEWSPAPERS

Charleston Daily Courier

Chicago Tribune

The Cincinnati Weekly Enquirer

The Daily Progress (Charlottesville, VA)

Detroit Advertiser and Tribune

Grand Rapids Daily Eagle

Harper's Weekly: A Journal of Civilization

Memphis Appeal

Mobile Daily Advertiser and Register

The Monitor (Monroe, MI)

Monroe Commercial

The National Tribune

The New York Herald

The New York Times

New-York Tribune

The Providence Daily Journal

The Record Commercial (Monroe, MI)

Richmond Dispatch

Richmond Enquirer
Richmond Examiner
Southern Illustrated News

COLLECTIONS
Chicago Historical Society
Columbia University, Rare Book and Manuscript Library, New York, NY
Duke University, Durham, NC
Emory University, Atlanta, GA
Gettysburg National Military Park, Gettysburg, PA
Henry E. Huntington Library, San Marino, CA
Historical Society of Pennsylvania
Library of Congress, Washington, DC
Little Bighorn National Battlefield
Monroe County Historical Museum Archives, Monroe, MI
Monroe County Library System, Monroe, MI
Museum of the Confederacy, Richmond, VA
National Archives and Records Service, Washington, DC
New York Public Library, Manuscript Division, New York, NY
Private Collection of John Merritt, Colorado Springs, CO
Rochester Public Library, Rochester, NY
United States Army Military History Institute, Carlisle Barracks, PA
The United States Military Academy Archives, West Point, NY
University of Michigan, Ann Arbor, MI
University of Virginia
Virginia Historical Society, Richmond, VA
West Virginia University Library
Yale University, Beinecke Rare Book and Manuscript Library, New Haven, CT

REGIMENTAL HISTORIES
Barrett, O. S. *Reminiscences, Incidents, Battles, Marches and Camp Life of the Old 4th Michigan Infantry in War of Rebellion, 1861 to 1864*. Detroit: W. S. Ostler, 1888.
Beach, William H. *The First New York (Lincoln) Cavalry from April 19, 1861 to July 7, 1865*. Reprint, Annandale, VA: Bacon Race Books, 1988.
Beaudry, Louis N. *Historic Records of the Fifth New York Cavalry, First Ira Harris Guard*. Albany, NY: S. R. Gray, 1865.

Beecher, Harris H. *Record of the 114th Regiment N. Y. S. V.* New York: J. F. Hubbard, Jr., 1866.

Benedict, G. G. *Vermont in the Civil War: A History of the Part Taken by the Vermont Soldiers and Sailors in the War for the Union, 1861–65.* 2 vols. Burlington, VT: Free Press Association, 1886–1888.

Bowen, J. R. *Regimental History of the First New York Dragoons (Originally the 130th N. Y. Vol. Infantry) During Three Years of Active Service in the Great Civil War.* N.p.: J. R. Bowen, 1900.

Buffum, Francis. *A Memorial of the Great Rebellion: Being a History of the Fourteenth Regiment New Hampshire Volunteers.* Boston: Rand, Avery & Co., 1882.

Carpenter, George N. *History of the Eighth Regiment Vermont Volunteers, 1861–1865.* Boston: Press of Deland & Barta, 1886.

Cheney, Norval. *History of the Ninth Regiment, New York Volunteer Cavalry, War of 1861 to 1865.* Poland Center, NY: Martin Merz & Son, 1901.

Chester, Henry W. "Campaigns of the 2nd Ohio Volunteer Cavalry." In *Report of the Reunion: The 2nd Ohio Cavalry, 25th Ohio Battery, Cleveland, Ohio, October 19, 1915.* Cleveland, Ohio: The O. S. Hubbell Printing Co., 1915.

Clark, Orton S. *One Hundred and Sixteenth Regiment of New York State Volunteers.* Buffalo: Printing House of Matthews & Warren, 1868.

Denison, Frederic. *Sabres and Spurs: The First Regiment Rhode Island Cavalry in the Civil War, 1861–1865.* Central Falls, RI: Press of E. L. Freeman & Co., 1876.

Farrar, Samuel Clarke. *The Twenty-second Pennsylvania Cavalry and the Ringgold Battalion, 1861–1865.* Pittsburgh: New Werner Co., 1911.

Foster, Alonzo. *Reminiscences and Record of the 6th New York V. V. Cavalry.* N.p.: Alonzo Foster, 1892.

Gardiner, William. *Operations of the Cavalry Corps Middle Military Division, Armies of the United States, from February 27 to March 8, 1865, Participated in by the First Rhode Island Cavalry.* Providence: Rhode Island Soldiers & Sailors Historical Society, 1896.

Gracey, S. L. *Annals of the Sixth Pennsylvania Cavalry.* Philadelphia: E. H. Butler & Co., 1868.

Haines, Alanson A. *History of the Fifteenth Regiment New Jersey Volunteers.* New York: Jenkins & Thomas, 1883.

Hall, Hillman A., et al., comps. *History of the Sixth New York Cavalry (Second Ira Harris Guard, Second Brigade—First Division—Cavalry Corps, Army of the Potomac, 1861–1865.* Worcester, MA: Blanchard Press, 1908.

Haynes, E. M. *A History of the Tenth Regiment, Vermont Volunteers.* Lewiston, ME: Journal Stream Press, 1870.

Hewitt, William. *History of the Twelfth West Virginia Volunteer Infantry: The Part It Took in the War of the Rebellion, 1861–1865.* N.p.: Twelfth West Virginia Infantry Association, 1892.

Isham, Asa B. *An Historical Sketch of the Seventh Regiment Michigan Volunteer Cavalry: From Its Organization, in 1862, to Its Muster Out, in 1865.* New York: Topics Publishing Co., 1893.

Krick, Robert K. *Ninth Virginia Cavalry.* Lynchburg, VA: H. E. Howard, Inc., 1982.

Lee, William O. *Personal and Historical Sketches and Facial History of and by Members of the Seventh Regiment Michigan Cavalry, 1862–1865.* Detroit: Ralston-Stroup Printing Co., 1901.

Lloyd, William Penn. *History of the First Reg't Pennsylvania Reserve Cavalry, from Its Organization, August 1861, to September, 1864.* Philadelphia: King & Baird Printers, 1864.

Lothrop, Charles H. *A History of the First Regiment Iowa Cavalry Veteran Volunteers.* Lyons, IA: Beers & Eaton Printers, 1890.

McDonald, William N. *A History of the Laurel Brigade, Originally the Ashby Cavalry of the Army of Northern Virginia and Chew's Battery.* Baltimore, MD: Sun Job Printing Office, 1907.

Moyer, H. P., ed. *History of the Seventeenth Regimental Pennsylvania Volunteers Cavalry.* Lebanon, PA: Sowers Printing Co., n.d.

Nash, Eugene Arus. *A History of the Forty-fourth Regiment New York Volunteer Infantry in the Civil War, 1861–65.* Chicago: R. R. Donnelley & Sons Co., 1911.

Norton, Henry, ed. *Deeds of Daring, or History of the Eighth N. Y. Volunteer Cavalry.* Norwich, NY: Chenango Telegraph Printing House, 1889.

Pickerill, W. N. *History of the Third Indiana Cavalry.* Indianapolis: Aetna Printing Co., 1906.

Preston, N. D. *History of the Tenth Regiment of Cavalry New York State Volunteers, August, 1861 to August, 1865.* New York: D. Appleton & Co., 1892.

Pyne, Henry R. *The History of the First New Jersey Cavalry.* Trenton: J. A. Beecher, 1871.

Rawle, William Brooke, ed. *History of the Third Pennsylvania Cavalry, Sixtieth Regiment Pennsylvania Volunteers in the American Civil War, 1861–1865.* Philadelphia: Franklin Printing Co., 1905.

Rodenbough, Theodore F., Henry C. Potter, and William P. Seal, eds. *History of the*

Eighteenth Regiment of Cavalry Pennsylvania Volunteers (163d Regiment of the Line) 1862–1865. New York: Wynkoop Hallenback Crawford Co., 1909.

Roe, Alfred Seelye. *The Ninth New York Heavy Artillery.* Worcester, MA: Published by the Author, 1899.

Slease, William Davis. *The Fourteenth Pennsylvania in the Civil War.* Pittsburgh: Art Engraving & Printing Co., n.d.

Stevenson, James H. *"Boots and Saddles": A History of the First Volunteer Cavalry Regiment of the War Known as the First New York (Lincoln) Cavalry, and Also as the Sabre Regiment.* Harrisburg, PA: Patriot Publishing Co., 1879.

Sutton, J. J. *History of the Second Regiment West Virginia Cavalry Volunteers, During the War of the Rebellion.* Reprint, Huntington, WV: Blue Acorn Press, 1992.

Tobie, Edward P. *History of the First Maine Cavalry, 1861–1865.* Boston: Press of Emery & Hughes, 1887.

Wildes, Thomas F. *Record of the One Hundred and Sixteenth Regiment Ohio Infantry Volunteers in the War of the Rebellion.* Sandusky, OH: I. F. Mack & Brothers, Printers, 1884.

PERIODICALS

Alexander, Ted. "Gettysburg Cavalry Operations, June 27–July 3, 1863." *Blue & Gray Magazine* 6, no. 1 (October, 1988).

Bakeless, John. "The Mystery of Appomattox." *Civil War Times Illustrated* 9, no. 3 (June 1970).

Beauregard, Erving E. "The General and the Politician: Custer & Bingham." *Blue & Gray Magazine* 6, no. 1 (October 1988).

Brewer, Wilmon. "The Capture of General Custer's Love Letters." *Yankee Magazine,* March, 1969.

Brooke-Rawle, William. "The Right Flank at Gettysburg." In *The Annals of the War,* edited by the editors of the *Philadelphia Weekly Times.* Philadelphia: Times Publishing Co., 1879: 467–484.

Bush, Garry L. "Sixth Michigan Cavalry at Falling Waters: The End of the Gettysburg Campaign." *Gettysburg: Historical Articles of Lasting Interest,* no. 9 (July 1993).

Calkins, Chris. "The Battle of Five Forks: Final Push for the South Side." *Blue & Gray Magazine* 9, no. 4 (April 1992).

———. "With Shouts of Triumph and Trumpets Blowing: George Custer Versus Rufus Barringer at Namozine Church, April 3, 1865." *Blue & Gray Magazine* 9, no. 4 (April 1992).

Campbell, William. "Stuart's Ride and Death of Latane." *Southern Historical Society Papers* 39 (1911): 86–90.

Crowinshield, Benjamin W. "Sheridan at Winchester." *Atlantic Monthly* 42 (1878).

Devin, Thomas C. "Fierce Resistance at Appomattox." *Civil War Times Illustrated* 17, no. 8 (December 1978).

Dorsey, Frank. "Gen. J. E. B. Stuart's Last Battle." *Confederate Veteran* 17 (1889): 76–77.

Dunphy, James J. "West Point Class of '61." *Research Review: The Journal of the Little Big Horn Associates* 7, no. 1 (January 1993).

Early, Jubal. "Winchester, Fisher's Hill, and Cedar Creek." In *Battles and Leaders of the Civil War*, IV: 522–530.

Frayser, Richard E. "A Narrative of Stuart's Raid in the Rear of the Army of the Potomac." *Southern Historical Society Papers* 11 (1883): 505–517.

Freeman, Douglas Southall. "Cavalry Action of the Third Day at Gettysburg: A Case Study." *Military Collector and Historian: Journal of the Company of Military Historians* 29 (Winter 1977).

Frost, Lawrence. "Cavalry Action of the Third Day at Gettysburg: A Case Study." *Military Collector and Historian: Journal of the Company of Military Historians* 29 (Winter 1977): 148–56.

Green, Israel. "The Capture of John Brown." *North American Review* (December 1885): 464–469.

Hall, Clark B. "Season of Change: The Winter Encampment of the Army of the Potomac, December 1, 1863–May 4, 1864." *Blue & Gray Magazine* 8, no. 4 (April 1991).

Hassler, William W. "The Battle of Yellow Tavern." *Civil War Times Illustrated* 5 (November 1966): 4–11, 46–48.

Hatch, Thom. "Custer vs. Stuart: The Clash at Gettysburg." *Columbiad: A Quarterly Review of the War Between the States* (Winter 1998): 44–60.

Horn, W. Donald. "Tom Custer's Civil War Wounds Considered." *Newsletter, Little Big Horn Associates* 24, no. 3 (1995).

Kidd, James H. "The Michigan Cavalry Brigade in the Wilderness." In *War Papers Read Before the Commandery of the State of Michigan Military Order of the Loyal Legion of the United States.* Vol. 1, From October 6, 1886, to April 6, 1893. Detroit: Winn & Hammond, Printers, 1893: 3–17.

Krolick, Marshall D. "Forgotten Field: The Cavalry Battle East of Gettysburg on July 3, 1863." *Gettysburg Magazine*, no. 4 (January 1991).

Ladd, David L. and Audrey J. "Stuart's and Gregg's Cavalry Engagement, July 3, 1863." *The Gettysburg Magazine*, no. 16 (January 1997).

Longacre, Edward G. "Alfred Pleasonton: The Knight of Romance." *Civil War Times Illustrated* 13 (December 1974): 13–28.

——. "Cavalry Clash at Todd's Tavern." *Civil War Times Illustrated* 16 (October 1977):12–21.

——. "The Long Run for Trevilian Station." *Civil War Times Illustrated* 18 (November 1979): 28–39.

——. "'A Perfect Ishmaelit': General 'Baldy' Smith." *Civil War Times Illustrated* 16 (December 1976).

Mackey, T. J. "Duel of General Wade Hampton on the Battle-Field at Gettysburg with a Federal Soldier." *Southern Historical Society Papers* 22 (1894): 122–126.

Manion, John. "Custer's Cooks and Maids." In *Custer and His Times. Book Two*, edited by John Carroll. Fort Worth, TX: Little Big Horn Associates, 1984: 150–206.

McCann, Donald C. "Anna E. Jones: The Spy Who Never Was." *Incidents of the War* 2, no. 1 (Spring 1987).

McIntosh, David Gregg. "Review of the Gettysburg Campaign." *Southern Historical Society Papers* 37 (1909).

McKim, Randolph Harrison. "General J. E. B. Stuart in the Gettysburg Campaign." *Southern Historical Society Papers* 37 (1909).

Merritt, Wesley. "Sheridan in the Shenandoah Valley." In *Battles and Leaders of the Civil War*, IV, 500–521.

Miller, Samuel. "Yellow Tavern." *Civil War History* 2 (1956): 57–81.

Miller, William E. "The Cavalry Battle Near Gettysburg." *Battles and Leaders of the Civil War* 3 (1887–88).

Monaghan, Jay. "Custer's 'Last Stand'—Trevilian Station, 1864." *Civil War History* 8 (September 1962): 45–58.

Moore, James O. "Custer's Raid in Albermarle County: The Skirmish at Rio Hill, February 29, 1864." *Virginia Magazine of History and Biography* 79, no. 3 (July, 1971): 338–348.

Mosby, John S. "The Ride Around McClellan." *Southern Historical Society Papers* 26 (1898): 246–54.

Nye, Wilbur. "The Affair at Hunterstown." *Civil War Times Illustrated* 9 (February, 1971): 22–34.

Oliver, J. R. "J. E. B. Stuart's Fate at Yellow Tavern." *Confederate Veteran* 19 (1901): 531.

O'Neil, Thomas E. "Two Men of Ohio: Custer & Bingham," *Research Review: The Journal of the Little Big Horn Associates* 8, no. 1 (January 1994).

——. "Custer's First Romance Revealed." *Newsletter, Little Big Horn Associates* 28, no. 2 (March, 1994).

Quaife, Milo Milton. "Some Monroe Memories." Burton Historical Collection Leaflet (May 1939). 9–12.

Ray, Frederick L. "George Custer and Stephen Ramseur." *America's Civil War* (July 2003).

Russell, Don. "Custer's First Charge." *By Valor & Arms: The Journal of American Military History* 1 (October 1974): 20–29.

———. "Jeb Stuart's Other Indian Fight." *Civil War Times Illustrated* 12 (January 1974): 10–17.

Ryckman, W. G. "Clash of Cavalry at Trevilians." *The Virginia Magazine of History and Biography* 75 (October 1967): 443–58.

Schultz, Fred L. "A Cavalry Fight Was On." *Civil War Times Illustrated* 23, no. 10 (February 1985).

Sergent, Mary Elizabeth. "Classmates Divided." *American Heritage Magazine*, February 1958.

Shriver, William H. "My Father Led J. E. B. Stuart to Gettysburg." Gettysburg National Military Park Library.

Starr, Stephen Z., ed. "Winter Quarters Near Winchester, 1864–65: Reminiscences of Roger Hanaford, Second Ohio Volunteer Cavalry," *The Virginia Magazine of History and Biography* 86 (July 1978): 320–38.

Thomas, Emory M. "The Kilpatrick-Dahlgren Raid." *Civil War Times Illustrated* 16 (February 1978): 4–9, 46–48.

Tucker, Glenn. "The Cavalry Invasion of the North." *Civil War Times Illustrated* 2 (July 1963): 18–24.

Urwin, Gregory J. W. "Yankee Horse Soldier: The Uniform and Gear of a Northern Cavalryman." *Combat Illustrated* 3 (Summer 1978): 20–23, 66–69.

Williams, Robert A. "Haw's Shop: A 'Storm of Shot and Shell.'" *Civil War Times Illustrated* 9, no. 9 (January 1971): 12–19.

BOOKS

Agassiz, George R., ed. *Meade's Headquarters, 1863–1865: Letters of Colonel Theodore Lyman from the Wilderness to Appomattox.* Boston: Atlantic Monthly Press, 1922.

Alberts, Don E. *General Wesley Merritt.* Columbus, OH: General's Books, 2001.

Alexander, John H. *Mosby's Men.* New York: Neale Publishing Co., 1907.

Allen, Stanton P. *Down in Dixie: Life in a Cavalry Regiment in the War Days from the Wilderness to Appomattox.* Boston: D. Lothrop Co., 1893.

Atkinson, Rick. *The Long Gray Line.* Boston: Houghton Mifflin, 1989.

Baltz, Louis J., III. *The Battle of Cold Harbor, May 27–June 13, 1864.* Lynchburg, VA: H. E. Howard, 1994.

Bearss, Ed, and Chris Calkins. *Battle of Five Forks.* Lynchburg, VA: H. E. Howard, 1985.

Blackford, Charles Minor, III, ed. *Letters from Lee's Army.* New York: Charles Scribner's Sons, 1947.

Blackford, William W. *War Years with Jeb Stuart.* New York: Charles Scribner's Sons, 1945.

Botkin, B. A., ed. *A Civil War Treasury of Tales, Legends and Folklore.* New York: Promontory Press, 1981.

Burr, Frank A., and Richard J. Hinton. *"Little Phil" and His Troopers: The Life of Gen. Philip H. Sheridan.* Providence: J. A. & R. A. Reid, Publishers, 1888.

Busey, John W., and David G. Martin. *Regimental Strengths at Gettysburg.* Baltimore: Gateway Press, 1982.

Bushong, Millard Kessler, and Dean McKain. *Fightin' Tom Rosser, C. S. A.* Shippensburg, PA: Beidel Printing House, 1983.

Calkins, Chris. *The Battles of Appomattox Station and Appomattox Court House, April 8–9, 1865.* Lynchburg, VA: H. E. Howard, 1987.

Carhart, Tom. *Lost Triumph: Lee's Real Plan at Gettysburg—And Why It Failed.* New York: G. P. Putnam's Sons, 2005.

———. *Sacred Ties: From West Point Brothers to Battlefield Rivals: A True Story of the Civil War.* New York: Berkley Caliber, 2010.

———. *West Point Warriors.* New York: Warner Books, 2002.

Carroll, John M., ed. *Custer and His Times: Book Two.* Fort Worth: Little Big Horn Associates, 1984.

———, ed. *Custer in the Civil War: His Unfinished Memoirs.* San Rafael, CA: Presidio Press, 1977.

———. *Four on Custer by Carroll.* New Brunswick, NJ: Guidon Press, 1976.

———. *General Custer and New Rumley, Ohio.* Bryan, TX: privately printed, 1978.

———. *They Rode With Custer: A Biographical Directory of the Men That Rode With General George A. Custer.* Mattituck, NY: J. M. Carroll & Co., 1993.

Carroll, John M., and W. Donald Horn, eds. *Custer Genealogies.* Bryan, TX: Guidon Press, n.d.

Carter, Samuel, III. *The Last Cavaliers: Confederate and Union Cavalry in the Civil War.* New York: St. Martin's Press, 1979.

Catton, Bruce. *The Army of the Potomac.* Vol. 1, *Mr. Lincoln's Army.* Garden City, NY: Doubleday & Co., 1951.

———. *The Army of the Potomac*. Vol. 2, *Glory Road*. Garden City, NY: Doubleday & Co., 1952.

———. *The Army of the Potomac*. Vol. 3, *A Stillness at Appomattox*. Garden City, NY: Doubleday & Company, 1953.

Cauble, Frank P. *The Surrender Proceedings: April 9, 1865, Appomattox Court House*. Lynchburg, VA: H. E. Howard, 1987.

Cheney, Norval. *History of the Ninth Regiment, New York Volunteer Cavalry, War of 1861 to 1865*. Poland Center, NY: Martin Merz & Son, 1901.

Coddington, Edwin B. *The Gettysburg Campaign: A Study in Command*. New York: Charles Scribner's Sons, 1968.

Coffin, Charles Carleton. *The Boys of '61; or, Four Years of Fighting, Personal Observations with the Army and Navy*. Boston: Estes and Lauriat, 1881.

Connell, Evan S. *Son of the Morning Star*. San Francisco: North Point Press, 1984.

Cooke, John Esten. *Wearing of the Gray*. Bloomington: Indiana University Press, 1959.

Custer, Elizabeth B. *"A Beau Sabreur."* In *Uncle Sam's Medal of Honor: Some of the Noble Deeds for Which the Medal Has Been Awarded, Described by Those Who Have Won It 1861–1886*, edited by Theodore F. Rodenbough. New York: G. P. Putnam's Sons, 1886.

———. *"Boots and Saddles"; or, Life in Dakota with General Custer*. New York: Harper and Brothers, 1885.

Davis, Burke. *To Appomattox: Nine April Days*. New York: Rinehart & Company, 1959.

———. *Jeb Stuart: The Last Cavalier*. New York: Holt, Rinehart & Winston, 1957.

Davis, William C. *Battle at Bull Run: A History of the First Major Campaign of the Civil War*. Garden City, NY: Doubleday & Co., 1977.

Delauter, Roger U., Jr. *Winchester in the Civil War*. Lynchburg, VA: H. E. Howard, 1992.

Denison, Frederic. *Sabers and Spurs: The First Regiment Rhode Island Cavalry in the Civil War, 1861–1865*. Central Falls, RI: Press of E. L. Freeman & Co., 1876.

Dowdey, Clifford, ed. *The Wartime Papers of R. E. Lee*. New York: Bramhall House, 1961.

Downey, Fairfax. *Clash of Cavalry: The Battle of Brandy Station, June 9, 1863*. New York: David McKay Co., 1959.

———. *The Guns at Gettysburg*. New York: David McKay, 1958.

Driver, Robert J., Jr. *1st Virginia Cavalry*. Lynchburg, VA: H. E. Howard, 1991.

DuPont, Henry A. *The Campaign of 1864 in the Valley of Virginia and the Expedition to Lynchburg*. New York: National Americana Society, 1925.

Dupuy, Ernest R. *Men of West Point*. New York: Williams Sloane Associates, 1951.

Early, Jubal. *Autobiographical Sketch and Narrative of the War Between the States.* Philadelphia: J. P. Lippincott, 1912.

Early, Jubal Anderson. *War Memoirs.* Bloomington: University of Indiana Press, 1960.

Eckenrode, H. J., and Bryan Conrad. *George B. McClellan: The Man Who Saved the Union.* Chapel Hill: University of North Carolina Press, 1944.

Eicher, David J. *The Longest Night.* New York: Simon & Schuster, 2001.

Farley, J. P. *West Point in the Early Sixties, with Incidents of the War.* Troy, NY: Pafraets Book Co., 1902.

Faust, Patricia L., ed. *Historical Times Illustrated Encyclopedia of the Civil War.* New York: Harper & Row Publishers, 1986.

Foner, Eric. *The Fiery Trial: Abraham Lincoln and American Slavery.* New York: W. W. Norton, 2010.

Freeman, Douglas Southall. *Lee's Lieutenants: A Study in Command.* 3 vols. New York: Charles Scribner's Sons, 1942–44.

———. *R. E. Lee: A Biography.* New York: Charles Scribner's Sons, 1962.

Frost, Lawrence A. *Custer Legends.* Bowling Green, OH: Bowling Green University Popular Press, 1981.

———. *General Custer's Libbie.* Seattle: Superior Publishing Co., 1976.

———. *Let's have a Fair Fight: General George Armstrong Custer's Early Years.* Monroe, MI: Monroe County Historical Museum, 1965.

Furgurson, Ernest B. *Chancellorsville, 1863: The Souls of the Brave.* New York: Alfred A. Knopf, 1992.

Gallagher, Gary W., ed. *The First Day at Gettysburg: Essays on Confederate and Union Leadership.* Kent, OH: The Kent State University Press, 1992.

———. *Shenandoah Campaign of 1864.* Chapel Hill: University of North Carolina Press, 2009.

———. *Stephen Dodson Ramseur: Lee's Gallant General.* Chapel Hill: University of North Carolina Press, 1985.

Glazier, Willard W. *Three Years in the Federal Cavalry.* New York: R. H. Ferguson & Co. Publishers, 1870.

Grant, Ulysses S. *Personal Memoirs of U. S. Grant.* Edited by E. B. Long. Cleveland: World Publishing Co., 1952.

Griffith, Paddy. *Battle Tactics of the Civil War.* New Haven, CT: Yale University Press, 1989.

Hanover Chamber of Commerce, Historical Publication Committee. *Encounter at Hanover: Prelude to Gettysburg.* Gettysburg, PA: Times and News Publishing Co., 1962.

Harris, Samuel. *The Michigan Brigade of Cavalry at the Battle of Gettysburg and Why I Was Not Hung*. Reprint, Rochester, MI: Rochester Historical Commission, 1992.

——. *Personal Reminiscences of Samuel Harris*. Chicago: Rogerson Press, 1897.

Hassler, William. *Colonel John Pelham*. Chapel Hill: University of North Carolina Press, 1960.

Hatch, Thom. *Black Kettle: The Cheyenne Chief Who Sought Peace But Found War*. Hoboken, NJ: John Wiley & Sons, 2004.

——. *The Custer Companion*. Mechanicsburg, PA: Stackpole Books, 2002.

——. *Osceola and the Great Seminole War: A Struggle for Justice and Freedom*. New York: St. Martin's Press, 2012.

Henderson, William D. *The Road to Bristoe Station: Campaigning with Lee and Meade, August 1–October 20, 1863*. Lynchburg, VA: H. E. Howard, 1987.

Heth, Henry. *The Memoirs of Henry Heth*, Edited by James L. Morrison. Westport, CT: Greenwood Press, 1974.

Hoke, Jacob. *The Great Invasion of 1863; or, General Lee in Pennsylvania*. Gettysburg, PA: Stan Clark Military Books, 1992.

Horn, W. Donald. *"Skinned": The Delinquency Record of Cadet George Armstrong Custer U. S. M. A. Class of June 1861*. Short Hills, NJ: W. Donald Horn, 1980.

Hutton, Paul A., ed. *The Custer Reader*. Lincoln: University of Nebraska Press, 1992.

Imboden, John D. "The Confederate Retreat from Gettysburg." In *Battles and Leaders of the Civil War*, Robert Underwood Johnson and Clarence Clough Buels. 4 vols. Reprint. New York: Thomas Yoseloff, 1956.

Johnson, Robert Underwood, and Clarence Clough Buels, eds. *Battles and Leaders of the Civil War*. 4 vols. Reprint, New York: Thomas Yoseloff, 1956.

Johnson, Rossiter. *The Fight for the Republic*. New York: G. P. Putnam's Sons, 1917.

Jones, Virgil Carrington. *Ranger Mosby*. Chapel Hill: University of North Carolina Press, 1944.

Katz, D. Mark. *Custer in Photographs*. New York: Bonanza Books, 1990.

Keller, S. Roger, ed. *Riding with Rosser*. Shippensburg, PA: Burd Street Press, 1997.

Kidd, James H. *Historical Sketch of General Custer*. Monroe, MI: Monroe County Library System, 1978.

——. *Personal Recollections of a Cavalryman with Custer's Michigan Brigade in the Civil War*. Reprint. Alexandria, VA: Time-Life Books, 1983.

Kines, Pat. *A Life Within a Life: The Story and Adventures of Libbie Custer, Wife of General George A. Custer*. Commack, NY: Kroshka Books, 1998.

King, W. C., and W. P. Derby, eds. *Camp-Fire Sketches and Battlefield Echoes of the Rebellion.* Cleveland, OH: N. G. Hamilton & Co., 1887.

Krick, Robert K. "An insurmountable Barrier Between the Army and Ruin: The Confederate Experience at Spotsylvania's Bloody Angle." In *The Spotsylvania Campaign*, edited by Gary W. Gallagher. Chapel Hill: University of North Carolina Press, 1998.

Leckie, Shirley A. *Elizabeth Bacon Custer and the Making of a Myth.* Norman: University of Oklahoma Press, 1993.

Lee, Fitzhugh. *General Lee.* Greenwich, CT: Fawcett Publications, 1961.

Lloyd, Harlan Page. "The Battle of Waynesboro." In *Sketches of War History, 1861–1865: Papers Prepared for the Ohio Commandery of the Military Order of the Loyal Legion of the United States, 1890–96.* Edited by W. H. Chamberlain. Vol. 2: 194–213. Cincinnati, OH: Robert Clarke Co., 1896.

Long, Armistead L. *Memoirs of Robert E. Lee.* New York: J. M. Stoddart, 1886.

Long, E. B. *The Civil War Day by Day: An Almanac 1861–1865.* Garden City, NY: Doubleday & Company, 1971.

Longacre, Edward G. *The Cavalry at Gettysburg: A Tactical Study of Mounted Operations during the Civil War's Pivotal Campaign, 9 June–14 July, 1863.* Lincoln: University of Nebraska Press, 1993.

———. *Custer and His Wolverines: The Michigan Cavalry Brigade, 1861–1865.* Conshohocken, PA: Combined Publishing, 1997.

Longstreet, James. *From Manassas to Appomattox: Memoirs of the Civil War in America.* Bloomington: Indiana University Press, 1960.

McClellan, George B. *McClellan's Own Story: The War for the Union.* London: Sampson, Low, Marston, Searle & Rivington, 1887.

McClellan, Henry B. *I Rode with Jeb Stuart: The Life and Campaigns of Major-General J. E. B. Stuart.* Boston and New York: Houghton Mifflin, 1885.

McCrea, Tully. *Dear Belle.* Middletown, CT: Wesleyan University Press, 1965.

McDonald, William N. *History of the Laurel Brigade.* Baltimore, MD: Sun Job Printing Office, 1907.

McPherson, James M. *Battle Cry of Freedom.* New York: Oxford University Press, 1988.

———. *This Mighty Scourge.* New York: Oxford University Press, 2007.

Mercer, Phillip. *The Gallant Pelham.* Wilmington, NC: Broadfoot, 1995.

Merington, Marguerite, ed. *The Custer Story: The Life and Letters of General George A. Custer and His Wife Elizabeth.* New York: Devin-Adair, 1950.

Meyer, Henry C. *Civil War Experiences Under Bayard, Gregg, Kilpatrick, Custer, Raulston, and Newberry 1862, 1863, 1864.* New York: Knickerbocker Press, 1911.

Mitchell, Adele H., ed. *The Letters of Major General James E. B. Stuart.* Stuart-Mosby Historical Society, 1990.

Monaghan, Jay. *Custer: The Life of General George Armstrong Custer.* Reprint. Lincoln: University of Nebraska Press, 1971.

Morris, Roy, Jr. *Sheridan: The Life and Wars of General Phil Sheridan.* New York: Crown Publishers, 1992.

Mosby, John S. *Mosby's War Reminiscences, Stuart's Cavalry Campaigns.* New York: Dodd, Mead and Company, 1898.

——. *Stuart's Cavalry in the Gettysburg Campaign.* New York: Moffat, Yard & Co., 1908. Reprint. Falls Church, VA: Confederate Printers, 1984.

Murfin, James V. *The Gleam of Bayonets: The Battle of Antietam and the Maryland Campaign of 1862.* New York: Bonanza Books, 1965.

Nanzig, Thomas P. *3rd Virginia Cavalry.* Lynchburg, VA: H. E. Howard, 1989.

Nesbitt, Mark. *Saber and Scapegoat: J. E. B. Stuart and the Gettysburg Controversy.* Mechanicsburg, PA: Stackpole Books, 1994.

——. *35 Days to Gettysburg: The Campaign Diaries of Two American Enemies.* Harrisburg, PA: Stackpole Books, 1992.

Nevins, Allan. *Ordeal of the Union.* Vol. 6, *War Becomes Revolution, 1862–1863.* New York: Charles Scribner's Sons, 1960.

Newhall, F. C. *With General Sheridan in Lee's Last Campaign.* Philadelphia: J. B. Lippincott & Co., 1866.

Norton, Chauncey S. *"The Red Neck Ties"; or, History of the Fifteenth New York Volunteer Cavalry.* Ithaca, NY: Journal Book & Job Printing House, 1891.

Nye, Wilbur Sturtevant. *Here Come the Rebels!* Baton Rouge: Louisiana State University Press, 1965.

Official Register of the Officers and Cadets of the U. S. Military Academy, West Point, NY, 1851–70. United States Military Academy Archives, West Point, NY.

O'Neil, Alice. *My Dear Sister: An Analysis of Some Civil War Letters of George Armstrong Custer.* Brooklyn, NY: Arrow & Trooper, 1994.

O'Neil, Thomas E. *Custer Chronicles.* Vol. I. Brooklyn, NY: Arrow & Trooper, 1994.

O'Neil, Thomas E., and Alice A. O'Neil. *The Custers in Monroe.* Monroe, MI: Monroe County Library System, 1991.

O'Neill, Robert F. *The Cavalry Battles of Aldie, Middleburg, and Upperville: Small but Important Riots, June 10–27, 1863.* Lynchburg, VA: H. E. Howard, 1993.

Pappas, George S. *To the Point, The United States Military Academy, 1802–1902.* Westport, CT: Praeger Publishers, 1993.

Bibliography • 351

Phipps, Michael. *Custer at Gettysburg*. Gettysburg, PA: Farnsworth House, 1996.

Pleasonton, Alfred. "The Campaign of Gettysburg." In *The Annals of the War*, edited by the Editors of the *Philadelphia Weekly Times*, 447–59. Philadelphia: Times Publishing Company, 1879.

Priest, John M. *Into the Fight: Pickett's Charge at Gettysburg*. Shippensburg, PA: White Mane Books, 1998.

Ray, Frederick E. *Alfred R. Waud, Civil War Artist*. New York: Viking Press, 1974.

Register of Delinquencies, 1856–61. United States Military Academy Archives, West Point, NY.

Register of Merit, 1853 to 1865, No. 3. United States Military Academy Archives, West Point, NY.

Regulations for the U. S. Military Academy at West Point, New York. New York: John F. Trow, Printer, 1857.

Reynolds, Arlene. *The Civil War Memories of Elizabeth Bacon Custer*. Austin: University of Texas Press, 1994.

Riggs, David F. *East of Gettysburg: Stuart vs. Custer*. Bellevue, NE: Old Army Press, 1970.

Robertson, John. *Michigan in the War*. Lansing: W. S. George & Co., 1880.

Robins, W. T. "Stuart's Ride Around McClellan." In *Battles and Leaders of the Civil War*, edited by Robert Underwood Johnson and Clarence Clough Buels, 4 vols. Reprint, New York: Thomas Yoseloff, 1956.

Ronsheim, Milton. *The Life of General Custer*. Reprint. Monroe, MI: Monroe County Library System, 1991.

Sanford, George B. *Fighting Rebels and Redskins: Experiences in the Army Life of Colonel George B. Sanford, 1861–1892*, edited by E. R. Hagemann. Norman: University of Oklahoma Press, 1969.

Schaff, Morris. *The Spirit of Old West Point, 1858–1862*. Boston and New York: Houghton Mifflin Co., 1907.

———. *The Sunset of the Confederacy*. Boston: John W. Luce and Company, 1912.

Scott, Winfield. *Memoirs*. New York: Sheldon & Co., 1864.

Sears, Stephen W., ed. *The Civil War Papers of George B. McClellan: Selected Correspondence, 1860–1865*. New York: Ticknor & Fields, 1989.

———. *George B. McClellan: The Young Napoleon*. New York: Ticknor & Fields, 1988.

———. *To the Gates of Richmond: The Peninsula Campaign*. New York: Ticknor & Fields, 1992.

Sergent, Mary Elizabeth. *They Lie Forgotten: The United States Military Academy,*

1856–1861, Together with a Class Album for the Class of May, 1861. Middletown, NY: Prior King Press, 1986.

Sheridan, Philip H. *Personal Memoirs of P. H. Sheridan.* 2 vols. New York: Charles L. Webster & Co., 1888.

Shevchuk, Paul M. "The Battle of Hunterstown, Pennsylvania, July 2, 1863." *Gettysburg: Historical Articles of Lasting Interest.* Dayton, OH: Morningside House, January 1991.

———. "Cut to Pieces: The Cavalry Fight at Fairfield, Pennsylvania, July 3rd, 1863." *Gettysburg: Historical Articles of Lasting Interest.* Dayton, OH: Morningside House, January 1991.

———. "The Lost Hours of 'JEB' Stuart." *Gettysburg: Historical Articles of Lasting Interest.* Dayton, OH: Morningside House, January 1991.

Siepel, Kevin H. *Rebel: The Life and Times of John Singleton Mosby.* New York: St. Martin's Press, 1983.

Stackpole, Edward J. *Chancellorsville: Lee's Greatest Battle.* Harrisburg, PA: Stackpole Co., 1958.

———. *From Cedar Mountain to Antietam.* Harrisburg, PA: Stackpole Co., 1959.

———. *Sheridan in the Shenandoah: Jubal Early's Nemesis.* Harrisburg, PA: The Stackpole Company, 1961.

Starr, Stephen Z. *The Union Cavalry in the Civil War.* 2 vols. Baton Rouge: Louisiana State University Press, 1979–1985.

Steere, Edward. *The Wilderness Campaign.* Reprint, Gaithersburg, MD: Olde Soldier Books, 1987.

Swank, Walbrook Davis. *Battle of Trevilian Station: The Civil War's Greatest and Bloodiest All-Cavalry Battle, With Eyewitness Memoirs.* Shippensburg, PA: Burd Street Press, 1994.

Taylor, James E. *The James E. Taylor Sketchbook: With Sheridan up the Shenandoah Valley in 1864.* Dayton: Morningside House, 1989.

Tenney, Luman Harris. *War Diary of Luman Harris Tenney, 1861–1865.* Cleveland: Evangelical Publishing House, 1914.

Thomas, Emory M. *Bold Dragoon: The Life of J. E. B. Stuart.* New York: Harper & Row Publishers, 1986.

———. *Robert E. Lee: A Biography.* New York: W. W. Norton, 1995.

Thomason, John W., Jr. *Jeb Stuart.* New York: Charles Scribner's Sons, 1930.

Townsend, George Alfred. *Rustics in Rebellion: A Yankee Reporter on the Road to Richmond, 1861–65.* Chapel Hill: University of North Carolina Press, 1950.

Tremain, Henry Edwin. *Last Hours of Sheridan's Cavalry.* New York: Bonnell, Silver & Bowers, 1904.

Trout, Robert J. *They Followed the Plume: The Story of J. E. B. Stuart and His Staff.* Mechanicsburg, PA: Stackpole Books, 1993.

———. *With Pen and Saber: The Letters and Diaries of J. E. B. Stuart's Staff Officers.* Mechanicsburg, PA: Stackpole Books, 1995.

Trowbridge, Luther S. *The Operations of the Cavalry in the Gettysburg Campaign.* Detroit, MI: Ostler Printing Company, 1888.

Tucker, Glenn. *Lee and Longstreet at Gettysburg.* New York: The Bobbs-Merrill, 1968.

———. *High Tide at Gettysburg: The Campaign in Pennsylvania.* Indianapolis, IN: Bobbs-Merrill Co., 1958.

Underwood, Robert, and Clarence Buel, eds. *Battles and Leaders of the Civil War.* 4 vols. New York: Century Co., 1888.

Urwin, Gregory J. W. *Custer Victorious: The Civil War Battles of General George Armstrong Custer.* Lincoln: University of Nebraska Press, 1990.

U. S. War Department. *Atlas to Accompany the Official Records of the Union and Confederate Armies.* Reprint, Gettysburg, PA: National Historical Society, 1978.

———. *The War of the Rebellion: A Compilation of the Official Records of the Union and Confederate Armies.* 128 volumes. Washington, D.C.: U.S. Government Printing Office, 1880–1901.

Utley, Robert M. *Cavalier in Buckskin: George Armstrong Custer and the Western Military Frontier.* Norman: University of Oklahoma Press, 1988.

Von Borcke, Heros. *Memoirs of the Confederate War for Independence.* 2 vols. New York: Peter Smith, 1938.

Wallace, Charles B. *Custer's Ohio Boyhood: A Brief Account of the Early Life of Major General George Armstrong Custer.* Freeport, OH: Freeport Press, 1978.

Warner, Ezra J. *Generals in Gray: Lives of the Confederate Commanders.* Baton Rouge: Louisiana State University Press, 1959.

———. *Generals in Blue: Lives of the Union Commanders.* Baton Rouge: Louisiana State University Press, 1964.

Wert, Jeffry D. *Custer: The Controversial Life of George Armstrong Custer.* New York: Simon & Schuster, 1996.

———. *Mosby's Rangers.* New York: Simon & Schuster, 1990.

———. *From Winchester to Cedar Creek: The Shenandoah Campaign of 1864.* Carlisle, PA: South Mountain Press, 1987.

Whitaker, E. W. to Charles E. Green. 4 February 1907. Pamphlet printed by the Michigan Custer Memorial Association, 1907, Custer Collection, Monroe County Historical Society, Monroe, Michigan.

Whittaker, Frederick. *A Complete Life of Gen. George A. Custer.* New York: Sheldon & Co., 1876.

Wiley, Bell Irvin. *The Life of Billy Yank: The Common Soldier of the Union.* Indianapolis, IN: Bobbs-Merrill Co., 1952.

Woods, C. J. *Reminiscences of the War.* Privately printed, ca. 1880.

Index